THE HOSPITALITY AND TOURISM INDUSTRY IN CHINA

New Growth, Trends, and Developments

Advances in Hospitality and Tourism

THE HOSPITALITY AND TOURISM INDUSTRY IN CHINA

New Growth, Trends, and Developments

Edited by

Jinlin Zhao, PhD

APPLE ACADEMIC PRESS

Apple Academic Press Inc.
3333 Mistwell Crescent
Oakville, ON L6L 0A2
Canada

Apple Academic Press Inc.
9 Spinnaker Way
Waretown, NJ 08758
USA

International Standard Book Number-13: 978-1-77188-652-9 (Hardcover)

International Standard Book Number-13: 978-1-315-14742-0 (eBook)

Library and Archives Canada Cataloguing in Publication

The hospitality and tourism industry in China : new growth, trends, and developments / edited by Jinlin Zhao, PhD.

(Advances in hospitality and tourism book series)
Includes bibliographical references and index.
Issued in print and electronic formats.
ISBN 978-1-77188-652-9 (hardcover).--ISBN 978-1-315-14742-0 (PDF)

1. Tourism--China. 2. Hospitality industry--China. I. Zhao, Jinlin, editor
II. Series: Advances in hospitality and tourism book series

G155.C6H67 2018   338.4'79151   C2018-903208-1   C2018-903209-X

CIP data on file with US Library of Congress

Apple Academic Press also publishes its books in a variety of electronic formats. Some content that appears in print may not be available in electronic format. For information about Apple Academic Press products, visit our website at **www.appleacademicpress.com** and the CRC Press website at **www.crcpress.com**

CONTENTS

ABOUT THE EDITOR

Jinlin Zhao, PhD

Professor, Director of Graduate Program, and Director of Asia and Pacific Development, Chaplin School of Hospitality and Tourism Management, Florida International University in Miami, Florida, USA

Jinlin Zhao, PhD, is a Professor, Director of Graduate Program, and Director of Asia and Pacific Development at the Chaplin School of Hospitality and Tourism Management at Florida International University in Miami, Florida, USA. He came to FIU in the fall of 2000 and was tenured in 2005. He started his teaching career in US in fall of 1992 when he became an assistant professor and coordinator of special studies in hospitality management at Western Carolina University (WCU), where he took the initiative in building the hospitality management degree program. The degree program was approved by the State of North Carolina in 1995. He was granted tenure and promoted an associate professor in 1999 at WCU. He has been a visiting professor at several universities, such as Hong Kong Polytechnic University, Macao City University, and Jinan University. In 2015, he was named "Municipal International Scholar" by the Shanghai Education Commission at the Shanghai Institute of Tourism. He was named a "Fulbright Specialist" by the Fulbright Foundation, USA, and was invited to teach at Northern University of Denmark in 2016.

Dr. Zhao is an active researcher. His area of research lies in competitive methods, the international environment and impact analysis, and multinational corporate strategy. He co-edited the book *Handbook of Hospitality Strategic Management* (London, Elsevier) in 2008. He also co-authored a book chapter in the same book. In 2010, he co-authored the book *Tourism Destination Management: Principles and Practice* (New Delhi, Kanishka Publishers). He is the author of *Instructor's Manual to Accompany-Strategic Management in the Hospitality Industry*, 3rd edition (Pearson/Prentice Hall Inc.) in 2008. He has also published many refereed articles in several research journals and five books/chapters, as well as other publications, and has given more than 70 presentations at international hospitality conferences. Dr. Zhao has guided and mentored graduate students in research, which has resulted in many publications in high-ranking academic journals and presentations at international conferences.

Dr. Zhao's industry experience includes pro-bono consulting activities in China, giving hotel management seminars and presentations in China, working as a foodservice manager during the 1996 Atlanta and 2004 Athens Olympic Games, and working as Training Manager for the 2008 Beijing Olympic Catering Project, in which he was in charge of recruiting and training 7,000 temporary employees. He also worked as a human resource expert for the 2010 Guangzhou Asian Games. He has worked with the Great Miami Convention & Visitors Bureau to conduct research.

Dr. Zhao earned his bachelor's degree in English at the Beijing Second Foreign Language Institute in 1979 and remained to teach at the institute until 1987. After he came to the United States in fall of 1987, he completed his Master degree at Indiana University of Pennsylvania in 1988. He earned his PhD degree in Hospitality and Tourism Management at Virginia Polytechnic Institute and State University in 1994.

ADVANCES IN HOSPITALITY AND TOURISM BOOK SERIES BY APPLE ACADEMIC PRESS, INC.

Editor-in-Chief:
Mahmood A. Khan, PhD
Professor, Department of Hospitality and Tourism Management,
Pamplin College of Business,
Virginia Polytechnic Institute and State University,
Falls Church, Virginia, USA
Email: mahmood@vt.edu

Books in the Series:

Food Safety: Researching the Hazard in Hazardous Foods
Editors: Barbara Almanza, PhD, RD, and Richard Ghiselli, PhD

Strategic Winery Tourism and Management: Building Competitive Winery Tourism and Winery Management Strategy
Editor: Kyuho Lee, PhD

Sustainability, Social Responsibility and Innovations in the Hospitality Industry
Editor: H. G. Parsa, PhD
Consulting Editor: Vivaja "Vi" Narapareddy, PhD
Associate Editors: SooCheong (Shawn) Jang, PhD,
Marival Segarra-Oña, PhD, and Rachel J. C. Chen, PhD, CHE

Managing Sustainability in the Hospitality and Tourism Industry: Paradigms and Directions for the Future
Editor: Vinnie Jauhari, PhD

Management Science in Hospitality and Tourism: Theory, Practice, and Applications
Editors: Muzaffer Uysal, PhD, Zvi Schwartz, PhD, and
Ercan Sirakaya-Turk, PhD

Tourism in Central Asia: Issues and Challenges
Editors: Kemal Kantarci, PhD, Muzaffer Uysal, PhD, and
Vincent Magnini, PhD

Poverty Alleviation through Tourism Development: A Comprehensive and Integrated Approach
Robertico Croes, PhD, and Manuel Rivera, PhD

Chinese Outbound Tourism 2.0
Editor: Xiang (Robert) Li, PhD

Hospitality Marketing and Consumer Behavior: Creating Memorable Experiences
Editor: Vinnie Jauhari, PhD

Women and Travel: Historical and Contemporary Perspectives
Editors: Catheryn Khoo-Lattimore, PhD, and Erica Wilson, PhD

Wilderness of Wildlife Tourism
Editor: Johra Kayeser Fatima, PhD

Medical Tourism and Wellness: Hospitality Bridging Healthcare (H2H)©
Editor: Frederick J. DeMicco, PhD, RD

Sustainable Viticulture: The Vines and Wines of Burgundy
Claude Chapuis

The Indian Hospitality Industry: Dynamics and Future Trends
Editors: Sandeep Munjal and Sudhanshu Bhushan

Evolving Paradigms in Tourism and Hospitality in Developing Countries: A Case Study of India
Editors: Bindi Varghese, PhD

The Hospitality and Tourism Industry in China: New Growth, Trends, and Developments
Editors: Jinlin Zhao, PhD

Labor in Tourism and Hospitality Industry: Skills, Ethics, Issues, and Rights
Abdallah M. Elshaer, PhD, and Asmaa M. Marzouk, PhD

ABOUT THE SERIES EDITOR

Mahmood A. Khan, PhD, is a Professor in the Department of Hospitality and Tourism Management, Pamplin College of Business at Virginia Tech's National Capital Region campus. He has served in teaching, research, and administrative positions for the past 35 years, working at major U.S. universities. Dr. Khan is the author of seven books and has traveled extensively for teaching and consulting on management issues and franchising. He has been invited by national and international corporations to serve as a speaker, keynote speaker, and seminar presenter on different topics related to franchising and services management. He is the author of *Restaurant Franchising: Concepts, Regulations, and Practices, Third Edition, Revised and Updated*, published by Apple Academic Press, Inc.

Dr. Khan has received the Steven Fletcher Award for his outstanding contribution to hospitality education and research. He is also a recipient of the John Wiley & Sons Award for lifetime contribution to outstanding research and scholarship; the Donald K. Tressler Award for scholarship; and the Cesar Ritz Award for scholarly contribution. He also received the Outstanding Doctoral Faculty Award from Pamplin College of Business.

He has served on the Board of Governors of the Educational Foundation of the International Franchise Association, on the Board of Directors of the Virginia Hospitality and Tourism Association, as a Trustee of the International College of Hospitality Management, and as a Trustee on the Foundation of the Hospitality Sales and Marketing Association's International Association. He is also a member of several professional associations.

LIST OF CONTRIBUTORS

Among the 17 contributors to this volume, ten are scholars who are teaching in the leading hospitality and tourism management programs at universities of China. In addition to two graduate students, contributors have all had overseas experiences in studying or working as visiting scholars in US, UK, and other Western countries. The other five scholars (including one PhD student) are teaching in US universities.

Huimin Gu
Dean of School of Hospitality Management, Beijing International Studies University, Beijing, 100024, China

Nan Hua
Associate Professor, Rosen College of Hospitality Management, University of Central Florida, Orlando, FL 32819 USA

Qiuju Luo
Associate Dean and Professor, School of Tourism Management, Sun Yat-sen University, Guangzhou, 510275, China

Xinying Ma
Graduate Student, College of Tourism and Service Management, Nankai University, Tianjin, 300071, China

Fang Meng
Associate Professor, School of Hotel, Restaurant and Tourism Management, SmartState Center of Economic Excellence in Tourism and Economic Development, University of South Carolina, Columbia, SC 29208 USA

Bo Qu
Program Director of International Hospitality Management, School of Tourism and Hotel Management, School of Economics and Trade, South China University of Technology, Guangzhou, 510006, China

Lianping Ren
Doctor of Hotel and Tourism Administration, Assistant Professor, Institute for Tourism Studies, Macao, China

Beiqi Shi
Associate Professor, Shanghai Institute of Tourism, Shanghai, 201418, China

Mohan Song
PhD Student, College of Business, Florida International University, Miami, FL 33191, USA

Jingna Wang
Assistant Professor, MICE Management Department, College of Tourism and Service Management, Nankai, Tianjin, 300071, China

Xiangxiang Xie
Associate Professor, Tourism College of Hainan University, Haikou, 570228, China

PCA	principal component analysis
PLSPM	partial least squares path model
PMSs	property management systems
RBV	resource-based view
SEZ	special economic zones
SMTEs	small medium tourism enterprise
SNIEC	Shanghai New International Expo Center
STA	smart tourist attraction
SZICEC	Shenzhen International Convention & Exhibition Center
TD	tourism destination
TDC	tourism destination competitiveness
TDC	tourism development committee
TDCM	tourism destination competitiveness models
TMT	top management team
TOPSIS	Technique for Order Preference by Similarity to an Ideal Solution
TTRA	Travel and Tourism Research Association
UGC	user generated content
UNESCO	United Nations Educational, Scientific and Cultural Organization
WOM	word of mouth
WTO	World Tourism Organization
WTTC	World Tourism & Travel Council

ACKNOWLEDGMENTS

I would like to take this opportunity to thank Dr. Joan Remington for her hard work in editing English language in this book. I also appreciate Ms. Sarah Black for her help in editing some of the chapters.

I would like to express my gratitude to my wife, Dr. Guixia Han. Without her support, I probably could not complete this book.

PREFACE

There have been great changes in the hospitality and tourism industry in China. The changes have been driven by the steady growth of GDP in China, the increasing middle-income population; life style changes of the Chinese people; and the fast infrastructure development of speed trains, airports, highways and seaports, linking the rapid development of many mega cities, mid-level cities, and townships. There is a great leap forward in information technology in China. All the value drivers have great impact on the booming of hotels, restaurants, meetings and conventions, cruise line industries, tourist attractions and destination developments. This book aims to present a comprehensive report to readers about the changes in the Chinese hospitality and tourism industry in recent years.

The Chinese GDP was growing by double digits for 30 years until 2011. Although the GDP growth in China has slowed down from 2012 to 2016, it is still one of the fastest growing economies in the world. The disposable income per city resident has increased from RMB 1002 in 1987 to RMB 31195 in 2015, an increase of 31 times. With much more money in their pockets, the Chinese have spent more than 60% of their disposable income on food and travel.

The Chinese social and life style has changed tremendously. During the 1980s and earlier when the Chinese were staying and cooking at home daily, life was simple in two ways: home and work, and work and home; perhaps some individuals would take short and local excursions as tours, because eating at a restaurant was considered a luxury activity. Traveling out of town was difficult (no fast transportation) and expensive. Today, the daily pace of life is so fast for the Chinese, and eating out has become very common. Traveling for business, escaping from busy life, and learning other regions and countries' cultures has converted their needs and wants. All these driving forces push the rapid development of the hospitality industry in China. The results from the China Tourism Research Institute (2017) show that the Chinese made 4.44 billion domestic trips in 2016, which is an 11% increase from that in 2015. The total revenue of domestic travel is RMB 3940 billion. In-bound travel from overseas visitors is 138 million, which is a 3.8%

increase from that of 2015. The revenue from in-bound travel is $120 billion. In 2016, 122 million Chinese travelled around the world, a 4.3 % increase compared to that in 2015. They spent $109.8 billion on overseas travels in 2016. The restaurant industry's revenue was over RMB 3400 billion.

The open-door policy in 1979 has attracted many multinational hotel and restaurant companies to enter the Chinese hospitality and tourism market. After the first joint-venture hotel, Beijing Jianguo Hotel, was built in 1982, many joint venture hotels have been built, between Chinese domestic companies and multinational hotel brands and companies. After the first KFC opened its door in Beijing in 1987, many international restaurant chains have expanded all over China in the last 30 years. These international expansions have stimulated the Chinese hoteliers and restaurateurs to build their own chains of hotels and restaurants. Domestic hotel chains, especially economic brand chains such as Home Inn, Jinjiang Star, and Seven Day Hotel, have all expanded throughout China. Large domestic restaurant chains have been established, such as Malan Noodles and Mother Dumpling Company. The negotiations of management contracts and franchise agreements have become tougher between foreign brands and Chinese hotel or restaurant owners. The competition has intensified in the hotel and restaurant industry in China. There was no cruise line industry, and not much of the MICE (meetings, incentives, conferences, exhibitions) industry in the 1980s; however, both industries have flourished in the last 10 years.

Information technology is very well applied in the hospitality and tourism industry. Hospitality and tourism education is booming, and the research in the hospitality and tourism industry is increasing. The issues discussed are well reflected in the chapters contributed by scholars from various universities in China and the United States.

The editor would like to express his whole-hearted thanks to all the contributors.

—Jinlin Zhao, PhD
Editor

CHAPTER 1

BUDGET HOTELS IN CHINA: RECENT DEVELOPMENT, CHANGES, AND CHALLENGES

LIANPING REN

Institute for Tourism Studies, Macao, China

CONTENTS

ABSTRACT

This chapter provides an overview of the development of the budget hotel sector in China. It reviews the historical development of this hotel sector in the past 20 years since the establishment of the first Jinjiang Inn in Shanghai, and describes the key players of this hotel sector. Recent development trends and the intense competition in this sector are also discussed.

1.1 INTRODUCTION

Development of the hotel industry as a whole started only after the reform and opening policy in China in 1978 (Zhang et al., 2005). Over the years, the Chinese hotel industry has undergone fast and dynamic development. Up until the beginning of the new century, public attention has been mainly on the number of star-rated hotels, statistics of which are mainly released by the China National Tourism Administration (CNTA). However, recent years have seen huge development in nonstar-rated hotels. According to Travel Daily (2015), the total number of star-rated hotels, up to the second quarter of 2015, was 11,282, including 96 One-Star hotels, 2,507 Two-Star, 5,447 Three-Star, 2,424 Four-Star, and 808 Five-Star hotels. On the other hand, according to the statistics released jointly by the Ministry of Commerce, People's Republic of China (PRC), and the China Hotel Association (2015), the number of mid-scale and lower scale budget hotels accounted for 45% of the total hotel numbers in China. Another 45% of the hotels are other types such as folk-style inns and small-scale but unique featured boutique hotels, both of which are not star rated. The majority of these hotels bear domestic brands. The above statistics have highlighted the portion of budget hotels out of the total number of hotels in China. Although most of the One-Star and Two-Star hotels in China, as rated by the Chinese Star Rating System, resemble the idea of budget hotels or limited service hotels, they are not included in the statistics for budget hotels. As a matter of fact, ever since the start of budget hotel development, the number of star-rated hotels, especially those under three stars, decreased significantly.

The concept of budget hotels is relatively new in China. It started only at the turn of the century with the opening of the first Jinjiang Inn in Shanghai in 1997 (Li, 2009). Prior to the establishment of the first Jinjiang Inn, there were a small number of hotels or hotel chains that resembled the idea of budget hotels, including Xinya Star, which was later acquired by Jinjiang Inn. But the scale and the standard of these hotels were not those of budget hotels strictly speaking. In China, the term "budget hotel" is interchangeable with "economy hotel," as Cai (2004) noted. On many occasions, it is also referred to as "limited service" or even "selective service" hotels, in comparison to its "full service" counterpart. Recent statistics released by Inntie and other websites have changed the term "budget hotel" into "limited service hotels," to include the mid-level hotels developed mostly by budget hotel chain companies, which provide upgraded room features and core service, but retain the idea of a no-frill hotel product.

Although budget hotels in China started late, its rapid development over the past 15 years or so has led to a lot of "wows" in the industry, domestically and internationally. Up to January 1, 2016, the numbers of hotels and hotel rooms that have been opened to the market have come to 21,481 (hotels) and 196,915 (rooms), respectively. The number of hotels of this type is almost double than that of the star-rated hotels. The table below shows the development trend and growth rate of budget hotels in China from 2005 to 2015. This hotel sector gained tremendous growth from 2005 to 2008, almost doubling the total hotel numbers every year. The growth pace slowed from 2009, but it has remained a double-digit growth rate up to now (Table 1.1).

1.2 KEY DOMESTIC PLAYERS IN THE BUDGET HOTEL SECTOR IN CHINA

Budget hotels in China are dominated by hotel chains. Over the years, the biggest names of budget hotel companies have been Home Inns, Huazhu, 7 Days Inn, and Jinjiang Inn. These companies have been on the top of the list consistently for the past decade. Other frequently heard names of budget hotel brands include Green Tree, Super 8, Vienna Hotels, 99 Hotel, Pod Inn, and so on. The majority of the well-known budget hotels and hotel

TABLE 1.1 Growth Rate of Budget Hotels and Rooms from 2005 to 2015 (Inntie, 2016)

Year	Hotels	Rooms	Growth (%)
2005	522	56,854	193.13
2006	906	98,817	73.81
2007	1,698	188,788	91.05
2008	2,805	312,930	65.76
2009	3,757	412,840	31.93
2010	5,120	544,210	31.82
2011	7,314	747,045	37.27
2012	9,924	981,712	31.41
2013	12,727	1,235,833	25.89
2014	16,375	1,525,471	23.44
2015	21,481	1,969,145	29.08

companies are Chinese indigenous brands, with a few exceptions such as Super 8, Ibis, and Holiday Inn Express. The following table shows the top 10 budget hotel brands in China, according to the latest statistics released by Inntie.com (2016). The statistics are based on hotels that have been opened up to January 2015 (Table 1.2).

Most of the companies listed above, however, have only undergone about 10 years of development or less. Jinjiang Inn is probably the oldest budget hotel brand in China, starting from 1997. But its expansion has not been the fastest. A possible reason could be that Jinjiang Inn undertakes more direct management rather than other business modes such as management contracts or franchising. Another possible reason could be that Jinjiang Inn is the only brand under the Jinjiang International Hotel Group, which has focused on full service hotel products since the start of hotel development in China. However, the recent acquisition and merger activity undertaken by the Jinjiang International Hotel Group is going to change its status in both the budget hotel sector and the hotel industry as a whole. This will be discussed later.

Home Inn is known as the second budget hotel chain in China according to time sequence. The first Home Inn was established in Beijing in 2002. The company gained tremendous growth, especially after 2004. It was listed on NASDAQ in 2006. Based on the budget hotel brand of Home Inn, the company has expanded to a mid-level hotel product such as Yitel, which is sold at a price between Three- and Four-Star hotels in China. Acquisitions

TABLE 1.2 Top 10 Budget Hotel Brands in China, by 2015 (Inntie, 2016)

Rank	Brand	Parent Group	Rooms	Hotels
1	Home Inn	Home Inn Hotel Group	233,518	2,135
2	7 Days Inn	Plateno Hotel Group	193,529	2,085
3	Hanting Inn	China Lodge	172,341	1,648
4	Jinjiang Inn	Jinjiang International Hotel Group	102,136	815
5	Green Tree	Green Tree Hotel Group	96,759	1,087
6	Motel	Home Inn Hotel Group	53,699	402
7	City Comfort Inn	Eastern Crown	23,835	256
8	Thankyou	Thankyou Hotel	22,791	412
9	99 Hotel	99 Hotel	22,287	387
10	Pod Inn	Zhuyou Hotel Group	21,126	306

of other budget hotel brands fostered a faster expansion that contributed to the No. 1 ranking of Home Inn in the budget hotel sector in China for many years.

The founder of Hanting Inn is the founding member of Home Inn: Mr. Qi Ji. He established Hanting Inn in 2005, 3 years after Home Inn was established. Hanting Inn was also listed on NASDAQ in 2010. Based on the brand of Hanting Inn, Mr. Ji and his team have developed the company into a hotel giant covering a full range of hotel brands, although the most well-known and biggest brand is still probably Hanting. The name of the company is China Lodge (or Huazhu), close to the Chinese meaning of Hanting. The company is currently aiming at further expansion, both domestically and internationally, by aligning with international hotel giants such as Accor (Huazhu Official Website, 2016).

7 Days Inn was founded in the same year as Hanting Inn, i.e., 2005. With an initial focus in the southern part of China, the brand also gained tremendous expansion nationwide, especially after it was listed on the New York Stock Exchange in 2009. In 2013, 7 Days Inn was privatized, and the brand became one of the multiple hotel brands under the Plateno Hotel Group, a company aiming at providing a whole series of hotel products, similar to other hotel companies such as China Lodge, Jinjiang, and Home Inn (Plateno Official Website, 2016).

In the international community, budget hotel companies in China, or companies that boast budget hotels as their main product, are more competitive than other hotel segments. According to the latest Hotels 325 (2016) ranking, there are four Chinese hotel companies ranked among top 20 in terms of the number of rooms and hotels. These are Shanghai Jinjiang International Hotel Group Co. (parent company of Jinjiang Inn, with 5,408 hotels, and 565,558 rooms), China Lodging Group (mainly budget hotels, with 2,763 hotels, and 278,843 rooms), Home Inns & Hotels Management (mainly budget hotels, with 2,257 hotels, and 255,319 rooms), and GreenTree Inns Hotel Management Group (mainly budget hotels, with 1,927 hotels, and 171,890 rooms). Looking at particular hotel brands, Chinese indigenous budget hotel brands have outperformed many others. Home Inn is ranked No. 2; Hanting Hotel, No. 8; 7 Days Inn, No. 10; GreenTree Inn, No. 14; and Jinjiang Inn No. 22 (Hotels 325, 2016).

Most of the major domestic budget hotel companies started with investment from domestic funds, but later opted to be listed publicly. For example, the Home Inns Hotel Group started by the joint investment of Ctrip (one

helps to lay a solid foundation for the Chinese brands to expand to overseas markets. The Chinese outbound market is growing tremendously. This has nurtured and will continue to nurture a large number of overseas hotels catering to Chinese customers. As a matter of fact, a few Chinese hotel companies have already taken this step and reached outside, as discussed in the previous section.

1.5 FURTHER TIERING OF THE BUDGET HOTEL SECTOR

If the emergence of budget hotels in China at the turn of the century satisfied the growing number of business and leisure travelers, it was largely due to the lack of clean and inexpensive accommodations in the market place. However, after 15 years or so, budget hotels are around every corner in the cities in China. At the same time, mass travelers have become more well-off and sophisticated in their hotel experience. The early batch of budget hotels that appeared in the market is obviously no longer the first choice for many travelers. Differentiation of disposable income has led to multiple tiers of consumers, who demand different kinds of budget hotels.

Another challenge that the budget hotels in China are facing now is declining profitability. The room rate of the budget hotels has not increased much, but the property cost, labor cost, and other costs have gone up dramatically. For example, when budget hotels started in China, the average salary for a front-line worker was about 800 RMB, but it is now over 2500 RMB. According to an anonymous calculation, the profitability of a budget hotel is as low as 10 RMB, which makes it hard for the companies to survive. While pushing up the room rate has proven to be difficult, looking for a differentiated hotel product would be a better solution.

In response to these changes, major budget hotel companies came up with the solution of further tiering budget hotels. For example, Home Inns official website (2016) displays five major Home Inn brands, including Yitel (targeting at mid-level travelers, better facilities and amenities, but with limited service), Home Inn Plus (simple but stylistic), Home Inn (the very first type of budget hotels under this company, and the major brand, covering 2500 hotels nation-wide), Motel (fashion and convenience), as well as Fairyland (mainly in Yunnan Province, with only 31 hotels) (Home Inns, 2016).

The effort in further tiering the budget hotel products is even more noticeable in the Plateno Hotel Group, now the parent company of 7 Days Inn.

Under Plateno, there are at least 14 brands devoted to limited service hotel products that offer different styles, levels, age groups, and even different gender-oriented hotel products. Mr. Nanyan Zheng, founder of 7 Days Inn, interpreted the ever-changing mass travelers' demand for more personalized and stylistic hotel products by saying that people no longer go to restaurants just to feed themselves, and they do not choose hotels just for a good night's sleep and a shower; instead, they look for a match of styles and personalities, experiential values, and imagination (Plateno Official Website, 2016). China Lodge (or Huazhu) has shown similar efforts in further tiering its hotel products. The official website of Huazhu displays eight different limited service hotel brands, ranging from mid-level brand of Joya Hotel to low-level inexpensive budget hotel brand of Hi Inn which only costs about 100 RBM per room night (Huazhu Official Website, 2016).

Among all the differentiation efforts, mid-level limited service or selective service hotels are the new targets for most of the budget hotel companies. Hoteliers have obviously noticed that, for so many years, the development focus has been either on luxury hotels or full service hotels or on low-level budget/economy hotels to meet the needs of mass travelers. But the market now is calling for mid-level hotels for both business and leisure purposes. So far, some of the more successful examples of developing mid-level hotel products include Vienna under the Vienna Hotel Group, All Seasons under China Lodge/Huazhu, Shanghai Trends Hotel, Fu Yi Fashion, Yitel under Home Inns, etc. (Inntie, 2016), but the number is far from enough.

However, along with this massive effort of providing a full range of hotel products to customers, the sudden emergence of so many brands of budget hotels causes potential confusion. For example, Plateno created 14 brands in two years' time between 2013 and 2015, and Huazhu has created eight. Many of the brands are only known to regional customers. The frequent acquisition and merger activities in this hotel sector further add to some of the confusion, as customers may have difficulty in recognizing the brands among the companies. The name of the companies and brands may be mismatched for a period of time after the acquisition activity. Therefore, empirical research is highly recommended at this point to investigate this issue.

Apart from the above efforts, the budget hotel companies in China have been pursuing other alliance strategies to gain competitive advantage to sustain and develop their brands. One such strategy is to partner with companies who produce cutting edge technology or products that can better meet the market's demand. Inntie (2016) regards this as "classic cross-sector marketing collaboration." For example, Huazhu collaborates with Didi (more like Chinese Uber) company to solve the difficulties of calling for taxies in most of the cities in China. The 99 Hotel Chain has pursued a similar activity. For another example, Pod Inn collaborates with Ali Pay (termed as Zhifubao in China), which is now one of the most convenient and popular payment methods in China.

1.6 CONCLUDING REMARK

In the past 20 years or so, the budget hotel (limited service) sector has undergone enormous development. Although the growth rate is declining, most of the major budget hotels are still massively expanding. As the profitability decreases, many of the smaller hotel companies either exit the market or are acquired by larger hotel companies, which means that the big budget hotel companies are getting bigger. To cater to the changing taste of customers and to meet the challenge of declining ADR and RevPar, major budget hotel companies are pursuing differentiation of product by further tiering their hotel products, with a focus on mid-level ones. Strategic alliances among the companies and between domestic companies and international hotel players are another big trend, which is going to create a synergy effect. Other strategies include forming alliance with other market-hot products and companies such as Chinese Uber (Didi) and Chinese Ali Pay (Zhifubao).

KEYWORDS

- **budget hotels**
- **mergers and acquisitions**
- **strategic alliances**

REFERENCES

Accor Press Release, (2014). Ground breaking alliance between Accor and Huazhu (China Lodging) creates a hotel giant in China. Retrieved from www.accor.com on June 29th, 2016.

Cai, L.A., (2004). State-owned economy and budget hotels in China – from commodity to brand. *Asia Pacific Journal of Tourism Research., 9*(1), pp. 29–42.

Chathoth, P. K., (2008). Strategic alliances in the hospitality industry. In: *Handbook of Hospitality Strategic Management*. Olsen and Zhao (eds.). Oxford, Butterworth-Heinemann.

China Tourism Daily, (2016). *Acquisitions in Hotel Industry*: Synergy effect and integration are the key. Retrieved from http://d.jiagle.com/news/1284601.html, accessed on June 28th, 2016.

Hilton Worldwide, (2016). http://news.hiltonworldwide.com/index.cfm/newsroom/detail/27688, accessed on June 30th, 2016.

Home Inns Official Website, www.homeinns.com, accessed on September 2016.

Hotels, (2016). Hotels 325 Special Reports. Retrieved from www.hotelsmag.com, accessed on September 6th, 2016.

Huazhu Official Website, (2016). www.huazhu.com, accessed on June 21st, 2016.

Inntie, (2016). Growth of limited service hotels in China from 2005 to 2015. Retrieved from www.innite.com on June 24th, 2016.

Inntie, (2016). The classic cross-sector marketing collaboration case – Limited service hotel + X. http://www.inntie.com/page120?article_id=209. Accessed on September 6th, 2016.

Kwansa, F. A., (1994). Acquisitions, Shareholder Wealth and the Lodging Sector: 1980–1990. *International Journal of Contemporary Hospitality Management, 6*(6), pp. 16–20.

Li, Z., (2009). *Success Road to Budget Hotels in China*. Shanghai: Shanghai Jiao Tong University Press.

Plateno Official Website, (2016). The strategic alliance between the two hotel giants – Plateno and Jinjiang. From: www.plateno.cc accessed on June 28, 2016.

Super 8, (2016). Super 8 Official website – About us. http://www.super8.com.cn/News/41119.html accessed on July 1st, 2016.

Travel Daily, (2015). The Average Occupancy of Star-rated Hotels is 54.61% in the Second Quarter. Retrieved from: http://www.traveldaily.cn/article/95218 (2016–06–24).

Zhang, H., Pine, R., & Lam, T. (2005). *Tourism and Hotel Development in China: From Political to Economic Success*. New York: The Haworth Hospitality Press.

CHAPTER 2

CO-CREATING VALUE WITH CHINESE HOTEL OWNERS: BASED ON GOVERNANCE MECHANISM THEORY

BO QU

School of Tourism and Hotel Management, South China University of Technology, Guangzhou, 510006, China

CONTENTS

ABSTRACT

The purpose of this chapter is to establish an integrated approach on how to choose governance mechanisms between multinational hotel corporations (MNHCs) and Chinese hotel owners (CHOs). Based on the governance mechanism theory and the institutional theory, this paper focuses on the following two questions: first, how partner differences affect the choice of governance mechanisms; second, how institutional differences affect the choice of governance mechanisms. The results show that: (1) The larger the cultural and goal differences between the MNHCs and the CHOs, the more the MNHCs will tend to select the contractual mechanism. Meanwhile, as the business relatedness difference increases, MNHCs will tend to choose trust mechanism. (2) The higher the marketization degree of the settling location, the more likely it is that the contractual mechanism will be chosen. The lower the marketization degree of the settling location is, there is greater possibility that the trust mechanism will be selected.

2.1 BACKGROUND: RELATIONSHIP BETWEEN MULTINATIONAL HOTEL CORPORATIONS (MNHCS) AND CHINESE HOTEL OWNERS (CHOS)

Effective development and integration of the Chinese market has become the essential strategy to enhance the international competitiveness of multinational corporations. Since China's reform and opening up in 1978 and access to WTO in 2001, and the current globalization of economic and information technology, the multinational companies are at an unprecedented pace to integrate into the Chinese market. Nonetheless, on the one hand, the social environment, competitive interaction, and competitive drive that the multinational companies face are more dynamic (LAN, 2015). On the other hand, the differences in regional systems caused by market segmentation will persist for quite some time in transitional China. Two forces at home and abroad require the multinational corporations to achieve the coordinate development from their professional strengths and weaknesses of a regional system that may face the inter-regional process with a more "flexible" approach.

The hotel and tourism industries have surpassed the oil and automobile industry to become the world's largest industry, and their contribution to the global GDP accounted for 9.1% in 2011 (the automobile industry accounted for 8.5% and the banking industry accounted for 11% in the same year). Its cross-regional business practices have been of concern and attention of scholars (Dunning, 1988; Contract & Kundu, 1998). Compared to manufacturing companies who tend to choose equity alliances like joint ventures (IJVs), the international hotel groups are more inclined to asset-light non-equity alliances such as management contracts, franchising, and other models for global expansion. The huge potential of the Chinese market has become a place of strategic importance for international hotel groups in the process of globalization. Since their arrival in 1982 to the Chinese market, more than 90% of the world's top 10 international hotel group brands have come to China and integrated into the Chinese market in a more rapid manner. Hotel investment has shifted from state-owned assets to private-owned capital. This is especially concerning the prompt development of the real estate industry, which has stimulated the unprecedented hurried development of high-star hotels. In recent years, there is the trend that five-star hotels are projected to become "compulsory exercise" in some places.

The InterContinental, Marriott, Accor, Shangri-La, and other well-known international hotel groups are branching out in China by virtue of their brands, networks, channels, management, and other core strengths. Cities such as Beijing, Shanghai, and Guangdong are chosen as a starting point, and gradually extend to Jiangsu, Zhejiang, Shandong, Liaoning, Fujian, Hainan, and other places, forming the coastal main axis zone. Wuhan and Chengdu, the bases of the second important zone, forms the branched axis of the Yangtze River and infiltrate nearby provinces (Wang, 2006). By the end of 2014, more than 20 international hotel groups managed thousands of hotels, which were 50 times as many as the 1990's after they entered China.

On the other hand, along with the accelerated expansion of the international hotel groups, disharmonies between the management and owners also tend to grow (Table 2.1). From the early individual "break up" events to the frequent outbreaks of "divorce" cases in recent years, almost all international hotel groups who have entered China have suffered cooperation crisis. The wake-up call for the industry has aroused the profound reflection of scholars and entrepreneurs: what happened to the management and the owners, and how can they achieve harmony?

2.2 CHALLENGERS FOR MNHCs IN CHINA

2.2.1 THE PROBLEM OF PARTNER DIFFERENCES BETWEEN MNHCs AND CHOs

In fact, the owners and management of the hotels cooperate in a way that combines the tangible assets of the owner and intangible assets of the management to gain the interests of clientele. Hotel owners and management may come from different countries and industries, and the diversities between them are the concept, customs, education, culture, and religion. According to the theory of human behavior (Alfred, 1890), the cultural difference is the

TABLE 2.1 (Continued)

No.	Time	Hotel Name	Location	Management Company	Hotel Owner	Contradictions/Results
17	2010	Metropark Hotel Minnan Xiamen	Xiamen	China Travel Service (HK) Group Corporation	Minnan Hotel Co., Ltd. affiliated with China Great Wall Asset Management Corporation	The hotel operating conditions were not ideal
18	2011	Crowne Plaza Beijing Lido	Beijing	Intercontinental Hotels Group	China Travel Service (HK) Group Corporation (mergers and acquisitions in 2011)	-
19	2011	Holiday Inn Dongguan	Dong-guan	Intercontinental Hotels Group	Cinese Group	Disagreement in management
20	2011	Crowne Plaza Hotel Huayu Sanya	Sanya	Intercontinental Hotels Group	Sanya Huayu	The proprietor was dissatisfied with the management and performance
21	2011	Beijing Marriott Hotel West	Beijing	Marriott Internationa	Beijing Jinyu Mansion	The hotel operating conditions were not ideal
22	2011	Crowne Plaza Shenzhen	Shenzhen	Intercontinental Hotels Group	Shenzhen Overseas Chinese Town Holding Company	High administrative fee and disappointing business performance
23	2012	InterContinental Shanghai Puxi	Shanghai	Intercontinental Hotels Group	Shanghai Yao Da Real Estate Development Co., Ltd.	The proprietor was dissatisfied with the management and performance while the management believed the management fees were in arrears and the proprietor interfered with the daily operation management

TABLE 2.1 (Continued)

No.	Time	Hotel Name	Location	Management Company	Hotel Owner	Contradictions/Results
24	2013	Gran Melia ShanghaiGran Melia Shanghai	Shanghai	Sol Meliá	Shanghai Xintian Shunhua Limited Com-panyShanghai Xintian Shunhua Limited Com-pany	Poor performance resulted in management conflict with the proprietor
25	2013	Honglou Grand Hotel	Shanghai	Days Inn World-wide, Inc.	China Honglou Group	Poor performance; terminated contract before the date of expiration
26	2016	DoubleTree Resort by Hilton Hotel Wuxi – Lingshan	Wuxi	Hilton Group	Yuanyi Group	Poor management of the hotel management company
27	2016	Kempinski Hotel Haitang Bay Sanya	Sanya	Kempinski Hotels	Keenwin Holdings	Bad management; aggressive proprietor

major external factor to influence behavior and cognition (Ludwig, 2012) and influences the business development strategies and cooperative performance by impacting the corporate management, organizational structure, and cooperative governance mechanisms (Barkema and Vermeulen, 1997; Min Wang, 2004; Junhua Wang, 2007). The motive of both owners and management is different. International hotel groups prefer to achieve market expansion and increase brand values, while the Chinese owners would like to achieve the "maximum combined value" (Zhu & Lv, 2011). Their diversified goals affect the choice of cooperative governance mechanisms (Su et al., 2007). Management is more concerned about whether the owners can provide sufficient tangible resources according to the contract, while the owners want to learn and gain management experience and exclusive knowledge from international hotel groups as much as possible under the premise of ensuring the hotel performance. The different goals of acquiring tangible resources and intangible knowledge result in the different choice of cooperative governance mechanisms. Additionally, both sides have different business areas, and the international hotel groups will work with a variety of hotel owners with business backgrounds, including governments, real estate developers, local hotel enterprises, and so forth. There are differences between these joint venture businesses and the hotel industry. The international hotel groups tend to choose control over hotel operations depending on the degree of difference between the owners and hotel businesses to ensure the effective operation of the hotel, its own profit, and the accomplishment of other targets. The international hotel groups are likely to enhance the operational control over the hotel business when the owners do not have any hotel business, hotel management, and operating experience. If cooperation exists with the owners who have certain experience in the hotel business, taking into account the high similarity on both sides, they might choose a more balanced control over both sides and tend to pass on business skills and experience, and expand the influence of the brand of the parent company in the local places by cooperation, as well as be familiar with the market environment of the local hotel industry (James, 1997; Lee, 2008; James, 2009). In contrast, the less experience the hotel business owners have, the more probable it is that they will be inclined to intervene with hotel operation and management out of the need to protect their assets. The management side considers that the interference of the owners weakens its control over hotel management to some extent and impacts the maximization of the hotels' values. However, most of the benefits are enjoyed by the owners, resulting in conflicts (Dimou et al., 2003; Dev, 2009). Therefore, the owners' familiarity with the hotel business is the important factor that management needs to consider to choose cooperation mechanisms.

2.2.2 THE PROBLEM OF INSTITUTIONAL ENVIRONMENT DIFFERENCES IN CHINA

In addition to considering the important external factor of "people (collaborators)", cross-regional business also needs to adapt to the exotic "system environment" or "social environment" (Wang and Lan, 2012). Scholars have systematically studied the horizontal expansion of business management mode under the background of unified market or market segmentation, but the applicability of these findings is relatively weak under the circumstance that the Chinese market is unified and segmented (Wu, 2006). In contrast, the Chinese scholars' research based on the dual characteristics of the Chinese market is more instructive for the international hotel groups to operate in China. Huang and Wang (2006) found that companies in different parts of China are faced with significant differences in institutional and market environments. The difference between the various provinces of China is significantly greater than the world average, and sometimes the degree of difference even approaches the level of difference between countries.

Compared with the behavior choice of multinational companies in a mature market economy environment, the degree of marketization difference caused by China's market segmentation constitutes the institutional constraints of the behavior choice. Due to the impact of market segmentation, the significant institutional barriers between provincial regions have led the enterprises to adopt market and nonmarket means to compete (Pi and Lan, 2014). In other words, the international hotel groups can employ more market-oriented means to deal with a variety of relationships in the areas with a high degree of marketization, because the institutional environment in these areas allows it to account for the past successful experiences and accumulations in hopes of better performance. As the international hotel groups expand to the second and third tier cities, in some areas with relatively low degrees of marketization, these groups may not be able to give full play to their professional advantage, and their accumulated experience in the past may not always be applicable. Therefore, this is the reason that the performance of international hotel groups in the second and third tier cities is not ideal. Previous market-oriented means are not necessarily effective, and they may need to be accompanied by more nonmarket means, including relations with the owners and government.

2.3 THEORY DEVELOPMENT

2.3.1 GOVERNANCE MECHANISM THEORY

The governance mechanism of cooperation between enterprises refers to the combination of legal (formal) and social (informal) control mechanisms to coordinate or protect the investment of resources between the partners, define each other's administrative duties, and distribute strategic alliance interest (Gulati, 1995; Bamford, Gomes-Casseres and Robinson, 2003; Man and Roijakkers, 2009). There are two views about governance mechanisms: control mechanism and trust mechanism. The earliest research on these two points of view come from the discussion and debate published in the Academy of Management Review by Ghoshal and Moran (1996a, b) and Williamson (1996). Subsequent research has raised concern regarding whether the cooperation between enterprises chooses the control mechanism or trust mechanism. Some scholars believe that the two are complementary, while some consider the two are substitutes, and some scholars (Das and Teng, 1998, 1999, 2001a, b) believe that the enterprises should balance the trust or control mechanism to achieve the optimal choice based on the risks the alliance face.

Hotel management contracts originate from the cooperative mode of profit-sharing lease after World War II (Beals, 1995; Child et al., 2005). The theoretical research on hotel management contracts lags behind compared with that on management contracts in the application and rapid development of the hotel industry. "Hotel Management Contract," as a jargon that has been given a specific meaning, appears later than its application in business (David and Peter, 1996; Chris, 2006; Xiang Zhang, 2014). Management contract effectively balances the interests between hotel management companies and hotel owners, and popularizes the advanced management experience of the hotel management companies to more hotels around the world, which has a far-reaching impact on the development of the global hotel industry (James, 1988). The most important feature of the early hotel management contract is the multiple principal–agent relationship. Previous research on hotel management contracts tends to believe that the relationship between owners and management is principal–employment (Eyster, 1997; Dimou, 2003). In recent years, with the changes in the market and rapid development of the international hotel industry, subtle changes have emerged in the status between owners and management in the constrained relationship and in the contract terms of hotel management. The form of employment relationship in hotel management contracts has gradually disappeared and is replaced by a strategic partnership of equality and reciprocity (Haast et al., 2005; Jagels, 2007). In order to conduct research with ease, this paper will define the business cooperation based on hotel management contracts. Management companies and hotel owners (organization) form the organizational alliance that takes advantages of the strengths, shares the risks, and provides the elements flowing in two ways through a contractual (or trust) relationship due to the expectations for the whole market and the wishes of the companies' business objectives. Cooperation based on strategic alliance differs from the joint-stock cooperation or the commission–employment cooperation relations of the traditional hotel industry. The business relationship is complex due to the high degree of interdependence on each other, and the cooperation alliance is easily affected by the uncertainties of the market environment and so on (Pearce, 1997; Prakash et al., 2003). Additionally, the "governance mechanism of hotel management" can be interpreted as what governance mechanisms (contract mechanism or trust mechanism) the management adopts to develop hotel and achieve better performance in the process of establishing alliance with the owners from the management's perspective.

The research on contract mechanism originates from the transaction cost theory, mainly due to the prevention of opportunistic behaviors of collaborators (Williamson, 1975, 1985, 1996). The transaction cost theory believes that the relationship between the companies in the case of opportunism and bounded rationality can be understood. Scholars with the perspective of contractual mechanism consider that the companies must implement strict control to achieve their strategic goals rather than alliance targets out of the high relational risk, the protection of their own interests, and prevention against partners' opportunistic behaviors when they are in alliance. The risk may be high or low due to the different environments, but the partner's selfish and opportunistic behaviors exist in any coalition. Therefore, it is necessary to suppress any opportunistic behaviors through formal contractual mechanism.

On the contrary, the trust mechanism believes that trust is an important element of cooperation between enterprises (Johansson and Mattsson, 1987; Lazerson, 1993; Ghoshal and Moran, 1996). Building and maintaining trust is an important challenge (Ghoshal and Bruch, 2003) and role to emphasize alliance in the informal governance mechanism. The assumption of the trust mechanism is that partners do not need too much official control to prevent other opportunistic behaviors when they are in the alliance, because they will do what is beneficial for the alliance. In contrast with the contractual mechanism, the common vision and trust are the "glue" of the alliance. The common goal brings information sharing and adaption to each other (Johansson and Mattsson, 1987; Madhok, 1995; Berger and Noorderhaven, 1997). The trust mechanism thinks that the excessive use of the control mechanism in an alliance easily leads to distrust between partners (Ghoshal and Moran, 1996; Lee and Cavusgil, 2006).

2.3.2 PARTNER DIFFERENCES AND GOVERNANCE MECHANISM CHOICE

The literature of alliance management shows that the cultural and organizational differences between the partners increase the difficulty of managing alliances (Inkpen and Beamish, 1997; Duan, 2007). Most conflicts are from each other's different management style and cultural background (Killing, 1983), which increases the difficulties of alliance management (Yan and Child, 2004). Although some studies have shown the factors affecting the governance mechanism choice (Geringer and Hebert, 1989; Blodgett, 1991a; Werner, 2002), such as cultural differences (Hennart and Larimo, 1998; Chang and Taylor, 1999; Child et al., 2005) and motivation differences (Calantone and Zhao, 2001), there is no direct evidence to show how the differences between partners affect the governance mechanism of alliances (Groot and Merchan, 2000). According to the literature analysis and business practices, the differences in culture, objectives, and business between the management and the owners have a certain influence on the stability of the alliance and governance mechanism of management contract. Consequently, these are the propositions as follows:

P1: The difference between MNHCs and CHOs affects the choice of governance mechanism on hotel management contracts.

Cultural differences add more difficulty to the alliance's communication, decision-making, and personnel management (Child and Markoczy, 1993). Alliance administrators must learn how to co-administer the alliance with local partners (Barkema, Bell, and Pennings, 1996). There are different conclusions about the influence of cultural differences on alliance performance. Economy of the other party, benefits, and strategic factors may cause failure of a strategic alliance. However, such factors originate from mutual cultural differences, which lead to disharmony among organizational practice and behaviors (Meschi, 1997). Egelhoff (1984) believed that, when joint enterprises are running business cross-region or cross-board, the larger the difference with the partner, the more necessary it is to adopt formal contractual management for the joint venture to strengthen its control. Jeffrey and Hugh (2007) conducted research on how cultural gaps would affect companies' business development overseas, and if these companies chose to establish international alliances with enterprises in host countries and conduct co-runs, or to set up independent subsidiaries that would abide by the parent company's strategic plans. Several propositions are raised regarding cultural differences and the choice of governance mechanism for management contracts.

P1a: The bigger the cultural differences are between MNHCs and CHOs, the more unfeasible is the adoption of a contract mechanism for a hotel management contract.

Strategic alliances are set up by independent organizations via contracts. Goals among the alliance might not be the same, and conflicts may even occur in cooperative competition, which results in appliance failure (Doz, 1996). Consequently, it is important to assess each other's strategic goals, and every company should evaluate the extent the alliance goal may satisfy members' goals. For tangible resource transactions, the contract needed for formal control will not create a high contracting cost (Tarun, 1998). However, it is a comparatively complex process of ability learning. The heavier rely on formal control by alliance members, the lower is the trust that is reflected (Das and Teng, 1998). When trust turns out to be quite weak among members, knowledge owners may fear that knowledge receivers would steal or disclose expertise without authorization, and knowledge transmission efficiency declines (Wang, 2000). Compared with formal control, social control provides more chances for coordination and communication, which may assist in transmitting and integrating information and help establish rapport (Uzzi, 1997).

Hotel owners would note to establish harmonious relations with the management party and build incentive mechanisms and constraint mechanisms against it, so as to realize maximum profit and high return. Through choice mechanism, payment mechanism, controlling power mechanism, reputation mechanism, market competition mechanism, etc., hotel owners set up complete incentive mechanisms for hotel management companies (Ren, 2009; Yuan, 2009). Howard (1998) analyzed the influence of financial management issues in hotel management contracts on each other's operation targets and hotel management goals, and the influence on owners and the management party's relation management and the arrangements of hotel organizational structure. Karen (1999) believed that the goals of cross-board operation by international hotel managing companies are quite similar, though the business goals of owner parties in different regions are diversified. When a management party signs a contract with the owner party, the management contract can only secure a benign interaction between the owner and the management party, and the hotel can only realize a long-term development target if mutual benefits are balanced and their pursuit for profits are satisfied. Chen Yong (2008) did a survey and interviewed some representatives of famous hotels in Shanghai, and found that the goal function is inconsistent with the profit pursuit between hotel owners and international hotel management companies. Through effective collaboration management methods, such as the incentive and constraint mechanism against the management party, efficiency can be improved. Therefore, here a proposition is raised against the goal difference and the choice of management contract governance mechanism.

P1b: The larger the goal difference between MNHCs and CHOs, the more apt is the adoption of a contract mechanism for a hotel management contract.

Scholars usually use business relatedness or industry similarity to evaluate the similarity in organizational business activities, products, and their industries (Luo, 1997; Merchant and Schendel, 2000; Lu and Xu, 2006). Business similarity will help realize economies of scale as well as knowledge and resource transfer. Paul (2005) traced the relations between chain hotel management companies and hotel owners in North America, and found that hotel owners, via cooperation with management, have parties, have become more and more familiar with hotel businesses, and their will for joining hotel management grows as well. After hotel businesses become completely known to the owner companies, they may rely on their advantages in capital and in acquiring governmental permission, to participate actively in the process of creating value in the hotel. Such activities may harm hotel management companies, and therefore, they would add some clauses into the contract to protect their own profits. High-level industry similarity, in particular among companies of quite-alike scale and quality, will incur fierce competition (Powell, Gouglas, Kenneth, and Jason, 2005). Product differentiation is hard to create among competitors; therefore, high industry similarity, compared with low, is even better to strengthen the influence of company mutual trust on relation governance (Zhang, 2014). The following proposition is raised on business differences and the choice of a management contract governance mechanism.

P1c: The larger the business differences between MNHCs and CHOs, the more likely is the adoption of a trust mechanism for a hotel management contract.

2.3.3 INSTITUTIONAL ENVIRONMENT DIFFERENCES AND GOVERNANCE MECHANISM CHOICE

The context reliance theory believes that both the performance of resource value and the effectiveness of strategic activities will be affected by the environment of the organization, and the effectiveness of various governance mechanisms will also be affected by environment uncertainty (Cavusgil, Deligonul, and Chun, 2004). At present, China is going through economic transition, and it should not ignore a significant feature of the exterior environment, i.e., high uncertainty. However, in such a dynamic environment, attention is quite limited to research on the questions like how the trade mechanism and relation mechanism would affect the alliance performance, which governance mechanism would be more effective, etc. (Li, Liu, and Xue, 2011). Environment uncertainty is a significant contingency factor for assessing the effectiveness of governance mechanisms, and such uncertainty refers to the range of environment variation and the degree of instability (Wong, 2011). The higher the environment uncertainty, the greater is the possibility of constant change in technical environment, market, product demand, and competitors. Environment is the cornerstone that a company can count on for survival and development (Narver & Slater, 1990), and it will affect a company's strategic decision and behavior. Companies must have a keen sense to adjust strategies automatically for survival and development in a variable environment. The institutional economy theories suggest that institutional environment directly influences a company's development strategy and is a significant element considered for deciding the strategy to conduct cross-region business. Regional institutional differences have an extensive effect on a company's development strategy, which involves manufacturing, retailing, service industry, financial industry, etc. In Chen's (1999) research on the effect of interior and exterior environment on the establishment of strategic alliance and its performance, he selected several variables such as economic motivation, alliance pattern, corporate cultural difference, and the management model in alliance companies for research. Chen considered that this way might cut transaction costs for such companies and make them more flexible in strategy. Cross-board companies running business in different regions should simultaneously think about the institutional environment of where their headquarters are settled and their difference with the target areas for investment. Wang (2011) studied the influence mechanism of institutional differences across the provinces in China for a company's choice of market access model in a cross-region. It was found that regional institutional differences measured by regulation systems and political networks would significantly affect companies in selecting their model for accessing China's market, where a co-governance model is the principal proposal under consideration.

Agreement or contract is a specific illustration of regulations and economic profits, which note more of one's own interest. The owner party intends more for maximum profits through its cooperation based on contracts. Therefore, as environmental uncertainty grows, it will further boost the management party's worry and concern on its sharing of resources and knowledge transferred to the owner party. Meanwhile, although contracts can provide formal protection for the management party, it is impossible to foresee all possible future events at the very beginning. As a result, if quite uncertain, it is impossible to completely avoid all opportunistic behaviors such as releasing or abusing expertise through the contracts. Moreover, trust built via cooperation can consolidate partnerships when risk increases in an uncertain environment. As the establishment of mutual trust asks for tangible and intangible resource investment and common efforts, both sides will not easily break it by a sunk cost.

In China, relations make it easier to cooperate. In particular, as environmental uncertainty is quite high, companies trust and rely more on relations when doing transactions. Cooperation based on relations has eliminated much worry and concern for knowledge transfer brought by such uncertainty (Li, Liu, and Xue, 2011). Consequently, in other words, in some regions in China where environmental uncertainty is high, a relation mechanism is more flexible and reliable than a formal trading mechanism, and the governance mechanism based on trust provides more chances for communication and coordination, which attains better performance (Gong and Xie, 2005).

Concerning international hotels run in different regions in China, the topic should first address the adaptability evaluation. Lu and Zhu (2010) studied Kempinski Hotel in Wuxi City. International hotel groups' domestication strategies in different regions of China were analyzed. It was believed that in the east, the management party usually chooses to build a good relationship with the owner party and takes advantage of the owner party's government relations to cut the cost on adapting to local relations. Zhang (2014) suggested that cross-board hotel management groups face provincial differences during their expansion in China, which have resulted from market attraction, regional competition, experience accumulation, etc. Additionally, the transportation system and tourism supply may also incur provincial differences. Therefore, regarding the choice of governance mechanism for strategic alliance after considering the features in hotel industry, several propositions are raised for regional institutional differences and the choice of governance mechanism of management contracts.

P2: The marketization degree of the region that MNHCs enters will affect the choice.

P2a: The higher the marketization, the more apt is the selection of the contract mechanism.

P2b: The lower the marketization, the more apt is the selection of the trust mechanism.

2.4 CONCLUSIONS

International hotel groups have entered the deep water zone in China's development strategy at a crucial strategic point where no advance means falling behind. The continual "divorce" with Chinese hotels owners is indicative of this. On the one hand, Chinese owners have attained stronger bargaining power after 30 years of study and knowledge accumulation. Companies entering the hotel industry are mostly outstanding firms in various areas, with their main business enjoying extraordinary advantages. Most hotel owners usually have powerful management experience and tradition, clear strategy orientation, and increasing hotel management experience. Alternatively, the areas for market integration by international hotel groups have been extended to second- and third-tier cities. While different from first-tier cities like Beijing, Shanghai, and Guangzhou, their institutional differences are clear. Such differences cause different owner parties. High-marketization areas can produce national professional firms, while low-marketization areas may create companies that count on relations. In other words, when a management party enters various areas, they face local institutional constraint, and constraints from companies formed in such an environment. Therefore, in order to achieve their cooperation targets, methods to get alone with the owner parties should vary against their features. If the "best" (best match) partner does not exist, it would become a significant measurement for China's market integration of how to "deal with" the owner party and how to comprehensively consider the influence of partners and institutional environment on their cooperation. The results show that (1) the larger the cultural differences and target differences, the more apt is the selection of the trust mechanism and (2) the higher the marketization, the more apt is the selection of the contract mechanism, while the lower the marketization is, the more apt is the selection of the trust mechanism

Theoretically, even though scholars in and abroad have done much research on hotel management contracts from multiple angles and levels, current research focuses more on the contract model or on the partnership from the perspective of hotel owners. However, when studying the cross-region expansion from the hotel group perspective, there is no systematic research on how to handle partner differences and regional institutional differences and on the influence of such differences on the choice of a partnership governance mechanism. The study involved in this paper concerns the integration of three different theories, including the strategic alliance theory, institutional theory, and inter-enterprise cooperation governance theory. The strategic alliance theory sets up the basis for this paper's framework, and it considers the management contract governance mechanism in the perspective of enterprise characteristics and environment characteristics. The institutional theory highlights the context of this paper, namely, market division and marketization differences that have resulted from economic transition, a special institution environment, and would have a direct and indirect effect on the choice. The inter-enterprise cooperation governance theory seeks to understand the foundation and key to a management contract, a non-equity alliance governance mechanism. Such understanding tries to establish the theoretical basis and the trust in a management contract governance mechanism and for building up a contract mechanism. The paper focuses on the influential factors (partner differences and regional institutional differences) for the choice of "nonequity alliance (management contract) governance mechanism (contract mechanism and trust mechanism)," and it is an extension and further exploration of current research, which enriches and replenishes the current research on the strategic alliance theory, institutional theory, hotel management contracts, and inter-enterprise cooperation governance mechanism theory.

KEYWORDS

- **Chinese hotel owners**
- **governance mechanism**
- **institutional difference**
- **multinational hotel corporations**
- **partner difference**

REFERENCES

Barden, J. Q., Steesma, H. K. & Lyles, M. A., (2005). The influence of parent control structure on parent conflict in Vietnamese international joint ventures: an organizational justice-based contingency approach [J]. *Journal of International Business Studies, 4*(36), 157–174.

Bell, C. A., (1993). Agreements with chain-hotel companies [J]. *Cornell Hotel and Restaurant Administration Quarterly, 21*(2), 27–33.

Birnberg, J. G., (1998). Control in interfirm co-operation relationships [J]. *Journal of Management Studies, 35*, 421–428.

Chen, D., Park, S. H., & Newburry, W., (2009). Parent contribution and organizational control in international joint ventures. *Strategic Management Journal, 30*(11), 1133–1156.

Chen, Y., (2008). An analysis of the current status of motivation and restriction on the agent of hotel management contracts: Based on An in-depth Interview and Questionnaire on 52 International Brand Hotels, *Tourism Science [J]*, *22*(1), 40–48.

Das, T., & Teng, B., (2001). Trust, control, and risk in strategic alliances: an integrated framework. *Organization Studies, 2*, 251–283.

Das, T. K., & Teng, B., (1998). Between trust and control: developing confidence in partner cooperation in alliances [J]. *Academy Management Review*, *23*(3), 491–512.

Das, T. K., & Rahman, N., (2010). Determinants of partner opportunism in strategic alliances: a conceptual framework [J]. *Journal of Business and Psychology, 25*(1), 55–74.

Deroos, J. A., (2010). Hotel management contracts-past and present [J]. *Cornell Hospitality Quarterly, 51*(1), 68–80.

Dev, C. S., Erramilli, M. K., & Agarwal, S., (2002). Choice between Non-Equity Entry Modes: An Organizational Capability Perspective [J]. *Journal of International Business Studies, 14*(33), 223–242.

Harris, P. J., & Mongiello, M., (2001). Key performance indicators in European hotel properties: General managers' choices and company profiles [J]. *International Journal of Contemporary Hospitality Management*, *3*, 120–127.

Lan, H., Wang, X., Wu, X., & Song, T., (2010). Research on market entry mode selection based on institution-based View: Developing Theoretical Framework and the Propositions, *Nankai Business Review* [J], *13*(6), 77–90.

Lee, Y., & Cavusgil, T., (2006). Enhancing Alliance Performance: The effects of contractual-based versus relational-based governance. *Journal of Business Research [J], 59*, 896–905.

Li, Y., Liu, T., & Xue, J., (2011). Governance mechanisms and distributor's knowledge transfer: the moderating effects of environment uncertainty, *Studies in Science of Science [J], 29*(12), 1845–1853.

Madhok, A., (2006). Revisiting multinational firms' tolerance for joint ventures: A trust-based approach [J]. *Journal of International Business Studies, 6*, 117–137.

Meirovich, G., (2010). The impact of cultural similarities and differences on performance in strategic partnerships: An integrative perspective. *Journal of Management and Organization [J], 1*, 127–139.

Rodriguez, A. R., (2002). Determining factors in entry choice for international expansion: the case of the Spanish hotel industry [J]. *Tourism Management,* 23, 597–607.

CHAPTER 3

DEVELOPMENT OF INTERNATIONAL BRAND HOTELS ON HAINAN ISLAND

XIANGXIANG XIE

CONTENTS

3.1 INTRODUCTION OF HAINAN ISLAND

3.1.1 LOCATION AND ECONOMICS

Hainan Province, located in the southernmost of Mainland China, is the nation's largest province with the smallest land area and biggest ocean area. This region consists of Hainan Island, the Paracel Islands, the Spratly Islands, the Zhongsha Islands, and the waters surrounding these islands. Hainan covers a total land area of 35,354 square kilometers. Additionally, it has a sea area of over two million square kilometers. Hainan province is referred to as "琼" in Chinese; it has the jurisdiction of 19 cities and counties, including Haikou City as the provincial capital, which is located in the north of the island. Furthermore, Sanya is the biggest tourist city in the province, which is situated at the south of the island. By the end of 2014, the population of residents in Hainan province had reached 9.035 million.

Geologically, Hainan Island is located on the northern edge of the area with tropical and subtropical monsoon climate. The island has gained the reputation as a "natural greenhouse" for its long summer without winter, with annual average temperature of 22~27. Hainan Island is also the native land of a tropical rain forest, which has rich resources of tropical flora and fauna. The island boasts growth of over 3,000 kinds of original tropical plant species and more than 500 kinds of distinct animal species.

Hainan Island used to be a part of Guangdong province before 1988, and it has become the youngest independent province in China since April 25, 1998, being a part of China's largest special economic zone. Agriculture, forestry, and fishery are the highlighted industries in the development of Hainan's economy. Under the idea of developing "Hainan International Tourism Island (HITI)" construction, the contemporary service industry led by the tourism industry is flourishing. Local economy has gradually become more diversified, modernized, and innovative than ever before. According to Hainan economic and social statistics, the gross domestic product (GDP) of Hainan province in 2015 was 370.28 billion yuan. Further, there was a growth rate of 7.8%. The province's investment in fixed assets was 335.54 billion yuan with an increase rate of 10.4%. The province's overall general public revenue was 100.10 billion yuan, which was up by 7.3% over the year of 2014 [1].

3.1.2 TOURISM INDUSTRY ON HAINAN ISLAND

Hainan, also known as the "Oriental Hawaii," is recognized as one of the most popular holiday destination in China in the official promotion. After April 25, 1988, when Hainan Province and the Economic Special Zone were established, the tourism industry entered a new development stage. The Hainan provincial government began to focus on viewing tourism as a vital industry in boosting the local economy. In particular, Sanya city has always been regarded by the tourism industry as a pillar of the economy. Due to this belief, Sanya city looked forward to construct an international, tropical, coastal holiday destination as a strategic goal. In 1992, China's State Council approved the establishment of the Yalong Bay National Tourism Resort. On January 1, 1996, the theme of China's

[1] http://hnrb.hinews.cn/html/2016-01/26/content_1_1.htm, 2015, the province's GDP growth of 7.8%

holiday tourism started in Sanya, Hainan, marking the beginning of China's tourism holiday format. In the same year, *Gloria Resort Sanya* was officially opened, which is the first resort in China mainland to be operated by Hong Kong-based Gloria Hotels & Resorts Group. It was rated as a "five-star hotel" at the end of the year, which is essential in Chinese resort development.

Based on the analysis of historical data, tourism development in Hainan can be roughly divided into four stages. The embryonic stage occurred before 2000, and the number of overnight tourists of Hainan province in 2000 reached 10.75 million by year 2000. That was the first time for the number to exceed 10 million tourists, thus laying a good foundation for subsequent development. The years 2001–2005 could be considered as the initial stage. The reason being that these years were able to overcome the "SARS" crisis in Asia. They then created success in the hospitality industry by having 15.16 million tourists in 2005. During the development stage, which was from 2006 to 2010, the island finally had over 20 million tourists in 2008. From years 2011 to 2015, Hainan Island achieved a breakthrough in the number of tourists ranging from 30 million to 50 million. In 2015, the annual reception of tourists reached 53.36 million with an increase of 11.4% over that of 2014. Furthermore, the total tourism revenue achieved 57.25 billion yuan, which was an increase of 13% from the previous year. Unfortunately, with the global economic crisis, inbound tourism was significantly affected. The number of Hainan's inbound tourists dropped to 0.6 million or 8.01%, and the tourism foreign exchange revenue was $247.65 million, which was a decrease of 6.8%.

The island experienced 3 noteworthy tourism years in 2003, 2008, and 2010. During 2003, the SARS crisis resulted in the decline of both Hainan's visitors and total revenue. The following year, 2004, there was a substantial growth in the number of visitors. Although the global financial crisis weakened the growth of the tourism industry in 2008, there were still a reasonable number of tourists to Hainan due to the Beijing Olympic Games. The policy of HITI popularized the name of Hainan Island worldwide. It also caused the number of tourists to continuously exceed previous records and numbers of 30 million (2011), 40 million (2014), and 50 million (2015), which laid a solid foundation for future tourism markets (see Figure 3.1).

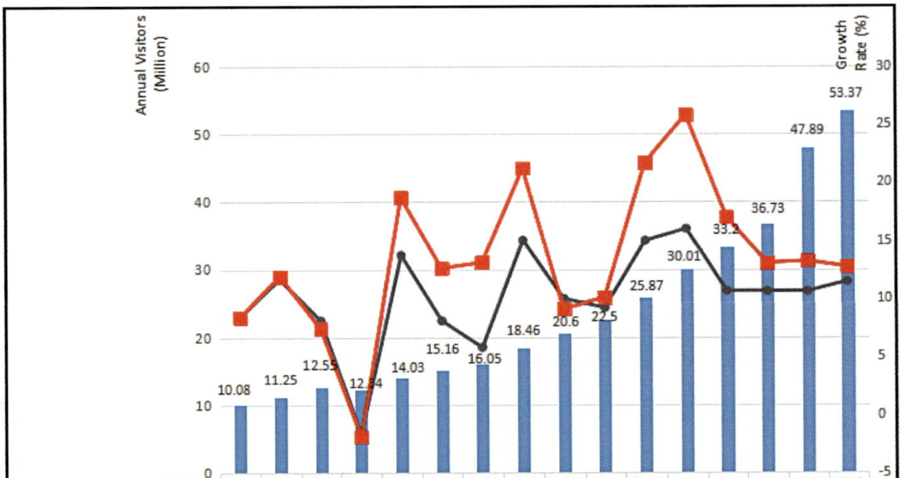

YEAR	2000	2001	2002	2003	2004	2005	2006	2007	2008	2009	2010	2011	2012	2013	2014	2015
Annual Visitors(Million)	10.08	11.25	12.55	12.34	14.03	15.16	16.05	18.46	20.6	22.5	25.87	30.01	33.2	36.73	47.89	53.37
Growth Rate of Visitor(%)	8.4	11.63	8.1	-1.7	13.7	8.1	5.8	15	9.97	9.2	14.98	16	10.63	10.61	10.6	11.43
Growth Rate of Income(%)	8.4	11.87	7.4	-1.9	18.7	12.6	13.1	21.2	9.1	10.1	21.68	25.8	17	13.04	13.2	12.7

FIGURE 3.1 Hainan Island tourism development in 2004–2015 (Source: Data from www.visithainan.org.cn collected by editor).

3.2 ANALYSIS OF INTERNATIONAL BRAND HOTELS ON THE ISLAND

3.2.1 BY YEAR: FROM 1996 TO 2016

In Hainan tourism development, the construction and development of the hospitality industry played an extremely important role. Hainan's first tourist hotel could be dated back to the year of 1963, when Hainan Overseas Chinese Hotel was established in Haikou City; it lasted for half a century since then and continues to provide high-quality services for both domestic and international tourists. Since the reform and establishment of the special economic zone, the Hainan hospitality industry has undergone more prosperous development. According to the data provided by the Hainan Tourism Development Committee (HNTDC), by the end of 2015, there were around 3,300 hotels with over 180,000 guestrooms. This consisted of tourist hotels, economy hotels, family hotels, holiday apartments, and other tourist accommodation industry. Among them, there were 144 star-rated tourist hotels, including 26 five-star hotels, 42 four-star hotels, and 64 three-star hotels.

In such a large tourist hotel system, international brand hotels have been shining stars. Back in 1994, the first five-star hotel in Hainan named *Haikou Huandao Tide Hotel* opened with the aid of Hong Kong investment. In 1996, Hainan's first international brand chain resorts called *Gloria Resort Sanya* opened at Yalong Bay and became China's first five-star resort. The second international brand hotel in Hainan, *Haikou Mandarin Hotel*, opened in 1997. In 2003, Hainan's first, top-ten international hotel group, Starwood Hotels and Resorts, opened its first resort, *Sheraton Resort Sanya*, on Hainan Island. It has been a driving force in the field of Chinese resort development. In the opening year of 2003, the total income of *Sheraton Resort Sanya* reached more than 100 million yuan, ranking the first place in the Asia Pacific region. It only took 3 years for the company to recover its full investment. From 2003 until 2005, the hotel was the host property for the Miss World Finals. It was a strong preference for the presidents who attended the Boao Forum for Asia (BFA) since 2003. In 2008, 2011, and 2013, the hotel was well known as the most popular place where the Chinese presidents held the most beautiful diplomatic activities for foreign presidents outside Beijing, the capital of China.

Since then, Hainan Island has become an even more popular tourist spot and attractive place of investment for international brand hotels. According to statistics, by the end of 2016, a total of 21 international hotel groups, 43 chain brands of 82 hotels opened around the island. These 30,238 guestrooms account for 16.8% of the total number of guestrooms on the island.

3.2.2 BY ROOM: FROM 400 TO 30,000

Generally, people believe that the opening of *Gloria Resort Sanya* in 1996 was the first international brand chain hotel in Hainan Island. There were 404 guestrooms in the hotel at that time. After nearly 20 years, the total number of Hainan international brand hotel guestrooms expanded to 30,238, which increased by 75 times as many guestrooms than those that were available in 1996 (see Table 3.1). The drastic increase in the number of new guestrooms was the proof of how international brand hotels increased in Hainan Island. There were 1,132 new guestrooms added in 2005 and another 2,163 guestrooms added in 2008. After 2010, the annual increase in new guestrooms was over 2000 rooms. There were 5,205 new guestrooms added in 2016, which was the largest growth rate of 20.8% as compared to the year of 2015. So, we can draw the conclusion that the year of 2010 was an important time frame for international brand hotels on Hainan Island.

TABLE 3.1 Development of International Brand Hotels on Hainan Island (2001–2016)

Year	2001	2002	2003	2004	2005	2006	2007	2008	2009	2010	2011	2012	2013	2014	2015	2016
New Rooms	359	333	948	0	1132	492	760	2163	748	2477	2403	3117	2462	3547	2510	5205
Total Rooms	1941	2274	3222	3222	4354	4846	5606	7769	8517	10994	13397	16514	18976	22523	25033	30238
Increase Rate (%)	22.7	17.2	41.7	0.0	35.1	11.3	15.7	38.6	9.6	29.1	21.9	23.3	14.9	18.7	11.1	20.8

(Source: Data from newspaper and internet collected by the editor).

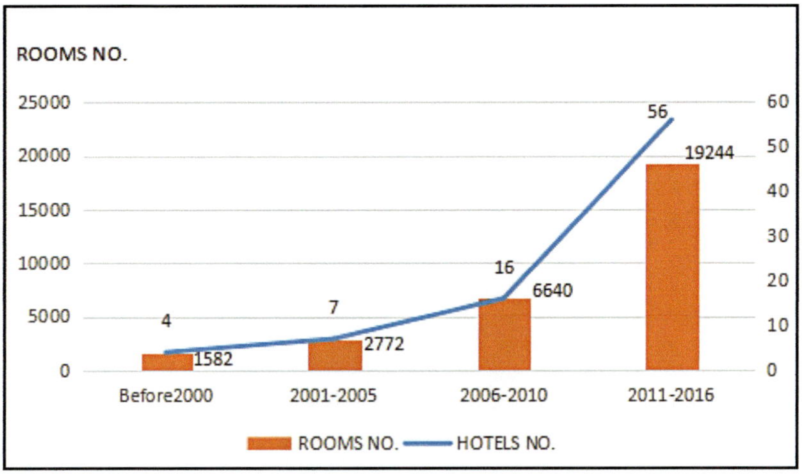

FIGURE 3.2 Increment of international brand hotels from 2000 to 2016 (Source: Data from newspaper and Internet collected by the editor).

As everyone knows, on January 4, 2010, the Chinese Central Government official website issued *"Opinions of the State Council on Promoting the Construction of Hainan International Tourism Island Development,"* which updated the development of HITI as a national strategy. This specific regional industrial policy led the international brand hotel investment boom, which played a pivotal role in promotion. From this point onward, the 5-year development cycle was much more significant (see Figure 3.2). In 2000, there were only 4 international brand hotels with 1,582 guestrooms. During 2001 through 2005, there were 7 new international brand hotels with a total of 2,772 guestrooms. From 2006 to 2010, there were 16 international brand hotels with 6,640 guestrooms. Surprisingly, from 2011 to 2016, there were 56 international brand hotels in operation with 19,244 guestrooms. This number had doubled in comparison to the number of rooms available 15 years ago. Obviously, the industrial policy and regional development strategy has promoted the value of the hospitality industry investment.

3.2.3 BY CITY: FROM SANYA TO WHOLE ISLAND

From the statistical data, Sanya, located at the southern tip of Hainan Island, has the highest concentration of international brand hotels. There

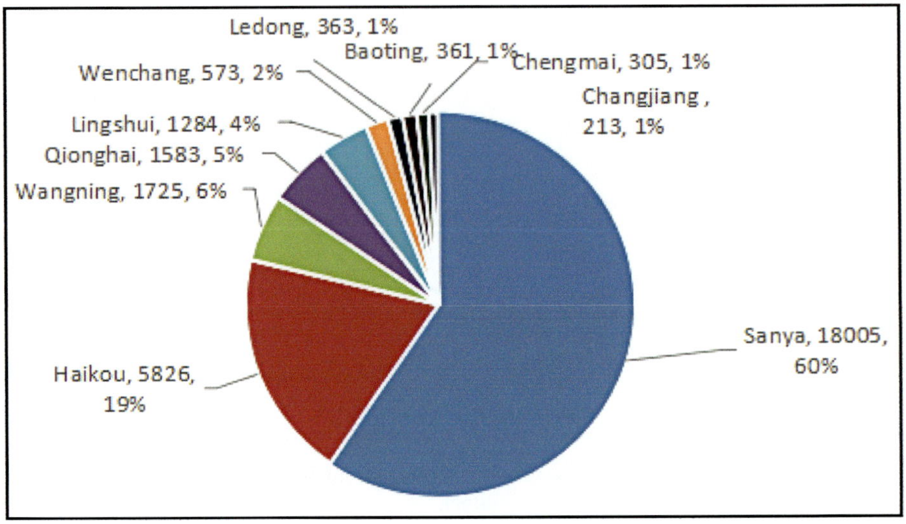

FIGURE 3.3 International brand chain hotels rooms on Hainan Island (by city).

are 44 international brand hotels with 18,005 guestrooms opened in Sanya (see Figure 3.3). In total, there are 82 international brand hotels opened on Hainan Island. The occupancy of Sanya is 53.7% of the total number of hotels and 59.5% of the total guestrooms, which exceeded Haikou in both the hotel numbers of 19.3% and the guestroom numbers of 20.7%. International brand hotels started in Haikou, flourished in Sanya, and followed by Wanning, Lingshui, and Qionghai along the east coast. Now, Wenchang, Baoting, Ledong, Chengmai and Changjiang are also making progress in such hotels. Thus, more and more international brand hotels will eventually reach and settle in the rest of the cities and counties across the island with the establishment of HITI.

3.2.4 BY BRAND: FROM STANDARD BRAND TO LUXURY BRAND

After successfully surviving the SARS crisis in 2003, Hainan tourism ushered in the new image of "Healthy Island, Longevity Island," and the hotel industry also entered a stage of growth. With the grand opening of *Sheraton Resort Sanya* at Yalong Bay in 2003, all famous international hotel groups began to attach great importance to Hainan Island. Most of them took Hainan

Island as the ideal place to showcase their first brands in China, in Asia, and even in the world. These brands made Hainan Island become a land full of all kinds of brands, from top luxury levels to economic brands.

Analysis of the distribution of international hotel groups, from the earliest Gloria Hotel Group (1996) to the most recent NH Hotel Group (2016), revealed 21 international hotel groups in Hainan Island (see Figure 3.4). Former Starwood Hotel Group was number one, opening 12 hotels with 4,409 guestrooms from 2003. The second largest group was the Wyndham Hotel Group with 11 hotels and 3,994 guestrooms. The InterContinental Hotel Group with 12 hotels and 3,882 guestrooms was among the top three. They were followed by the Hilton Hotel Group (9 hotels with 3,270 guestrooms) and the Marriott International Group (8 hotels with 3,100 guestrooms).

There are already 43 international hotel brands in Hainan Island. There are 6 hotels branded as Day Inn, followed by the brands of Holiday Inn, Hilton, and Marriott with 4 hotels each. The Starwood Hotel Group is the most successful for its brand numbers, frequency, scope, and coverage. It consists of St. Regis, the luxury collection, Westin, Sheraton, and Four Points by Sheraton, and other high-end brands landed in Sanya, Haikou, Wanning,

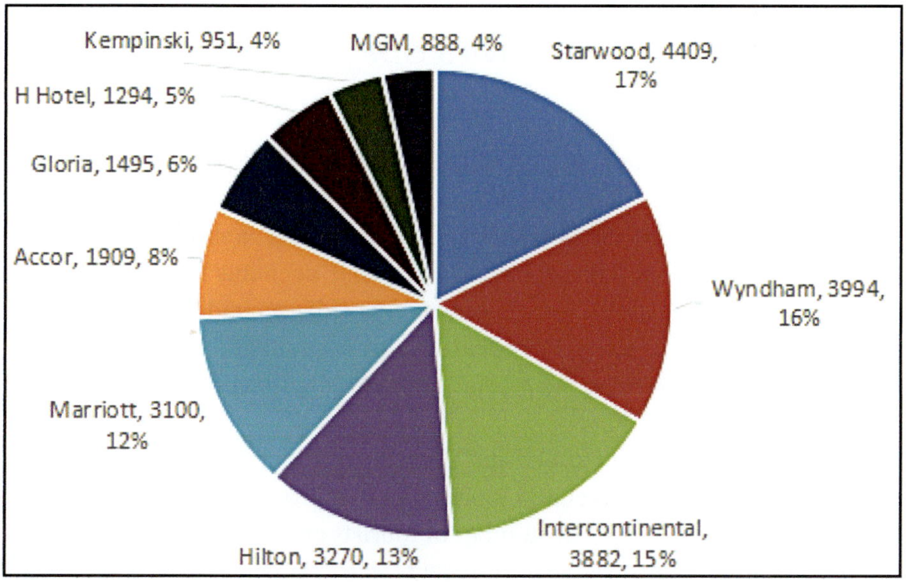

FIGURE 3.4 First 10 Hotel Groups on Hainan Island (2016) (Remark: The two Kempinski Resorts in Sanya were replaced by other brands in 2016).

Lingshui, and other cities around Hainan Island. For fast expansion and good business, the Starwood Hotel Group set up the first Hainan regional general manager who is in charge of all the hotels and brand development on Hainan Island. With the completion of the merger with the Marriott Group in September 2016, the Marriott Group will have more than 30 hotels with its classic brands and will probably rank the first on Hainan Island.

At the beginning of international brand hotels coming to Hainan Island, the management groups were from Hong Kong and Southeast Asia, including *Gloria Resort Sanya* operated by the Hong Kong Gloria Hotel Group and *Haikou Mandarin Hotel* managed by the Mandarin Oriental Hotel Group from Singapore. The Starwood Hotel Group, an American company and one of top 10 in the world, began to operate *Sheraton Resort Sanya* at Yalong Bay in 2003, which attracted and stimulated other famous hotel group development on the island. The following table shows the distributions of international brands in cities and counties on the island (see Table 3.2). It is easy to see that Sanya is the first choice of the brand name hotels on Hainan Island.

3.3 KEY DRIVERS OF INTERNATIONAL BRAND HOTELS IN HAINAN

3.3.1 INCREMENT OF CHINA'S GDP AND TOURISM CONSUMPTION

Since the reform and opening up of the country in 1978, China's economic growth has entered a stage of sustained and rapid development. According to the data reported by the World Bank, China's GDP was 11007.72 billion US dollars in 2015 (see Figure 3.5). China's GDP accounts for 17.75% of the total of the world's GDP. China is now the world's second largest economy after the USA. The Chinese President Xi Jinping said at the G20 summit in Hangzhou that China was the world's second largest economy, with a per capital GDP over $8,000.

With the income growth and the institution of public holidays, Chinese people's awareness of travel and tourism also improved with more time and more interest in traveling. The number of tourists and money spent by tourists are both increasing year by year. In recent years, statistics show that China's domestic tourism, total tourism income, and tourism consumption abroad have the highest ranking in the world. "*2015 National Economic and Social*

TABLE 3.2 List of The First Show of International Hotel Brands on Hainan Island

Year	Brand	Group	Hotel	City	Remark
1996	Gloria	Gloria	Gloria Resort & Hotel Sanya	Sanya	Upgraded by MGM
1997	Mandarin	Mandarin	Meritus Mandarin Haikou	Haikou	Replaced by Owner
2001	Holiday Inn	Intercontinental	Holiday Inn Sanya Yalong Bay	Sanya	First Holiday Inn
2002	Crowne Plaza	Intercontinental	Crowne Plaza Hainan	Haikou	Replaced by Owner
2003	Sheraton	Starwood	Sanya Sheraton Yalong Bay	Sanya	First Sheraton
2003	Sofitel	Accor	Sofitel Hotel BFA Qionghai Boao	Qionghai	Replaced by Owner
2006	Hilton	Hilton	Hilton Jinmao Sanya Yalong Bay	Sanya	First Hilton
2007	Days	Wyndham	Days Hotel & Suites Sanya Resort	Sanya	First Days
2007	Kempinski	Kempinski	Kempinski Resort, Sanya Bay	Sanya	Replaced by Mid-Club
2008	Banyan Tree	Banyan Tree	Banyan Tree Resort Sanya	Sanya	First Banyan Tree
2008	Howard John	Wyndham	Howard Johnson Resort Sanya Bay	Sanya	First Howard Johnson
2008	Le Meridien	Starwood	Wangning Le Meridien, Shimei Bay	Wangning	First Le Meridien
2008	Pullman	Accor	Pullman Sanya Yalong Bay	Sanya	First Pullman
2008	Ritz Carlton	Marriott	Ritz Carlton Sanya Yalong Bay	Sanya	First Ritz Carlton
2009	Mandarin	Mandarin	Mandarin Oriental Resort Sanya	Sanya	First Mandarin
2009	Marriott	Marriott	Marriott Sanya Yalong Bay	Sanya	First Marriott
2010	Conrad	Hilton	Conrad Resort Sanya Haitang Bay	Sanya	First Conrad
2010	Double Tree	Hilton	Doubletree Sanya Haitang Bay	Sanya	First Double Tree
2010	Grand Metro	CTS	Grand Metro Park Resort Sanya	Sanya	First CTS
2010	Intercontinental	Intercontinental	Intercontinental Resort Sanya	Sanya	First Intercontinental
2010	Mission	Mission	Mission Hills Haikou	Haikou	First Mission

TABLE 3.2 (Continued)

Year	Brand	Group	Hotel	City	Remark
2010	Ramada	Wyndham	Ramada Hotel & Suites Boao	Qionghai	First Ramada
2011	MGM	MGM	MGM Sanya Yalong Bay	Sanya	First MGM
2011	St. Regis	Starwood	St. Regis Sanya Yalong Bay	Sanya	First St.Regis
2012	Anantara	Minor	Anantara Sanya Resort and Spa	Sanya	First Anantara
2012	Shangri la	Shangri-La	Shangri-La Hotel Haikou	Haikou	First Shangri la
2013	Raffles	Accor	Raffles Sanya Qingshui Bay	Lingshui	First Raffles
2013	Westin	Starwood	Westin Sanya Haitang Bay	Sanya	First Westin
2015	Alila	Alila	Alila Resort Xiangshui Bay	Lingshui	First Alila
2016	Hampton	Hilton	Hampton by Hilton Sanya Bay	Sanya	First Hampton
2015	HuaLuxe	Intercontinental	Huayi Hotel Haikou	Haikou	First Hua Luxe
2015	Park Hyatt	Hyatt	Park Hyatt Sanya Yalong Bay	Sanya	First Park Hyatt
2016	Edition	Marriott	Edition Sanya Sanya Haitang Bay	Sanya	First Edition
2016	Grand Hyatt	Hyatt	Grand Hyatt Sanya Haitang Bay	Sanya	First Grand Hyatt
2016	Langham	Langham	The Langham Hotel Haikou	Haikou	First Langham
2016	NH Hotels	H Hotel	NH Hotels Sanya Phoenix Airport	Sanya	First H

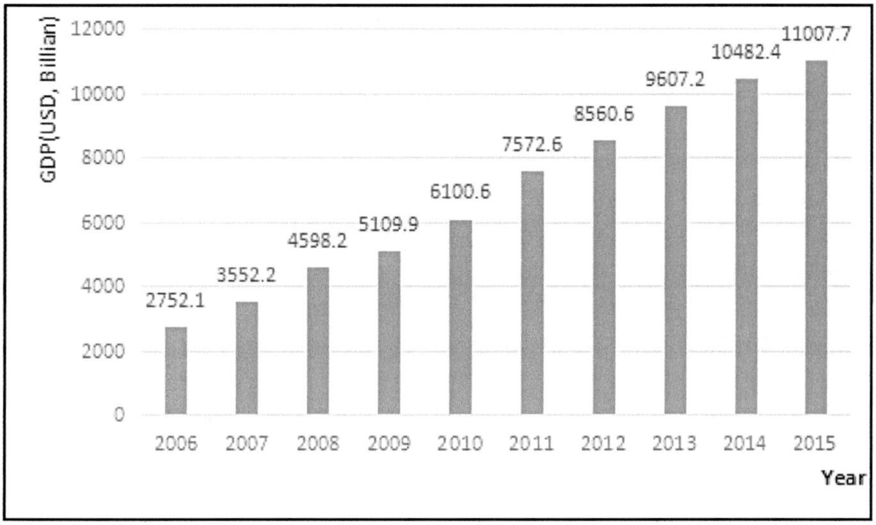

FIGURE 3.5 GDP of China from 2006 to 2015 (Source: http://www.tradingeconomics.com/china/gdp).

Development Statistics Bulletin" published by the National Bureau of Statistics showed that China's domestic tourists reached 4 billion passengers, with an increase of 10.5% over the previous year [2]. Domestic tourism revenue was ¥34.195 billion with 13.1% growth. The number of inbound tourists was 133.82 million with an increase of 4.1%, and international tourism revenue was $113.7 billion with an increase of 7.8%. A total of 127.86 million passengers traveled abroad in 2015, with growth up by 9.7%. According to the World Tourism & Travel Council (WTTC), China tourism's contribution on the GDP reached 10.1%, which was more than that of education, banking, and the automotive industry.

3.3.2 ABUNDANT TOURISM RESOURCES ON HAINAN ISLAND

In China, Hainan Island is the only tropical coastal island with rich and unique resources for tourism development, such as sunshine, ocean, islands, beaches, forests, animals, hot springs, caves, pastoral, customs, and

[2] http://www.stats.gov.cn/tjsj/zxfb/201602/t20160229_1323991.html, Statistical Communique on National Economic and Social Development in 2015

monuments. Hainan Island is one of the most abundant and intensive tropical coastal tourism resources in the world. There are more than 300 days of sunshine, over 2 million square kilometers of sea area, and over 1,823 km of the coastline on the island. Significantly, there are 60 beaches and bays that can be used for tourism, including Yalong Bay, Sanya Bay, Dadong Bay, Shimei Bay, and Clear Water Bay. In addition, there are more than 50 golf clubs that can host international golf tours and 8 state forest parks with tropical rain forests. Hainan Island also has some classic ethnic minorities including Li, Hui, and Miao with their special music, dance, clothing, food, architecture, and customs that are very distinctive.

With its rich and unique resources, Hainan has developed a full array of holiday travel products and services such as coastal resorts, island resorts, mountain resorts, cruise vacation, holiday village, attractions, shopping, golf, low altitude flight, and others.

3.3.3 GOOD TOURISM INFRASTRUCTURE CONSTRUCTIONS

Since 1988, Hainan has established fast and convenient means of three-dimensional transportation infrastructure and other facilities. Tourists can reach Hainan Island by plane, train, car, or ship.

3.3.3.1 Airports and Airlines

Sanya Phoenix International Airport opened on July 1, 1994, and Haikou Meilan International Airport opened on May 25, 1999. Both airports reached 10 million passengers in 2011 and more than 15 million passengers in 2015. On March 17, 2016, Hainan Boao Airport officially implemented trial operations and became the third airport in Hainan Island. In 2016, three airports located on Yongshu Reef, Meiji Reef, and Zhubi Reef completed successful test flights by Chinese airplanes [3]. They enabled the development of remote, oceanic island tourism. At present, the two international airports of Sanya Phoenix and Haikou Meilan are undergoing expansion. Sanya also has a new plan to build Sanya International Airport within the coming 10 years.

[3] http://news.xinhuanet.com/local/2016-01/06/c_1117692073.htm, China 's Nansha Yongshu reef new airport test flight successfully

3.3.3.2 Rail Transportation

A crossing-sea train (Haikou-Guangzhou, K408/407) was developed on Hainan Island on December 5, 2004. Currently, there are six railway lines connecting the island and the mainland, namely Haikou-Xi'an, Haikou-Shanghai, Haikou-Zhengzhou, Haikou-Harbin, Sanya-Beijing West, and Sanya-Changchun. On December 30, 2015, Hainan Western Ring High-Speed Railway officially opened with a total mileage of 345 km from Haikou to Sanya by the western side. It was linked with the existing Hainan Eastern Ring High-Speed Railway, which opened in 2010 with a total mileage of 308 km. Thus, the only ring island high-speed railway in the world, Hainan Island Ring High-speed Railway, was built with a total length of 653 km, covering 12 cities and counties and 87% of the population in the province (see Figure 3.6)[4]. It takes 3.5 hours to travel around the island in the shortest time, which can save much time for the residents and tourists.

3.3.3.3 Ports and Cruise

Hainan Province has already opened 24 ports among the existing 68 natural harbors, including the three biggest ports, namely Haikou Port, Yangpu Port, and Sanya Port. On August 8, 2015, the cruise ship, Voyager of The Seas, docked at Sanya Phoenix Island International Cruise Terminal. The stop enabled Hainan's first 150 thousand tons of cruise terminal to be officially put into use. At the same time, Sanya Phoenix Island International Cruise Terminal will facilitate the construction of two more terminals of 150 thousand tons and 225 thousand tons, which will be able to anchor the world's largest cruise ships.

3.3.4 SPECIAL SUPPORTING POLICY FROM THE CENTRAL GOVERNMENT

On January 4, 2010, the China Central Government website issued a signature document named "*Several Opinions of State Council on Promoting the Construction and Development of Hainan International Tourism Island*"

[4] http://usa.chinadaily.com.cn/epaper/2015-12/31/content_22885515.htm, New high-speed rail circles Hainan

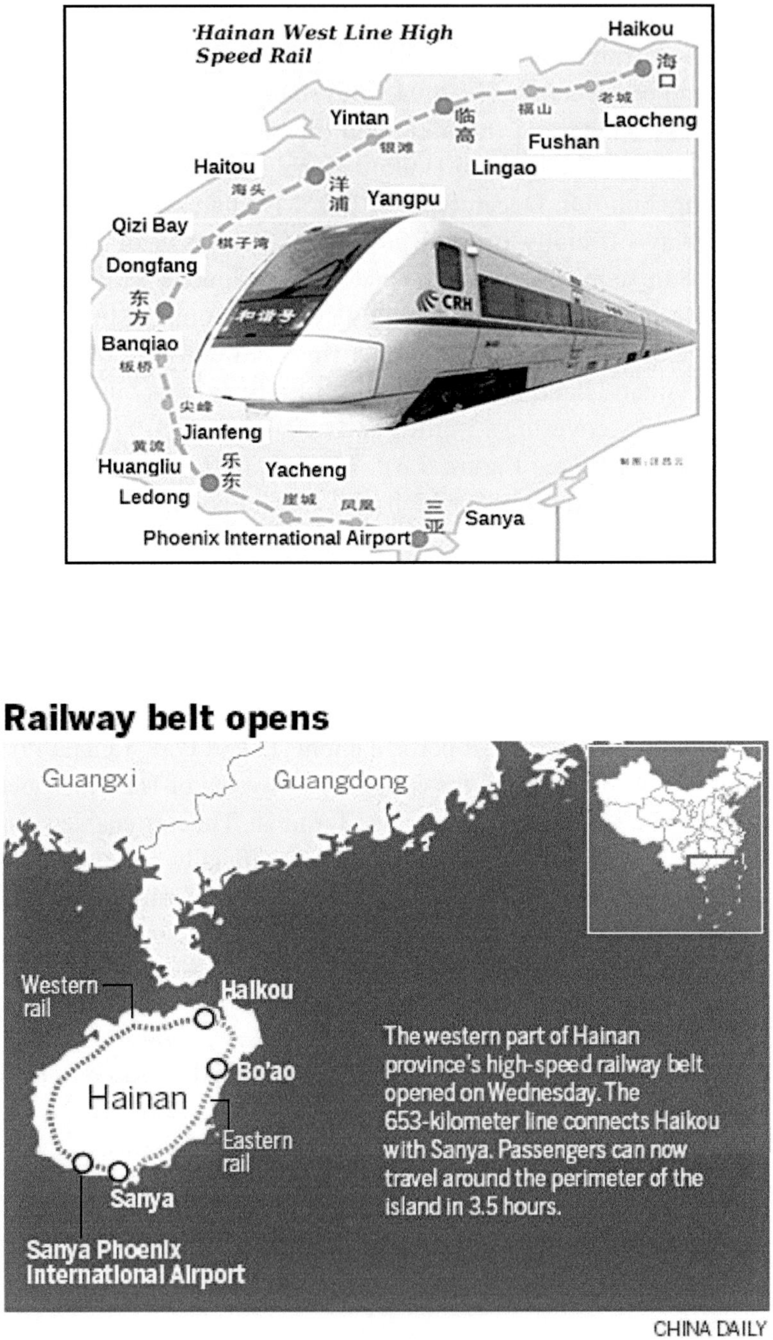

FIGURE 3.6 High-speed railway around Hainan Island (Source: http://usa.chinadaily.com.cn/epaper/2015-12/31/content_22885515.htm).

(No. 44 of State Council in 2009), [5] which was the first official regional tourism development strategy issued by the State Council to Hainan Island and played an important role as a major national strategic deployment. The document included the key general requirements of HITI as follows:

(1) How to strengthen the construction of ecological civilization and the ability of sustainable development.
(2) How to improve the tourism management and related services by taking advantage of the unique characteristics and advantages of Hainan Island.
(3) How to develop modern service industry vigorously for the transformation and upgrading of service industry.
(4) How to accelerate the integration of the process with urban and rural areas by the modern tropical agriculture.
(5) How to strengthen infrastructure construction for enhancing the service ability.
(6) How to promote social construction improvement of people's livelihood and human intellectual property.
(7) How to make full use of local resources to develop new smart and comprehensive industry.
(8) How to strengthen the organization and coordination of the implementation of the safeguard measures.

All these requirements will be used to build an open, green, civilized, and harmonious world-class travel and leisure island and popular holiday destination in 2020.

With the issuance of the document being issued, many new policies have been implemented including visa on arrival or visa free, duty-free shopping for residents, duty refund for foreigners, event games, lottery, and others.

3.3.4.1 The Visa-free Policy Renewed for Foreigners on Arrival

Since October 31, 2000, a visa-free policy began to take effect in Hainan; this policy is for a tourist group with 5 and more people from 21 countries staying on the island for less than 15 days without a visa. In October 2011, the Central Government added five more countries, namely Finland, Denmark, Norway, Ukraine, and Kazakhstan, to the visa-free country list.

[5] http://www.gov.cn/zwgk/2010-01/04/content_1502531.htm, Opinions of the State Council on Promoting the Construction and Development of Hainan International Tourism Islands

At the same time, the minimum requirement for tour groups from Russia, South Korea, and Germany was reduced from 5 persons to 2 persons, and the residency time limit was extended from 15 days to 21 days. Until now, the visa-free policy for 26 countries in Hainan Island is the most convenient visa policy in China's mainland.

3.3.4.2 The Tax Refund Policy for Foreigners Upon Departure

From January 1, 2011, Hainan Island was the China's first region to implement the policy of tax refunds for foreigners when they depart from Hainan Island. Overseas visitors can obtain a refund totaling 9% of the invoice value. After more than 4 years of trials, Beijing and Shanghai began to implement the same policy starting July 1, 2015. This policy was extended to Tianjin, Fujian, Liaoning, Anhui, and Sichuan from January 1, 2016; to Jiangsu, Qingdao, Shenzhen, Shaanxi, and Yunnan from April 1, 2016; to Guangdong on July 1, 2016; and to Shandong on September 1, 2016. In other words, the amount of refund that the overseas visitors can obtain actually is 9% of the invoice value.

3.3.4.3 The Duty-free Policy to Chinese Residents

On April 20, 2011, the first duty-free shop operated by the China Duty Free Group opened at Sanya downtown, marking the formal implementation of an offshore duty-free policy for Chinese citizens. At that time, the Sanya duty-free shop in downtown was not only a shopping mall but also a popular attraction spot for more than 100 million tourists each year. Because the shop had a very good business and the huge demand, a newer and bigger duty-free shop, Sanya Haitang Bay International Duty-free Shopping Center, opened on September 1, 2014. The business area of the new shop was increased from 10 thousand square meters of the former city shop to 70 thousand square meters. It is now the largest single duty-free shop in the world covering nearly 300 international brands. The Sanya Haitang Bay International Duty-free Shopping Center has already received more than 9.2 million customers totally in the past 2 years and has created a new record of duty-free sales of over 8 billion yuan.[6] Obviously, it became a major highlight of the tourism market in Hainan Island.

[6] http://finance.china.com.cn/roll/20160827/3880060.shtml, The world's largest single duty-free shops in Sanya reached 8 billion yuan income in the past two years

3.3.5 TOURISM INVESTMENT STRATEGY AND LOCAL GOVERNANCE

Over the past 30 years, the government of Hainan Province continued to promote a strategy to attract large companies to invest in big projects in its tourism industry. There are several landmark projects that encourage the tourism industry to develop rapidly. Early in 1996, the State Council approved the Sanya Yalong Bay National Resort District, which was the first coastal tourism resort in China, which is still running well among the former 13 national resort districts. On April 25, 2005, the most exquisite 180-meter-high statue of Buddhist Guanyin was set up on the ocean at the Sanya Nanshan Cultural Tourism Zone, which is very popular with more than 4 million visitors yearly. The Haikou Mission Hills Golf Resort, the world's second biggest golf paradise, was opened in 2011 with eleven different styles of golf courses; it hosted the World Cup of golf many times, attracting some world-class golf masters including Tiger Woods. At the same time, there were many tourism attractions, hotels, resorts, restaurants, yacht ports, and other kind of enterprises to be operated. At the end of 2016, there were 55 A-grade tourist attractions, including six AAAAA-grade tourist attractions.[7]

The Hainan Province government has issued several regulations to promote the development of the tourism industry. One document named "*Hainan International Tourism Island Construction and Development Plan*" was promulgated in 2010, which was in response to the State Council policy on the construction of HITI. On January 27, 2016, a document "*A Number of Opinions on Improving the Quality and Level of Development of the Tourism Industry in Hainan Island*" (Hainan Government [2016] No. 7) promulgated by the people's government of Hainan Province was used to implement the "*State Council's Opinions on Promoting the Reform and Development of Tourism*" (State Council [2014] No. 31) and the "*State Council Office's Opinions on Further Promoting Suggestions on Tourism Investment and Consumption*" (State Council Office [2015] No. 62). The province now is implementing these policies.

From the beginning, Hainan Island positioned the tourism industry as a pillar industry, developing relevant industrial policies with innovating

---

[7] http://hnrb.hinews.cn/html/2016-01/29/content_1_12.htm, Behind the beautiful performance of Hainan tourism development

tourism management systems. On May 28, 2009, Hainan took the lead in the reformation of the tourism administration department, establishing the first Tourism Development Committee (TDC) around China mainland, renaming the Hainan Tourism Bureau to the Hainan Tourism Development Committee and entrusting them with updating responsibilities for the co-ordination of traffic rights, ports, transportation, culture, business, and other related departments to integrate tourism management functions. The head of the committee also worked as an assistant to the province governor to show the importance of the new organization.

Moreover, all the cities, including Sanya city, have made some innovations to regulate the tourism marketing. On October 10,2015, China's first "*Tourist Police*" was established in Sanya (see Figure 3.7), which effectively curbed frauds in tourism sales.[8] The National Tourism Administration designated Sanya as a national model. There are at least 34 cities or counties in 16 provinces that established a system of tourist police.

FIGURE 3.7 Sanya Tourist Police founded in October 2015.

[8] http://news.xinhuanet.com/legal/2015-10/10/c_1116782818.htm, The first tourist police team was formally established in Sanya, Hainan

3.3.6 WORLD-CLASS SPECIAL EVENTS & FESTIVALS

Since the inception of the BFA in 2001, Hainan Island has become the host of all kinds of momentous and landmark events and festivals, which made Hainan Island a focus over the world. In fact, the events and festivals in Hainan Island have ranged from beauty contests to political events and from sports to music, arts, and others.

The beauty contests began with the China Silk Road Model Contests in 2001. The Miss World Finals were the most popular events, held six times in Hainan Island in 2003, 2004, 2005, 2007, 2010, and 2015. Miss World 2010, the 60th anniversary of the Miss World pageant, was held on October 30, 2010, at the Crown of Beauty Theater in Sanya, Hainan Island, China. Finally, Alexandria Mills of the United States won the coveted crown as Miss World 2010, triumphing over 115 beautiful and talented young women from all around the world. The Elite Model Look 25th/26th World Finals were held in Sanya, Hainan, in 2008/2009, which was the world's most prestigious, widely covered, and most influential modeling contest. The world-class beauty contests indeed contributed to make Hainan Island as an international tourism destination.

In terms of political events, Hainan Island was the founding place and permanent venue of the BFA. BFA has grown into an important international event comparable to the Davos World Economic Forum. Every year, thousands of state heads, ministers, CEOs, and business men brought enormous marketing value to Hainan Island. Hainan is an especially good place to hold a military parade ceremony to welcome foreign presidents and dignitaries.

There are also sports, music, and arts events. Hainan International Road Cycling Race, also called Tour of Hainan, started in 2006 and is a 2.HC class event approved by the International Cycling Union. Tour of Hainan 2016 was held during October 22-30, 2016, in a total of 9 stages and a total mileage of 1512 km, passing through 18 cities and counties in Hainan Island (see Figure 3.8).[9] The 2008 Beijing Olympic Torch Passing arrived in Hainan Island on May 4, 2008. Haikou Mission Hill created World Golf Star & Professional Invitational in 2011 and held World Cup golf game every two years since 2012, which was attended by Tiger Woods. The Volvo Ocean Race, the

---

[9] http://news.xinhuanet.com/sports/2016-10/22/c_1119766619.htm, 2016 Hainan Island International Road Cycling Race opened on Oct. 22nd

FIGURE 3.8 Course outline of Tour of Hainan 2016.

longest ocean race in the world, stopped at Hainan Island twice in 2012 and 2015. These were the only stop in Asia and spawned Hainan International Regatta Race held annually in March in the Hainan Island sea since 2010.

The World Women's Surfing Competition is also held every year at Sun & Moon Bay of Wanning City, Hainan Island.

In addition to the above, there are also other local events and festivals featuring music, beer, food, art, culture, and business held in different counties and cities in Hainan Island. These events and festivals brought national leaders, entertainment stars, business partners, medias, and visitors to experience Hainan Island landscape and culture, bringing with them the world's attention, which made Hainan Island increasingly better known, understood, and accepted. Of course, more people will come to Hainan Island, and more businesses will participate in the hospitality industry, including international brand hotels.

3.3.7 TOURISM PROMOTIONS AND ROADSHOWS AROUND THE WORLD

Based on these tourism resources, products, policies, and investments, the Hainan government departments, tourism enterprises, and industry organizations are constantly planning and executing many international and domestic market and promotion activities that continue to shape Hainan Island as a world tourism destination. In the past 10 years, Hainan continued to participate in first-class tourism exhibitions including ITB (International Tourism Exchange Berlin), MITT (Moscow International Travel & Tourism Exhibition), KITF (Kazakhstan International Tourism Fair), and ITEHK (International Travel Expo Hong Kong), where the main tourist source countries and regions over Asia, Europe, America, Australia, and the Middle East are present. More, Hainan also participates in the Miami International Cruise Conference every year to promote its place in the Cruise and Yacht industry to the world. Hainan also created its own branded tourism exhibition, Hainan Rendez-Vous, in 2010, which was Asia's first lifestyle exhibition and a unique opportunity to penetrate the Chinese high-end consumer market. The 2016 Hainan International Tourism Trade Fair attracted many valued investors and visitors from around the world. At the same time, Hainan tourism promotion benefited from the China-Russia Tourism Year and China-USA Tourism Year with more and more tourists from Russia and America in the most recent 2 years. Data showed that Russia was the number one origin country of visitors to Hainan Island. The number of American tourists has kept going up from 2010 even during the global economic crisis.

3.4 KEY EFFECTS OF INTERNATIONAL BRAND HOTELS ON HAINAN ISLAND

3.4.1 NEW BRAND HOTELS CHANGED THE SUPPLY-NEED STATUS OF HOSPITALITY

The most immediate impact of the international brand hotels in Hainan Island is that they changed the supply of the hotel market, in terms of their quantity and quality of supply. The number of international brand hotel guestrooms was over 30,000. Due to the rapid growth of international brand hotels, the five-star hotels and four-star hotels in Hainan Island have brought direct competitive pressure. In Sanya, for example, the average daily rate (ADR), occupancy (OCC), and revenue per available room (RevPAR) showed a downward trend generally in the past 20 quarters. Table 3.3 shows the ADR, OCC, and RevPAR of the first quarter from 2011 to 2016 (see Table 3.3).

More importantly, these hotels, on behalf of the international standard hotel facilities, products, and services, also enriched Hainan Island's hotel supply system. They can provide a new choice for Chinese and foreign tourists, allowing tourists to enjoy high-quality products and services of these

TABLE 3.3 Sanya Five-Star Hotel and Four-Star Hotel Performance in Q1 of 2011 to 2016

Hotel star	Year/quarter	No. of star hotels	ADR (Yuan)	OCC (%)	RevPAR (Yuan)
Five star	2011/Q1	10	1688.75	79.56	1343.57
	2012/Q1	9	1789.84	75.97	1359.74
	2013/Q1	9	1819.61	76.53	1392.55
	2014/Q1	9	1544.99	82.75	1278.48
	2015/Q1	11	1537.53	79.54	1222.49
	2016/Q1	13	1379.29	79.44	1095.71
Four star	2011/Q1	16	486.28	84.29	409.89
	2012/Q1	20	460.81	79.22	365.05
	2013/Q1	17	460.54	69.93	322.06
	2014/Q1	16	454.58	70.98	322.66
	2015/Q1	16	393.73	75.53	297.38
	2016/Q1	17	359.79	75.62	272.07

international brand hotels. For example, the former *Gloria Resort Sanya* opened in 1996 with the first open-style lobby facing the ocean without any windows and with air conditioning. Sanya Marriott Resort opened with the first wedding chapel in 2008 (see Figure 3.9). The Ritz Carlton Hotel *Sanya* built the first botanical garden with all kinds of animals and plants, and Sanya MGM Resort brought the first chocolate waterfall to China in 2011. All these new products and services offer visitors a whole new experience and fun to their holidays.

3.4.2 NEW SYSTEMS IMPROVED HOTELS MANAGEMENT AROUND THE ISLAND

Management modes and quality of service are the core comparative advantages of the international brand hotels, among which talents are the key of the style. In the early days when international brand hotels came to Hainan Island, senior management were all foreigners including the general manager, directors, and many department heads. These foreign managers had different concepts and methods of hotel management and

FIGURE 3.9 Hainan's First Wedding Chapel at Marriott Resort Sanya Yalong Bay, in 2008.

leadership, especially when dealing with customer relationships, staff care, brand promotion, and a high level of leadership. These objectively promoted Chinese employees to change service consciousness and management philosophy and to improve the quality of local staff growth. It also improved the management level of other hotels. At present, the new international brand hotels have begun to appoint local people as general managers or only keep at most two foreign staff when opening a new brand hotel. More and more Chinese professional managers have been trained and appointed as general managers of the international brand hotels. In China, with the exception of Beijing, Shanghai, and Guangzhou, Yalong Bay at Hainan Island, was recognized as the top level of hotel service and management because of the Ritz Carlton, St. Regis, Park Hyatt, MGM, Sheraton, Hilton, and the other international brand hotels located around the bay.

3.4.3 NEW CONSUMPTION PROMOTED ECONOMIC DEVELOPMENT

The economic index is always an important index for the evaluation of the development of a new industry in terms of creating new consumption, providing new employment opportunities, increasing local fiscal revenue, and promoting related industries. In the past 6 years, the international brand hotels created 30,000 new jobs at least, including more than 50 general managers, more than 500 department managers, and thousands of supervisors and captains. These new jobs will increase the annual household income to improve the quality of life significantly.

3.4.4 NEW CULTURE FASTENED THE SOCIAL IMPRESSION

International brand hotels bring new cultural phenomenon, including new language culture, new consumption concepts, new service concepts, new design ideas, new management theories, and a new way of life. The Hainan Island local society and the community provide a pluralistic and open world, with employees of different nationalities, from different regions, and all kinds of popular culture in this intersection, collision, integration, and development. Lifestyle and social thought have had a more or less influence on the local people's life philosophy, and gradually, the international brand hotels have adapted the local culture in their designs and architecture.

3.4.5 NEW HOTEL BUILDINGS ENRICHED THE CITY LANDSCAPES

International brand hotel management is a system consisting of the design, construction, decoration, and operation of the property. Its architectural form is a local landmark. The Y shape of the old *Gloria Resort* or the later double Y of the MGM were both classical benchmarks at Sanya Yalong Bay or in Hainan Island and even in China. Sanya is a wonderful place to reflect on the ingenious application of Chinese traditional construction culture in the hospitality industry, where you can see the hall layout at the Sheraton, the summer palace miniature at the Ritz Carlton (see Figure 3.10), and the royal columns at the St. Regis. These enriched the landscape of the local city, as guests were enjoying comfortable guestrooms and delicious foods. The unique resorts and hotels gathered at different bays are the wonderful landscape in Hainan Island. They also create a good place to experience, visit, and learn for the Chinese hotel industry.

FIGURE 3.10 Chinese traditional construction of Ritz Carlton Sanya Yalong Bay.

3.4.6 NEW BRANDS ENHANCED THE REPUTATION OF HAINAN ISLAND

One hotel can become an international and world-class brand due to its visibility, customer and employee satisfaction, and reputation. These world-class brand hotels in Hainan Island brought Hainan Island to the worldwide marketplace through its global distribution system. Take Marriott International Group for example; when Marriott Resort Sanya opened in 2008, all the information about Sanya and Hainan Island was spread to the world through the advertisement, TV, websites, Facebook, Twitter, and other media of the Marriott International Group. At the same time, the other international hotel groups can also provide a variety of channels and resources to promote Hainan Island, in which the membership system, partners, and investors play an important role.

3.5 TRENDS OF THE HOSPITALITY INDUSTRY ON HAINAN ISLAND

3.5.1 TOURISM INDUSTRY WILL PLAY NEW ROLES FOR CHINA'S ECONOMY

According to data announced by the Chinese government, China's GDP growth rate was 6.9% in 2015. [10] The downward pressure on the economy was a general consideration. As is well known, China's economy entered the new normal, namely the speed of economic development from rapid growth to a turn for high-speed growth; the economic structure is optimized and upgraded, and the economic driving force is transformed from factor driven and investment driven to innovation driven. At the same time, China's tourism industry in 2015 continued to achieve steady growth, with estimated annual reception of domestic and foreign tourists of more than 4.1 billion; the total tourism revenue reached 4.13 trillion RMB, which contributed to 10.8% of GDP with 7.34 trillion RMB directly and indirectly. Obviously, under the new normal of the Chinese economy, the strategic value of the tourism industry is significantly improved and is positioned for economic transformation and upgrade as a key driving force.

---

[10] http://www.stats.gov.cn/tjsj/zxfb/201602/t20160229_1323991.html, Statistical Communique on National Economic and Social Development in 2015

3.5.2 HOSPITALITY INDUSTRY IS STILL LEADING THE TOURISM INDUSTRY

Reviewing the history of China's tourism industry for more than 30 years, the hospitality industry has been one of the three pillars of the tourism industry, leading the development of tourism industry in China. On April 28, 1982, the first Chinese foreign joint venture hotel, Beijing Jianguo Hotel, was opened as a starting point of China's tourist hotel development. On September 1, 1993, the first Chinese national tourism industry standard "*The Foreign-related Tourist Hotel Star Classification and Assessment in China*" (GB/T 14308-1993) began to operate. It was renewed with three revisions of 1997, 2004, and 2010, which played a positive and important role in promoting the standardization and internationalization of China's tourist hotel industry. Thus, the hospitality industry in China was the earliest utilization of foreign capital, the earliest implementation of standards, and the earliest international industry, and it also set up the benchmark to other elements of the tourism industry, promoting the stable and sustainable development of China's tourism industry.

The hospitality industry is a capital-intensive, technology-intensive, personnel-intensive, and emotion-intensive industry, with a positive effect on tourist destinations. The positive effects included the provision of financial resources, research and technology, outstanding management personnel, advanced international awareness, greater scale employment, destination image promotion, international communication, and so on. The hospitality industry has become the most important part of the tourist destination and tourist city. All the large hotel groups have entered the Chinese tourism market.

3.5.3 TRENDS OF INTERNATIONAL BRAND HOTELS ON HAINAN ISLAND AFTER 2017

3.5.3.1 More and More International Brand Hotels will be Opened

According to projected estimated statistics, from 2017–2020, there will be 21 hotel group's 51 international brand hotels opening with new rooms of 17,754 in Hainan Island. They will continue to the growth of 58.7% from the present. In 2017 alone, there will be 23 international brand hotels constructed with 8,828 new guestrooms, which accounts for 49.7% of the total

FIGURE 3.11 Atlantis Hotels Sanya, Hainan, is coming in 2018.

new guestrooms. From the hotel group distribution, the Marriott Group will open 15 hotels & resorts (including the original nine Starwood hotels), with 4,169 guestrooms, thus accounting for 23.5% of the total new guestrooms; this is followed by the IHG with 7 hotels, Hyatt with 5 hotels, and Hilton and Accor with 4 hotels each.

In addition, the most noteworthy addition is the Atlantis Sanya, which will be opened with 1314 guestrooms and the biggest ocean garden in the world (see Figure 3.11). [11] The investor of Kerzner International has confirmed the discovery of artifacts from the lost civilization of Atlantis in Sanya Hainan, China. The site, which encompasses over 62 hectares, will be home to the new five-star Atlantis Destination Resort. Holidaymakers from across the globe will uncover a mysterious and captivating world as they explore the myth and wonder of Atlantis. Guests will realize larger-than-life experiences as they come face-to-face with exotic marine life, are exhilarated by the Aquaventure water slides, and indulge in masterful culinary delights. The find in the South China Sea has revealed a new understanding of the Atlantis civilization. The resort's new design combines regional architectural hues and the aquatic theme that is synonymous

[12] http://www.atlantissanya.com, Sanya Atlantis Hotel Official Website

with the two existing Atlantis Destination Resorts in The Bahamas and Dubai. An unprecedented marine experience will be discovered in Atlantis Hainan. It will provide once-in-a-lifetime entertainment. There is something for everyone in the imaginative world of Atlantis, which includes superb accommodation, restaurants by world-renowned chefs, a vibrant range of bars and lounges, indulgent spas and luxury boutiques, extensive slides and rides at Aquaventure Waterpark, a dolphin interaction and education center, an interactive Atlantis Kids Club, magnificent event spaces, and endless stretches of beach, fresh and salt-water pools, lagoons, and marine exhibits as well.

3.5.3.2 More and More Luxury Brands Will Land on Hainan Island

Ritz Carlton Resort Sanya Yalong Bay began to welcome guests on April 25, 2008; it was recognized as the first top-rated luxury resort in Hainan Island. Since then, Banyan Tree Resort at Luhuitou Bay (2008), Mandarin Oriental Resort at Xiaodong Bay (2009), Conrad Resort at Haitang Bay (2010), St. Regis Resort at Yalong Bay (2011), Raffles Resort at Tufu Bay (2013), and Park Hyatt Resort at Sunny Bay (2015) opened consecutively and yielded a good return on the market. In the coming 4 years, the first Waldorf, the first Four Seasons, the first Fairmont, the first Bulgari, the First Jumeirah, the first One & Only, the first Andaz, the first Indigo, and the first Autograph are going to be opened around Hainan Island as well as the second Mandarin Oriental, the second St. Regis, and the second and third Ritz Carlton are also under planning. Thus, all the world's first luxury resort brands will finish their management or investment in Hainan, thus playing a new role and presenting a new world of luxury resort in China.

3.5.3.3 More and More Cities and Counties Will Have International Brand Hotels

From the view of regional distribution, Sanya is still the most popular and the first choice destination of international brand hotels' strategic development. Over the next 4 years, 23 new international brand hotels will be opened in Sanya. In the next 4 years, 23 new international brand hotels with 8,840 guestrooms will be opened in Sanya, which accounted for 45.1% of the number of newly opened hotels and 49.8% of the number of new guestrooms on the whole island. Lingshui County will open 10 hotels, with more than 9 hotels in Haikou City, showing its incorporation advantage of the Grand Sanya Tourism Circle. There are many international brand hotels under planning and construction in Wanning, Qionghai, Wenchang, Baoting, Ledong, Dingan, and other cities and counties, either in East of Hainan Island or in the Central and Western areas of Hainan Island.

3.5.3.4 More and More impacts by International Brand Hotels Will Occur

The most important thing is that the current oversupply of the market situation will continue to develop for a period of time. International brand hotels bring the international perspective, concept, behavior, culture, and personnel. They will have a deeper impact on the development of the Hainan Island hotel and the tourism Industry. One of these effects is that China's local brand hotels will become more powerful under the multiple forces of self-promotion and more international mergers and acquisition. Further, these changes will improve the experience in Hainan Island and benefit the Chinese and foreign tourists. Hainan Island can also take a step closer to become an international tourism destination with the hospitality industry thoroughly internationalized.

3.6 CONCLUDING REMARKS

- Hainan Island is a unique tropical island and the most popular coastal tourism destination in China, being one of the regions with the fastest growing tourism in the country.
- Hainan Island abounds in hotels that are highly ranking internationally, playing a role in the development of the hospitality industry in China, and even in the Pacific and Asia region.
- Based on quality resource endowment and infrastructure improvement, the national industrial policy plays a key role in the rapid expansion of the international brand hotels in Hainan Island.
- International brand hotels have brought great changes to Hainan Island, especially to the establishment of great international reputation and the improvement of service and management quality. It has some negative effects such as income decline and quality damage.

- In terms of hospitality, the tourism industry is a new field and new power of economic development and enhancement of consumption in China. It is predicted that the hospitality industry in Hainan Island will confront intense competition in the future, and both the government and business partners should be well prepared to face these challenges.

KEYWORDS

- **branding**
- **development**
- **drivers**
- **effects**
- **Hainan Island**
- **hospitality industry**
- **international brand hotels**
- **internationalization**
- **tourism**
- **trends**

CHAPTER 4

THE EXPANSIONS OF CHINESE COMPANIES IN FOREIGN HOSPITALITY INDUSTRY

KUN YANG[1] and JINLIN ZHAO[2]

[1]*College of Business Administration, Central Michigan University, MI 48859, USA*

[2]*Chaplin School of Hospitality and Tourism Management, Florida International University, Miami, FL 33199, USA*

CONTENTS

4.1 OVERLOOKING CHINESE COMPANIES' HIGH-PROFILE OVERSEAS EXPANSION SPREE

The Chinese hospitality industry started its substantial development and relationship with international markets after the China Open Policy in 1979. It is one of the earliest Chinese industries to receive foreign investment and to link its business to the international market. While inward foreign direct investment (FDI) entered the Chinese hospitality industry, limited outward FDI entered the foreign hospitality markets at the same time. This phenomenon continued until the early 2000s, when more and more China-based hotel companies moved forward to foreign markets. Some transactions targeted eminent companies or locations with the highest bids in history, which have drawn attention from the public worldwide (e.g., Anbang's acquisition of Waldorf Astoria Hotel).

Back to the early 1990s, a few individual hotel owners started their overseas investments. Qifeng Li opened the ChaoQun Hotel (later renamed Chinatown Holiday Inn) in New York. It is considered the first Chinese investment in the US hospitality industry. Sam Zhang, another hotelier, owns the Mc Sam hotel group, which has 25 hotels in New York and a 7.5% stake in Trump Entertainment Resorts. He was ranked "the busiest Chinese developer in New York" and was honored in 2007 as "Developer of the Year" by Hilton Hotels. Besides targeting the US, some Chinese companies set their sights on Asian countries in the last decade. For example, Shenzhen Dong-Meng Technology Company and Suzhou Youth Travel Services invested in hotels in Nepal and Fiji, respectively, in 2006. Shenzhen New Century company acquired a Marriott Hotel for $60 million in 2010.

In the late 2000s, more and more large-scale transactions occurred, and they took the place of the early piecemeal and small-scale foreign investments. Perhaps, the earliest large-scale cross-border acquisition is between Jinjiang International Hotels Development, Thayer Lodging Group, and Interstate Hotels and Resorts in 2009. Jinjiang partnered with the Thayer Lodging Group and invested $153.5 million dollars to acquire the leading US-based global hotel management company, Interstate, which operates 380 hotels throughout the world. One year later, Jinjiang bought 50% ownership of the Intercontinental Hotel & Resort Group, the biggest hotel group in the world in terms of number of guest rooms. In 2015, Jinjiang acquired a French hotel company, Groupe Du Louvre, Europe's second largest budget hotel operator for 1.3 billion Euros. After this purchase, Jinjiang International could incorporate more than 1,100 hotels and 91,154 rooms in 46 European countries into its international network and entered the Top 10 worldwide.

The largest hotel transaction by Chinese companies as of early 2016 is Anbang Insurance Group's purchase of the Waldorf Astoria, the iconic hotel in Manhattan, from Hilton International for $1.95 billion US dollars. Anbang also made a tender offer to Starwood who was in talks with Marriott about its acquisition. It offered $12.8 billion for Starwood shortly after striking a deal to buy Strategic Hotels from Blackstone for $6.5 billion.

Another insurance company, Sunshine Insurance Group, acquired the Baccarat Hotel from Starwood for $230 million US dollars in 2015. In the same year, it spent 463 million Australian dollars (400 million US dollars and purchased an Australian hotel from Starwood, called the Hyde Park Sheraton Hotel in Sydney. Besides insurance companies, real estate companies also actively engage in foreign hotel acquisitions. A good example is Wanda, which expended 3.4 billion US dollars in total and bought three buildings/lots in the U.K. (One Nine Elms), US (Wanda Vista Tower), and Spain (Edificio España building). All three projects are located in either CBD, downtown, or central landmark areas.

Auto companies and Airlines also joined the feast of foreign acquisitions with a large amount of capital. In 2014, Hainan Airlines enriched its portfolio investment by purchasing an additional 8.3% of stock in the Spanish NH Hotel Group, the third largest hotel group in Europe with more than 380 hotels providing close to 60,000 rooms in 26 countries. Hainan Airlines has now become the largest single stockholder of the NH Hotel Group with a 29% shareholding. Wanxiang, an auto company, teamed up with San Francisco-based Geolo Capital and invested in US hotels in California in 2015. In the same year, a Chinese conglomerate and investment company, Fosun International Limited, won the bid on Club Mediterranee, the French holiday group, at the price of €939 million.

Other small- to medium-sized private companies such as ChongQing Kangde and Sichuan Xinglida stepped into the overseas travel market. Sichuan Xinglida, a real estate developer, bought Torrance Marriott South Bay Hotel for 74 million US dollars and the Los Angeles Airport Marriott for 160 million US dollars in 2013 and 2014, respectively. Kangde Industrial Group and Kai Yuan Group made investments in Spain and Germany as well.

Besides US and European markets, Chinese companies also targeted developing countries such as Cambodia and Malaysia. China Sunshine Hotel opened a resort in Cambodia, and Fosun Capital Group holds shares of the Malaysian restaurant, the Secret Group.

Global lodging transactions have increased 13% to more than $28 billion in 2015, according to data compiled by Bloomberg. Chart 4.1 shows the trajectory of foreign investments in terms of deal amount in the past few years. Starting in 2013, the amount rocketed up to $1185.57 million. It reached $4623.16 million in 2015. According to the China Ministry of

CHART 4.1 Transaction amount.

Commerce, Chinese overseas acquisitions reached 142 deals in the first quarter of 2016, totaling 16.56 billion US dollars. The number of deals and transaction amounts increased about 50% more than that in 2015. According to first Pacific Davis, the percentage of Chinese investors will grow from 4% to 10% in global hotel investments. Predictions are that investments will go beyond 200 million pounds in the next 3 years (Table 4.1).

Compared with hotel transactions, restaurant transactions are modest in scale. Most restaurant foreign expansions occurred in Southeast Asia. Europe and the US are also the main target markets of Chinese restaurants. Quanjude Beijing Duck was one of the first movers who entered the US market in 1996. However, it stayed open for a very short period. Taiwanese restaurant Din Tai Fung opened its first store in California in 2000. Later, Wang Xing Ji and China's famed Hai Di Lao brought its hot pot to California in 2012 and 2013, respectively. Meizhou Dongpo, the upscale Sichuan restaurant, opened its first US franchise at the Westfield Mall in Century City, California, in December 2013. It opened in Las Vegas in 2015, and in Irvine, California, in 2016. It launched its Casual Concept Dongpo Kitchen in Los Angeles. Pavilion Hot Pot opened its first restaurant in New York in 2015. Other than the US, Europe is also a hot spot for Chinese restaurant investment. For example, The Family Li Imperial Cuisine opened its flagship store in Paris in 2014. Quanjude has started its strategic plan of re-entering the US market after getting more foreign investment since 2015 (Table 4.2).

TABLE 4.1 List of Major Foreign Investment by Chinese Firms

Year	Investor/Acquirer	Hotel invested/ Target	Location of the target	Status	Deal amount (USD mil)	% acquisition	Potential partnership
1990s	Qifeng Li	ChaoQun Hotel (later renamed Chinatown Holiday Inn)	New York, USA	Open	Not known	N/A	N/A
1997	Sam Zhang	McSam Hotel Group (25 hotels)	New York, USA	Open	Not known	N/A	N/A
2009	Jinjiang International Hotels Development	Interstate Hotels & Resorts	USA	Completed/ in talks to sell the Interstate	153.5	50	Thayer Lodging Group
2010	Jinjiang International Hotels Development	Inter-continental & resort group	USA	Completed	990	50	
2010	Shenzhen New World Group	Marriott Downtown	LA USA	Completed	60	100	
2011	China Sunshine Hotel	Sunshine Angkor Palace Resort	Combodia	Open			
2013	Wanda Group	One Nine Elms / Green Property	UK	Completed	1100	100	
2013	Kai Yuan Group	Golden Tulip Hotel	Frankfurt, Germany	Completed	11.57	100	
2013	Sichuan Xinglida Group Enterprises Co.	Torrance Marriott South Bay hotel	LA, USA	Completed	74	100	Diamond Rock Hospitality Co.
2013	Hazens	Sheraton Gateway	LA, USA	Completed	96	100	
2014	Hainan Airlines	NH Hotels	Spain	Completed	315.77	25.5	

TABLE 4.1 (Continued)

Year	Investor/Acquirer	Hotel invested/ Target	Location of the target	Status	Deal amount (USD mil)	% acquisition	Potential partnership
2014	Fu Wah Group (HK)	The Melbourne Park Hyatt	Melbourne, Australia	Completed	119.78	100	
2014	Anbang Insurance Group	Waldorf Astoria	New York, USA	Completed	1950	100	Hilton
2014	Greenland Holding Group	Atlantic Yards	Brooklyn, USA	Completed		70	
2014	Kangde Industrial Group	Barceló Santiago Hotel / Barceló Group	Spain	Completed	10.12	100	
2014	Keck Seng (HK)	Sofitel Hotel	New York, USA	Completed	273	100	Accor/ Sofitel
2014	Chinese Strategic Holdings Ltd	Manage Tinian Dynasty Hotel and Casino /Hong Kong Entertainment	Northern Mariana Islands, USA	Completed		N/A	
2014	Wanda Group	Edificio España building	Spain	Completed	292	100	
2014	Fosun Capital Group	Secret Recipe	Malaysia	Completed	31.13	<100	Secret Recipe
2014	Portofino Hotels	Portofino Hotel and Resort	Lao's	Under construction	N/A	N/A	N/A
2014	Wanda Group	Wanda London One	London, UK	Completed	1102.18	100	
2014	Sichuan Xinglida Group Enterprises Co.	Los Angeles Airport Marriott	LA, USA	Completed	160	100	Diamond Rock Hospitality Co.

2015	Fosun International	Club Mediterranee	Paris, France	Completed	1034.96	98	Thomas Cook
2015	WanXiang Group	Ventana Inn & Spa Hotel	California, USA	Completed	400	Not known	Geolo Capital
2015	Sunshine Insurance Group	Hyde Park Sheraton-hotel/Starwood	Sydney, Australia	Completed	335	100	Starwood
2015	Sunshine Insurance Group	Baccarat Hotel / Starwood	New York, USA	Completed	230	100	Starwood
2015	Jinjiang International Hotels Development	Groupe Du Louvre	France	Completed	1653.43	100	
2015	Wanda Group	Wanda Vista Tower (will be in construction)	Chicago, USA	Completed	900	100	
2015	China International Travel Service (CITS)	Combodia Siem Reap Hotel	Cambodia	In talk	69.77	100	Cambodia government
2015	Zhongke Holding and Fangde Real Estate	Lasavong Plaza project	Vientiane, Lao's	Under construction			
2015	Yunnan Huanglong Group, Yunnan Xingyao Group, & Lao's Longfu investment company	Vientiane Heaven Steps project	Vientiane, Lao's				
	In talk	N/A	N/A	Lao's Longfu investment company			
2016	Anbang Insurance Group	Strategic Resorts & Hotels Group	USA	Completed	6500	100	Blackstone Group LP

TABLE 4.2 List of Major Chinese Restaurant Foreign Expansion

Year of completion	Restaurant expanded abroad	Location of the target	Result
1996	Quanjude Beijing Duck	California, USA	Closed
2000	Din Tai Fung (Taiwan)	California, USA	Open
2012	Wang Xing Ji	California, USA	Open
2013	Sichuan Haidilao Catering Co.	California, USA	Open
2013	Meizhou Dongpo	California, USA	Open
2014	The Family Li Imperial Cuisine	Paris, France	Open
2014	Singapore Leaf	California, USA	Closed
2015	Little Sheep Mongolian Hot Pot	Texas, USA	Open
2015	Lion Pavilion Hot Pot	New York, USA	Open
2015	Meizhou Dongpo	Nevada, USA	Open
2015	ChickenPapa	California, USA	Closed
2016	Little Sheep Mongolian Hot Pot	Oregan, USA	Open
2016	Meizhou Dongpo	California, USA	Open

4.1.1 SOME OBSERVATIONS OF HOTEL TRANSACTIONS

4.1.1.1 Target Parent Firms Are Eminent; Some of Them Are Partnering with the Chinese Acquisition Firms

The majority of the target parent firms are leading hotel groups or hotel management companies in the world. They range from Hilton, InterContinental, Hyatt, Starwood, and Marriott from the US to Accor, Groupe Du Louvre, and Club Mediterranee from France, and Barceló Group from Spain. Keck Seng, a Hong Kong-based property investment company looks to grow relationships with Accor and Sofitel, starting from the acquisition of the Sofitel Hotel in New York. From the perspective of Starwood, the Sunshine Insurance Group shares their long-term strategic vision for Baccarat Hotels and is an excellent partner for the growth of Starwood brands. Anbang Insurance Group reached an agreement with Hilton before the acquisition of the Waldorf Astoria and promised to have Hilton manage the hotel for 100 Years. Furthermore, Jinjiang and Thayer Lodging Group are partners in the acquisition of Interstate Hotels and Resorts. Wanxiang, Geolo Capital Diamond Rock Hospitality Co., and Sichuan Xinglida Group have already worked together multiple times on acquisitions.

Besides partnering with companies, some Chinese firms work with foreign governments on hotel/resort development. China International Travel Services and the Cambodian government are in talks concerning investing in the Cambodia Siem Reap Hotel in 2015. The partnership will benefit both Chinese acquirers and the foreign target firms by facilitating the Chinese learning process and helping foreign target firms develop their brands while freeing cash to explore new markets.

4.1.1.2 Motives May Differ Across Diversified and Limited Diversified Chinese Firms

Normally, the motivations of acquisitions include following customers, accessing competitive advantages from the targets, and bringing back competencies to the domestic, Chinese market or other host markets. Looking at these hotel transactions, diversified acquisition firms account for a considerable percentage of the acquirers. Of these acquirers, only approximately one-fourth are hotel groups or travel services. Three quarters of the acquirers are in related or unrelated industries such as real estate, auto, and insurance. Some firms started implementing a diversification strategy from these hotel transactions. This may imply that a certain number of the hotel transactions are motivated by diversifying capital allocations instead of acquiring hotel-related strategic assets, which is the traditional motive of acquisitions.

4.1.1.3 The Deals Are Featured by High Bid Prices; Some Are the Highest in History

The hotel transactions are characterized by the high bid price from the Chinese to the foreign firms. Some bids are the highest on record. For instance, Anbang Insurance Group paid Hilton $1.95 billion dollars for the Waldorf Astoria; it is among the highest prices ever paid for a hotel (Bagli, 2014). Another insurance company, Chinese Sunshine, bought the Baccarat at the price of about $2 million per room, which was the second highest on that basis for a New York hotel (Brandt and Levitt,2015). The offering price range of Jinjiang International taking over Groupe Du Louvre is about 11 times Groupe Du Louvre's operating profits for the financial year before the acquisition (Chinese Chamber of Commerce in The Netherlands, 2015). At this time, Anbang is still in a bidding war, the most prominent so far, with

Marriott on the acquisition of Starwood Hotels. Anbang raised its bid to $14 billion (US dollars or RMB?), 4% higher than Marriott's offer, pressing to raise its offer to win the battle. In addition, the preemptive offer Anbang made in early 2016 for Strategic Resorts & Hotels Group is about $450 million US dollars more than what Blackstone paid for Strategic in December 2015. According to the data compiled by Bloomberg, it will be the top US real estate purchase by a buyer from Mainland China.

These high bid prices demonstrate the optimistic attitude of Chinese acquirers on the future growth of hotels or real estate in foreign markets. They compete with other bidders by offering higher price in order to seal the deal. However, it is doubtful whether the potential gain is worth paying the high premium. This brings a question of how close the acquirers' estimate is to the actual value of the transactions. Fosun finally clinched the control of French Club Med after 2 years of bidding when all other bidders dropped out. The deal cost Fosun 939 Euros, equivalent to $1034.96 million US dollars, the fourth highest price in the history of hotel transactions by Chinese companies in the past 8 years. In addition to the large acquisition prices, Anbang and Wanda planned to spend a significant amount to renovate the Waldorf-Astoria and to reconstruct the landmark skyscraper Edificio España building, respectively. This leaves a question of how soon these acquirers will recoup the investment outlay.

While these investments may have high yield return in the Chinese market due to one of the fastest economic growth rates in the world, it is common for companies in the Chinese market to experience rapid investment returns (e.g., Chinese real estate industry). However, it is doubtful the mechanism works the same way in developed economies, which have stable, well-established infrastructure and economic and legal systems as well as secure but relatively slower economic growth.

4.1.1.4 The private firms and state-owned firms showed different characteristics in the foreign acquisitions

From the ChaoQun Hotel and Mc Sam hotel group to Wanda, Kai Yuan, Portofino Hotels, Kangde, Fu Wah, and Fosun, private firms have played an active role in investing in foreign hotel businesses since the late 1990s. However, the deal amount is normally on a small scale. The majority of large transactions are made by state-owned firms or firms that have close ties with the government, such as Jinjiang International and Anbang Insurance Company. While these firms may meet the goals of national strategies (e.g., to preserve the value of national assets), private firms may conduct more market-driven transactions and are becoming the main actors of foreign acquisitions.

4.1.1.5 Target Locations are Concentrated in Certain Regions/Cities of USA (New York, Chicago, California) and Europe (Spain and France)

Chinese buyers generally follow the rule of thumb for the hospitality industry: "location, location, and location." Target locations are concentrated in certain cities/states. New York, Chicago, and California are among the hottest places for Chinese acquirers in the US; Spain (Madrid), France (Paris), and Germany (Frankfurt) are frequently chosen in Europe; Melbourne in Australia is among the top list of location choices.

The majority of the target hotels are either landmarks (e.g., the Edificio España Building in Madrid; Waldorf Astoria in Manhattan, etc.) or located in busy, well-known areas with a rich history and large amount of customer traffic and demand (e.g., One Nine Elms in London, Wanda Vista Tower in Chicago, etc.). On the one hand, these locations could determine higher hotel RevPAR. On the other hand, the location preferences may result from the imprinting effect of the abnormal domestic Chinese real estate market, indicating an overoptimistic attitude toward the future growth of foreign real estate markets. Moreover, the target choices serve as tools establishing or enhancing the publicity of the company in both China and foreign markets.

4.1.1.6 Target Countries not Limited to Developed Countries but also Developing Countries such as Laos and Cambodia

In addition to US and European countries, Chinese firms also targeted developing countries, particularly in South Asia. In 2011, the China Sunshine Hotel Group entered a joint venture with a Cambodian company to open the Sunshine Angkor Palace Resort, a five-star hotel with 259 rooms. In early 2014, the Fosun Capital Group invested 2,105 million Yuan in the Malaysian restaurant chain, Secret Recipe, and became its second largest shareholder.

Besides Cambodia and Malaysia, Laos has become one of the popular tourist target countries of Chinese customers. Several projects are either in negotiation or under construction, such as the Portofino Hotels' Latsavong-Portofino Hotel, China International Travel Service (CITS) acquiring the Cambodia Siem Reap Hotel, and the Latsavong Plaza project by Zhongke Holding and Fangde Real Estate (see details in Table 4.1).

Different from investments in developed countries where Chinese firms tend to explore strategic assets and focus on learning from the foreign target, investing in developing countries will enable the Chinese to exploit their current competitive advantages and facilitate the local partners' learning process.

4.1.2 TYPE OF CHINESE INVESTORS IN GLOBAL HOTEL INDUSTRY

There are two significant characteristics of hotel transactions: one is that many hotels conducted acquisitions through partnerships, and the other is that some of them are diversified while some have lower levels of diversification. We take the two as dimensions of a matrix depicting the different types of Chinese acquirers. Please refer to Chart 4.2 for details. Based on different levels of diversification and dependence on partners, we categorize four types of acquirers. They are industry explorer, opportunity hunter, trailblazer, and asset optimizers (see Chart 4.2).

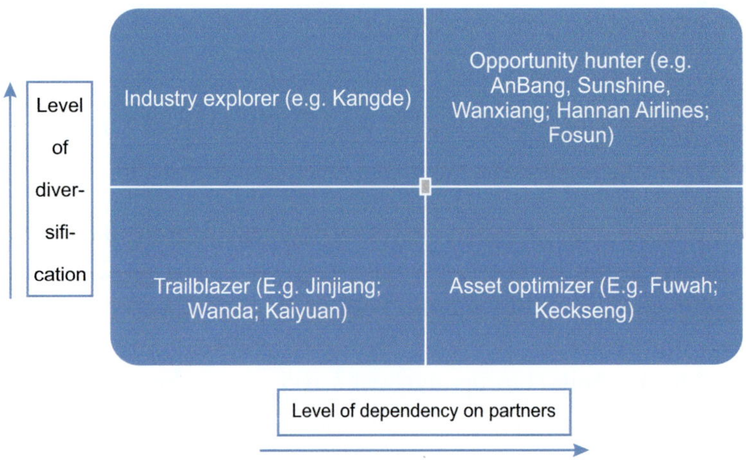

CHART 4.2 Types of Chinese investors in foreign hotel industry.

4.1.2.1 Industry Explorers

Diversified firms that invest abroad with limited partnerships in foreign investments are industry explorers. These firms have businesses in different fields, which are normally related, such as real estate and hotels. Kangde Group, a Chong Qing-based private company, has spread its business in real estate, property management, hospitality management, and construction engineering. It purchased the Santiago Hotel of the Barcelo Group in early 2014. This is the first of its overseas mergers and acquisitions (M&As), signifying the acceleration of its overseas strategies. The company has limited partners during foreign expansion. Instead, it explores opportunities mainly on its own and takes a majority of the investment risk. In addition, foreign markets have different cultures, customer preferences, legal requirements, and institutions from their home markets. Thus, there will be a long learning curve for industry explorers. Industry explorers are more likely to experience slow growth or hurdles in a foreign operation due to the long learning curve and limited partnership.

4.1.2.2 Opportunity Hunter

Opportunity hunters are normally diversified firms with a broad extent of partnerships. They normally have access to abundant cash or credit from banks. For example, insurance companies, real estate companies, airlines, etc. They are hunting for opportunities for their portfolio investment across borders. A considerable motivation for purchasing hotels is the optimistic estimates on the hotel property for the future in foreign markets. This is because they usually choose a location near or at landmarks in the most popular cities such as New York, Paris, and London. Furthermore, landmark buildings are common among the targets, for example, the Waldorf Astoria in Manhattan, the Edificio España building, etc. Hotel property purchasers are not necessarily experts in hotel operation. This is a particularly dominant phenomenon for the Opportunity Hunters. They purchase the properties and are more likely to keep the original management teams or management companies for future operation. They tend to be very flexible in switching "subsidiaries" when there are other investment opportunities.

They also have a large number of partnerships in foreign markets to help their expansion. For example, Anbang bought New York's landmark

Waldorf Astoria in 2015 from Hilton. Hilton Worldwide Holdings Inc. and Anbang have reached an agreement on the management of the Waldorf for the next 100 years. Hilton will stay as the hotel management company after the acquisition. Their partnership has moved further. Hilton's major owner, Blackstone, sold Strategic Hotels & Resorts Inc. to Anbang for $6.5 Billion in March 2016. It ranks as the largest US real estate purchase by a buyer from mainland China, according to data compiled by Bloomberg (Yu, 2016). Given the large extent partnerships help with familiarization with the local market and diversification spreading the investment risks in different areas, Opportunity Hunters have more possibilities to experience stable development.

4.1.2.3 Trailblazer

Trailblazers are more concentrated in the hospitality industry with limited partnerships. Their motives of acquiring foreign hotels are mainly learning from the advanced foreign peers, and/or following the customers, and/or expanding markets outside China. Trailblazers tend to be more professional hoteliers. They are limited in their diversification and build limited partnerships with foreign companies. For example, the Kai Yuan Group bought Golden Tulip Hotels in Germany. Its focus was to learn advanced management techniques and expand its markets to Germany.

Besides, acquiring established hotel properties, trailblazers are brave enough to build their own property from scratch. A good example is Wanda, which planned to build Wanda Vista Tower in Chicago and the London One Project near the Thames. Trailblazers are more likely to experience barriers during development, while heavily relying upon the development of the global hotel industry.

4.1.2.4 Asset Optimizers

Asset Optimizers are limited diversified firms that are good at establishing partnerships with leaders in the global hospitality industry. For example, Fu Wah, a private Hong Kong real estate developer, bought the Melbourne Park Hyatt Hotel. Fu Wah has a portfolio of real estate assets across China. Its hotel portfolio comprises the Regent Beijing hotel, the Park Plaza Wangfujing Hotel, and the Sandalwood Beijing Marriott Executive Apartment.

Similar to Fu Wan, the Hong Kong-listed company, Keckseng Group, is an investment firm specializing in real estate and long-term hotel investments in North America and Asia. Its 12 hotel properties are in seven countries. These firms focus on the hotel industry and are more likely to experience stable development. However, they rely heavily on the global hotel industry because of limited diversification.

4.2 THE INFLUENTIAL FACTORS OF FOREIGN HOTEL ACQUISITIONS

4.2.1 GOVERNMENT POLICY

The most significant factor encouraging Chinese companies to invest abroad is the government policy. The Chinese government has been opening the gate of foreign investments wider and wider for Chinese companies interested in exploring foreign soil during the past few years, following the Go Out policy that encourages Chinese enterprises to invest abroad. The China government has removed some barriers to business expansion and relaxed restrictions and requirements for Chinese firms to get approval for foreign investments. Furthermore, with the new strategy of "the Silk Road Economic Belt and the 21st-Century Maritime Silk Road," more Chinese companies are encouraged to seek foreign investment opportunities along the Belt and Road. In addition, the free trade zone policy also boosts outbound investment.

Industry-wide policies play a critical role in stimulating cross-border investments. One example is the large amount acquisitions by insurance companies, which are quite active in cross-border M&As in recent years (e.g., Anbang Insurance Company, Sunshine Insurance Company). This phenomenon is largely inspired by the relaxed regulatory restrictions on overseas investment by the China Insurance Regulatory Commission.

Statistics indicate that Chinese direct foreign investments rose from $3 billion US dollars in 1991 to 35 billion US dollars in 2003. It reached $92 billion US dollars in 2007. According to KPMG reports, China's outward FDI reached a historic high of 118.02 billion US dollars in 2015. Dealogic data show that, as of March 1, 2016, China is the top acquiring nation globally with 34.7 billion US dollars in 2016 YTD (222 deals) for the first time and accounts for a record high volume share (49%). The 2015 outward M&A flows in the hotel industry has grown 197% over 1 year. Starting from 2009, the main hotel M&A deal amount has skyrocketed from approximately $153.5 million to 4623.16 million US dollars (Please refer to Chart 4.1).

The above data vividly demonstrate the critical role of government policy on the buying spree of Chinese firms' cross-border investments. The government policy will continue affecting Chinese outbound investment. The release of the 13th Five-Year Plan in March 2016, particularly the principle of "openness," would continue encouraging Chinese firms to explore foreign markets. However, it is worth noting that government policy may not be compatible with market-driven motivations and is likely to lead to imprudent M&As.

4.2.2 CHINESE YUAN'S DEPRECIATION

Currency is a barometer of the economy. The Chinese Yuan is sliding, particularly after being anointed as one of the world's elite currencies. Its devaluation is a sign of the Chinese economy's weakness. Most banking economies are expecting the Chinese Yuan to continue slipping. Meanwhile, it is predicted that the Chinese government will help its economy by making exporters more competitive, driving the currency to slide further.

Consequently, Chinese companies are seeking ways of maintaining the value of their cash and alleviating suffering from the potential economic slowdown. Purchasing foreign assets such as companies/properties before the Chinese Yuan's value slumps is a good option to preserve and secure their cash value.

4.2.3 THE DOMESTIC GROWTH SLOW DOWN IN THE HOSPITALITY INDUSTRY ENCOURAGES CHINESE HOSPITALITY COMPANIES TO SEEK FOREIGN MARKETS TO KEEP ASSET VALUE

Besides government policy, China's economic slowdown and volatility in the stock market also motivate Chinese firms to diversify their capital allocation to improve their overall risk/return profile. Overseas investment in developed countries is a good option. According to Dealogic, China is the top cross-border acquirers in the US with 23.5 billion US dollars as of March 2016. In 2015, China ranked as the eighth largest cross-border acquiring nation in the US, with 20.6 billion US dollars via 115 deals. Firms are cautious about Greenfield investment, and acquisitions on premium assets can hedge against the financing risks. As the chair of Portfolio Hotels, Nanyan Zheng stated, “I personally think it is the best way to preserve the state-owned asset by acquiring valuable resources and asset abroad.”

4.2.4 FOLLOWING THE CUSTOMERS

Another important motivation of the foreign investment is Chinese tourists’ demand. Outbound tourism continues growing. The number of Chinese outbound tourists has increased 20% from 2010 to 2014, according to China’s domestic economy and social development statistics for 2014. Moreover, Chinese immigrants have become the largest immigrant group in the world. These Chinese travelers and immigrants demand Chinese style hospitality services, including Chinese food and beverage; this will attract more Chinese firms to invest in foreign markets with a high density of Chinese travelers or Chinese populations.

Hospitality companies respond to this trend by following customers to where they need accommodations in cross-border travels. For instance, Fosun acquired Club Med to serve customers in China and Brazil. The Fu Wah Group purchased the Melbourne Park Hyatt to serve increasing numbers of Chinese customers in Australia. As the chair of Portofino Hotels, Mr. Nanyan Zheng said, Portofino Hotels investing abroad can “serve the authentic rice congee for Chinese tourists in foreign countries.”

4.2.5 AMBIDEXTROUS STRATEGY

Springboard strategy (Luo & Tung, 2007) is exclusive for emerging markets. It applies to many Chinese hotel foreign investments quite well. Chinese firms acquire high-quality targets in order to obtain, upgrade, transform, or improve their competitiveness and compete in domestic markets. In the meantime, they are able to enhance foreign exposure, obtain market share, or grasp opportunities to optimize their assets. Thus, Chinese firms tend to embrace ambidextrous strategy to acquire foreign firms.

4.3 UPDATES ON THE PREVIOUS FOREIGN INVESTMENTS

It is too soon to conclude the results of recent Chinese overseas investments in the foreign hospitality industry. Several Chinese companies, however, are having trouble convincing their western peers that they are a credible M&A counterparty. Some Chinese firms listed on the US stock market encountered hurdles, and they must follow restrictions and practice transparency in order to do business successfully in the US

We have some updates on several large acquisitions. For example, Wanda real estate had to reassess the Madrid skyscraper and the historic landmark building, Edificio Espana, following the acquisition in summer 2014. The Madrid city authorities refused to allow Wanda to demolish the building's facade before reconstructing it. It is reported that Wanda has started dismissing employees in its Madrid office after talks with the city government failed.

Anbang Insurance Company provides a lesson in troubled China-US relations. The Waldorf Astoria lost US Diplomats after Anbang took it over because of concerns about security. The US State Department has been using the Waldorf Astoria as home base for US diplomats during the United Nations General Assembly for decades. Due to the concerns about China-based hackers and other forms of electronic espionage, it shifted hotel accommodations to the nearby New York Palace Hotel. Anbang has been very active and conducted high-profile acquisitions in 2015 and early 2016. Besides the Waldorf Astoria, it bought Strategic Hotels & Resorts from the Blackstone Group for about $6.5 billion. It also pursued Starwood while Marriott tried to take it over. It interrupted the deal between the two large hotel corporations by raising the bid from $12.8 billion to $14 billion US dollars, 4% higher than Marriott's bid. A few weeks later, Anbang withdrew its offer and stated that it was due to market concerns. It also breached the rule of exceeding 15% of an insurer's offshore assets threshold for overseas investments.

The listed hotel companies, Plateno Group (previously 7 Days Inn, now acquired by Jinjiang) and Home Inn, were privatized in 2012 and 2015, respectively, after years of IPO. Huazhu Hotels Group Ltd (NSDQ: HTHT) is the only Chinese hotel group on the US stock market. The privatization is mainly due to the irreconcilable divergence of estimates on the listed firm's value between the capital market and the listed firms themselves.

Privatization is a wise choice to avoid take over by competitors who may take advantage of a low stock price.

However, there is some positive news. The US-Chinese joint venture that owns Interstate Hotels & Resorts (Jinjiang & Thayer), the largest independent hotel operator in the US, planned to sell the company in July 2015 and expected to fetch a price of more than $600 million from the potential sale. Interstate expanded its business and grew quickly since the acquisition in 2010. The potential sale indicates success of the acquisition by Jinjiang and Thayer in 2010, which may lead to a high yield return after only 6 years of postacquisition operations.

4.4 PROSPECT AND WARNINGS

The unprecedented foreign expansion spree has encouraged many more Chinese firms to invest abroad. Meanwhile, several first movers have experienced challenges in foreign markets. Some transactions were not market driven, leading to the question of whether the Chinese firms are ready for FDI. Before making a strategic decision, firms should consider the following questions, despite the favorable governmental policies. That is, what, how, when, and where to acquire?

4.4.1 NON-MARKET DRIVEN DEALS MAY LEAD TO UNFAVORABLE RESULTS

It is not difficult to observe that a certain amount of foreign hotel transactions was driven by the government's support, particularly the state-owned firms such as Jinjiang or companies closely tied to the government such as the Anbang Insurance Group. Some acquisitions are based on national strategies with the purpose of protecting state-owned assets. These M&As are usually backed by extensive capital from the state-owned bank. The non-market driven M&As have an innate drawback of deprioritizing the potential gain/loss in and after the transaction and neglecting the readiness of the firm to go abroad. Among the recent M&As, the state-owned acquirers or government-related acquirers has the highest bid. They tend to offer far higher prices than the target's firm value in the absence of assessing the appropriateness of the target selection.

4.4.2 WHAT TO ACQUIRE? – IDENTIFY THE PREMIUM STRATEGIC ASSET

Regardless of whether it is a market-driven or nonmarket-driven deal, Chinese companies should consider several critical questions closely before making strategic decisions. They need to consider what to acquire, how to acquire, when to acquire, and where to acquire.

Acquirers should have a clear goal of each M&A transaction. What to acquire, i.e., what competitive advantages the acquirer will obtain from the purchase is the first question they need to answer. Furthermore, the acquirers need to consider whether the perceived target firm's strategic asset sustains market value after integration. Research shows that normally the acquirers' market value suffers from the M&As at least in the short term, while the target firms' market values rise on average 25% upon the M&As. Therefore, it is crucial to balance out the transaction cost plus the potential loss from the purchase and the potential benefits/advantages for the acquirers. Typically, the acquirers are motivated by acquiring strategic assets such as the targets' complementary resources, business system, business model, location, or patents, target market's low labor cost or low production cost, the target market's under-supplied demand, and so on. Some Chinese acquirers overestimated the target hotel companies' resources or neglected scrutinizing the targets' financial performance before investing in the ventures.

One example is TCL that acquired the French company, Thomson, in 2014. It did not check Thomson's balance sheet carefully before the purchase, nor did it hire M&A professionals to conduct the deal. When the Boston Consulting Group warned TCL that the venture had excessive risks, the top management team (TMT) just ignored it. Moreover, TCL did not clearly know the brand was old and tired in both America and Europe. It failed to assimilate Thomson's people, and it did not retain the TMT of Thomson. Chinese managers' lacking international experience became a major constraint. Cultural clashes occurred inevitably. TCL ended up purchasing the wrong asset—brand equity that was supposed to be synergized with TCL's low production cost to succeed in the global TV market. This dream-like marriage between the two companies lasted 3 years before it broke.

In Anbang's bidding war for the Starwood with Marriott, it offered $12.6 billion for the purchase. However, it is still not clear what the strategic asset is from this acquisition. If Anbang were to pursue the deal, there remains the question of whether Anbang could capably run Starwood. None of the investors in Anbang's consortium has much hotel experience. We think Anbang's withdrawal from the bid is a wise decision. Before acquisitions, it should clarify what essential assets it acquires and ensure its own current capacities are compatible with the target's competiveness.

Some Chinese acquirers are under the impression that the acquirer should dominate or integrate the target firm, which led to postacquisition issues and losing the chance to obtain the real strategic asset it needs through the acquisition. The management team at Anbang's Belgian acquisition left after a few months amid complaints about Anbang's management style. Lenovo had some initial hiccups with the IBM's TMT and corporate culture. It did not realize the most valuable asset for Lenovo is the IBM business model. Instead, it deemed IBM customers as the most important assets for Lenovo. Soon, it lost quite a few top talents. After some efforts, Lenovo leadership coaxed most of the TMT to stay with Lenovo and took a hands-off approach to the US-run PC company. They now fully trust its leadership to keep the business moving forward.

In the context of acquiring firms from developed countries, Chinese firms should be clear about its role of learner or teacher. A possible feasible approach is to keep the original TMT while motivating them to achieve higher goals. Wanda set a good example with their approach on managing AMC Theaters and fully motivating the TMT by converting the TMT to partners. According to the report, AMC achieved a 200% profit margin in 2012.

4.4.3 HOW TO ACQUIRE?

As Table 4.1 shows, a certain number of transactions are between more than two parties, that is, the acquirer has partners. As stated above, Chinese firms' foreign investment has experienced an early stage of the learning curve, encountering hurdles from the political, cultural, or legal perspectives. They must have a deep understanding about the local culture, foreign law, hiring practices, and so on, in order to survive. A quick way to clear these obstacles is through the help of partners from the local market. Particularly, partnership is crucial in the early stage of foreign investment. Partnership includes joint venture partners (e.g., Jinjiang with Thayer), operation partners (e.g., Anbang with Hilton on Waldorf-Astoria), or partners with the original TMTs (e.g., Wanda with AMC theatre TMT; Lenovo with IBM TMT). For instance, Wanda has partnerships with foreign hotel management companies including Accor, Starwood, Hilton, and Hyatt in China. It can extend the partnerships outside China to help it familiarize with local markets.

4.4.4 WHEN TO ACQUIRE? – THE READINESS OF THE FIRM

Regardless of how precious an opportunity is, firms must be fully ready to operate on foreign soil. First, the firm should have a clear strategic goal of investing abroad. That is, will it go abroad to expand markets, to acquire some strategic assets that are not available at home, or to synergize its competitive advantages with the target firms, and so on? Second, it should have the ability to assess the value of the target firm and identify the target's real resources. In other words, does the target truly have the resources the firm needs? Third, it must have enough resources or support to purchase the target. Fourth, it should have enough resources to inject more capital for postacquisition investment. Fifth, the firm must be ready to handle the postacquisition integration issues such as organizational culture clash, cultural differences, economic differences, legal system differences between the home market and host market, and so on.

4.4.5 WHERE TO ACQUIRE?

The location selection depends on the strategy. If the Chinese firm's strategy is to upgrade, transform, or improve their competitive advantages, then they need to seek high-quality targets that are more common in North America, Europe, and other developed economies. Developing economies and emerging economies are the ideal locations for Chinese firms to exploit their current competitive advantages and leverage value in the expanded markets.

4.4.6 FOLLOWING THE JAPANESE MODEL?

In history, Chinese firms are not the first group of firms from emerging economies that entered developed economies for large-scale foreign investments. About two decades ago, Japan was as hot as China is today in terms of rapid domestic economic growth and ambitious foreign investments. After the "Plaza Accord," the agreement between the government of France, US, Japan, West Germany, and the U.K. to depreciate the US dollars, the Japanese Yen largely appreciated in the short term. This triggered movement of the Japanese Yen outbound, particularly to the US on a considerably large scale. An unprecedented ambitious acquisition spree by Japanese firms occurred (e.g., blind purchase of Rockefeller Center). Some observers say that it is similar to what is happening with China now. The "Plaza Accord" led to a Japanese asset price bubble and a plunging Japanese stock market later on. Many Japanese firms bankrupted and sold their overseas assets at low prices to remedy the loss in the domestic market. This ended with a serious recession, the so-called "Lost Decade." If the Chinese Yuan continues sliding and Chinese firms continue the blind cross-border purchase without learning from the Japanese lesson, the same tragedy is possible. Chinese firms should be able to identify a real quality asset for acquisition accurately, estimate the bid price rationally, and clarify the strategic motives of the acquisition in order to succeed in cross-border acquisitions in the long run.

4.5 CONCLUDING REMARKS

Chinese companies' high profile, cross-border expansion is unprecedented in history. It not only boosts Chinese companies' confidence in growth in both domestic and foreign markets, but also warns against the risks of this adventure. Chinese companies' foreign expansion relies mainly on capital advantages instead of other competencies such as technology, marketing capacity, and innovation. They differ from traditional multinational corporations whose foreign operation is supported by the competencies that the local firms lack. Without the competencies that are the souls of the companies' existence, Chinese acquirers' success tends to be more dependent than traditional multinationals on other factors such as the target firms' competitiveness, the target firms' management team, Chinese government policies, and Chinese domestic market's development.

Besides the vulnerability of the Chinese acquirers, the transactions are characterized by high bid price and multiple motivations including non-market driven motives, all of which add more uncertainty to their future growth. There are four types of acquirers with different levels of diversification and dependence on partners. The Opportunity Hunters are more likely to go through stable development. Trailblazers are brave explorers with limited diversification and partnerships; thus, there are more possibilities for them to experience hindrances during foreign expansion. Asset Optimizers tend to come through stable development while heavily depending on the global hotel industry. Industry Explorers experience a long learning curve with limited partners and have a greater likelihood to undergo slow growth particularly in the early stage of expansion. Among these acquisitions, there are a certain amount of nonmarket-driven deals (e.g., driven by government policy or supported by national strategies). This raises some concerns about the readiness of the Chinese acquirers that have operated in foreign markets. Thus, it is crucial for these firms to clarify what to acquire, how to acquire, when to acquire, and where to acquire assets before marching to the foreign markets.

One significant feature of the hospitality industry is the distinction between hotel owners and hotel operators or management teams. The former is the capital investor, and the latter is the brand or intellectual property provider. In the cross-border hotel business, Chinese acquirers are playing a role of the owners taking on most of the risk, and the foreign targets are serving as the intangible strategic asset provider, who obtain cash flow from the acquisition for further investment in other locations or spreading its brand name. Foreign targets tend to have lower risk and high yield from the M&As. For Chinese acquirers, there is a tendency to place less emphasis on capital investment (hardware), more on management (software), and develop independent intellectual property in order to obtain a solid stand in the global service industry. A good example is Wanda, which formed Wanda Hotel and Resort Management Company, while conducting cross-border acquisitions. It has established "Wanda Realm," super five-star "Wanda Vista," and the upscale luxurious brand "Wanda Reign." Wanda's strategy is to walk on two legs: one is to acquire foreign hotels and the other is to establish its own brands. We are looking forward to the implementation of this two-legged walking strategy.

KEYWORDS

- **motives**
- **overseas expansion**
- **type of investors**
- **warning prospect**

REFERENCES

AFP (2016). China's Wanda says reassessing Madrid project. Retrieved from http://www.dailymail.co.uk/wires/afp/article-3420518/Chinas-Wanda-says-reassessing-Madrid-project.html.

Ahrens, F., (2009). *Thayer Lodging Joins Chinese Firm to Buy Interstate Hotels*. Retrieved from http://www.washingtonpost.com/wp-dyn/content/article/2009/12/18/AR2009121802096.html.

Atlas, T., & Lakshmanan, I. A. R., (2015). *Waldorf Astoria Loses U.S. Diplomats After China Purchase*. Retrieved from https://www.bloomberg.com/news/articles/2015–06–18/diplomats-flee-ny-s-waldorf-astoria-on-china-spying-fears.

Bloomberg, (2015). *China's Wanxiang Teams-up With Pritzker for $1 Billion in Hotels*. Retrieved from http://www.chicagobusiness.com/article/20150814/NEWS12/150819873/chinas-wanxiang-teams-up-with-pritzker-for-1-billion-in-hotels.

Bray, C., & Picker, L., (2016). *Marriott-Starwood Deal Is Interrupted by a Chinese Suitor*. Retrieved from https://www.nytimes.com/2016/03/15/business/dealbook/starwood-receives-unsolicited-bid-putting-marriott-plan-in-doubt.html?_r=0.

Charles, V. B., (2014). Waldorf-Astoria to Be Sold in a $1.95 Billion Deal. Retrieved from http://www.nytimes.com/2014/10/07/nyregion/waldorf-astoria-hotel-to-be-sold-for-195-billion.html?_r=0.

China Chamber of Commerce in the Netherlands, (2015). China Jinjiang Hotels to buy Louvre Hotels for €1.5 billion. Retrieved from https://www.dccchina.org/2015/01/china-jinjiang-hotels-to-buy-louvre-hotels-for-e1–5-billion-euros/.

China Cuisine Association, (2016). "China restaurant industry development report 2015".

China Travel News, (2014). *Hainan Airlines Secures Top Stakeholder Position in NH Hotels*. Retrieved from http://www.chinatravelnews.com/article/86423.

Cole, M., (2014). *Hong Kong's Fu Wah Group Buys Melbourne Park Hyatt for A$135m*. Retrieved from http://www.mingtiandi.com/real-estate/outbound-investment/hong-kongs-fu-wah-group-buys-melbourne-park-hyatt-for-a135m/.

Direct China Chamber of Commerce, (2015). *China Jinjiang Hotels to buy Louvre Hotels for €1.5 billion*. Retrieved from http://www.dccchina.org/2015/01/china-jinjiang-hotels-to-buy-louvre-hotels-for-e1–5-billion-euros/.

Editor of Chicago Architecture, (2015). *Everything You Ever Wanted to Know About the Wanda Vista Tower*. Retrieved from http://www.chicagoarchitecture.org/2015/06/18/everything-you-ever-wanted-to-know-about-the-wanda-vista-tower/.

Edwin, G., (2016). *Irvine Marie Callender's Closed to Make Way for Meizhou Dongpo*. Retrieved from http://www.dealogic.com/media/market-insights/ma-statshot/.

Eisen, D., (2014). *Interstate Maintains Strong Growth Here and Abroad*. Retrieved from http://www.wsj.com/articles/owners-of-interstate-hotels-resorts-in-talks-to-sell-company-1438117845.

Gold, J., (2014). China's famed Hai Di Lao brings its hot pot to San Gabriel Valley. Retrieved from http://www.latimes.com/food/la-fo-gold-20140531-story.html.

Global Newswire, (2014). China Lodging Group (Huazhu Hotels Group) Forms a Strategic Alliance with Accor. Retrieved from http://www.sec.gov/Archives/edgar/data/1483994/000117184314005898/newsrelease.htm.

Hammond, E., David, R., & Nair, D., (2015). *Hotels Exploring a Sale or a Merger*. Retrieved from https://skift.com/2015/11/06/intercontinental-hotels-exploring-a-sale-or-a-merger/.

Karmin, C., & Mattioli, D., (2015). The independent hotel operator could fetch more than $600 million. Retrieved from http://www.wsj.com/articles/owners-of-interstate-hotels-resorts-in-talks-to-sell-company-1438117845.

KPMG's New Report, (2016). *China Outlook*, Retrieved from https://home.kpmg.com/cn/en/home/insights/2016/03/china-outlook-2016.html.

Liu, Y., (2014). *Keck Seng to Buy Sofitel Hotel in Manhattan*. Retrieved from http://www.scmp.com/business/companies/article/1573381/keck-seng-buy-sofitel-hotel-manhattan.

Liu, Y., (2014). Analysis on the status quo and strategy of China hotel multinationals foreign operation, *Hotel Modernization, 3*, 52–54.

Luo, Y., & Tung, R. L., (2007). "International expansion of emerging market enterprises: A springboard perspective". *Journal of International Business Studies. 38*(4), 481–498.

Nadja, B., & Levitt, D. M., (2015). *Starwood to Sell NYC's Baccarat Hotel to Chinese Insurer*. Retrieved from http://www.bloomberg.com/news/articles/2015–02–09/starwood-to-sell-nyc-s-baccarat-hotel-to-chinese-insurer.

People's Daily Online, (2004). UN report: China becoming major investor abroad. Retrieved from http://en.people.cn/200401/07/eng20040107_132003.shtml.

PR Newswire, (2013). *Kai Yuan Hotel Brand Marching into Frankfurt Germany*. Retrieved from http://www.prnasia.com/story/77313-1.shtml.

Song, L., (2015). *Asset-light Investment is the Basis for China Hotels Expanding to the World*. Retrieved from http://www.chinadaily.com.cn/hqcj/xfly/2015–02–28/content_13291843.html.

Shanghai Daily, (2015). *FTZ Policies Boost Foreign Investments*, Retrieved from http://www.china.org.cn/business/2015–11/17/content_37083096.htm.

Wanda Group, (2014). *Wanda Group Acquires Landmark Skyscraper in Madrid*. Retrieved from http://www.wanda-group.com/2014/latestnews_0610/721.html.

Xiao, L., (2014). *Wanda Speeds Foreign Expansion*, the first project London one is coming to the market. Retrieved from http://news.xinhuanet.com/house/sh/2014–10–14/c_1112822406.htm.

Yu, H., (2016). *Blackstone Said to Sell Hotels to Anbang for $6.5 Billion*. Retrieved from http://www.bloomberg.com/news/articles/2016–03–12/blackstone-said-selling-strategic-hotels-to-anbang-for-6–5-bln.

CHAPTER 5

CHINESE HOTEL MERGERS AND ACQUISITIONS (M&AS)

NAN HUA,[1] and HUIMING GU[2]

Rosen College of Hospitality Management, University of Central Florida, Orlando, FL 32816, USA

School of Hospitality Management, Beijing International Studies University, Beijing, China

CONTENTS

5.1 INTRODUCTION

With increasing expansion of the middle class and continued economic growth of China, the hospitality industry has been gradually recognized as a center for companies to reshape the investment landscape and secure long-term competitive advantages. As a result, some Chinese companies have started to aggressively acquire both hotel management companies and properties, trying to accomplish vertical integration of businesses in travel and tourism. Some have focused on acquiring well-established brands and managerial expertise to extend and enhance their domestic lodging businesses, while others have tried to diversify into the hotel businesses by acquiring existing hotel companies to reduce risks associated with developing new products or services and achieve greater market power. In contrast, international hotel companies have continued to increase their presence across China by focusing on gaining market share through strategic alliance, franchise, management contracts, joint ventures with local partner, and other light-asset strategies. Therefore, this chapter is designed to provide a brief description of Chinese hotel mergers and acquisitions (M&As) in its three development stages and offer several insights and reflections relevant to the industry, academia, and government agencies.

5.2 THE PRE-M&A PERIOD

Since the founding of the People's Republic of China in 1949, the hotel industry in China can be considered to have experienced three major stages related to M&As: The pre-M&As period, the initial M&A period, and the active M&A period. The pre-M&As period spanned the years around 1980 and early 2000. The 1980s saw joint ventures between Chinese governments and diaspora/investors from Hong Kong that created the first group of modern hotels such as the Beijing Jian Guo Hotel, the White Swan Hotel, the China Hotel, and the Zhaolong Hotel Beijing (Gu et al., 2012). During the 1980s, over 50% of foreign investments in China went into hotel development. At the same time, international hotel companies were also attracted to the Chinese hotel market by promising projections of rapidly growing domestic market and international arrivals. Gradually, management contracts, franchising, and joint ventures were featured as the favorable entry modes. Particularly, the form of joint venture directly attracted foreign capital investment and management knowhow, and played a critical role in setting the foundation for more sophisticated M&As thereafter (Gu et al., 2012).

5.3 THE INITIAL M&A PERIOD

As a result, the initial M&A period of Chinese hotel companies started in 2009, when Jinjiang Hotels from Shanghai acquired Interstate Hotels and

Resorts in the US for 309 million US dollars with Hotel Acquisition Company in a 50:50 partnership arrangement (Gu et al., 2012). This acquisition can be considered as the milestone of Chinese companies' overseas acquisition in the hotel industry due to its large size, transaction complexity, and access to the top markets of Chinese outbound travelers in the North American market. In addition, Jinjiang gained comprehensive access to management knowhow in all the acquired hotel and resorts. In the same year, China's Wuxi farmer entrepreneur Jubao Xie acquired 75% stake in the Golden Horse Holiday Inn in the heart of Manhattan in New York City (21jingji, 2015). The hotel, which has 500 rooms, is the first 50-story hotel acquired by a Chinese in New York (21jingji, 2015). The Chinese government also attempted to bid over £1 billion to acquire 37% of Maybourne in 2011, showing clear intention to enter a major European hotel market. Maybourne owned historical properties of The Berkeley, Claridge's, and The Connaught hotels in London at that time (Hotel Online, 2011). Although the deal did not finalize by the end due to a series of court actions, it was clear that the Chinese government would pursue similar opportunities when they present themselves.

5.4 THE ACTIVE M&A PERIOD

The active M&A period started in 2013, when a wide variety of Chinese companies began to actively and aggressively explore M&A opportunities in the hotel industry around the world. Domestic hotel markets faced challenges of low rate of return on investment, relatively small percentage of chain hotels and large hotel groups, and lack of influential brands around 2011. In particular, the growth rate of operating income for star-rated hotels increased slower than that of GDP between 2011 and 2013. Even negative growth of operating income was observed in 2013. It was recognized that most high-end hotel supplies were driven by the real estate bubble, instead of demand (Hotel Expo China, 2015). As a result, this excess supply problem led to business performance decline and, between 2010 and 2013, payback for high-end hotels in China increased from 25 years to 62 years, and many four or five-star hotels were looking for potential buyers (hc360, 2015). These challenges forced the hotel industry to make significant adjustments and presented increasingly more opportunities for M&As in China and made overseas M&As increasingly more attractive.

In addition, four factors were critical in leading China into this new era. The first was the legal factor since China ushered in the "Tourism Law" in 2013, introducing orderly competition to the tourism market (CNTA, 2013). The second was the policy factor, with "National Tourism and Leisure Program (2013-2020)" formally furthered the acknowledgement and policy support in 2009 that the tourism and hospitality industry is a strategic pillar industry of the national economy (qyj.saic.gov.cn, 2016). The third was the information and technology factor, as the advancement and application of information technology in the tourism industry had completely changed the traditional workshop-style industry to an industry that utilized Internet and mobile technologies (Lvyou168, 2014). And lastly, the consumer factor, reflected by more diverse and quality-oriented demands for tourism products and services, drove tourism market segmentation to be more specialized and differentiation oriented (People's Central Government of the People's Republic of China, 2014). As a result, enormous market potentials were generally recognized for the hospitality and tourism industry for the years to come.

China's foreign direct investment in the hospitality and tourism industry reached 100.8 billion US dollars in 2013 (China.com, 2016). In particular, the real estate markets in the UK and the US attracted the largest amounts of Chinese capital, showing significant increases from 1.3 billion US dollars in 2012 to 2.3 billion US dollars in 2013 and from 64 million US dollars in 2012 to 3.1 billion US dollars in 2013 (Newsdh, 2014).

According to statistics in 2014, Chinese enterprises invested 116 billion US dollars overseas, marking an increase of 15.5% from 2013 (Ministry of Commerce, 2015). This trend of overseas M&As continued in 2015 and is expected to continue for the foreseeable future. Two key driving forces are behind this trend. On the one hand, a significant supply increase at about 40% in China in 2015, coupled with relatively low return on assets at only 1%, forced companies to look outside of China for growth opportunities. On the other hand, China produced over 100 million Chinese outbound tourists in 2015, spending 229 billion US dollars (CNTA, 2016). When overseas tourist destinations attracted more and more Chinese visitors, more expansion opportunities were presented to Chinese hotel investors, resulting directly in more international M&A transactions.

CTS HK Metropark Hotel Co. Ltd. successfully acquired the entire shareholding in Kew Green Hotels on August 8, 2015, and became the sole shareholder of Kew Green Hotels; it further obtained 44 hotels' ownership and management rights in the UK and 11 more hotel management rights to successfully enter the UK hotel market. After the acquisition, CTS HK Metropark Hotel Co., Ltd. further enriched the franchise hotel brand on the basis of the existing "Metropark International," "Metropark," and "Traveler," etc., and had under its ownership or management nearly 140 hotels in and out of China. Nearly 30,000 rooms were distributed in three major countries, including the UK covering more than 30 cities such as London, Leeds, Birmingham, Lincoln, Portsmouth, and Brighton; Greater China covering more than 40 cities such as Hong Kong, Macau, Beijing, Nanjing, Hangzhou, and Chongqing; and a hotel in Africa (Prnasia, 2015).

Jinjiang International and Plateno Group formally signed a strategic cooperation agreement on September 18, 2015 (Traveldaily, 2015a). Further, Home Inns announced a definitive agreement to merge with Capital Hotels Group (Hong Kong) on December 7 (Jiemian, 2015). These M&As created several important benefits for both the acquiring and target companies, such as economies of scale and stronger bargaining power for procurement and booking. Increased membership base also brought a significant increase in revenue from direct sales channels, in addition to synergistic effects in areas such as regional strategic planning and brand coverage. On the other hand, these merged companies also faced challenges to integrate management platforms, management styles, and similar brands. In addition, Chinese companies were also the third largest buyer of Australian hotels by volume in 2015, acquiring some famed properties such as Hilton Sydney (AU$442 million) and Sydney's Sheraton on the Park (AU$463 million) (ACNW, 2015).

5.4.1 THE CREATION OF THE CHINA TOURISM GROUP

The 18th CPC National Congress pointed out: We must unswervingly consolidate and develop the public sector of the economy, carry out various forms of public ownership, deepen the reform of state-owned enterprises, improve the management system of state-owned assets, and promote and channel the state-owned capital to important sectors and key areas critical to the national security and national economic lifeline, and constantly enhance the vitality of state-owned economy, control, and influence. In September 2015, the CPC Central Committee and the State Council issued the "Guiding Opinions on Deepening the Reform of State-owned Enterprises," from reforming the general requirements to classifying the reform of state-owned enterprises, improving the modern enterprise system, the state-owned assets management system, and developing the mixed ownership economy. The guiding opinions comprehensively put forward the objectives, tasks, and major measures for the reform of state-owned enterprises in the new era. In this context, the tourism group in accordance with national requirements to actively carry out a series of initiatives such as M&As; the formation of economies of scale; the introduction of strategic partners to enhance management efficiency; and the creation of vertical industry synergy (Lxsnews, 2016).

In particular, state-owned Assets Supervision and Administration Commission of the State Council of the People's Republic of China (SASAC) guided and helped the incorporation of CITS Group Corporation and China Travel Service (HK) Group Corporation to create the China Tourism Group (CTG) in July 2016 (Traveldaily, 2016a).

A few special characteristics should be noted for this transaction. First, the merger of the CITS Group Corporation and China Travel Service (HK) Group Corporation is not driven by the market, but by the government. In order to strengthen the strategic influence of state-owned capital in a competitive market and guide the healthy development of the tourism industry in China, SASAC transferred CITS to the China Travel Service (HK) Group and set up the CTG as the only tourism-based corporation group under the SASAC.

Second, this merger quickly formed a large and comprehensive tourism company, with monopoly resources to a certain degree. This newly formed company of the CTG will undoubtedly become the leading company in the tourism industry in China. In terms of travel agencies, CTG integrated three strong veteran travel agencies of CITS, China Travel Service Head Office Co., Ltd. and the China Travel Service (HK), which boast a network of 1,826 business outlets throughout the country and more than 20 countries and regions overseas; in terms of hotels, the CTG has four featured brands, and holds and manages more than 140 hotels in Mainland China, Hong Kong, Macao, and the UK; in terms of scenic areas, the CTG holds and manages many leisure resort resources, in addition to traditional tourist attractions; moreover, the business of CTG spans China tax-free zones, tourism real estate, tourism finance, banking, logistics, recreation vehicles (RV), cruise and other fields (Traveldaily, 2016d).

Third, the CTG is created to lead the development of China's tourism industry and to build a strong tourism brand for China. After the merger, the strategic optimization in the tourism industry in China is improved, along with a more complete industry vertical integration and stronger brand equity. At present, the CTG has the first China Tourism Bank, has held China Motor Show for five consecutive years, and has set up a cruise company that runs a route between Sanya and the South China Sea.

5.4.2 THE M&AS LEAD BY JINJIANG INTERNATIONAL

Jinjiang International, as Shanghai SASAC's subordinate enterprise, has accelerated capital operations and has frequently carried out M&As. Jinjiang invested 1.3 billion euros to acquire 100% stake in the French Louvur Group in the European market in March 2015; this transaction is expected to introduce to the Chinese hotel market the brands, human capital, and technologies accumulated over the years by this famous European hotel management group. Jinjiang acquired 19.8% stake in Lvmama at a price of nearly 500 million yuan in June 2015, which introduced the Online Travel Agencies (OTA) business model in Jinjiang's traditional hotel businesses. Moreover, it spent 8.27 billion yuan to acquire about 81% stake in the Plateno Group in September 2015, which significantly improved revenue from direct sales channels; formed complementary advantages in regional distribution, brand coverage, and other aspects; and created a synergistic effect (Ccstock, 2015; Traveldaily, 2015a). By continuously increasing holdings of Accor Group shares, as of March 31, 2016, Jinjiang held 14.98% 'of the shares of Accor Group, with 13.07% of the voting rights, and became Accor Group's largest shareholder. In April 2016, Jinjiang spent 17.49 billion yuan and acquired 80% stake in Vienna hotel to further expand its limited hotel services and broaden its regional layout plans. In December 2016, Jinjiang Hotels and Jinjiang Shares, Jinjiang Capital, Shanghai Lianyin Venture Capital Co., Ltd., Tibet Hony, Guosheng Investment, and other qualified investors invested 1 billion yuan to build Wehotel platform to improve connections between domestic and international hotel systems and to build a sharing economy platform based on Mobile Internet to reduce dependence on OTA distributions (Traveldaily, 2016b).

Located at the financial center of Shanghai, Jinjiang took full advantage of its capital operation and carried out a series of large M&As in the hotel industry at home and abroad, created economy of scales, and quickly became the largest hotel company in China and the first Chinese hotel company that ranked in the top five worldwide. Several observations can be made. First, the reform process of state-owned enterprises has been carried out with high efficiency and clear direction. Through efficient M&As, Jinjiang started to fill the gap in the hotel industry to achieve deep integration and reform of the state-owned capital, international capital, and private capital. At present, Jinjiang has a total of more than 6,000 hotels, more than 64 million rooms (suites), covering 55 countries or regions; the combined brand series cover high, medium, and economic brand levels, with a diverse group of brands. For example, Jinjiang has J.HOTEL, Jinjiang, Kunlun, Yan Garden, Jinjiang capital, Jinjiang, and other well-known brands; Louvre has Golden Tulip, Première Classe, Campanile, and other brands; Plateno owns Maison Albar (Amber), H12, Portofino, Lavande, Coffeetel, ZMAX Hotel, Xana Hotelle, IU, and 7 Days Inn, which total over a dozen hotel brands (Traveldaily, 2015a).

Second, Jinjiang's execution of hotel companies' "Going out" strategy set an excellent example for other domestic enterprises (Sina.com, 2015). Jinjiang is one of the companies that is emphasized and supported by the Shanghai SASAC to execute the "Going out" strategy. In the past 2 years, Jinjiang started from the initial output of brands, with the non-capital bundled alliance strategy, and advanced to the acquisition of the Louvre Group, continued capital operations in the European hotel market and output of brands, in addition to a number of strategic investments in the Accor Group that increased its impact on the international hotel market. Jinjiang has effectively expanded its businesses and services both vertically and horizontally, established the connection between the domestic and international hotel markets, and promoted the strategy of creating global distribution and realizing multinational operations. From the Chinese government's perspective, Jinjiang has set a solid foundation for hotel and tourism companies in China to execute the strategy of "Going out."

Third, Jinjiang's membership system is powerful, which significantly improves the income proportion from its direct sales channel. After the acquisition of Plateno (Traveldaily, 2016c) and the Louvre Group, Jinjiang brands maintained its advantages in innovation and appeared to have created a synergistic effect. The establishment of the global hotel sharing platform of WeHotel is instrumental in enhancing Jinjiang's resource integration and market power, advancing connections between domestic and international hotels systems, and improving operational efficiency and reducing service costs (Traveldaily, 2016b). In addition, WeHotel provides opportunities to open up inventories between the various hotels; integrate member information in Jinjiang, Louvre, Plateno, and Vienna; build loyalty programs and sales channels; and help reduce the dependence on OTA distribution (Traveldaily, 2016b). In addition, Jinjiang has a total of more than 100 million members, which can be integrated to provide more secure, more personalized services for domestic and foreign business, leisure, and outbound travelers.

5.4.3 THE M&AS LEAD BY THE BTG HOTELS GROUP

As one of the pilot units to lead the state-owned enterprise reform, the BTG Hotels Group invests in private capital, introduces new management, and carries out a series of reform measures over the past 2 years. A subsidiary of BTG Hotels, Xinyandu, increased its investment and purchased a total stake of 65% of Shijiazhuang Ykinns to add more capital influence in the economy hotel segment, improve the integration of operational capital, and set the foundation for its strategic expansion plan in the Beijing-Tianjin-Hebei area in June 2014 (BTG Hotels Group, 2016). BTG Hotels increased its investment three times to a total of about 549 million yuan in cash to buy 92.697% stake in Nanyuan shares, successfully implementing its "brand + capital" strategy to accelerate expansion in the southern market from June to December 2014 (BTG Hotels Group, 2016).

BTG Hotels and Shanli Village (Beijing) Tourism Investment Management Co., Ltd. jointly funded the establishment of the Beijing BTG Village Hotel Management Co., Ltd. in March 2015 to manage "Shanli Village" and "Shanli Retreat" branded hotels, officially entering the countryside B&B segment. BTG Hotels initiated the process of privatizing Home Inns in June 2015; by cash and share purchase, BTG Hotels acquired 100% stake in Home Inns in April 2016 (Traveldaily, 2015b). After the acquisition, BTG Hotels increased its shares to 725 million, of which the CTG holds 248 million shares, or 34.25% of total shares outstanding, as the company's controlling shareholder; Ctrip Shanghai holds 105 million shares of BTG Hotels, as the company's second-largest shareholder with a shareholding ratio of about 14.47% (Traveldaily, 2015b).

In March 2016, BTG Hotels, Flying Pigs (formerly Ali Travel), and Beijing Shiji Information Technology Co., Ltd. set up a joint venture to establish a hotel brand alliance relying on the Internet as the core foundation (Xinhuanet, 2017). This joint venture will provide comprehensive services including brand operations, technical support, and large data linkage for independent, small-, and medium-sized chain hotels.

5.5 SEVERAL INSIGHTS AND REFLECTIONS

M&As are widely recognized as one of the key corporate strategies to achieve greater economies of scale and scope, market power, access to innovative capabilities, new knowledge beneficial for long-term survival, and synergy. In addition, they are known to reduce the risks associated with new product/service development and reshape a firm's competitive scope.

A number of factors have been identified to have significant influence on M&A adventures. For example, it appears that the size of the host and source countries has a significantly positive relationship with M&A activities. This observation appears to support the key country choices of recent Chinese companies in their M&A adventures. In addition, three frequently argued obstacles, namely geographic distance, language barrier, and cultural differences, do not seem to apply to the Chinese M&A activities (Lu and Zhao, 2015).

As the source country, China shows several characteristics that could be instrumental in cross-border M&A activities. First , Chinese outbound travelers have increased in record numbers, reaching 109 million in 2015 (People.com, 2016). The majority of them chose to stay in three or higher star hotels, which has driven growth in the global hotel industry. In addition, Chinese insurers and other state-owned companies that had not invested in the hotel industry appear to emerge as large acquirers domestically and internationally, which is likely due to the appeal of growth potential of the hotel industry and their own diversification needs.

Approaching Chinese cross-border M&A activities from the host country perspective, several factors appear to play a significant role in attracting Chinese investors, including, but not limited to, political and economic stability, GDP, tourism revenue, market size and growth, availability of infrastructure, investment incentives, local tourism assets such as beaches and cultural sites, cost factors, and a reputation as attractive business destination.

The tourism industry in China is ushering in the best momentum of development in recent years. The state's strong support for the development of the tourism industry, the continuous promotion of state-owned enterprise reform, and unprecedented attention to the capital market have provided tourism enterprises opportunities to grow bigger and stronger. As a result, domestic M&As have been taking a significant upswing. At the macro level, the "One Belt and One Road" strategy, the Beijing-Tianjin-Hebei area, and the Yangtze River Economic Zones, as well as the new urbanization process have created new opportunities for investment growth. In addition, government decentralization, the initiatives to reduce taxes, the promotion to take advantage of modern information and technology, particularly with an emphasis on using the Internet, mobile network, and Internet of Things as key platforms, would stimulate and increase efficiency and market power on the supply side of the Chinese hotel industry. The rise of the domestic middle class, which is expected to reach 330 million by 2025, would inject stronger purchasing power into the industry, but would be expected to have new consumption needs and wants to satisfy (CNTA, 2015). It is likely that the hotel industry has to adapt to this dynamic demand group by introducing significant changes on the supply side, which tends to lead to M&As. At the micro level, intensified competition and the desirability to gain more market power and economies of scale and scope appear to play a critical role.

The administrative means was used to carry out the reform of state-owned enterprises, such as the creation of the CTG. However, whether synergy will be created from this type of M&As is still to be tested by time. In particular, among those keys to be considered are competition in the travel agency business, integration of business units, internal personnel adjustments, and new business development. In addition, capital advantages were used to merge and acquire enterprises in the hospitality industry to achieve economy of scales and market power, such as Jinjiang International and BTG Hotels Group. However, they showed different development directions. Jinjiang acquired Platinum Tao, Vienna, the Louvre, and the Accor Group, and yet did not reorganize the management nor introduce professional managers. It appears that both acquiring and acquired firms are still maintaining their independence overall and are in the initial stage of cooperation. As a result, the effect of these acquisitions is not expected to surpass expectation. On the other hand, after a series of M&As, such as the acquisition of Home Inns, the BTG Hotels Group introduced the management of Home Inns, adopted professional manager systems, and realized separation of ownership and management and a higher degree of marketization, although their different customer base, back-end operation, and maintenance could still pose challenges in the field of limited service hotel success for smooth promotion of unified operation and collaborative development (Ctnews, 2015).

However, integrating merged companies to create synergy appears to pose significant challenges. In particular, how to handle complex relationships between brands and unify different systems to obtain a successful transition is a big test. For example, in May 2016, Jinjiang Hotel unexpectedly sold the hotel management company Interstate Hotels & Resort 6 years after the acquisition (Traveldaily, 2016e). From the industry's perspective, this may declare a strategic failure to transform Jinjiang hotel management company. Human resources and loyalty program integration appear to also put pressure on the merged companies, because corporate culture differences and layoffs tend to increase the tension between the acquiring and target companies. This is particularly true if such an M&A transaction involves companies from different industries.

KEYWORDS

- **BTG group**
- **China tourism group**
- **Jinjiang International**
- **M&A**

REFERENCES

21jingji, (2015). Ctrip Initiated M&A Funds for Oversea Hotel, Chinese Companies Started the Global Mode of Hotel Asset Acquisition. http://epaper.21jingji.com/html/2015–07/20/content_5971.htm.

ACNW, (2015). Asian Investors Acquired Hilton Sydney for ¥442 Million. http://www.acnw.com.au/article-27372–1.html.

BTG Hotels Group, (2016). 2015 Annual Report. http://money.finance.sina.com.cn/corp/view/vCB_AllBulletinDetail.php?stockid=600258&id=2301470.

Ccstock, (2015). Jinjiang International' 8.3 Billion Acquisition of Plateno Brings Controversies. http://www.ccstock.cn/gscy/qiyexinxi/2015–09–23/A1442944370861.html.

China.com., (2016). China and Europe Plan to Create a New Blueprint of Tourism, the Number of Chinese Companies Entering Europe Reaches 7, 148. http://m.china.com.cn/yidian/doc_1_10_778582.html.

CNTA, (2013). Tourism Law of the People's Republic of China (Full Text). http://www.cnta.com/zwgk/fgwj/fl/201506/t20150610_17641.shtml.

CNTA, (2015). Forbes Magazine Remarks: *The World Tourism Industry is Good News for the Next 20 Years*. http://www.cnta.gov.cn/ztwz/lyzs/lywjckd6q/201507/t20150710_741619.html.

CNTA, (2016). Reasons for Chinese Outbound Tourism Growth Spurs (*Rational View of Inbound and Outbound Tourism I*). http://www.cnta.com/xxfb/xwlb/201601/t20160119_758473.shtml.

Ctnews, (2015). *The Capital Collaboration Drama of BTG Hotels Group and Homeinns*. http://www.ctnews.com.cn/zglyb/html/2015–06/15/content_109250.htm?div=-1.

Gu, H., Ryan, C., & Yu, L., (2012). The changing structure of the Chinese hotel industry: (1980–2012). *Tourism Management Perspectives*, *4*, pp. 56–63.

hc360. Analysis Report: What is the Current Status of Chinese Star Hotels under the Sky? http://info.hotel.hc360.com/2015/03/050907589533.shtml (accessed March 5, 2015).

Hotel Expo China, (2015). *Analysis Report of Current Status of Star Hotels in China*. http://www.hotelexpochina.com/news/185304532.html.

Hotel Online. (2011). News for the Hospitality Executive. http://www.wvvw.hotel-online.com/archive/archive-35224.

Jiemian, (2015). Homeinns Merges with BTG, *Giant Fights Emerge in the Chinese Hotel Industry*. http://www.jiemian.com/article/465406.html.

Lu, Q., & Zhao, X., (2015). Brand Integration After Cross-border M&A Evidence from China Hotel Industry. *Management & Engineering*, *20*, pp. 68.

Lvyou168, (2014). China's Outbound Tourism Markets' Rapid Growth, IT Factors Can Not Be Underestimated – Network and Mobile Devices to Increase Chinese Tourists Outbound Travel Frequency, *Consumption and Freedom Substantially*. http://focus.lvyou168.cn/tourism_analysis/20140716/33649.html.

Lxsnews, (2016). Tourism Mergers and Acquisitions Continue, *Industry Competition and Collaboration Tend Subtle*. http://www.lxsnews.com/index.php?m=content&c=index&a=show&catid=3&id=8005.

Ministry of Commerce, (2015). China's Foreign Investment Cooperation and Development Report. http://fec.mofcom.gov.cn/article/tzhzcj/tzhz/upload/zgdwtzhzfzbg2015.pdf.

Newsdh. ￥3.1Billion, the Real Estate Industry in US Attracted Tremendous amounts of Chinese Capital. http://www.newsdh.com/?uid-1-action-viewnews-itemid-118857 (accessed Feb. 18, 2014).

People.com., (2016). Outbound Tourists for 12 Consecutive Years Have Maintained Double-Digit Growth, *China Becomes the Lasting Source of Power of the Global Tourism Industry*. http://paper.people.com.cn/rmrb//html/2016–01/28/nw.D110000renmrb_20160128_1–22.htm.

People's Central Government of the People's Republic of China, (2014) Several Opinions of the State Council on Promoting the Reform and Development of Tourism. http://www.gov.cn/zhengce/content/2014–08/21/content_8999.htm.

Prnasia, (2015). HKCTS hotels acquired the UK's second largest hotel management company Kew Green Hotels. http://www.prnasia.com/story/128424–1.shtml.

qyj.saic.gov.cn., (2016). Notice of the State Council on Printing and Distributing the "13th Five – Year Plan" Tourism Development Plan. http://qyj.saic.gov.cn/wjfb/gwyfb/201612/t20161230_173878.html.

Sina.com., (2015). *Jinjiang Shares*: "Going Out" Strategy Upgrade, the Acquisition of Luff Group Brings more Brand Recognition than the Actual Assets. http://vip.stock.finance.sina.com.cn/q/go.php/vReport_Show/kind/company/rptid/2633392/index.phtml.

Travel Daily, (2015a). Jinjiang Acquired 81% of Plateno's Shares, *Becoming One of the Top Five Hotel Companies Worldwide*. http://www.Traveldaily.cn/article/95670.

Travel Daily, (2015b). Frequence M&As in the Hotel Industry, *Industry Leaders May Emerge Shortly.* http://www.Traveldaily.cn/article/97743.

Travel Daily, (2016a). *Resource Integration Accelerates in the Tourism Industry*, Well Diversified Industry Leaders Gradually Emerge. http://m.Traveldaily.cn/article/106118.

Travel Daily, (2016b). *Investing and Financing Briefing*: Trend of Integration: Jinjiang Invested Heavily to Create We Hotel. http://www.Traveldaily.cn/article/109751.

Travel Daily, (2016c). *Merger of Jinjiang and Plateno*: Average Occupancy of Plateno in Q2 reaches 81.81%. http://www.Traveldaily.cn/article/106260.

Travel Daily, (2016d). China Tourism Group: Sales Surpass ￥10 Billion, *Speeding up Oversea Strategic Deployment*. http://www.Traveldaily.cn/article/109000.

Travel Daily, (2016e). Jinjiang Sold Intercontinental, *Hotel Management Strategies May Have Failed*. http://www.Traveldaily.cn/article/103829.

Xinhuanet, (2017). The O2O Plot of Ctrip and BTG Hotels Group. http://news.xinhuanet.com/tech/2017–01/12/c_1120293550.htm.

CHAPTER 6

NEW DEVELOPMENTS OF THE CHINESE RESTAURANT INDUSTRY

JINLIN ZHAO[1] and MOHAN SONG[2]

[1]*Chaplin School of Hospitality and Tourism Management, Florida International University, Miami, FL 33199, USA*

[2]*College of Business, Florida International University, Miami, FL 33199, USA*

CONTENTS

6.1 INTRODUCTION

Chinese people always mention "民以食为天" (food is the basic need of man). It means that food is as important to the people as heaven. In Chinese history, food scarcity is deeply embedded and ingrained in people's consciousness. While China is known for its rich cuisine culture, food consumption has dramatically changed from meeting basic physiological needs to an occasion for enjoyment (Zhao and Li, 2001). According to the China Hotel Association report, compared with RMB 700 billion (about 103 billion US dollars), which contributed to 1% of China's GDP in 2004, the total revenue of the Chinese restaurant industry is estimated to reach RMB 3500 billion (over 500 billion US dollars) in 2016, and the revenue was RMB 3,231 billion (about 475 billion US dollars), which contributed 4.3% to the China GDP in 2015 (China Cuisine Association, 2016). In detail, from Figure 6.1, it is obvious that restaurant industry revenues have grown rapidly from 2010–2016. Figure 6.2 shows the top 10 provinces' revenue contributions to the Chinese restaurant industry in 2015 (China Hotel Association 2016; Wu, 2016).

6.2 GENERAL BUSINESS ENVIRONMENT

Many factors have impacted the rapid development of the restaurant industry in China. Factors in the political environment, focus especially on the new Food Safety Law and anti-corruption rules; in the technological environment, it is mobility and online to offline (O2O)- internet+ restaurants; in the social cultural environment, it is the lifestyle changes of the Chinese people; and in the economic environment, there is focus on infrastructure development and the increase in the mid-income population; further, public awareness of green practices in the ecological environment has great influence on the industry's development. The following sections will discuss these issues and their importance to the Chinese restaurant industry.

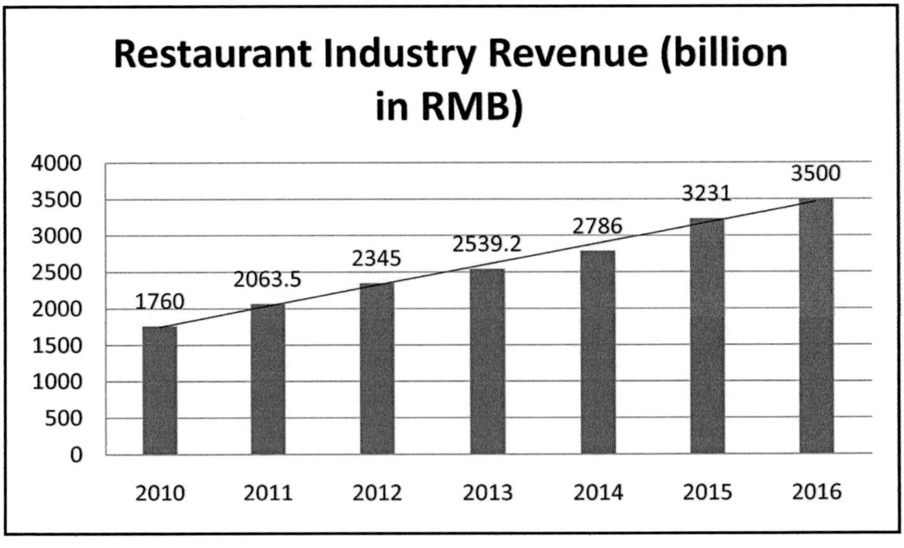

FIGURE 6.1 Restaurant industry revenue in 2010-2015 (billion in RMB).

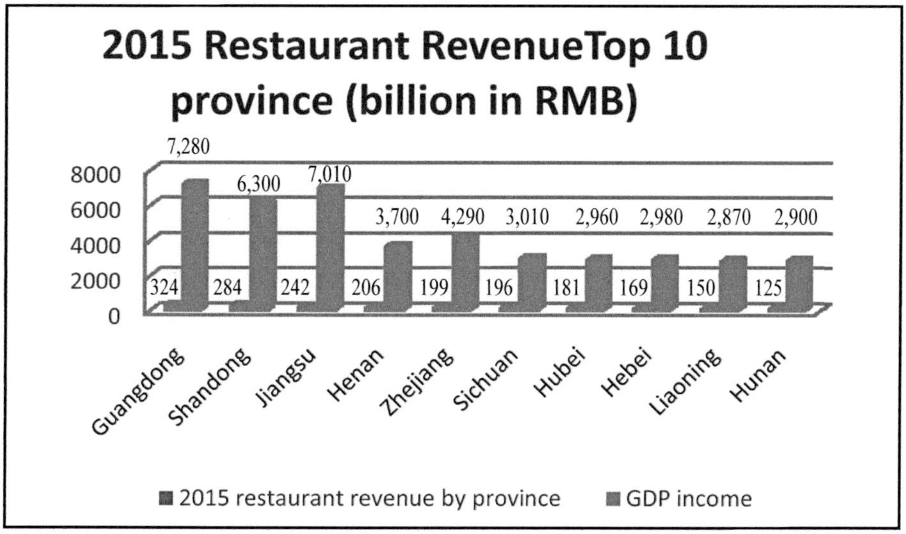

FIGURE 6.2 Top 10 provinces in restaurant revenue in 2015 (billion in RMB).

6.2.1 POLITICAL ENVIRONMENT

The Chinese restaurant industry has benefited from political reform. The government has boosted the restaurant industry by establishing government policies, laws, and regulations in recent years. A series of preferential policies have made a positive impact on the industry.

6.2.1.1 Food Safety Law for Food Industry

The Chinese restaurant industry is growing rapidly. However, there are rising concerns over food safety in China (Broughton, 2010), particularly in food ingredients, food processing, and cooking methods. Food safety has always been an issue in China due to the lack of knowledge about contamination and hygiene standards (CCTV Finance, 2014 & 2016; Deluca, 2016; Huehnergarth, 2014). There are some profit-driven illegal practices by individuals or companies. Even after the establishment of Food Safety Law in 2009, thousands of food safety violations from tainted milk to the use of illegal additives in food production still took place. In 2014, Shanghai health inspectors found that McDonalds, KFC, and Pizza Hut used expired meat supplied by Husi Food Co., a subsidiary of Illinois-based OSI Group (Li, 2014). A Chinese court fined the company 2.4 million yuan (about 365,000 US dollars) and 10 employees involved in the incident received up to 3 years of imprisonment (Filloon, 2014). The incident caused McDonalds to suffer a revenue decrease of 14.5% in its Asia, Pacific, Middle East, and Africa regions in August 2014 (Forbes.com). Because Husi Food Co. provided 20% of supplies for McDonalds restaurants in Japan, the scandal also caused the company a net loss of $186.2 million in Japan in 2014 (WSJ.com).

In order to strengthen food safety regulations, after nearly 2 years of drafting and commenting, investigating, and discussion, on October 1, 2015, China's newly revised Food Safety Law was enacted and made effective. The new Food Safety Law ("FSL 2015") has substantially revised the existing law including tightened scrutiny of use of additives and raw food materials; packaging and labelling; importation; sourcing and sale tracking requirements; detailed recall procedures; third party liabilities; and the obligations of catering service providers (Bird & Bird, 2015). The government will implement the law in full swing.

6.2.1.2 Anti-Corruption Rules for Food Industry

The revenue of top-tier restaurants dramatically declined after the Chinese President Xi Jinping launched eight rules of anti-corruption movement (CPC, 2012). According to the data from the New York Times, revenues in the high-end restaurants in Beijing continue to struggle and have to face the decline of 35% and the decline of 20% in Shanghai (Florcruz, 2015). In the past, Chinese government officials represented the majority of high-end restaurant and private club diners, which influenced and contributed to a big portion of revenue to restaurants and entertainment venues. However, restaurants and hotel food & beverage departments were among the victims of the anti-corruption law as banquets and meetings were cancelled. At the same time, the decline in food consumption led to the decline in beverage consumption. Beer sales at restaurants and entertainment venues were gloomy, as many officials did not dare to eat out or even go to karaoke parlors. Based on the data from the website of the Beer Professional Committee at the China Food Industry Association, after the anti-corruption rules were implemented, the output of beer fell 17% in the month of December 2012 alone. Over the full year, total beer production fell 1% instead of increasing like usual (Florcruz, 2015; Hite, 2015; Wu, 2013). The mid-income population is increasing quite rapidly and prefer to dine at high-end restaurants, and the high-end restaurants have changed their menus and lowered their prices to attract those eaters. The total revenue in 2013 and 2014 did not decrease but still increased as one can see from Figure 6.1.

6.2.2 TECHNOLOGICAL ENVIRONMENT

The Chinese restaurant industry has not changed much in its traditional food preparation techniques (Zhao and Li, 2001). However, information technology (IT) has given huge momentum to the restaurant industry. The IT industry has improved greatly in its ordering, delivering, and other service techniques. For example, the restaurant industry works closely with the IT industry and explores and exploits all kinds of mobile applications and those technological developments that boost the industry's development. China's online food delivery industry contains four types of online to offline (O2O) models: group purchase apps like Groupon; review apps like Yelp; food delivery apps; and food order apps. According to a recent report, group purchase apps contributed RMB 76.94 billion to the market share from January to June in 2015, and the trend is still growing, driven by the continuous improvement of technology and logistics (China Finance, 2015: Pintu, 2015). Until 2016, transactions within the industry yielded RMB 176.15 billion.

The 2015 restaurant industry report provided the market segmentation of the restaurant industry of O2O. Basically, the market has been divided into two parts: "what to eat" and "sharing after eating." Under the segment of "what to eat," three branches exist as "delivery," like 饿了吗; "make food at home," like recipe apps; and "eat in the restaurant," like reservation apps and Groupon apps. Under the segment of "sharing after eating," two branches exist as "review apps" and "social media apps" (Pintu, 2015).

6.2.2.1 Mobility and All Kinds of Applications

Online food ordering is growing dramatically because of its ease, speed, and precision to both consumers and restaurants (Kimes, 2011). While young Chinese generations are using more mobile apps for ordering food instead of using a PC, online review/ordering mobile apps are becoming popular in recent years. One can easily find 125 mobile apps for food ordering on a website. Based on 360 Mobile Assistant download results, in one week, "饿了吗" (are you hungry), "大众点评" (Dianping), and "美团外卖" (Meituan), ranked as top 3 downloaded apps. They have been downloaded more than 400 thousand times in one week. Among those, "饿了吗" (are you hungry) enjoys a 34.6% market share and is ranked first (Pintu, 2015). Consumers review different restaurants, get information about restaurant trends, order, and pay through apps. Based on Figure 6.3, the O2O market share increased dramatically from 2010 to 2015.

According to the report, white-collar workers accounted for 61.8% among all users, college students contributed 29.1% to the market share, while residential communities and the other markets comprised the remainder (Pintu, 2015; Zou, 2016). A total of 85% market share is from top-tier cities and provincial capital cities, which is due to high transaction numbers per customer and population density in major cities (Pintu, 2015). Based on the research from 2015 restaurant industry report, top-tier residents have their own preference in choosing different food delivery apps. Beijing people prefer delivery service, Shanghai people prefer ordering service, Guangzhou people are fond of food-related social media, and Shenzhen people prefer both delivery and ordering service. The demographic report tends to divide male and female into two groups; males are inclined to use order and

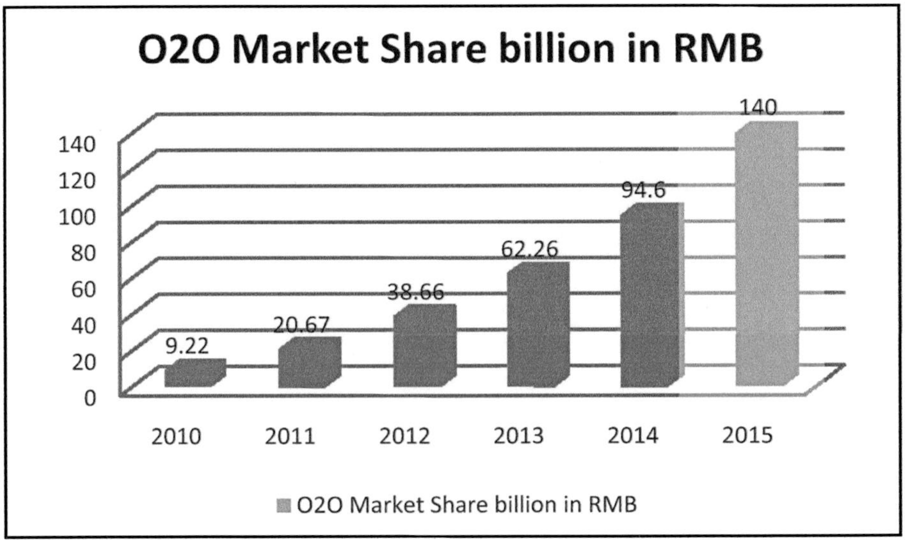

FIGURE 6.3 Online to offline market share from 2010 to 2015 (billion in RMB).

review apps, while females prefer using delivery and recipe applications (Pintu, 2015).

Simultaneously, instead of a traditional restaurant concept, more entrepreneurs contribute to restaurant industry innovation (Figure 6.4). For example, "farm to table" is increasing its popularity in top-tier and second-tier cities in China (World Federation of Chinese Catering Industry, 2016). The concept, similar to "Blue Apron," comes from "eat healthy and eat green" but has been extended to "eat conveniently" by delivering fresh washed vegetables and clean meat and seafood to consumers. Based on Figure 6.5, 71% of people are willing to use "farm to table" apps in terms of saving time

FIGURE 6.4 Food delivery and mobile payment.

FIGURE 6.4 Food delivery and mobile payment.

and money. Moreover, instead of going to a restaurant, people can find a good chef to come to the consumer's house and cook for them through apps (China Hotel Association, 2016). Chefs also can invite consumers to his/her "restaurant" – an independent kitchen to have a meal. People can find such invitations through "有饭"(have a meal), "觅食" (foraging), "回家吃饭" (eat at home), "妈妈的菜" (Mom cooks), "一起吃" (eating together), and "蹭饭" (have meals for free). Through these meals, people start to build social networks. However, because of the lack of regulations and policies, it is reported that some delivery companies and chefs operate with no business licenses, and some stores have food safety issues. Because "farm to table" groups of people are concerned about the food safety issues, the online food delivery industry pays attention to food quality and safety. Since 2015, popular apps started to build their own network with restaurants to track offline food safety and service quality in hopes of building a long-term relationship with partners (Figure 6.5).

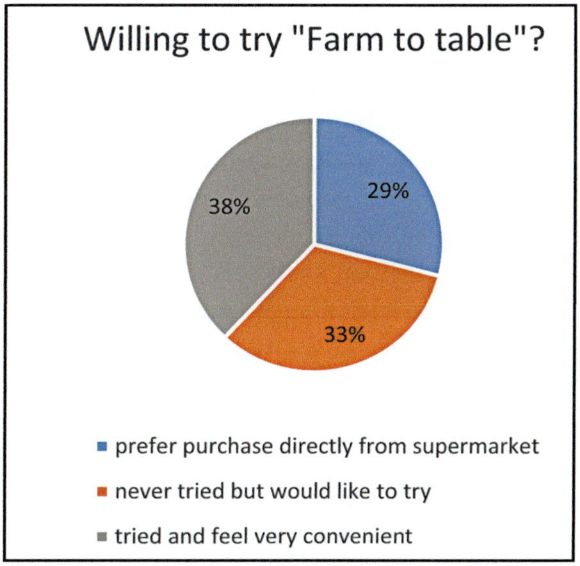

FIGURE 6.5 Willingness to use "farm to table."

6.2.2.2 Mobile Payment

China's fast developing e-commerce is becoming another very important technological support for O2O, and it leads the mobile payment industry. Mobile payment is known for its convenience and is used in ordering and delivering in the Chinese restaurant industry, such as Ali Pay and Wechat Pay. CNN shared a video regarding "surviving a day in China's biggest city, Beijing, without carrying a wallet (no cash nor credit card)" (Ripley, 2016). In the video, people can pay by mobile phone, regardless of whether you buy a coffee or eat in a fine-dining restaurant. According to the report, 55% of China's Internet users have made a mobile payment, versus only 19% of Internet users in the US. On top of technology, people experienced the convenience of mobile payment by scanning QR codes (Pasquier, 2015).

6.2.3 SOCIAL CULTURAL ENVIRONMENT

In the 1980s and earlier, the Chinese people were mostly staying and cooking at home daily, and even family and friend reunions or any other events mostly took place at home. This was because at that time, eating in a restaurant was considered a luxury event and the disposable income for Chinese was very low at the time. The choices of menu items changed from limited and rationed food supply from 1953 to the earlier 1980s, more food in the later 1980s, to the abundant food choices and the end of food coupons in 1993. Chinese people's food choices changed from limited food, meat, and vegetables to large amounts of meat and seafood consumption. There was a shift from rice, wheat flour, and vegetables to meat and seafood consumption among city residents in China, which caused many health-related diseases. However, at present, most city residents want to select healthier and green items for food choices in a restaurant.

Due to fast the pace of life and more disposable income, the Chinese people from urban to rural areas are changing their eating habits dramatically. More and more people are choosing to eat in the restaurant or order food online instead of cooking and eating at home. Urban Chinese people are more likely to spend time eating in a restaurant before going home instead of suffering peak time traffic. On the one hand, it is sensible to take public transportation at off-peak time. On the other hand, eating in a regular restaurant does not cost much more money than cooking at home. The Chinese social and life style has changed tremendously. In the old days, Chinese people wanted to save money and eat at home; moreover, there were not that many restaurants in China. Today, for most of them, it is common practice to go to a restaurant to feed themselves; to celebrate a birthday or reunion; or to get together for any reason. People choose a good restaurant as an important leisure activity on weekends or holidays.

6.2.4 ECONOMIC ENVIRONMENT

The Chinese GDP had been growing double digits for 30 years until 2011. Although the GDP growth in China has slowed down around 7% from 2012 to 2016, it is still one of the fastest growing economies in the world. The disposable income per city resident has increased from RMB 1,002 in 1987 to RMB 31,195 in 2015, which is 31 times increase (www.baidu.com). With much more money in their pockets, the Chinese people have spent more than 60% of their disposable income on food and travel. The infrastructure development contributes greatly to the restaurant industry's development in China. According to the Ministry of Transport, China has 121,000 km (75,186 miles) of railways which includes 19,000 km (11,806 miles) of high-speed rail (HSR). The freight on the railways was 3.36 billion tons in 2015. A total of 2.357 billion Chinese people travelled on the trains in 2014. China has 4.04 million km highway and 210 airports including 26 airports with passenger traffic over 10 million annually. China has 120,000 km of water ways http://www.moc.gov.cn/jigou/). All these transportation developments enhance the Chinese people's travel experience, enabling them to taste all regional foods and cuisines. All these developments help to transport and deliver all the food materials in the fastest way nationwide.

6.2.5 ECOLOGICAL ENVIRONMENT

The Chinese government announced a big commitment made by President Jinping Xi at the Paris Weather Summit to reduce carbon emissions to 40% by 2030. This move will definitely improve the country's environment, which will lead to better food production. The government seriously realized the impact of global warming and soil and water pollution on the food industry and wants to change the food supply chain system to serve safe food for its people.

People have gained more information about sustainable development and want to embrace the green practices. Now, 87% of the Chinese are looking for healthier and green menu items when eating out. In 2013, Unilever China signed an agreement with the China Culinary Association to train Chinese restaurant managers and chefs to select the food materials from sustainable sources. In doing so, the recognized benefits include saving energy, reducing air and water pollution, and reducing food waste in food production and providing customers with balanced menu choices.

6.3 COMPETITIVE ANALYSIS OF THE CHINESE RESTAURANT INDUSTRY

6.3.1 BRANDS AND PRODUCTS

Before the open-door policy took place in 1979, the Chinese restaurant industry was fragmented and closely related to the characteristics and cultures of various regions. Originally, there were four well recognized cuisines: Shandong, Huaiyang, Sichuan, and Cantonese, and four more were added later: Hunan, Northeast, Fujian, and Hui cuisines. These became the eight cuisines in various regions in China. Before the rapid infrastructure development, each region of people based on the local culture would stick to the local food materials, taste, color, aromas, and even decoration style of the restaurants. There were only individual restaurants or maybe a few restaurants under the same name in a city, but no large restaurant chains.

In 1987, KFC opened its first store in Beijing, China. The Chinese people started to have exposure to a restaurant chain and began to learn about the importance of a brand and market share. International restaurant chains with various brands have played a very important role in the development of domestic restaurant chains and brands in China. Massive travel and tourism industry development and customer demand propel the restaurant chains' development, as people have more disposable income and may sometime want to have the same cuisine they are used to when they are traveling into other regions.

6.3.1.1 International Restaurant Chains and brands

KFC was the pioneer, which started its first store in Beijing, China, in 1987. This was followed by McDonalds, which opened its first store in Shenzhen, China, in 1990. Pizza Hut also opened its store in China in 1990. To safeguard the standard and quality of the food and system, these companies did not use franchises as an expansion tool at the beginning, but the companies owned and operated the stores in China. Later, there were some joint ventures between these companies with their Chinese partners. KFC opened its franchise system to Chinese investors in 1992. Under YUM China, KFC and Pizza Hut had 6400 stores in China in 2015, making them the largest restaurant chain in China. McDonald's started its franchise practice in 2014, and it has 2200 stores in China now. Starbucks entered in 1999 and had 2000 stores by the end of 2016. Subway started in 1995 and has 657 stores at present. Burger King entered the Chinese market late in 2005, but it already has 1416 stores. There are also a number of Papa John's Pizza, Dairy Queen and Carl's stores in China. The competition is thus fierce.

6.3.1.2 Domestic Restaurant Chains and Brands

Most domestic restaurant chains developed during the 1990s. The 2016 China Restaurant Survey Report, based on the annual revenue and service styles, named the top 50 specialty restaurant chains with a total revenue of RMB 50 billion. Among this category, Hangzhou Foodservice Group with a total revenue of RMB 5.5 billion is ranked No. 1, followed by Shanghai Xinghualou Co. Ltd as No. 2, and Shangdong Kairui Catering Company as No. 3. The report also listed top 20 hotpot chains with a total revenue of RMB 45 billon. In this category, Sichuan Haidilao Co. Ltd. was listed as No. 1, Beijing Hangjihuang as No.2, and Neimenggou Little Lam Tail as No. 3. It also reported top 10 fast food companies with RMB 12 billion. Ajisen ranked first, Zkungfu as second, and Beijing Qing-Feng Dumpling as third. There were also top 10 catering companies with a total revenue of RMB 18 billion, and top 10 Western and leisure style companies with a total revenue of RMB 10 billion.

According to the 2016 China Restaurant Survey Report, it is interesting to learn that the hotpot category made RMB 45,600 per seat with 14.15% net profit, the highest among all categories in 2015. The fast food category made RMB 48, 500, the highest revenue per seat, but its net profit was 6.41%. The Western and leisure category made RMB 40,400 with a net profit of 8.34%. The specialty category cropped RMB 36,800 with a net profit of 7.38%. The sale in the catering category was RMB 22,000 per seat with 8.2% of net profit. The highest costs for all categories were raw materials, labor, and rent.

6.3.2 ENTREPRENEURS

A report from 2016 China Restaurant Industry Survey Report informs that there were 5,074,852 restaurants or eating places in China. Most of the restaurants are owned or operated by individual entrepreneurs. Some of the entrepreneurs are more successfully expanding their single restaurant into a multiple brand restaurant chain. Here are some interesting stories:

In 1993, Mr. Jianxin Ren opened his Malan noodle restaurant in Lanzhou, Gansu Province. In 1996, he registered his brand, opened his first Malan Noodle, and set up his headquarters in Beijing. He has focused on the quality of food materials, balanced the menu, and improved the cooking technique, store design, and logistic development. The company had 100 owned and franchised stores in 2015. Its sale was RMB 250 million in 2015. In 2007, it opened its first store in the US in Los Angeles.

In 1996, Mr. Guoqiang Wu left his reporter job and started his restaurant business in Changzhou, Jiangsu Province, China. He converted a 30-square meter Chinese restaurant, which was losing 10,000 RMB monthly, into a Mother Dumpling Restaurant. He hired a woman from Northwest China, who was well known for her dumplings. It was very successful. Later, in 1996, he started to deliver dumplings to locals. In 1997, he opened a larger store in Changzhou, followed by two more stores between 1997 to 1998. However, because of the wrong locations and unclear positioning, the two stores failed and caused him a loss of RMB 200,000! He did not stop there, but opened a store in Suzhou in September 1998. Then, he opened stores in several cities in the Jiangsu Province. In September 1999, the first Mother Dumpling Restaurant opened on the busiest shopping street, Nanjing Road in Shanghai, and proved very successful. In 2003, the company invested RMB 50 million to build its quick-frozen dumpling factory. Now the company has expanded to 19 provinces with 500 stores. More than 50 million customers visit its stores annually. In 2002 and 2004, the company opened its restaurants in Indonesia and Australia.

One evening in September 2009, Mr. Xuhao Zhang and Jia Kang (two graduate students at Shanghai Jiaotong University) were competing in a computer game at their dormitory. Around 10 o'clock, they were so hungry and tried to call KFC and McDonalds for food delivery, but none of them had a delivery service, which triggered them to develop their food delivery system—ele.me "饿了么". They both put their tuitions and allowances for room and food for a total RMB 30,000 and purchased more than 10 motorcycles for food delivery. In two to three months, the news quickly spread throughout universities' campuses in Shanghai. They had to deliver about 1000 orders a day. The system at the beginning was: a customer called for an order, an associate searched for a restaurant and placed the order, picked up the order from the restaurant and delivered the food to the customer, and then received a commission from the restaurant. For each delivery, they made only RMB 5. Soon, they found that there were too many orders to handle. With the help from a student, a computer programmer, they created an "Internet Food Order System". From 2009 to 2011, ele.me dominated the food deliveries throughout university campuses in Shanghai. In the second half of 2011, the company received a one million US dollar investment from Jinshajiang Capital to boost its ordering system. In December 2011, the company reached 10,000 orders per day and became the largest food ordering website. The investments were pouring into ele.me, with over one million US dollars from Trjcn.com in January 2013, 25 million US dollars from Sequoia Capital, Trjcn.com, and Jinshajiang Capital in November 2011, 80 million US dollars from dianping.com in May 2014, 350 million US dollars from five companies in January 2015, $1.1 billion US dollars from two companies in August 2015, and $1.25 billion US dollars from Ali Capital in December 2015. The total capital of ele.me was estimated up to $4.5 billion. By September 2014, the company's food delivery system covered more than 200 cities in 'China.

6.3.3 THE CUSTOMERS

6.3.3.1 What Do Customers Need and Want

One online big data analysis (Leung, 2014) showed some interesting explorations of restaurant customer behavior: The reason for eating out besides meals at work are as follows: 61.9% of the people go out eating with friends, 20.7% with family members, 11.5% for business socialization, and 5.7% of them who do not want to cook!!! Because of the fast pace of life, customers do not have patience for waiting at a restaurant. A total of 22.4% of the customers will wait for 10 minutes, 70.1% will wait for 10–20 minutes, and 7.5% for 21–30 minutes. Taste is always the No. 1 consideration for the customers: 37.9% of them prefer spicy hot food, 25.3% favor light meals, and 20.7% favor heavy meals. The choice of regional cuisines is broken down as 50.6% for Sichuan, 31.6% for Hunan, 29.3% for Cantonese, 26.4% for Huaiyang, and 18.4% for Shangdong. A total of 36.8% of the consumers choose the hotpot as their first choice in cooking style and 33.9% choose grill as the second choice. The reason for restaurant selection is as follows: 80% choose based upon taste, 62% for health safety, 57% for price, 21% for eating environment, and 18% for service quality (searchina.com). A study from the China Culinary Association (2016) indicates that taste ranks as the No. 1 reason to dine out, followed by food safety, eating environment, price, and restaurant image as the other important factors. For food item choice decisions, 64% of choices are made by females and 36% by males. Most customers will eat out twice a week and the price ranges between RMB 50–60; 80.2% of the customers will choose a price below RMB 100 per person, 13.6% for RMB 100 to 200, 3.3% for RMB 200-300, and only 0.9% for RMB 400 and above. Most of them will have 2-4 people as a group when eating out (Luo, 2015). A total of 82.4% of the 1990s generation use Wechat to make a restaurant reservation and 79% of the 1980s generation also do so.

6.3.3.2 Wedding Party

According to (xishiwang.com), a report found the cost of a wedding luncheon or dinner among the top 20 cities in China in 2012 and 2013. For an average wedding luncheon or dinner cost, a wedding couple spends RMB 4,441 per table for 10 guests and the wedding dinner size is normally around 16 to 18 tables in Shanghai. This wedding dinner costs the highest (a total over 70,000 Yuan) among the 20 cities. From No. 2 to No. 10 cities, an average wedding dinner costs RMB 3,308 per table for 10 guests. Prices range from city to city: RMB 2,800 in Hangzhou, RMB 2,582 in Ningbo, RMB 2,499 in Beijing, RMB 2,413 in Dalian, RMB 2,313.5 in Shenzhen, RMB 2,219 in Guangzhou, RMB 2,183.5 in Nanjing, RMB 2.140 in Qingdao, and 2,098.5 Yuan in Tianjin. The wedding dinners often take place at four- or five-star hotels or well-known restaurants in a city. According to jia.com (2016), wedding dinner in the first-tier cities costs RMB 2000 to 5000 a table for 10 persons, RMB 1500 to 3000 for the second-tier cities, RMB 1000 for the third-tier cities, and RMB 800 at the county level.

6.3.3.3 Conference and Exhibition Participants

Conference and exhibition participants also contribute to the restaurant industry. According to meetingschina.com, 10.87% of hotels will quote RMB 4,000 and above for a meal serving 10 persons at a table; 17.39% of hotels charge RMB 3,000–4,000, 33.7% of hotels charge RMB 2,000–3000, and 38.04% of hotels charge RMB 2000 and below. In 2015, there were 8,157 exhibitions in China. Imagine if 100 exhibitors participate at a banquet, taking RMB 2000 for a table of 10 persons, then the total cost will be RMB 163 million. This does not include millions of participants who will eat out!

6.3.3.4 Domestic Travelers

Domestic travelers will also contribute to the restaurant industry. Imagine with the 4.44 billion trips the Chinese people made domestically in 2016, and if each person travelling for 2 days paid RMB 20 for a day, the contribution to the restaurant industry would be RMB 177.6 billion!

6.3.4 SUBSTATIONS–SUPERMARKET

If one wants to eat but does not want to cook at home, you either call for food delivery, or before you go home after work, you can stop by any supermarket and shop for a variety of ready-to-eat and all cooked food items in Hualian or Huarun Chinese Supermarket or Walmart/Sam Club and Carrefour. It is quite convenient and costs much less than eating at a restaurant or through food delivery.

6.3.5 SUPPLIERS

6.3.5.1 Investment in Safe Food Supply Chains

According to Perkowski's (2014) report, there were large capital investments in safe Chinese food supplies. In 2013, Shuanghui International acquired US Smithfield Foods for $4.7 billion in order to obtain a safe meat source from US. In 2014, Kohlberg Kravis Roberts (KKR) invested $270 million to Joycom, a subsidiary of COFCO Meat, a Chinese food company, to produce high quality meat and seafood. US Tyson Foods Inc. invested hundreds of millions of dollars to build super-sanitary chicken farms in China and its revenue reached $1.1 billion in 2015. Jacky Ma of Alibaba, FOSUN, and COFCO in China and two European companies invested into the three largest dairy companies to boost Chinese dairy production. Deere & Company invested $190 million into three factories in agricultural equipment and engine productions to modernize the agricultural industry in China.

6.3.5.2 Investments in O2O Food Platform

From the above story of the development of ele.me by Xuhao Zhang and Jia Kang, several companies invested $4.5 billion in the company. One can therefore expect that there is so much capital pouring into online food delivery systems. In the first half of 2015, more than 90 companies invested into O2O systems, including food delivery, specialty food, food supply logistics, and C2C private kitchens. Baidu.com invested RMB 20 billion into its O2O Nomi.com system to provide assistance from group sales to luxury service. It also invested $310 million for its Baidu delivery system. In 2016, Alibaba took over top.chinaz to enter the food service business and added RMB 6 billion additional investment. In 2013, Alibaba created its taodiandian (taotao.com). Alibaba and Tencent were two larger investors who supported the merger between dianping.com and meituan.com, which were two large food delivery platforms.

6.3.6 COMPETITION

The western fast food companies led by KFC and Pizza Hut under Yum enjoy greatly its expansion in China with more than 6700 stores, followed by McDonalds with 2200 stores. They are the largest restaurant companies among international or domestic companies in China. The western restaurant companies have used large-scale purchasing power, large market shares, good franchise and operation systems, large investment capital, and good management teams as competitive tools to compete in the Chinese restaurant industry. They promote and market their products and give incentives to the customers. From 2013–2015, Yum China sales were 6.905 billion, 6.934 billion, and 6.909 billion US dollars and net profit was 777 million, 713 million, and 757 million US dollars, which were half of the revenue or net profit of each of the three years. However, both Yum and McDonald's growth have slowed down. Even though they have started a 24-hour food delivery service, offered new menu items, and given e-coupons and price discounts, there are other factors affecting growth. The reasons for slow growth can be that the Chinese people are not interested in Western food, the saturation of the market, their slow response to the challenge of O2O platform, and the scandal of using expired meat. They cannot increase their sale and expand the market like in the old days. Yum China's sales declined 14% and 16% in Quarters 3 and 4 in 2014. KFC's revenue declined 4% and Pizza Hut's revenue dropped 5% in 2015. McDonald's revenue was 25.41 billion US dollars and net profit was 4.53 billion US dollars in 2015, but it exhibited a 9% drop in revenue and 17% drop in net profit compared with the results of 2013. Now, McDonald's wants to sell its franchise system for 20 years for 2 billion US dollars, and there are many companies bidding for it. Yum China plans to go public and sell 20% of its stock, and several international or domestic companies are interested in the deal (Jin, 2016). After bidding for 6 months, on January 9, 2017, the CITIC Group obtained 52% and Carlyle got 28% of McDonald's China's stocks. The joint venture will operate

7300 stores in China for 20 years. The two companies paid 2.08 billion US dollars. McDonald's still holds 20% of the shares (news.xinhuannet). Yum China has split from Yum! Brands and has become YUMC, which started to trade on New York Stock Exchange on November 1, 2016 (yumchina.com).

The competition among domestic Chinese restaurant companies is fierce. For the customer market, high-end restaurants changed their operational strategies from "chasing luxury and comprehensive restaurant" to "originality and boutique restaurant." Restaurant owners started to use the Internet as a resource to market their business, such as Weibo marketing, WeChat official account marketing, order, and delivery through apps and other marketing strategies. Besides, innovative restaurants in rural areas are growing with tourism. For example, "农家乐", the Chinese "farm to table," makes the possibility of visiting the farm, picking up fresh vegetables and fruits, feeding cows and other livestock and eating at the farm. The competition is intensified because the online IT companies (Baidu, Taobao, Tencent) have joined the restaurant business. They have invested into the O2O food service platform (as aforementioned). Regardless of whether it is a small individual restaurant or a large restaurant chain, O2O food delivery can help the operations and the customers enjoy the convenience and quick service.

However, due to the fast speed of development and the lack of regulations and policies, the restaurant industry still faces many problems and the urgent need to change from "bold economy" to "intensive economy."

6.4 CONCLUDING REMARKS

The Chinese restaurant industry has developed very quickly in the last 20 years. This is because of the fast growth of GDP and more disposable income and the increase in the mid-income population. The information technology plays a critical role linking restaurants and customers by promoting and marketing the restaurant business, delivering food to the customer, as well as providing logistical service to the restaurants. The international restaurant companies have taken a very important role in helping the Chinese to develop their restaurant chains.

The future of the Chinese restaurant industry is bright. There will be more opportunities to develop community food service and food service for the increasing aging population. However, the restaurant industry needs to make additional efforts in food safety and security as well as sustainable practices in operations. The strict implementation of laws and regulations, coupled with more involvement from the IT industry will assist in providing safe, tasty food, and improved convenient service to the ever-changing customers.

KEYWORDS

- **anti-corruption policy**
- **Chinese restaurant industry**
- **development**
- **environment**
- **mobile payment**
- **restaurant market segmentation**

REFERENCES

Bird & Bird, (2015). *China Tightens Food Safety Law*. Retrieved from http://www.twobirds.com/en/news/articles/2015/global/food-law-jul/china-tightens-food-safety-law.

Broughton, E. I., & Walker, D. G., (2010). Policies and practices for aquaculture food safety in China. *Food Policy, 35*(5), 471–478.

Canglanfushi, (2016). *China Top 100 Restaurant Ranking in 2014*. Retrieved from http://wenku.baidu.com/link?url=QacVly3HwYY0mtfRZTgjrXN7cnIg31fd3JV-Ht8Wzt-MgG6RyRdMgqFeyRj7y1mXRmqFLGTA7j2gfQAdtufW2bdo667G1ITNtvPRFmys-N23q.

China Cuisine Association, (2016). Restaurant Industry have increased 11.2% in the first half year in 2016. Retrieved from http://www.ccas.com.cn/Article/HTML/107870.html.

CCTV Finance, (2016). *The Exposure from CCTV*: Something You Will Never Know about Take-out Kitchen. Retrieved from http://www.backchina.com/news/2016/09/26/450271.html.

China Finance, (2015). China Restaurant Industry Annual Report in 2015: *Apps Change the Industry*. Retrieved from http://finance.china.com/fin/kj/201505/17/6289026.html.

China Hotel Association, (2016). *China Restaurant Industry*, Annual Report in 2016. Retrieved from http://www.chinahotel.org.cn/ChoiceOSP/forward/findContent.do?id= c8e3a6a76dd445dea72b2dead7f082ae&childMId1= c8e3a6a76dd445dea72b2dead7f082ae&childMId2=&childMId3=&contentId= 6b9dda6257b34dd6bdd92bac135ad8ba.

Deluca, & Michael, (2016). Food Scandals regulation and the administrative process in modern China. Retrieved from http://www.thereviewatnyu.com/all-articles/2016/2/8/food-scandals-regulation-and-the-administrative-process-in-modern-china.

Fast Food in China http://factsanddetails.com/china/cat11/sub73/entry-4477.html.
Filloon, W., (2014). Ten Jailed in China for Supplying Expired Meat to McDonald's, KFC. http://www.eater.com/2016/2/1/10887058/china-tainted-meat-kfc-mcdonalds-prison.
Florcruz, & Michelle, (2015). *China's Food & Beverage Industry Rebounding Amid Anti-Corruption Drive*. Retrieved from http://www.ibtimes.com/chinas-food-beverage-industry-rebounding-amid-anti-corruption-drive-1924543.
Hite, & Brittany, (2015). *China's Beer Industry Goes Flat with Anti-Corruption Campaign*. Retrieved from http://blogs.wsj.com/chinarealtime/2015/02/06/chinas-beer-industry-goes-flat-with-anti-corruption-campaign/.
http://www.meetingschina.com/news10871.html (the cost analysis of main conference halls and meal service in the first half year of 2015 in China).
http://searchina.com (reasons for choosing a restaurant.).
http://news.xinhuanet.com/info/2017–01/10/c_135968968.htm (CITIC and Carlyle used $2.08 purchases McDonald's stocks).
http://www.yumchina.com/News/Index/2016–1-213 (YUMC completed its separation from YUM! Brands).
Huehnergarth, & Nancy, (2014). *China's Food Safety Issues Worse Than You Thought*. Retrieved from http://www.foodsafetynews.com/2014/07/chinas-food-safety-issues-are-worse-than-you-thought/#.WC369elrKcM.
Interview with Guoqiang, Wu, CEO of Jiangsu Mother Dumpling Group, Co. http://xiaochi.liansuo.com/news/8052.html.
Jia, (2016). *How Much to Cost for a Wedding in Beijing, China?* Retrieved from http://zixun.jia.com/article/427432.html.
Jin, L., (2016). *Lightning*. McDonalds would like to cut short stores because Chinese People are Not Fond of Fast-food Any More. http://finance.qq.com/a/20160714/033659.htm.
Kimes, S. E., (2011). The current state of online food ordering in the US restaurant industry.
Li, Z., (2014). China's tainted meat scandal explained, http://www.cnn.com/2014/07/29/world/asia/explainer-china-meat-scandal/.
Luo, H., (2015). What does 2015 food and drink data tell you? http://o2ocanyin.baijia.baidu.com/article/298577.
Leung, W., (2014). Data tells your Chinese food consumption behavior. http://blog.sina.com.cn/s/blog_6eb5d96a0102vfqe.html.
Martin, A., (2015). *Food Scandals Push McDonald's Japan Into Loss*. https://www.wsj.com/articles/food-scandals-push-mcdonalds-japan-into-loss-1423121899.
OperationAnalysisofMalanNoodlehttp://www.askci.com/news/dxf/20160620/13505131167.shtml.
Pasquier, Martin, (2015). O2O: *Why China Leads the "Online to Offline" Revolution?*. Retrieved from http://www.innovationiseverywhere.com/o2o-why-china-leads-the-online-to-offline-revolution/.
Pintu Website, (2015). *China Restaurant Industry O2O,* Annual Report in 2015. http://file.pintu360.com/upload-by-admin/other/20151118/02cb063c-adb7–44f1–8829–027c0b-d2e0a5.pdf.
Perkowski, J., (2014). *China's Growing Food Problem/Opportunity*. http://www.forbes.com/sites/jackperkowski/2014/09/25/chinas-growing-food-problemopportunity/#5c865014235a.
Ripley, & Will, (2016). *How to Get By in Beijing Without a Wallet*. Retrieved from http://money.cnn.com/2016/04/08/technology/beijing-mobile-payments-no-wallet/.

Trefis Team, (2014). *McDonald's Faces Declining Sales In Asia After China Food Scandal,* http://www.forbes.com/sites/greatspeculations/2014/09/11/mcdonalds-faces-declining-sales-in-asia-after-china-food-scandal/#740dceaa561e.

Wenxuecity, (2017). He only wanted to have something to eat, fortunately he has a RMB 31.5 billion business at age of 31. Retrieved from http://www.wenxuecity.com/news/2017/01/02/5892150.html.

World Federation of Chinese Catering Industry, (2016). *Find a New Path? Restaurant Featured Health Food in Local Flavors Restaurant.* Retrieved from http://www.wacc.cn/info.php?act=detail&id=1553.

Wu, & Ji, (2016). O2O only share 4.3% of the 3.2 trillion market in Restaurant Industry. Retrieved from http://www.iyiou.com/p/29351.

Wu, & Jingna, (2013). *How the High-End Restaurants Cope With the Crisis After Anti-Corruption Regulations Issue.* Retrieved from http://cn.nytimes.com/china/20130301/cc01restaurant/.

Zhao, J., & Li, L. (2001). The restaurant industry in China: assessment of the current status and future opportunities. *Journal of Restaurant and Foodservice Marketing, 4*(4), 155–172.

Zou, & Renchuan, (2016).*The Current Issue in Restaurant Industry*. Retrieved from https://www.gtja.com/content/default/market/xinsanban/market_cy_20160526/_jcr_content/left-par/download/file.res/%E9%A4%90%E9%A5%AE%E8%A1%8C%E4%B8%9A%E5%8F%91%E5%B1%95%E7%8E%B0%E7%8A%B6.pdf.

CHAPTER 7

E-TOURISM EVOLUTIONARY EFFECT: STUDYING E-TOURISM IN CHINA

BEIQI SHI

Shanghai Institute of Tourism, Fengxian Qu, Shanghai Shi, China

CONTENTS

7.1 A HUGE CAKE—INTRODUCTION TO TOURISM IN CHINA

The tourism industry is an important economic driver in many countries. Contributions of this industry are more salient in economies where tourism accounts for a substantial share of the gross domestic product (GDP). With increasing disposable income, more public holidays, and faster transportation, China's domestic and outbound travel has grown unprecedentedly in recent years. In 2011, the number of inbound tourists reached 135 million with an international tourism (foreign exchange) revenue of 48.464 billion US dollars. The number of domestic tourists jumped to 2.641 billion with a revenue of RMB 1930.539 billion. The number of outbound tourists climbed to 70.25 million. The total revenue of tourism hit

RMB 2.25 trillion. China had 120 million outbound visitors in 2015, and they spent 104.5 billion US dollars, which is an increase of 12% and 16.7% compared with that of 2014. There were 133.8204 million inbound tourists, including foreigners and tourists from Hong Kong, Macau, and Taiwan. There were 56.8857 million overnight stays in China, which is an increase of 4.1% and 2.3%, respectively, compared with the same period in 2014. The total revenue of tourism hit RMB 4.00 trillion. Figure 7.1 shows domestic and inbound tourism statistics in 2011–2015.

In addition, the latest data released by the World Tourism Organization (WTO) shows that China's revenue from international tourism in 2015 amounted to 11.4 billion US dollars, taking Spain's former ranking as second in the world. The US remains the first with 17.8 billion US dollars. Spending by Chinese travelers increased 25% in 2015 to reach 292 billion US dollars, as total outbound travelers rose by 10% to 128 million visitors.[1]

It is evident that e-business is an essential prerequisite for successful organizations in the emerging, globally networked, internet-empowered business environment, especially for the tourism industry. With the emergence of the Internet, travel planning (e.g., travel information search and booking) has always been one of the main reasons that people use the Internet. An increasing number of Chinese travelers use the Internet to search

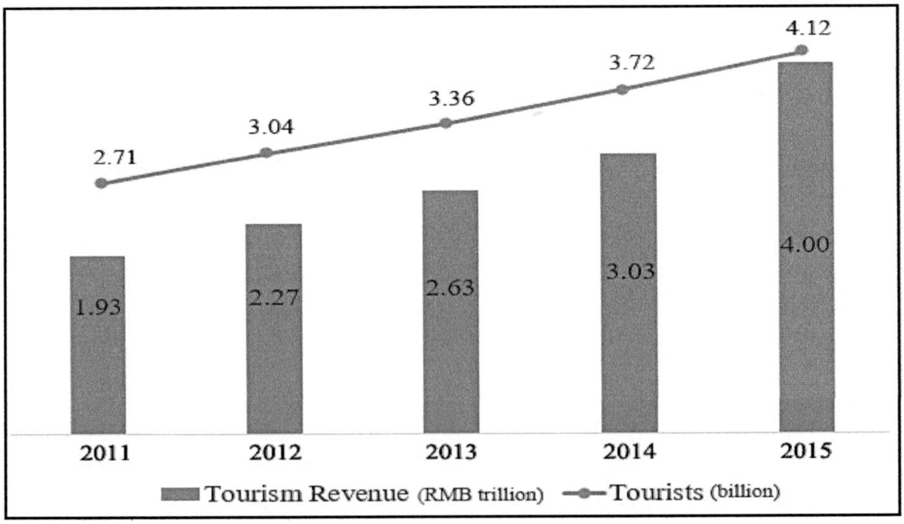

FIGURE 7.1 2011-2015 bulletin of domestic and inbound tourism statistics (Source from China National Tourism Administration).

[1] (http://media.unwto.org/press-release/2016-05-03/exports-international-tourism-rise-4-2015).

for tourism information, share travel experiences, and make reservations. Electronic-tourism (E-tourism) is booming. According to a report published by iResearch in 2011, online travel arrangement and reservation services accounted for RMB 131.39 billion, an increase by 33.9% over the previous year (http://www.iresearch.com.cn/View/161323.html). In 2015, online travel arrangement and reservation services accounted for RMB 432.63 billion, and it is expected that in 2016, the account will reach 542.09 billion RMB.[2] Figure 7.2 is the Gross Merchandise Volume of China's online travel arrangement and reservation services in 2011–2015. Ctrip, Tuniu, and CY were the top three largest Online Travel Agencies (OTAs) by transaction values in 2015. The three accounted for 50% of total OTA market share. CY increased its market share in 2015 with 3.7 percentage points higher than that in 2014 and Tuniu increased by 3.3 percentage points compared with that in 2014.[3]

Users can obtain and share travel information freely from user-generated content (UGC) websites. UGC is playing an important role for China online tourism. UGC can generate traffic and attract users by providing accurate travel needs for OTAs and other suppliers. Meanwhile, they can help users make better decision for travel planning. There exist two different business models in the China online travel UGC market. One focuses on vertical search and price comparison like Qunar. The other is mainly concentrated on online travel blogs such as Mafengwo.

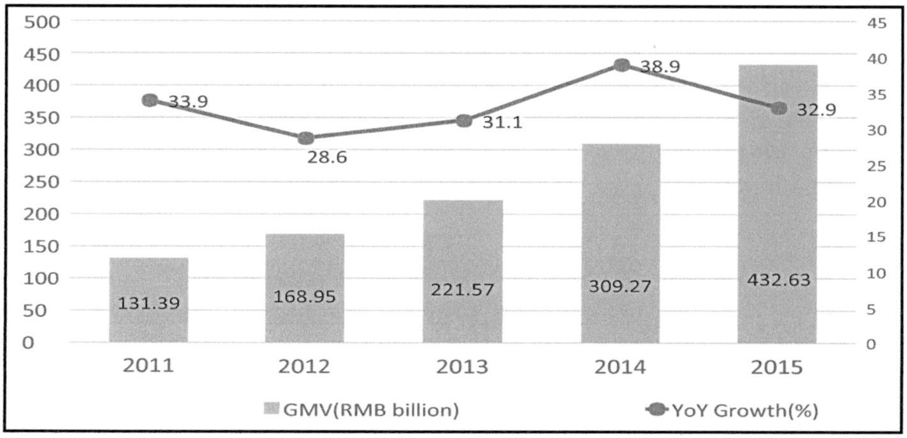

FIGURE 7.2 Gross Merchandise Volume of China's online travel arrangement and reservation services in 2011-2015 (Source from iResearch).

[2] (http://report.iresearch.cn/content/2016/05/260893.shtml)

[3] (https://www.chinainternetwatch.com/17141/online-travel-agent-market-2015/)

The Internet has also greatly shaped the evolution of channel distribution systems in the tourism industry, which caused channel conflict between service suppliers (e.g., hotels and airlines) and their intermediaries (e.g., OTAs). Suppliers intend to cease the direct offering and booking of their own fares on their websites.

Thus, currently, electronic-tourism (e-tourism) is booming. E-tourism has gained more support than ever from the government recently. "Beautiful China—2014 Year of Smart Travel" is the slogan of China National Tourism Administration (CNTA) in 2014, which expresses the government's desire to encourage tourism firms and authorities to use advanced technology to enhance the quality of tourism services.[4] Moreover, the Internet Plus concept was first presented by Premier Li Keqiang in March 2015 when delivering the government work report. The action plan will integrate mobile Internet, cloud computing, big data, and the Internet of Things (IoT) with modern manufacturing, to encourage the healthy development of e- commerce, industrial networks, and Internet banking and to help Internet companies increase their international presence.[5] The future development of Chinese tourism will focus on improving productivity and applying the Internet Plus approach to create new market growth and drive innovation.

The purpose of this review is to provide essential knowledge related to E-tourism in China. E-tourism has closely been connected to progress of information and communication technologies (ICTs). It illuminates ICT developments and main implications of ICT in tourism. The review intends to investigate the main factors, which driving users' E-tourism website motivation and stickiness are the key issues to the forming of a critical mass of users and the probability of making a sales increase. The evolution of channel distribution systems in the tourism industry is also explored in the review.

7.2 THE KNIFE—INFORMATION COMMUNICATION TECHNOLOGIES APPLIED IN TOURISM

ICTs is an extended term for information technology (IT) that stresses the role of unified communications and the integration of telecommunications (telephone lines and wireless signals), computers as well as necessary enterprise software, middleware, storage, and audio-visual systems, which

[4] (http://en.cnta.gov.cn/focus/travelnews/201507/t20150707_721217.shtml)
[5] (http://english.gov.cn/policies/latest_releases/2015/07/04/content_281475140165588.htm)

enable users to access, store, transmit, and manipulate information. ICTs is, undoubtedly, the key to the conceptualization and development of E-tourism. In this section, firstly, the applications of ICTs for E-tourism are described. Then, the benefits of ICTs are discussed. Finally, ICTs and Internet application in China's tourism industry are explored.

7.2.1 APPLICATIONS OF ICTs FOR E-TOURISM

ICTs with the ability to support tourism in an intelligent way has been discussed, developed, and envisioned for quite a long time. ICTs have been applied in tourism since the early adoption of computer reservation system (CRS) in airlines in the 1950s and in the transformation to global distribution systems (GDSs) in the 1980s. Hotel property management systems (PMSs) and hotel CRS systems appeared shortly afterwards, bringing switch companies into the market as well in order to improve interconnectivity and interoperability.

Since the Internet brought revolutionary changes to the structure of the industry, ICTs provided E-tourism principals, airlines and hoteliers, an opportunity to sell directly. The implications of ICTs on the tourism distribution system has been developed rapidly. The most recent developments in E-tourism applications are at the destination level. By employing Internet, Intranet and Extranet, some destination management organizations (DMOs) have successfully integrated this function in promoting their destination (Francesca and Frank, 2009; Bornhorst and Ritchie, 2010).

As the "smart" technological environment encompasses connected physical and digital infrastructures, the IoT has the potential to rapidly become a new reality as a technological infrastructure. The basic idea of the IoT is the pervasive presence around us of a variety of objects to interact with each other and cooperate with their neighboring objects to achieve common goals. The innovations driven by the IoT have important implications for tourism development because travel involves movement through time and space, and this "smart" environment will grow to be aware of, and be able to address, the traveler's contextual needs in a pervasive yet non-intrusive way (Wang et al., 2013; Guo et al., 2014).

With the popularity of E-Word of Mouth (E-WOM), social recommender systems aim to relieve information and interaction overload by applying various techniques that ultimately present the most relevant and attractive information to users. These personalized recommendations based on social interactions or preferences are viewed as a huge opportunity for vendors (Zhang et al., 2010; Ye et al., 2011).

The intersection of social media and location-based services (LBS) resulted in the development of location-based social networks or location sharing services, which allow user to broadcast location or geotag content as 'crowdsourcing geospatial data' (CGD). Specifically, visitor behavior and travel flow patterns within a tour destination are closely related with geographic location. Meanwhile, CGD derived from non-authoritative sources consisting primarily of end-users participating in social media and web-based activities can be primarily geospatial in nature or could simply be an associated geospatial characteristic of non-geospatial information, which shifts from a data-sparse to a data-rich paradigm (Heipke 2010, Sui and Goodchild, 2011).

7.2.2 BENEFITS OF ICTs

ICTs, as the backbone of process innovations, has improved the reliability, compatibility, and interconnectivity of numerous terminals and applications in recent years. The development of the Internet and ICTs has made many significant impacts on the operation, structure, and strategy of organizations as well as on communication with consumers.

Benefits of ICTs to organizations aim at escalating efficiency, productivity, and flow. The wider impacts of this massive technology push on the business of tourism, destinations and subsequent innovations still have to be investigated (Werthner & Klein, 2006; Schegg, et al., 2008). Yuan et al. (2006) pointed out the prospects of technology are confronted and modified by the organizational features and specific managerial objectives that map ICTs implementation in visitor bureaus. Blake et al. (2006) demonstrated that productivity in tourism enterprises can be improved by introducing new ICTs, but favorable impacts are especially obtained where ICTs were combined with other strategic and managerial measures such as competence building and human resource management. Katsoni (2011) drew the attention of all the stakeholders in the tourism sector to the need to support and promote ICT as the most effective tool for tourism regional planning, tourist information access and dissemination as well as the tourism regional development participants' need for organizational change. Museums and other (heritage) attractions are rapidly moving into these areas, and evidence is emerging that ICTs can improve understanding, attraction, and accessibility for tourists and lead to higher organizational efficiency (Nielsen and Liburd, 2008; Hjalager, 2010). Blake et al. (2006) explored that ICTs shifts the power balance of tourism distribution channels. Buhalis and Amaranggana (2015) studied smart tourism destinations. They illustrated that big data can analyze computationally to reveal patterns and trends and smart tourism destinations should make an optimal use of big data by offering the right services that suit users' preference at the right time.

Each tourist carries a unique blend of experiences, motivations, and desires. ICTs can empower tourists with more knowledge and encourages them to seek exceptional value for money and time. In this respect, tourists can find information anywhere and anytime in accordance with where the users are and what the situation is through the latest technology, including, smart phone application, augmented reality, and LBS. Learning of the rich historical and cultural backgrounds of scenic spots in a limited time is difficult for nonlocal and foreign tourists during their visit. Huang et al. (2015) involved developing a smart tourism application system for historical and cultural scenic spots for tourists based on visual search technology. The results of the experiment indicated that the current accuracy of the image search identification is 86%. Reino et al. (2007) assessed technology-mediated heritage interpretation. The result revealed that with a traditional interpretative technology-based heritage interpretation can enhance displays′ multisensory provision and visitors′ perceived interactivity. UGC related to travel can be posted on specific travel-related websites or on more generic social networking websites. This content reflects the experiences of the tourist at specific destinations or with other travel products. Burgess et al. (2009) listed the benefits of online travel recommendations as shown in Table 7.1.

7.2.3 EXPLORATION OF ICTs AND INTERNET APPLICATION IN CHINA'S TOURISM INDUSTRY

In order to explore the level of adoption of ICTs and Internet applications in China. Ma and Buhalis (2003) focused on the supply sides (such as airlines, hotels, tour operators, visitor attractions, and the tourism authorities) of the Chinese tourism industry; they found that in the early 21st century, the development was first started in airlines and then extended to hotels, tour

TABLE 7.1 Benefits of Online Travel Recommendations*

Category		Benefits
Content	Argument; extreme opinions	Well-reasoned, logical, persuasive reviews can positively influence purchase decisions
Source	eWOM and 'weak' ties	Sources more plentiful; Access to more reviews than with WOM
	Credibility	Credible as source as nothing to lose by offering advice; Consumers and independent bodies can be neutral source
Nature of Recommendations	Influence	More likely to influence as tourism is an 'experience' product
	Filter	Can assist tourists to manage the wealth of data

* From Burgess, et al. (2009).

operators, attractions and DMOs, with the first two sectors taking the lead. Airlines and hotels developed in terms of their ICTs adoption within the organization and the awareness of ICTs. At that time, though some changes have taken places in tour operators, visitor attractions, and DMOs, ICTs applications in these sectors are limited.

Lu and Lu (2004) investigated online tourism service development in China from three perspectives: the tourism website, the tourism website user, and the tourism website provider. The results showed that the majority of tourism website providers are regional tourism destination organizations that mainly provide comprehensive local tourism information and online services. It further showed the level of regional economic development has a significant impact on the construction of these local tourism websites.

According to a survey report of the China Tourism Academy,[6] e-commerce associated with tourism continues with the provision of the traditional services of air tickets, hotels, and consulting businesses. Moreover, a new emerging trend includes booking tickets for attractions and travel group purchase. The survey shows that the three most popular online services include booking airline tickets, booking hotels, and looking for tourism information, which was used by 61%, 45.4%, and 44.6% of respondents, respectively, in Figure 7.3.

Smart tourism has rapidly developed in China. Smart tourism destination initiatives coined firstly officially by China's State Council of Chinese

[6] (http://www.cnta.gov.cn/html/2011-9/2011-9-14-23-1-76970.html)

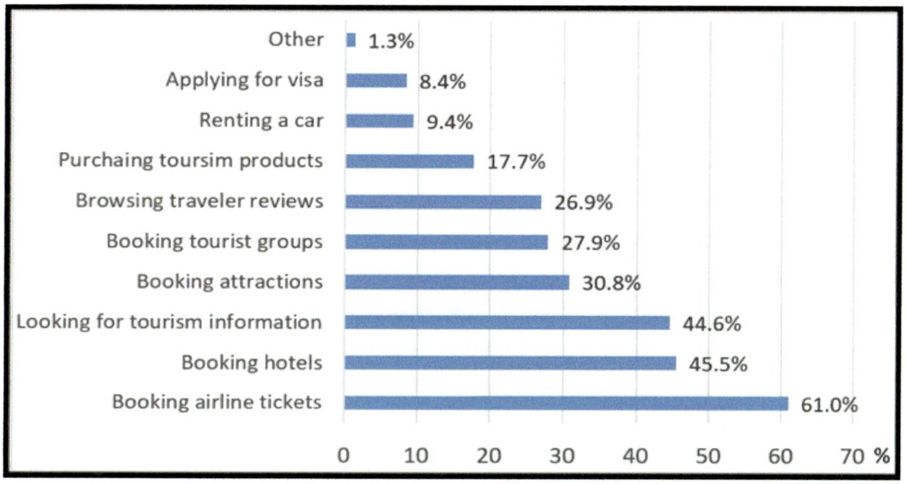

FIGURE 7.3 Online leisure trip-planning activities*. (*Source from:http://www.cnta.gov.cn/html/2011-9/2011-9-14-23-1-76970.html)

Central Government in 2009 refer to a platform on which information related to tourist activities, the consumption of tourism products, and the status of tourism resources can be instantly integrated and then provided to tourists, enterprises, and organizations through a variety of end-user devices (Huang and Li, 2011; Zhang et al., 2012). Further, in 2014, CNTA proposed the slogan "Beautiful China—2014 Year of Smart Travel."

Zhang, Li, and Liu (2012) proposed the component application architecture (CAA) framework of smart tourism comprising three levels, namely, capabilities, attributes, and applications. Smart tourism is generally dependent on the following four core information technologies: IoT, mobile communication, cloud computing, and artificial intelligent technology. These technologies connect the physical infrastructure, information infrastructure, social infrastructure, and commercial infrastructure of tourism, and supply smart tourism value to multiple stakeholders.

Wang et al., (2013) took Nanjing as an example for a smart tourism destination. Nanjing published "Nanjing Tour Assistant," a mobile application for smartphones and tablets. This application provides not only comprehensive information about local attractions, but also LBS that equips tourists with a better understanding of the attractions and things surrounding them as well as coupon information from merchants and restaurants nearby. In essence, DMOs are now playing an active role in helping tourists design their own travel experience. The "Nanjing Tour Assistant" application (http://www.

cnta.gov.cn/html/2011-9/2011-9-14-23-1-76970.html) provides connections with "*Sina Weibo*," a Twitter equivalent in China. Thus, tourists who share the same interest (i.e., Nanjing as a tourism destination) are connected to share stories and exchange travel tips. As such, not only are tourists involved in experience creation, but this co-creation is also real-time and multidirectional (service provider-tourist, tourist-tourist, tourist-service provider). It demonstrated that the initiative of a smart tourism destination has enhanced the tourist experience through co-creation and sharing. The micro-blog owned by the Nanjing Tourism Development Committee has attracted more than 200,000 fans. Through constant conversations with tourists, the local DMO can acquire more insights on the demands and preferences of tourists.

Guo et al., (2014) stated that there is a trend of embedding application of tourism IoT in China's scenic spots. They attempted to combine the Internet of Things (IoT) technology with the development of the smart tourism industry and smart tourism cities from technical viewpoint.

Wang et al. (2016) proposed a methodological approach of assessing tourist preference of smart tourist attraction (STA). Fuzzy comprehensive evaluation methods and analytic hierarchy processes were applied to the STA evaluation of Hongshan Zoo, a popular tourist attraction in China. Findings suggested that "information system," "intelligent tourism management," "smart sightseeing," "e-commerce system," "smart safety," "intelligent traffic," "smart forecasting," and "virtual tourist attractions" are tourists' key evaluation factors of STA.

7.3 WHY E-TOURISM?—FROM CONSUMERS' PERSPECTIVE

While E-tourism develop rapidly in China, it is required to understand the attitude and behavior of China's Internet travelers to offer better service. What are the general factors affecting E-tourism adoption? What drives users' E-tourism website stickiness? This section attempts to answer these questions.

7.3.1 FACTORS AFFECTING THE E-TOURISM ADOPTION

7.3.1.1 Autonomy

E-tourism services offer travel portals to make the traveler self-dependent and provide all information on single click. E-tourism services have made it possible for travelers reaching everything about a destination properly before going to destination and trip planning according to their convenience. Travelers learning about the tourism information has evolved from the completely passive mode to an active online information searching mode.

7.3.1.2 Culture

Culture is regarded as the collective programming of the human mind that distinguishes the members of one human group from another. Cultural values are the deepest and most relevant aspect of a cultural manifestation, albeit intangible. Although the virtual world is not culturally neutral, the norms and values that govern cultural groups are also represented online. According to Hofstede's cultural framework, national culture is the shared values of people within a certain national environment. There are five cultural dimensions: power distance, individualism, masculinity, uncertainty avoidance, and long-term orientation (Hofstede, 2001). Yoon (2009) explored the effects of national culture values on consumer acceptance of e-commerce in China, which showed that uncertainty avoidance and long-term orientation had moderate effects on the relationship between trust and intention to use and that masculinity also had a moderate effect on the relationship between perceived usefulness and intention to use and the relationship between perceived ease of use and intention to use. Zhang et al. (2013) investigated 200 participants on the influence of mood and social presence on consumer purchase behavior in consumer-to-consumer (C2C) e-commerce. They found that two cultural dimensions (individualism and uncertainty avoidance) have significant impacts on purchase intention. The results indicated that Chinese consumers tend to value group decisions, order, and security in their purchase behaviors. In a culture with high uncertainty avoidance, people are likely to create more formal regulations and do not put up with abnormal ideas and behaviors.

Michopoulou and Moisa (2016) have taken deep insight into the impact on culture on tourist's online information search behavior between the UK and China. According to their study, as a country with higher levels of uncertainty avoidance, travelers from UK appear to feel more threatened by uncertain situations and try to avoid them. Now, Chinese travelers are more open at using the online booking systems, while British travelers raise safety and security issues. Chinese travelers are more independent. They prefer to DIY their trip. The Chinese travelers' plan is not detail oriented, and they are happy to change plans as they go along and obtain new information. When purchasing, the British travelers focus their search around various websites and the process is price-driven. On the contrary, the Chinese travelers access the popular OTA with a good reputation. It is indicated that the Chinese travelers' search process is brand-driven, which is affected by long-term orientation.

7.3.1.3 Sensory Attraction

E-commerce websites exhibit elegant and colorful web pages, providing visual stimulations which can help travel consumers reduce stress and fatigue while spending money. In addition, purchasing travel products online can not only complete the actual purchase needs, but also enable the consumers to get much information and some fun that cannot be found in traditional travel agencies.

Jeong et al. (2012) revealed that exposure to a travel website significantly affected the majority of cognitive and overall destination images. Additionally, an experimental design was shown to be an effective method in measuring changes in destination image. Rodríguez-Molina et al. (2015) demonstrated that destination image is more positive when emotional messages are employed on the website and when the individual does not experience overload. The work also demonstrated the moderating role of involvement in the effect of the factors manipulated in the study (message type and information-overload) on tourist destination image. Law and Bai (2006) found that the importance of website design is widely recognized and that a number of website development evaluation instruments have appeared in the tourism field.

7.3.2 IMPACTORS DRIVING CUSTOMER'S E-TOURISM WEBSITE STICKINESS

Website stickiness, i.e., visit duration, is a key performance metric for website managers. It is also defined as repetitive visits to and use of a preferred website. Some travel and tourism e-commerce websites attract a large number of users who "stick" to their sites, while others never reach the critical threshold to become "fashionable" among users. Website stickiness is the key to the forming of a critical mass of users and the ability of a website to attract and retain customers.

To prevent users from switching to competitors, on-line companies are implementing various technologies and investing substantial resources to enhance the "stickiness." Lin (2007) indicated that improving the contents and format of the website would enhance the web user's positive attitude toward the website, which in turn will increase his/her stickiness intention. Trust in the context of e-commerce was another key issue for stickiness. Xu and Liu (2010) illustrated that information and services including the type of goods, goods guiding information, online communities, and convenient payment channels improve user's satisfaction and trust, which in turn will increase user's online stickiness. Website interface was the major media between the retailers and consumers that affected stickiness. Chen and Lin (2015) surveyed 376 e-tourism website users in China and examined "perceived fashionability" in forming users' e-tourism website stickiness in comparison with four commonly studied rational factors: system quality, information quality, security and e-shopping value. They implicated that managers of e-tourism websites should deliver rational factors to attract a critical mass of users to inspire perceived fashionability and subsequently induce customers' stickiness to the website. Providing discounts or low price alone was unlikely to achieve stickiness. In addition to rational factors, the perceived fashionability, as an important factor of social influence, plays a key role in forming website stickiness. The authors suggested that managers should monitor users' website visit behavior since fashion keeps changing.

Fashionability is a prime impact of social influence. Social influence may be particularly prominent in a collectively oriented society like China (Zhu and He, 2002). However, being social is not just about sharing connections; it is also about providing different ways for people to interact. In shopping as a social experience, people often want to get their friends' opinions before buying. Social commerce can help consumer buy where they connect. Therefore, many e-commerce companies integrate social media into e-retail sites and add e-commerce functionality to social networks. They want to use friends' preferences to help consumer make better purchasing decisions. The preference is online Word of Mouth (WOM). WOM exerts a powerful influence on consumers' purchase behavior especially in the presence of experience travel-related product purchases (O'Neill et al., 2002; Morgan et al., 2003). Online WOM has various advantages such as convenience, speed, one-to-many, many-to-many, and the absence of face-to-face interaction. Ye et al. (2011) conducted an empirical study to identify the impact of online user-generated reviews on business performance using data extracted from a major online travel agency in China. The results showed that traveler reviews have a significant impact on online sales, with a 10% increase in traveler review ratings boosting online bookings by more than 5%. Zhang et al. (2010) compared consumer reviews and editor reviews on the online popularity of restaurants. This study showed that consumer-generated ratings about the quality of food, environment, and service of restaurants and the volume of online consumer reviews are positively associated with the online popularity of restaurants, whereas editor reviews have a negative relationship with consumers' intention to visit a restaurant's webpage. Luo and Zhong (2015) demonstrated that travel-related e-WOM communication via SNS relied on existing social relationships, ties of which can be categorized as strong, moderate, or weak. The effect of transmitted information was stronger than that of influential decision-making. The communication network studied was found to be structured, loose-knit, flat, and of high centrality.

7.4 WHY E-TOURISM?—FROM MERCHANTS' PERSPECTIVE

E-tourism not only facilitates the travelers, but it also gives opportunities to merchants to develop their business across the world. As Internet-based e- commerce removes all geographical boundaries, firms get a scope for getting business across boundaries. Therefore, new commercial formats have developed by ICTs during the last two decades. The E-tourism industry has greatly evolved and modernized. It is intended to explore the E-tourism evolution in China.

7.4.1 RELATIONSHIPS ON TOURISM DISTRIBUTION CHANNEL

Since tourism products are often viewed by consumers as value-added chains of different service components that form service networks, the tourism supply chain has several characteristics (Zhang et al., 2009). First, tourism is a coordination-intensive industry in which different products/services (transportation, accommodation, and so on) are bundled together to form a final tourism product. Second, as services cannot be stored for future use, a tourism product is perishable. Third, tourists need to travel to the destinations where tourism products are produced to consume these products. Fourth, tourism products are complex in nature. Finally, the tourism industry often faces higher demand uncertainty and more complex dynamics than its counterparts because of intensive competition among service providers.

Figure 7.4 shows the relationship on the tourism distribution channel. Because vertical relationships are in the nature of the channel structure, vertical relationships based on ICTs have a main effect on performance in China. Overall, ICTs reduce transaction costs, and therefore, ICTs allow for a larger volume and control of information flow among sellers and buyers. Tourism service suppliers formerly offer products to intermediaries or sell tickets to offline consumer. In the past, intermediaries had a huge information competitive advantage over suppliers, and it was difficult for a supplier to develop an effective multichannel distribution. In the e-tourism era, while the channel conflict between service suppliers (e.g., hotels, airlines, and destinations) and their intermediaries in the tourism industry has become increasingly intense recently, more service suppliers have added a direct online channel to their existing distribution channels. Suppliers intend to direct offering and booking of their own fares on their website.

Most airline companies in China globalize their operations more easily, and they can also get effective access to distant consumers just with the ICTs tools. The emergence of hotel direct online channels has made the situation more serious, because hotels now have the option to reach consumers directly with very low costs. The quality of the travel agency's offer on the Internet, such as personalized and individualized service and the ease of using the channel, impacts customer trust in the travel agency. Travel agencies can increase their competitiveness by having online presence because

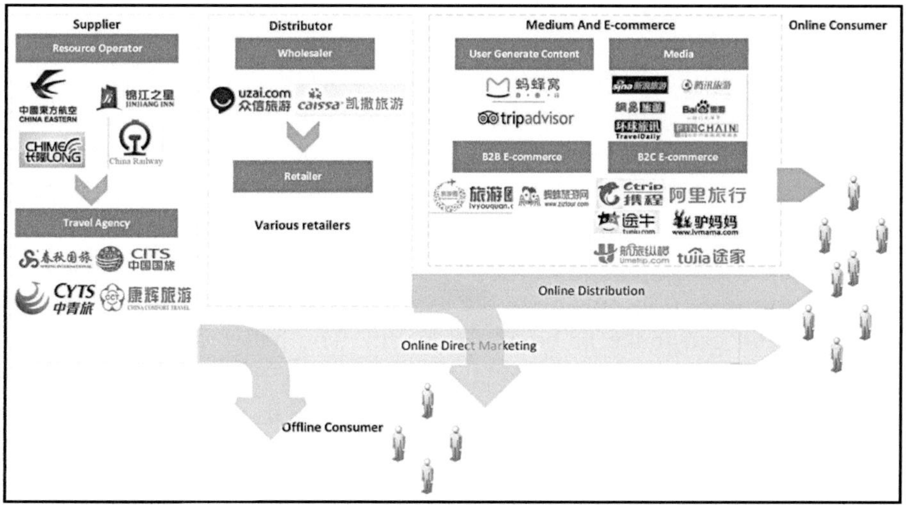

FIGURE 7.4 The relationship on tourism distribution channel in China.

consumers consider the travel agency's online channel as a value-added service. The price premium charged by intermediaries has been significantly reduced by the adoption of a direct online channel.

Meanwhile, ICTs also leads to changes in horizontal relationships because they add more incentives for cooperation between competitors and provide a communication platform with lower costs of coordination, especially for small medium tourism enterprise (SMTEs) such as such as small-scale hotels, transport companies, and rental businesses.

7.4.2 MOBILE PAYMENTS IN CHINA

It was found that credit card and debit card users—the so-called "plastic money" segments—spend more money in total on their trip than cash users. Further, of the two plastic money segments, credit card users are the bigger spenders (Thrane, 2015). However, for travel e-commerce brands focused on China, a market where top OTAs are today garnering over 70% traffic and transactions from mobile applications, the experience during check-out can make or break their business. Alternative modes of payment are already a big hit in China. Tourists are quite familiar with mobile payment. According to iResearch, the GMV of China third-party mobile payment attained 10.17 trillion Yuan in Q4 of 2015, shooting up 69.7% compared with 2014, and its growth was much lower than in Q4 of 2014.[7]

There are multiple ways of making a point-of-sale mobile wallet payment: NFC (an NFC-enabled device communicates via an RFID link with a contactless transmitter attached to a POS device), QR codes (QR code-based systems manage payment details in the cloud rather than in the device and can be carried out on any smartphone), and Bluetooth technology and apps.

Figure 7.5 is a pie chart that illustrates the market share of online payment services regarding transaction volume in Q2 of 2014, according to iResearch, a provider of information product, service, and solution in China.

Thus, for instant gratification, the experience of mobile payment during the check-out can make or break E-tourism. The battle over the Chinese e-payment market is raging fiercely now that Apple Pay and Samsung Pay have taken to the field in China. Apple Inc. launched its mobile payment system in China on February 18, 2016, in a bid to change the strategic landscape of mobile payment market amid the popularity of alternative mobile systems associated with Alibaba and Tencent.

[7] http://www.iresearchchina.com/content/details7_21238.html

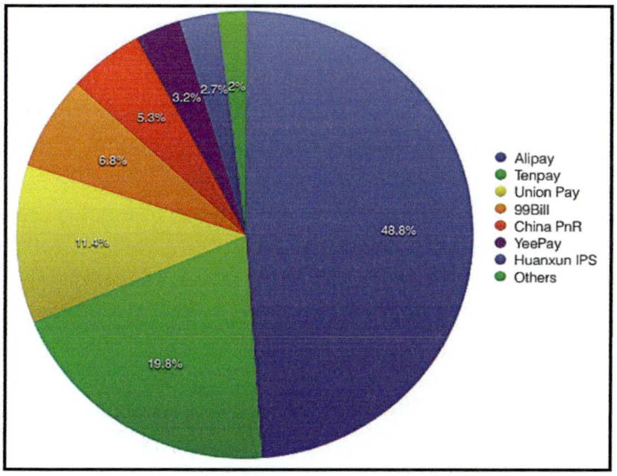

FIGURE 7.5 Market share of online payment services (Source: http://www.iresearchchina.com/content/details7_21238.html).

Alipay has already bridged the gap between trust and travel e-commerce transactions for outbound tourist. WeChat Crossborder Payment (WePay) is not particularly new, but to a lot of businesses outside China, it can still seem like magic. WePay is launching support for overseas vendors in nine different foreign currencies (USD, GBP, HKD, JPY, CAD, EUR, AUR, NZD, and KRW). Thus, mobile payments create convenient transaction for both tourists and vendors.

KEYWORDS

- **benefits**
- **e-tourism**
- **ICTs**

REFERENCES

Berne, Carmen, Margarita Garcia-Gonzalez, & Jose Mugica, (2012). "How ICT shifts the power balance of tourism distribution channels." *Tourism Management, 33*(1), 205–214.

Blake, Adam, M., Thea Sinclair, & Juan Antonio Campos Soria, (2006). "Tourism productivity: evidence from the United Kingdom." *Annals of Tourism Research 33*(4), 1099–1120.

Bornhorst, Tom, J. R., Brent Ritchie, & Lorn Sheehan, (2010). "Determinants of tourism success for DMOs & destinations: An empirical examination of stakeholders' perspectives." *Tourism Management, 31*(5), 572–589.

Buhalis, Dimitrios, & Aditya Amaranggana, (2015). "Smart tourism destinations enhancing tourism experience through personalization of services."*Information and Communication Technologies in Tourism*. Springer International Publishing. 377–389.

Burgess, Stephen, et al., (2009). "User-generated content (UGC) in tourism: Benefits and concerns of online consumers." *ECIS*.

Chen, Ye, & Zhibin Lin, (2015). "Fashionability vis-à-vis rationality: investigating factors driving users' e-tourism website stickiness." *Current Issues in Tourism*, 1–17.

D'angella, Francesca, & Frank, M., & Go, (2009). "Tale of two cities' collaborative tourism marketing: Towards a theory of destination stakeholder assessment." *Tourism Management, 30*(3), 429–440.

Guo, Yang, Hongbo Liu, & Yi Chai, (2014). "The embedding convergence of smart cities and tourism internet of things in China: An advance perspective." *Advances in Hospitality and Tourism Research 2*(1), 54–69.

Heipke Christian. (2010). "Crowdsourcing geospatial data." *ISPRS Journal of Photogrammetry and Remote Sensing 65*(6), 550–557.

Hjalager, & Anne-Mette, (2010). "A review of innovation research in tourism." *Tourism Management 31*(1), 1–12.

Hofstede, Geert, H., & Geert Hofstede, (2001). *Culture's consequences: Comparing Values, Behaviors, Institutions and Organizations Across Nations*. Sage, USA.

Huang, C., & Li, Y., (2011)." In the 12th five-year plan, the system research of smarter tourism under the background of smarter cities" In: *Proceedings of Annual Conference of Tourism Tribune*, 55–68.

Huang, Cheng Ming, & Sheng Chih Chen, (2015). "Smart tourism: exploring historical, cultural, and delicacy scenic spots using visual-based image search technology." *Applied Mechanics and Materials*, vol. 764, Trans Tech Publications.

Jeong, Chul, et al., (2012). "Enhancing destination image through travel website information." *International Journal of Tourism Research, 14*(1), 16–27.

Law Rob, & Billy Bai, (2006). "Website development and evaluations in tourism: a retrospective analysis." *Information and Communication Technologies in Tourism*, 1–12.

Lin, Judy Chuan-Chuan, (2007) ."Online stickiness: its antecedents and effect on purchasing intention." *Behavior and Information Technology, 26*(6), 507–516.

Lu Jie, & Zi Lu, (2004). "Development, distribution and evaluation of online tourism services in China." *Electronic Commerce Research, 4*(3), 221–239.

Ma, Jennifer Xiaoqiu, Dimitrios Buhalis, & Haiyan Song, (2003). "ICTs and Internet adoption in China's tourism industry." *International Journal of Information Management, 23*(6), 451–467.

Michopoulou, E., & Moisa, D., (2016). *Global Dynamics in Travel, Tourism, and Hospitality*. Pappas, Nikolaos, & Ilenia Bregoli, (eds.). IGI global.

Morgan, Nigel, J., Annette Pritchard, & Rachel Piggott, (2003)."Destination branding and the role of the stakeholders: The case of New Zealand."*Journal of vacation Marketing, 9*(3), 285–299.

Nielsen, N. C., & Liburd, J. J. (2008). "Geographical information and landscape history in tourism communication in the age of Web 2.0. The case of the Salt River Bay National Park in St. Croix of the US Virgin Islands."*Journal of Travel & Tourism Marketing, 25*(3–4), 282–298.

O'Neill, M., Adrian, P., & Steven, C., (2002). "Wine production as a service experience–the effects of service quality on wine sales." *Journal of Services Marketing, 16*(4), 342–362.

Rodríguez-Molina, M. A., Frías-Jamilena, D. M., & Castañeda-García. J. A., (2015). "The contribution of website design to the generation of tourist destination image: The moderating effect of involvement." *Tourism Management, 47*, 303–317.

Reino, Sofía, Nicole Mitsche, & Andrew Frew, J., (2007). "The contribution of technology-based heritage interpretation to the visitor satisfaction in museums." *Information and Communication Technologies in Tourism*, 341–352.

Reino, Sofía, Nicole Mitsche, & Andrew Frew, J., (2007). "The contribution of technology-based heritage interpretation to the visitor satisfaction in museums." *Information and Communication Technologies in Tourism*, 341–352.

Schegg, R., Liebrich, A., Scaglione, M., & Ahmad, S. F. S., (2008). An explorative field study of Web 2.0 in tourism. In: *Information and Communication Technologies in Tourism.* O'Conor, P., Hopken, W., & Gretzel, U. (eds.), *Proceedings of the International Conference in Innsbruck*, Austria: Springer, pp. 152–163.

Sui, D., & Michael, G., (2011). "The convergence of GIS and social media: challenges for GI Science." *International Journal of Geographical Information Science, 25*(11), 1737–1748.

Thrane, C., (2015). "Does method of payment affect total trip expenditure?" *Tourism Economics, 21*(3), 669–676.

Vicky, K., (2011). "The role of ICTs in regional tourist development." *Regional Science Inquiry 3*(2), 95–111.

Xu, J., & Zilong, L., (2010). "Study of online stickiness: its antecedents and effect on repurchase intention." *e-Education, e-Business, e-Management, and e-Learning. IC4E'10. International Conference on*. IEEE.

Wang Dan, Xiang Robert Li, & Yunpeng Li, (2013). "China's "smart tourism destination" initiative: A taste of the service-dominant logic." *Journal of Destination Marketing & Management, 2*(2), 59–61.

Wang, X., et al., (2016). "How smart is your tourist attraction?: Measuring tourist preferences of smart tourism attractions via a FCEM-AHP and IPA approach." *Tourism Management, 54*, 309–320.

Werthner, H., & Klein, S., (2006). ICT-enabled innovation. In B. Walder, K., Weiermair, & A., Sancho-Perez (Eds.), *Innovation and Product Development in Tourism*. Berlin: Erich Schmidt Verlag, pp. 71–83.

Ye, Q., et al., (2011). "The influence of user-generated content on traveler behavior: An empirical investigation on the effects of e-word-of-mouth to hotel online bookings." *Computers in Human Behavior, 27*(2), 634–639.

Yuan, Yu-Lan, Ulrike Gretzel, & Daniel Fesenmaier, R., (2006). "The role of information technology use in American convention and visitors bureaus."*Tourism Management, 27*(2), 326–341.

Zhang, L., Li, N., & Liu, M., (2012). "On the Basic Concept of Smarter Tourism and Its Theoretical System."*Tourism Tribune, 27*(5), 66–73.

Zhang, Xinyan, Haiyan Song, & George Huang, Q., (2009). "Tourism supply chain management: A new research agenda." *Tourism Management, 30*(3), 345–358.

Zhang, Ziqiong, et al., (2010). "The impact of e-word-of-mouth on the online popularity of restaurants: A comparison of consumer reviews and editor reviews." *International Journal of Hospitality Management, 29*(4), 694–700.

Zhu, J. J., & He, Z., (2002). "Perceived characteristics, perceived needs, and perceived popularity adoption and use of the Internet in China." *Communication Research, 29*(4), 466–495.

CHAPTER 8

THE DEVELOPMENT AND CHANGE OF THE CRUISE INDUSTRY IN CHINA OVER THE DECADE (2006–2016)

XINLIANG YE

Shanghai University of Engineering Science, Songjiang District, Shanghai, China

CONTENTS

ABSTRACT

China's cruise industry has experienced great changes during the 2006–2016 decade. From initial skepticism to the current affirmation, China has become an important cruise market in the world, with a bright future highly anticipated by global cruise lines. During the decade, constant improvements have been made in the cruise industry chain as well as in port distribution for cruise ships, thereby continuously increasing the influence of the industry. The flagship of China's cruise industry, the Port of Shanghai is the busiest port in the country, with Wusongkou International Cruise Terminal, the biggest port in Asia and the fifth largest port in the world.

As the cruise tourism market matures, tourists begin to view cruise tourism from new perspectives, resulting in greater demand for cruise tourism. However, some bottlenecks and problems occurred during the development of the industry, e.g., the domination of the Chinese market by foreign cruise ships, the slow growth of domestic cruise ships, the shortage of upstream and downstream in the cruise industry chain, limited economic contribution, and an obvious lack of richness and diversity in cruise routes. In addition, the cultivation of the cruise tourism consumption culture is still in the initial stage in China, and there is a big gap between supply and demand of talent for cruise tourism. In the future, solutions for port operation, policy innovation, talent cultivation, etc. are required to ensure sound and rapid development of China's cruise market.

8.1 INTRODUCTION

Cruise tourism first originated in Europe and America. With cruise tourism markets in Europe, America, and other developed regions becoming increasingly saturated after decades of growth, cruise lines begin to transition their development focus to the Asia-Pacific region. With one-third of the world's population and vigorous economic growth, the region instills energy into the development of tourism, promotes further development of maritime tourism, and provides new momentum for economic development. Due to rapid economic growth, residents' strong power of consumption, and a great demand for tourism, China is validated as a key target market for international cruise lines, who invest more into the Chinese market, including more neotype luxury cruise ships.

In over a decade's development, China's cruise market expanded its scale and increased market potential. The development surpassed all expectations and the growth rate rose quickly, e.g., from over 10,000 men-times (what exactly is men-times?) in 2006 to over 2,000,000 men-times (clarify men-times) at present. Cruise tourism has shown strong demand and vitality in

China. China is now the key place of departure for Asia-Pacific cruise routes and an important tourism destination. As an integral part of the global cruise industry, China's cruise industry has exhibited greater international influence day by day and has played an important role in the international marketplace.

8.2 LITERATURE REVIEW

8.2.1 RELATED DOMESTIC AND OVERSEAS RESEARCH

Cruise tourism started early in foreign countries. Europe and America have formed mature development modes and conducted considerable research on the cruise industry, achieving abundant relative academic research results.

Regarding economic contributions of the cruise tourism, Mescon and Vozikis (1985) and Braun et al. (2002) evaluated the contribution of cruise economy in Miami, the Cruise Capital of the World, and in Canaveral, etc. by employing the input-output model; the results indicate that cruise tourism imposed positive effects on the development of cruise ports and the local economy. The results essentially matched the data of economic contribution of cruise tourism to peripheral regions. Diakomihalis (2007) attempted to study the contribution of cruise tourism to the economic development of Greece by adopting the tourism satellite account. However, it was difficult to obtain data with this method due to the complexity and diversity of data in the process of data collection. Andy et al. (2007) conducted statistical analysis on the consumption preference, consumption behaviors of tourists and crews, number of people, etc. of cruise tourism in Costa Rica in Latin America and found that there was barely any difference between the contribution to the local economy made by cruise tourists and that of other tourists. Thus, doubts were raised about the vigorous promotion of cruise tourism by the local government. Chase (2002) analyzed the impact of the tourism export industry on tourism destinations based on a theory of the comparative advantage of tourism exports, focusing on the comparative advantages of an island economy in developing cruise tourism. The impacts of cruise tourism on tourism destinations were evaluated via modeling, and the effectiveness of the Barbados's economic model for evaluating the impacts on tourism destinations was verified.

Regarding the cruise tourism market, Andriotis and Agiomirgianakis (2010) found during the investigation of cruise tourists' behaviors in the

Mediterranean Sea that the tourists in this region preferred tourism activities such as visiting historical relics, city sightseeing, shopping, excursions, visiting museums, dining, and swimming. Teye and Paris (2011) investigated the activities of cruise tourists in the Caribbean region, and the results showed that tourists preferred activities such as tasting specialties, group touring, sightseeing, port shopping, entertainment, communication with locals, and city sightseeing. Petrick, Li, and Park (2007) adopted decision-making variables to classify cruise tourists into two categories, i.e., complicated consumption decision-making tourists and quick decision-making tourists of high brand loyalty. Gabriel (2010) issued questionnaires to cruise tourists in Cartagena to determine consumption and expenditure structure. The results indicated a significant difference in tourists' expenditure preferences. From the research on the motivations for cruise tourism, Hung and Petrick (2011) knew that major motivations include cultural exploration, and relaxation, recreation and entertainment, sightseeing, social motivation, and the need to pursue innovation. Hosany and Witham (2010) conducted research on the relationship between tourists' experience and satisfaction and the intention for recommendation; they discovered that among the three dimensions (i.e., education, entertainment, and beauty appreciation), beauty appreciation had the most significant impact on satisfaction and the intention for recommendation of cruise tourists, followed by entertainment and education.

Blas (2014) studied the relationship between cruise tourists' satisfaction for the culture of a tourism destination and their future behavioral intention. By comparing the differences between cruise tourists from the UK and the US and tourists from Germany and Italy, the conclusion was made that the image of tourism destinations had a direct impact on tourists' satisfaction, which in turn directly affected their future behavioral choice such as returning to the destination or recommending it to others.

Regarding the environmental impact of cruise tourism, Butt (2007) investigated the management and handling of cruise ship pollutants by cruise ports and the impact of cruise ships on ports. The emission reduction measures proposed to fully recycle the pollutants. Jones (2011) studied the social and environmental impacts of mega cruise ship manufacture and found that large cruise ships had greater influence on coral reef. Related data revealed the fact that large cruise ships produced sediment disturbance much greater than natural water flow, which might cause significant adverse effect on corals in the offshore area of a port. Hrvoje Caric (2014) believed that the change in cruise tourism usually reflected the transition of the external environment.

Cruise ships would produce larger impact on the main environment. With the continual growth of the industry, such impact might escalate, such as economic development, sustainability, and new laws and regulations for the cruise tourism industry.

8.2.2 RELATED DOMESTIC RESEARCH

With respect to economic benefits of the cruise tourism industry, Wang et al. (2010) studied the economic output effect of China's cruise industry from the perspective of cruise industry chain. Miao et al. (2013) studied the accelerating effect of tourist consumption on China's cruise industry from the perspectives of the demand for and the market supply of cruise tourism. Zhang et al. (2012) and Zhang et al. (2008) analyzed the features and problems found in China's cruise tourism and offered some policy-related suggestions for the development of cruise tourism in China. Liu et al. (2012) compared the development of cruise tourism in China, Japan, and South Korea; discussed the problems found in the cruise tourism industry of China in terms of the industry chain, port, tourism route, etc.; and put forward some countermeasures.

Regarding the study of consumption in the cruise tourism market, Ye et al. (2007) suggested to develop cruise tourism products to satisfy tourists' demands in the Shanghai Market based on market demand. Sun et al. (2010) introduced the customer value spatial model into marketing of cruise tourism and suggested some strategies for the marketing of cruise tourism. Cai et al. (2010) analyzed core industrial factors and the competition potential of cruise tourism and established the competition potential evaluation system for cruise tourism. Evaluations were conducted from the perspective of resource abundance, tourism operation performance, enterprise operation, financial and insurance services, and traffic conditions. The factor analysis method was adopted to evaluate and analyze the top eight cruise tourism cities of China. Zhang et al. (2010) studied data of the international cruise tourism market, summarized the basic features of international cruise tourists, and predicted the demand of China's cruise tourism market. Yang et al. (2011) conducted analysis on the features of China's cruise tourism market and provided some countermeasures and suggestions. Jia et al. (2013) analyzed the factors influencing the demand for cruise tourism and established the prediction model for cruise tourism demand on the basis of BP neural network. Tests were performed based on statistical data from the U.S.

cruise market and a prediction was made regarding the demand for cruise tourism in China. Zhang et al. (2013) established the tourist consumption decision-making model for structural equation analysis of the data obtained. The results showed that motivation, opportunity, and capability had positive effects on decision-making of cruise consumers. Sun et al. (2015) applied the X-12-ARIMA and TRAMO/SEATS seasonal adjustment models in the research on the data from the North American cruise market. The results showed that the cruise market in North America continued to expand and presented more significant monthly and seasonal features.

In terms of port development, Wang et al. (2008) analyzed the development status of port tourism resources and put forward a strategy for China's development of port tourism, aiming at promoting the construction of cruise tourism bases. Ye et al. (2014) completed questionnaire surveys and interviews and proposed the establishment of a standard system for home port services of cruise tourism. Countermeasures were recommended for standardized construction of cruise home ports from both national and local perspectives. Wu et al. (2015) set up the competitive evaluation system for international cruise ports by utilizing the cloud model evaluation method to convert qualitative description into quantitative measurement to conduct comparative competitiveness evaluation between the Port of Barcelona and the Port of Kotor in Europe, and the Port of Shanghai and the Port of Tianjin in China.

8.2.3 RESEARCH REVIEW

Research on literature of domestic and overseas cruise industry development revealed the following features and trends. In foreign studies, the focus of cruise industry research both at home and abroad lies in the economic effects of cruise tourism and tourists' consumption behaviors. In contrast, studies on cruise tourism in China are usually focused on marketing and port development. Researchers highly value the impacts of the traveling mode of cruise tourism on the industry. Meanwhile, the focus also rests in the economic effect of the cruise tourism on local economic development. The research methods become diversified, and the research system is continuously enriched and perfected; the transition occurred from mostly qualitative research in the early stage to current quantitative research. Empirical analysis for quantitative research is emphasized, although qualitative research is still far from being sufficient. The research on the cruise industry still needs to be developed to a greater depth and breadth.

8.3 DEVELOPMENT OF MARKETS IN CHINA IN THE PAST DECADE

8.3.1 CONTINUOUS SCALE-UP OF CHINA'S CRUISE INDUSTRY OVER THE DECADE

The past decade is a period for China's cruise industry to lay a solid foundation and keep expanding. We can see this from the improvement of supporting facilities for the cruise industry, the steady infrastructure construction of cruise ports, the perfection of custom clearance policies for cruise tourists, the raising of the cruise port service level, the extension of the port cruise industry chain inland, and the accelerated cultivation of cruise culture. With respect to hardware, supporting infrastructure related to cruise ports, such as the passenger transport buildings, and surrounding commercial facilities have improved gradually. With respect to software, a set of cruise port tourist service standards are in embryo; cruise tourist service procedures are optimized, and the satisfaction of tourists is then greatly enhanced.

The routes of cruise ships starting from Chinese ports are mainly the China–South Korea Route, Sanya–Vietnam Route, Cross–Straight Route, and Hong Kong–Taiwan Route. Most of the routes are medium- and short-term routes (usually 4 to 7 days), among which, the China–South Korea Route and the China–Japan Route are dominant, accounting for over 98% of the market.

After a decade's growth, China's cruise tourism market keeps scaling up, with more market potential being explored, cruise tourism brand images being formed rapidly, and tourists' recognition of cruise tourism being enhanced. In the development process, the trips and tourist number of home port cruise ships increase fast, while those of visiting port cruise ships decrease obviously (Figure 8.1). Since 2014, China's cruise tourism has experienced explosive growth, resulting in a total of 466 navigation trips operated by 10 major cruise ports of the country, with year-on-year growth of 15%. The outbound and inbound cruise tourists reached 1,723,400, with year-on-year growth of 43%, indicating a strong momentum of growth (Figure 8.2). In 2015, the

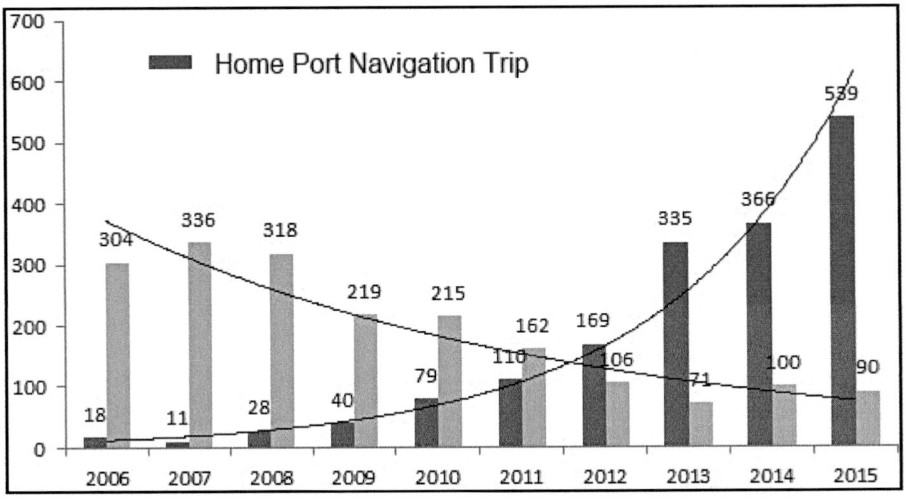

FIGURE 8.1 Home port cruise ships and visiting port cruise ships received by China during 2006–2015. Source: Statistics of CCYIA (data of Hong Kong and Taiwan excluded)

number of navigation trips operated by 10 major cruise ports reached 629, and outbound and inbound cruise tourists reached 2,480,500, making China the fourth largest market for cruise tourist source. Today, the sector of cruise tourism has achieved a consensus that China is an emerging market of the

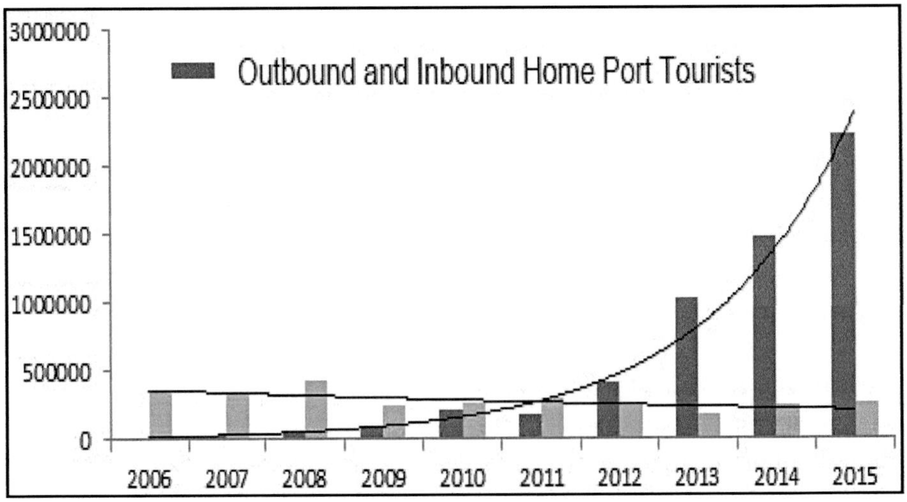

FIGURE 8.2 Statistics of outbound and inbound home port tourists and visiting port tourists received by china during 2006–2015.

world where cruise tourism has the fastest growth. In the future, China is expected to become the largest cruise market in the world.

8.3.2 IMPROVEMENT OF DISTRIBUTION OF CRUISE PORTS IN CHINA OVER THE DECADE

Over the decade, China established five separate port clusters in the Rim-Bohai-Sea area, the Yangtze River Delta, the regions on both sides of the Taiwan Strait, the Pearl River Delta, and the southwest coastal region. On this basis, regional cruise tourism markets developed around cruise ports in Tianjin, Shanghai, Xiamen, Shenzhen, and Sanya. Each port cluster has its own locational advantages and highly developed traffic patterns to form a tightly connected network with surrounding tourist attractions featured in three-hour, non-stop arrival at almost all tourism destinations in the region.

Shanghai's cruise industry developed the fastest among inland cities of China. In 2003, Shanghai first proposed the development plan for a cruise home port, playing an exemplary role for the country. At present, Shanghai has built an international cruise combination home port on the basis of the Shanghai Port International Cruise Terminal and Shanghai Wusongkou International Cruise Terminal, realizing the objective of "Two Terminals for One Port". Attributed to its unique market and locational advantages, the Port of Shanghai became the largest cruise tourism hub in the Asia-Pacific Region and the eighth largest cruise home port in the world in 2015. Due to an increased imbalance between demand and supply, in June 2015, Phase 2 Project of Shanghai Wusongkou International Cruise Terminal commenced. When completed, the port will harbor four large cruise ships at the same time.

The main construction of Phase 2 of Tianjin Dongjiang Cruise Home Port was completed at the beginning of 2014, and it is capable of harboring a maximum 220,000 tons cruise ship. The number of international luxury cruise ships visiting the Port of Tianjin has increased yearly, which is attributed to the development of the port itself as well as its proximity with Beijing (the nearest port to Beijing), making it a cruise center in north China. Sanya Phoenix Island International Cruise Terminal was officially completed and opened for navigation in 2006, which is the first 80,000 tons cruise terminal in China. Xiamen is one of the first ports receiving international cruise ships in Mainland China. In May 2014, the Port of Xiamen became the fourth international cruise home port of China.

8.3.3 INCREASED INPUT OF TRANSPORT CAPACITY INTO CHINESE MARKET BY INTERNATIONAL CRUISE LINES OVER THE LINES OVER THE DECADE

Currently, international cruise lines are optimistic about the prospects of China's cruise market and have paid more attention to the Chinese market, with more and more new luxury cruise ships entering the Chinese market. In 2006, there was only one home-port cruise ship in operation. By the end of 2015, there were as many as 12 home port cruise ships operating in China. Many cruise lines state that more luxury cruise ships of higher classes will be launched in the Chinese market in the future. The Allegra, the first home port cruise ship in China, only has a tonnage of 2,850 tons and a passenger capacity of 984. By 2016, China has 18 home port cruise ships, showing an obvious trend of increasing cruise ships entering the Chinese market, including two cruise ships of over 160,000 tons, six cruise ships of 100,000~160,000 tons, six cruise ships of 70,000~100,000 tons and four cruise ships below 70,000 tons. Royal Caribbean International placed its state-of-the-art cruise ship, the Quantum of the Seas, into the Chinese market, and plans to bring the Ovation of the Seas, one of its quantum-series ships, into the Chinese market. By then, China will have 17 home port cruise ships in operation, forming an obviously larger fleet of cruise ships (Figure 8.3).

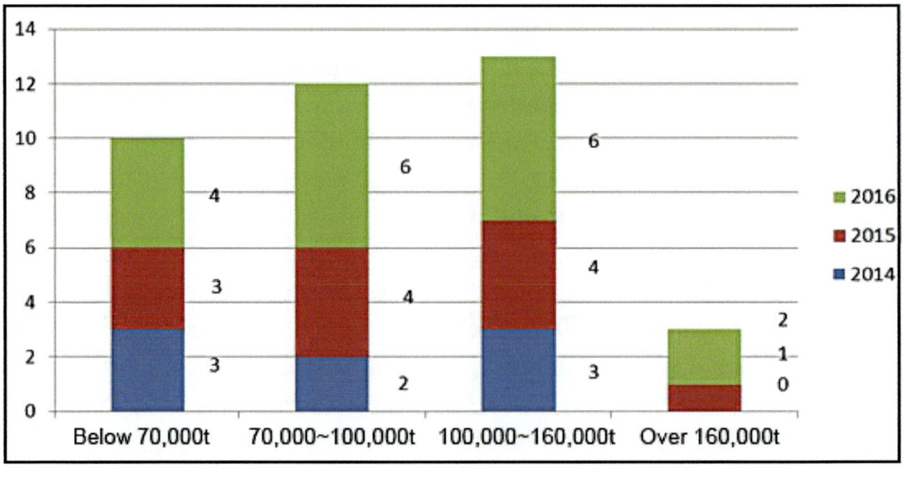

FIGURE 8.3 Improvement in shipping ability of China's cruise ship fleet.

8.3.4 *RAPID GROWTH OF ONLINE CRUISE TOURISM IN CHINA*

According to the experiences of the international cruise industry, it is essential to build appropriate marketing channels. For cruise ticket sales, the travel agency has always been the most used and recognized distribution channel. With increased demand in the Chinese cruise market and continuous growth of the industry, travel agencies started to develop cruise business (Figure 8.4). In December 2012, the cruise channel went online at LY.com. In September 2014, ctrip.com initiated a cruise ticket reservation platform in Chinese. With traditional outbound tourism being impacted by cruise tourism, conventional travel agencies established cruise tourism departments, one after another, to cope with competition between outbound tourism and cruise tourism. Tier-2 and tier-3 cities also began to step into the cruise market, leading to a gradual increase in the market size.

Source: Estimates made by big data research based on the data from CLIA

The online cruise tourism platform has an important position in cruise ticket sales. In 2015, total income of China's cruise market recorded CNY 4.53 billion, with the quantity of outbound tourism reaching 2,185,000 tourists. Of this revenue, CNY 1.33 billion came from the online cruise reservation platform, accounting for 29.3%, with the online reservation market increased by 60.1% on a year-on-year basis (Figure 8.5). Of all online cruise

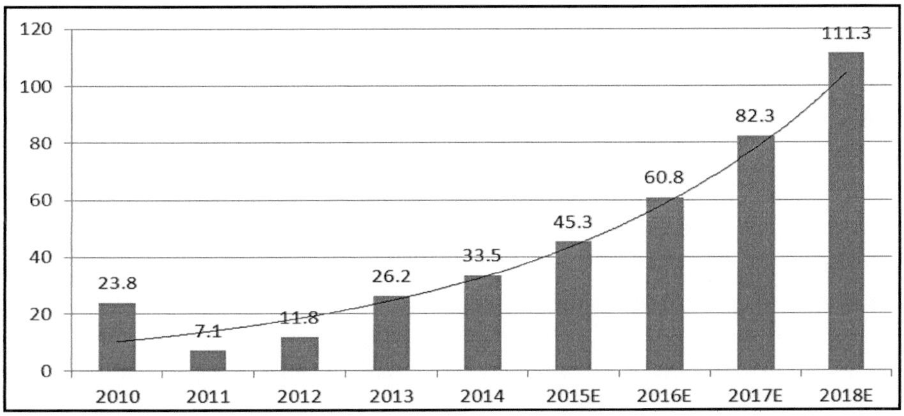

FIGURE 8.4 Income scale of China's cruise market during 2010–2018 (unit: hundred-million yuan).

reservation platforms, the trade amount from OTA accounted for 48.7% and company-owned online platforms of travel agencies accounted for 24.3%. OTA has become the platform with the fastest growth among all online platforms.

8.3.5 CONTINUOUSLY STRENGTHENED POLICY SUPPORT

To further direct, normalize, and promote healthy development of cruise tourism in China, central and local governments have introduced a series of preferential policies to establish an ideal environment for the development of cruise tourism. To seize the opportunity for developing cruise tourism, the NDRC (National Development and Reform Commission) duly unveiled the *Guidance for Promoting the Development of the Cruise Industry in China* in June 2008. For the purpose of standardizing the development of the cruise tourism, the Ministry of Transport introduced the *Guiding Opinions of the Ministry of Transport on Promoting the Continuous and Healthy Development of the Cruise Transport Industry in China* in March 2014. To advance coordinated development of ports, in April 2015, the Ministry of Transport introduced the *Planning for Distribution of Cruise Terminals in Coastal Areas of China*. In May 2015, the State Council issued the *Notification for Distributing Made in China 2025*, demanding breakthroughs be made in terms of design and construction of luxury cruise ships. To extend

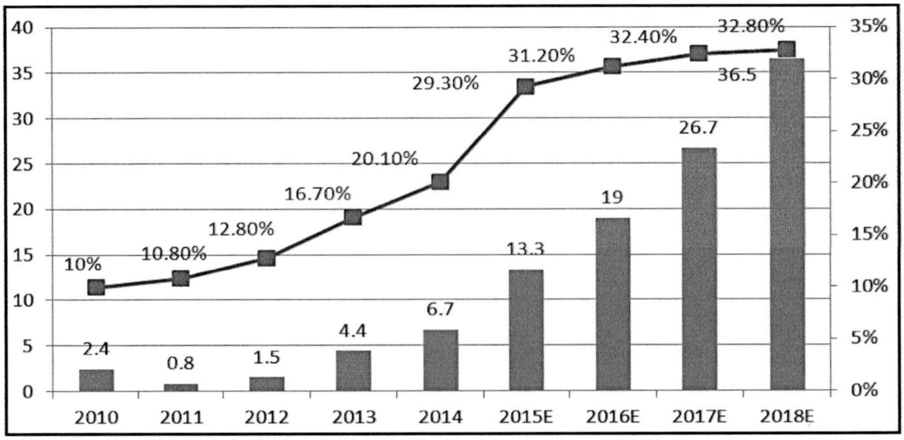

FIGURE 8.5 Revenue of China's online cruise market and its proportion in total incomes during 2010–2018. Source: Big Data Research

China's cruise industry chain and improve the industry status in the world, in August 2015, the Ministry of Transport publicized the *Opinions for Further Promoting Tourism Investment and Consumption* issued by the State Council, requesting the establishment of domestic R&D, design, manufacture, and independent supporting systems for large cruise ships and encouraging qualified domestic ship manufacturers to research, develop, and manufacture large and medium-sized cruise ships. In September 2015, the Ministry of Industry and Information Technology of the People's Republic of China and the NDRC jointly issued the *Implementation Suggestions on Promoting the Development of the Tourism Equipment Manufacture Industry*, in which five key tasks were specified, with the top priority task being "quickening up the realization of independent design and manufacture of cruise ship." To promote breakthroughs in the upstream industry chain, the 13th Five-Year-Plan has clearly stated to provide vigorous support for breakthroughs in core technologies (design, manufacture, etc.) of the cruise industry. The substantial support from central and local governments has provided ideal opportunities for the development of the cruise industry, continuously enhancing the advantage and competitive edge of China's cruise tourism.

For the purposes of eliminating development bottlenecks as early as possible; promoting innovations in system and mechanism; establishing policy, regulation, and standard; conducting reforms and seeking breakthroughs with respect to service and market; enhancing functionality of cruise home ports as well as exploring new modes and ideas for the cruise industry, the National Tourism Administration has successively approved the demonstration regions for cruise tourism in Shanghai, Tianjin, Qingdao, and Shenzhen, which have played positive leading roles in promoting the development of China's cruise industry.

8.4 ANALYSIS OF ISSUES IN THE DEVELOPMENT PROCESS OF THE CRUISE INDUSTRY IN CHINA IN THE PAST DECADE

8.4.1 MARKET DOMINATED BY FOREIGN CRUISE SHIPS AND SLOW DEVELOPMENT OF DOMESTIC CRUISE SHIPS

Today, foreign cruise lines still have dominance in China's cruise tourism market. Foreign cruise ships have occupied an absolutely dominant position in the Chinese market, with over 95% of market share held by three international cruise giants: Royal Caribbean International, Carnival Cruise Lines, and Genting Hong Kong Limited. Economic benefits of the cruise industry result in an increasing contradiction between the rapid growth of the cruise industry and a limited economic contribution to China's development. An extremely high industrial barrier makes it difficult for local cruise lines who own a single cruise ship to obtain profit based on their operational costs as newcomers. The expansion of transport capacity develops very slowly, and local cruise lines have little voice in the market.

Most Chinese cruise ships are second-hand ships that have been withdrawn from the mainstream European and American markets. In terms of hardware, such cruise ship can hardly compete with international cruise lines. In terms of software, services are still in the exploration stage, showing the lack of competitive edge. From the perspective of passenger source, outbound passengers account for over 90% of the cruise market of China. The proportion of international passengers is quite low, showing significant reduction in inbound cruise tourism. Local cruise tourism based on coastal tourism resources of China have not been fully developed, which cannot satisfy the strong demand for domestic cruise tourists. Presently, the problems of structural imbalance between demand and supply of cruise tourism are quite serious.

Regarding the development of local cruise ships, restrictions of some core policies on the development of the cruise industry need to be further relaxed to promote the development and growth of local cruise lines. For example, many companies having sufficient capital are deterred by the policies in different areas including purchasing of cruise ships, taxes, cruise routes, operational items, staffing of cruise ships, etc. Such policies have restricted the construction and development of local cruise lines. A rapidly developing market requires continuous policy innovations. However, the current policies greatly limit the cruise industry.

8.4.2 LACK OF UPSTREAM AND DOWNSTREAM OF THE CRUISE INDUSTRY CHAIN AND LIMITED ECONOMIC CONTRIBUTION

At present, the most important mode of cruise tourism is for Chinese passengers to take a foreign cruise ship for outbound tourism. China's cruise industry chain mainly focuses on port construction, operation, travel agencies, etc. Ticket sales income from cruise tourism, consumption on cruise ships, and consumption at tourism destinations flow to foreign companies. In addition, China has benefited less than expected from its rapidly growing cruise industry due to the incomplete support of the cruise industry and insufficient support of commercial facilities for the cruise economy. Coastal cities have made huge input in construction of cruise ports, which turned out to be incapable of earning profits due to few profitable items. Currently, only Shanghai Wusongkou International Cruise Terminal has earned profits.

In the upstream of the cruise industry chain, the core of the cruise economy is cruise ship companies, with economic-added value accounting for over 50% in the total cruise economy, followed by the cruise manufacture industry which has a share of approximately 20%. At present, the cooperation between international cruise lines and domestic companies is still limited to purchasing ships from international cruise lines for operation or directly procuring a cruise brand for operation, not involving the design and manufacture of cruise ships and even more links in the whole cruise industry chain. For a long time, the design and manufacture of cruise ship as well as the supporting industry chain were concentrated in Europe, led by European shipyards from Italy, Germany, and France, with an annual production of merely eight vessels. In China, vessel design, manufacture and maintenance, which are of high added value and high technologies, are still not available. In comparison with Japan and South Korea., China's cruise ship manufacturing industry lags behind in terms of technology and innovation and is even further behind European countries.

With respect to the service standard for cruise ports, it is essential to establish a standard service system to normalize the development order of international cruise home ports and improve the quality of service of international cruise home ports. In China, the cruise industry is still an infant with no mature port management system established. Currently, there is still a lack of a normalized service standard system set up for this emerging sector. Due to the lack of sufficient experience in operation and management of cruise port and the low level of maturity of the domestic cruise tourism market, domestic cruise ports are still operated and managed at low levels, resulting in an urgent need to promote the experiences in operation and management of cruise ports.

In addition, there is also a lack of certain service standards for cruise tourism service. Travel agencies need to further improve their services and optimize passenger service procedures. All procedures related to tourist reception need further optimization and upgrading.

8.4.3 LACK OF RICHNESS AND DIVERSITY IN CRUISE ROUTES

Over 90% of home port cruise ships departing from China have Japan and South Korea as their destinations. In terms of cruise line route distribution, they prefer to arrange cruise routes lasting for 4–6 days. Japan and South Korea are the closest destinations for routes starting from China. Passengers also hope to visit more places at the same price. With passengers demanding higher diversity of destinations, China's cruise tourism has become less attractive due to the simplicity of cruise routes, resulting in a low rate of repeat bookings. Current rapid growth is mainly attributed to strong demand, which is unfavorable for the development of cruise tourism in the long run, as it limits the healthy and long-term development of the market.

8.4.4 SLOW CULTIVATION OF THE CRUISE TOURISM CONSUMPTION CULTURE

Cruise tourism originated in Europe and America and is an emerging mode of tourism in China. Despite the development over the decade, the cruise culture is still far from being mature. People have not obtained deep cognition for cruise tourism. The research conducted on cruise tourism is rather superficial. Cruise tourism is still very strange to many Chinese people, who barely understand the essence of the industry.

Some passengers even have some misunderstanding of cruise tourism during their first trips, showing a certain unwillingness for such a mode of tourism. With respect to price, most products of cruise tourism are package prices, with most costs included in the price during the trip, resulting in a rather high price. Chinese customers are not quite used to purchasing the entire tourism product before the trip starts. Regarding the cognition of consuming groups, cruise tourism is believed to be a comfortable and relaxing experience, which is, according to traditional understanding of Chinese people, more suitable for the elderly rather than for young people. In terms of the cruise dining culture, Chinese tourists are not very adaptable to foreign specialties. When arriving at the destination, it is unusual for passengers to conduct visiting tours, which is difficult to understand for some passengers. Besides, some passengers are doubtful about the safety of cruise ships, which is an important reason for them to give up or not to take part in cruise tourism.

8.4.5 SERIOUS IMBALANCE BETWEEN SUPPLY AND DEMAND OF CRUISE TOURISM TALENTS

Strong talent reserve is always a guarantee for healthy development of the cruise industry in its development process. Currently, China has a lack of professionals in the cruise industry. With the rising of China's cruise market, there is more demand for international cruise management and service talent. It is expected that there will be a big gap between the demand and supply of the talents required for management, operation, technology, navigation, etc. in both upstream and downstream of the industry chain, resulting in the increasingly growing contradiction between the rapid growth of cruise tourism and the lack of professionals. However, despite such a trend, there are still few disciplines set up for the cruise industry in China's higher education system. The situation has only been slightly eased during the past few years. Such contradiction between demand and supply has, to some degree, increased the difficulties in improving service quality of cruise ports.

It is estimated that the gap in talent for cruise tourism will have reached nearly 300,000 by 2020. Presently, only over 1,000 graduates from cruise-related disciplines are provided each year, leading to an extremely huge gap.

8.5 PREDICTION AND ANALYSIS OF FUTURE DEVELOPMENT OF CRUISE INDUSTRY IN CHINA

8.5.1 CONTINUOUS EXPANSION OF THE CRUISE TOURISM CONSUMPTION MARKET WITH AN OBVIOUS TREND OF DEMAND DIVERSITY

In recent years, the demand for outbound tourism of Chinese citizens has grown greatly. Since 2012, China is the largest outbound tourism market in the world, with overseas average consumption per capita ranking first in the world, being the most important passenger source market with consumption attraction. In the next three decades, China will still face a prime period for rapid growth of tourism.

Welcoming the development of the cruise tourism and the era of mass tourism, more and more passengers are willing to participate in cruise tourism to truly experience the charm of the industry. More and more cruise tourism travel agencies are promoting the development of the cruise tourism market. People have a better understanding of cruise tourism including cruise lines and ships. The cruise tourism culture will continue to grow and mature in the country. There will be more abundant cruise tourism products along with an increased pace of innovation to satisfy the diversified demands of tourists. The diversity of cruise tourism products will give Chinese tourists more options on where to spend their cruise holidays as well as maintain and promote the attraction of cruise tourism to tourists and engender customer loyalty. With increased enthusiasm for cruise tourism, more and more Chinese tourists will to experience such a mode of travel with special value.

8.5.2 ACCELERATED PORT INTEGRATION WITH THE TREND OF OLIGOPOLISTIC COMPETITION

The distribution of cruise ports in China has been improved, with more and more ports under construction. Local governments have invested great amounts of funds in port construction. However, China is still exploring how to operate and manage cruise ports, mostly utilizing the current operation and management mode of cargo terminals. In terms of cruise port profits, berthing charges are still the main profit item of a cruise port. The lack of diversified profitable items results in poor profitability of ports and prolonged recovery of the huge investment made on these ports. When developing a cruise economy, it is necessary to provide supporting facilities for the cruise industry based on cruise ports. Huge funds are required to build public and commercial facilities, leading to a great demand for funds in the later period of construction.

At present, the China Merchants Group has initiated home port projects separately in Shenzhen, Xiamen, Qingdao, and Tianjin, and holds the ownership of Shanghai Wusongkou International Cruise Terminal via Sinotrans & CSC Holdings Co., Ltd. Sanya Phoenix Island International Cruise Terminal is owned by China Communications Construction Company Ltd. Such large state-owned enterprises have strong financial power and can make continuous interference for cruise ports, possibly leading to oligopolistic competition of cruise ports.

8.5.3 ACCELERATED GROWTH AND INCREASED MARKET INFLUENCE OF LOCAL CRUISE TOURISM

The future of the cruise industry is promising. China is currently exploring its own path to develop local cruise tourism. Chinese capital has been invested in SkySea Golden Era, Chinese Taishan, and Brilliant of the Seas (Diamond Cruise). The country has successfully introduced policies to encourage innovation in the areas of cruise ship design, manufacture, operation, and management. China has plenty of cruise port resources supported by ideal maritime conditions of the East Sea, Rim-Bohai-Sea region, Huanghai Sea, and South China Sea. Abundant tourism resources are located in the coastal areas of China. A solid foundation has been laid in the field of ship design and manufacture, and local tourism companies have developed strong influence in this regard. Besides, China is the largest source of passengers in the world. All these factors create good conditions for developing local cruise tourism.

In the future, with more emphasis placed on the cruise industry by the Chinese government; Chinese cruise tourism fleet and onshore tourism destinations with Chinese characteristics being established; local cruise tourism routes being developed; and domestic and overseas tourists being attracted to coastal, island, and maritime tours, China will have much bigger influence in the cruise market.

8.5.4 CONTINUOUS IMPROVEMENT OF LAWS, REGULATIONS, AND STANDARDS FOR THE CRUISE INDUSTRY

In the progress of promoting continuous development of the cruise industry, central and local governments have successfully introduced new policies to vigorously support the cruise industry, including some guidance policies. To better promote the development of the industry, more policies need to be introduced and completed. Currently, China still borrows the experiences in cargo ship management in its cruise-related policies, which is unfavorable for the development of the cruise industry. In the future, efforts will be made to introduce and complete the policies related to cruise ship manufacture, purchasing taxes, passenger customs clearance, visa-free transit, cruise tourism service standard, set-up of headquarters of foreign cruise lines, taxes and fees for in-operation cruise ships, cruise financial issues, offshore cruise development, cruise talent cultivation, etc. Breakthroughs will be made for existing policy restrictions and integrated with the development mode of the international cruise industry.

8.6 RECOMMENDATION ON PROMOTING SOUND AND ORDERLY DEVELOPMENT OF CRUISE INDUSTRY IN CHINA

8.6.1 CRUISE PORT OPERATION AND MANAGEMENT

With regard to port operation and management, policy support from the government should be obtained and fully implemented. The Experimental Area for China Cruise Tourism Development, which has been respectively set up in Shanghai and Tianjin, continuously innovates the mode of developing cruise tourism and explores new concepts for cruise tourism. The experimental areas have become the example and leading models for the development of China's cruise industry. The experimental areas are set up as the model to achieve the conversion from hardware construction to the integration of both hardware and software, and to perfect the cruise industry chain. In the process, the core focus should be cruise home ports, with the emphasis laid on the integration of upstream and downstream of the industry chain as well as the cultivation of all-round service functions.

It is necessary to continue policy innovation and execute the centralized supervision pattern over cruise tourism characterized by the Administrative Localization and One-Station Service, to provide convenient and highly efficient customs clearance services for cruise lines, agencies, and ship enterprises. It is also important to optimize customs clearance procedures, paperless customs clearance, integrated customs clearance and single-window customs clearance; reduce costs of customs clearance; improve customs clearance capability; and enhance the customs clearance efficiency of the ports.

In addition, the formulation of cruise port reception service standards should be reinforced to continuously promote international and standardized services of cruise ports. Service management standards should be prepared, including cruise port construction, safety management, emergency handling, and supervision and examination. Service quality standards should also be established, including information services, passenger building space, passenger building comfort levels, and cleanliness. Moreover, port operation standards should be built together with the passenger service quality standards, including passenger landing, arrival, shopping and catering, and suites and VIP lounge.

8.6.2 OPERATION AND MANAGEMENT OF CRUISE LINES

Cruise products and services: cruise tourism routes should be enriched and the cruise ship departing ports should be diversified. More departing ports (such as Dalian, Qingdao, Yantai, Zhoushan, Shenzhen, Guangzhou, Beihai, and Haikou) are put into operation besides the main cruise ports in Shanghai, Tianjin, Sanya, and Xiamen. The diversity of departing ports will contribute to diversified cruise routes, increase market coverage of cruise tourism, and provide more opportunities for tourists. Entertainment, catering, services, etc. on board will be more diversified and innovated to provide a positive experience for tourists.

Market access and openness: Efforts should be made to encourage cruise consumption, support the establishment and business operation of cruise lines, develop the ship supply system, assist the R&D and manufacture of cruise ship, etc. The visa-free policy for foreigners at cruise ports should be promoted and implemented; a more convenient and relaxed commercial tourism environment should be created; the duration of stay in visa-free transit can be extended from 72 hours to 144 hours for some national public employees; and the visa-free transit can be realized not only in the airports but also in the sea, land and airports; thus, linked visa-free transit policy at relevant transit ports can be fulfilled.

Financial and credit support: Funds should be raised for cruise development. The innovation of cruise financial services and products should be increased, with domestic funded cruise lines fostered. In terms of vessel leasing, the limit that any Chinese capital company cannot lease vessels for operation until it has at least one free vessel should be eliminated. Local cruise lines should be encouraged to lease cruise ships for operation. In the Experimental Area for China Cruise Tourism Development, measures should be taken to facilitate direct cross-border investment made by enterprises and encourage enterprises in the experimental area to conduct direct investment, with cross-border receipt and payment as well as exchange with banks.

Tax preferences and reduction/exemption: export rebates are applicable to the domestic commodities supplied to overseas cruise ships in the Experimental Area for China Cruise Tourism Development, which are treated as general trade. Bonded goods policy is applicable to commodities directly imported and transferred to overseas cruise ships, which are treated as general trade. The functions of bonded warehouse of cruise ship should be enhanced, with public bonded logistic centers established.

8.6.3 IMPROVEMENT OF SPECIAL LAWS AND REGULATIONS ON CRUISE TOURISM

Cruise tourism is an emerging type of tourism in China, and the cruise industry has dual attributes of transport and tourism. Due to the hysteresis quality of the laws, there are only a few laws and regulations in effect for cruise tourism in China. Sometimes there are even no laws or regulations for reference; therefore, it is urgent to perfect the laws and regulations on cruise tourism. When handling cruise tourism events, the most common practice is to follow the regulations in *Tourism Law* and *Maritime Law*. Where there is a difference between a cruise ticket contract and an ordinary transport contract, it is required to prepare a special cruise ticket contract with details about the obligations and rights of the travel agency, cruise lines, and tourist, so as to settle effectively or avoid irrational occupation of ship by tourists. There are still no special laws and regulations for the supply of cruise ship. As a result, the cruise ship supply industry cannot play the role of significantly pulling the development of a port economy.

Regarding environmental pollution caused by the cruise industry, the current legislative regulations are not so rigid, and poor results are realized due to weak operability. China has established an environmental protection legal system based on *Environmental Protection Law, Marine Environment Protection Law*, and *Law on Environment Impact Assessment*. However, there is still a big gap in the area of compensation for pollution and damages caused by cruise companies. Mostly, administrative penalties are adopted for responsibility identification and control of maritime pollution, and there is a lack of effective compensation and remedial mechanism for the loss of the maritime environment. As a result, it is necessary to formulate special laws and regulations for cruise industry environment control and to ensure there is always a legal basis for penalties and compensation.

8.6.4 PERFECTION OF TALENT CULTIVATION MODE

Currently, the educational structure for cruise tourism in China is rather simple. Due to the strict requirements for cruise talent and their practical abilities, it is necessary to implement guidelines of industry-university-institute cooperation and insist on the close integration of theories and practice. With respect to cultivation of talents, it is required to establish a comprehensive educational system covering undergraduate education, higher occupational education and training. Students of undergraduate education can assume core positions due to their solid knowledge foundation, in-depth education on operation and management theories, and the strong ability to learn and innovate. Talents of higher occupational education can handle basic theories of cruise tourism and apply the knowledge with better innovation; thus, they can be cultivated to become an important force for cruise operation and management. Training is mainly carried out for in-service staff to improve their understanding of cruise tourism.

Cruise tourism requires highly internationalized talents; so, more schools run by international partnerships are preferred. Besides academic education, it is also required to increase the input into occupational education and training to continuously better the education and training system for cruise tourism.

8.7 CONCLUSION

China's cruise industry has steady development in 2017. As China's economy has shifted from a high speed growth stage to a high quality development stage, the development of cruise tourism has also undergone transformation from rapid growth to quality improvement. China's cruise market now focuses on transforming and upgrading of the market structure. The industry transforms from the demand for big ships and new ships to understanding of the laws of the market. The industry needs to constantly enhance on new product developments, product quality and improve the experience and satisfaction of tourists, and provide an assurance for people's yearning for a better life.

KEYWORDS

- **cruise industry**
- **cruise line chains**
- **cruise tourism**

REFERENCES

Chase, Gregory Lee, (2001). *The Economic Impact of Cruise Ships in the 1990s*: Some evidence from the Caribbean. PhD, Kent State University, p. 150.

Cong Jianmei, (2012). *Research on the Development Strategy of Chinese Cruise Tourism Based on SWOT Analysis [D]*. Dalian Maritime University.

Dumana Teoman, & Mattilab Anna, S., (2005). The role of effective factors on perceived cruise vacation value. *Tourism Management,* vol. 26, pp. 311–323.

Guo Xu, (2013). Research on China's cruise tourism [J]. *Special Economic Zone*, *9*, 104–106.

Henthorpe, T., (2000)."An analysis of expenditures by cruise ship passengers in Jamaica" *Journal of Travel Research*, pp. 246–250.

James Macbeth, (1985). *Ocean Cruising*: A study of affirmative deviance. PhD, Murdoch University, pp. 152–198.

Liu Jun, (2011). A *Research on the Development of Chinese Cruise (Travel) Motherland from the Perspective of Regulation [D]*. Fudan University.

Luan Hang, (2008). *Research on Regional Economy Driving Capacity of Cruise Port [D].* Dalian Maritime University.

Mackay Careen, (2003). "Are we having fun yet?" *An Ethnographic Study of a Group Cruise Tour. PhD*. The Pennsylvania State University, pp. 242.

Mahmoodzadeh, Abbas, G., (1989). *Cruise Ships and Small Island Economies*: Some evidence from the Caribbean region. Kent State University, 195.

Marc Mancini. *Cruising*: *A Guide to the Cruise Line Industry*. Copyright 2000 by Delmar. a division of Thomson Learning, *21*(45–47), pp. 96–108.

Qu Hailin, & Elsa Wong Yee Ping (1999). A service performance model of Hong Kong cruise travelers' motivation factors and satisfaction. *Tourism Management*, *20*(2), pp. 237–244.

Wang Hong, et al., (2014). *Olympic Green Paper*: China Cruise Industry Development Report [M]. Beijing: Social Sciences Academic Press (CHINA), *9*.

Wang Hong, et al., (2015). *Olympic Green Paper*: China Cruise Industry Development Report (2014) [M]. Beijing: Social Sciences Academic Press (CHINA). *10.*

Wynen, Nancy, H. A., (1991). *Survey of the Cruise Ship Industry*, 1960–1990. M. A., Florida Atlantic university, pp. 109.

Xie Li Heng, (2003). A summary of research on value creation in resource-based Alliance.[J]. *Journal of Management Sciences in China, 6*(1),81–86.

Xu Hong, & Gao Lin, (2010). Discussion on cruise tourism based on supply chain angle [J]. *Journal of Beijing International Studies University*, *1*, 58–62.

Yan Hongye, (2012). *Research on Cruise Line Planning [D].* Dalian Maritime University.

Yang Lifang, (2009). *Research on Spatial Strategy of Chinese Cruise Economy [D].* JiNan University.

Zhao Shamei, (2012). *Research on the Change of World Cruise Tourism Market and Its Impact on China's Cruise Tourism Development [D].* Hainan University.

Zhou Huanhuan, (2013). A summary of domestic cruise tourism research [J]. *Oriental Corporate Culture*, *20*, 169–170.

Zhu Wenting, (2010). *Research on the Structure and Optimization of Cruise Tourism System [D]*. Shanghai Normal University.

CHAPTER 9

PROFILE AND TREND OF THE EXHIBITION INDUSTRY IN CHINA

QIUJU LUO

Associate Dean and Professor, School of Tourism Management, Sun Yat-Sen University, Guangzhou, China

CONTENTS

ABSTRACT

Against the backdrop of the global economic crisis and the ongoing evolution of international business, the event industry in the Asia-Pacific region enjoys increasing growth. In recent years, the event industry in China has been booming, and it exerts a considerable impact with regard to economic, social, and environmental aspects. The state and municipal governments actively invest in event facility construction and upgrade industry structures accordingly. They also focus on improving intelligent information systems and on cultivating high-level, elite events within the industry, both of which are conducive to the stable development of the event industry.

Currently, the event industry is composed of exhibitions, conventions, and festivals. Of these components, exhibitions account for the leading role in the event industry worldwide, and the research data for it are relatively comprehensive. On this basis, this chapter aims to analyze the current development status of exhibitions in China and compare the competitiveness of major exhibition cities, in order to predict the development trend of exhibition cities in China.

9.1 PROFILE OF THE EXHIBITION INDUSTRY IN CHINA AND ANALYSIS OF ITS COMPETITIVE SITUATION

To evaluate the development status of the exhibition industry in different Chinese cities reliably, the following indicators were chosen for comparison: number of exhibitions, exhibition area, average exhibition area, number of exhibition venues, number of large-scale exhibitions, percentage of international exhibitors and buyers, as well as the number of exhibitions certified by the Global Association of the Exhibition Industry (known by its original French initials UFI). In general, there are six main characteristics of the exhibition industry in China:

(1) The number of exhibitions in China is tremendous and the degree of concentration is relatively high.
(2) In 2015, there were 29 cities whose total exhibition area was above 1 million square meters, with the exhibition area of Shanghai alone over 10 million square meters.
(3) In 2015, there were 16 cities whose average exhibition areas were above 10,000 square meters.
(4) In 2015, exhibitions with an exhibition area of around 100,000 square meters to 500,000 square meters ranked first by number, while those with an exhibition area of below 100,000 square meters ranked second.
(5) There are a great number of scaled exhibition venues in China, and the exhibition area is relatively sufficient.
(6) There are 124 UFI members in China at present, of which 108 exhibitions are certified. However, they are mainly distributed in Shanghai, Beijing, Shenzhen, and Guangzhou, which is highly uneven.

9.1.1 NUMBER OF EXHIBITIONS

The number of exhibitions held in one city could, to a great extent, illustrate the developing status of the exhibition industry of that city. The number of exhibitions held in China is tremendous and the degree of concentration is relatively high. According to data of the China Exhibition Economic Committee, in 2015, the total number of exhibitions held in China was 8,157, and of that, four cities accounted for more than 400 exhibitions each: Shanghai, Chongqing, Beijing, and Guangzhou. There were 2,395 exhibitions held in those four cities, accounting for 29.36% of the national total. In addition, there were 18 cities with 100 to 400 exhibitions in 2015, and their total number of exhibitions came to 3,549, accounting for 43.51% of the total. Altogether 22 cities had more than 100 exhibitions or 72.87% of the total (see Table 9.1).

9.1.2 EXHIBITION AREA

The total exhibition area and the number of exhibitions are related, and to some extent, reflect the development status of city-level exhibition industries overall. In 2015, there were 29 cities whose total exhibition area was

TABLE 9.1 Cities with More Than 100 Exhibitions in 2015

Ranking	City	Number of exhibitions	Ranking	City	Number of exhibitions
1	Shanghai	749	12	Hefei	181
2	Chongqing	749	13	Xiamen	193
3	Beijing	415	14	Xian	180
4	Guangzhou	482	15	Jinan	148
5	Ningbo	136	16	Nanchang	121
6	Changchun	123	17	Chengdu	195
7	Nanjing	225	18	Zhengzhou	255
8	Shenyang	350	19	Taiyuan	108
9	Tianjin	260	20	Wuhan	336
10	Hangzhou	297	21	Qingdao	201
11	Changsha	104	22	Guiyang	136

Source: 2015 China Exhibition Statistical Reports; 2016 China Exhibition Economic Committee.

above 1 million square meters, with the exhibition area of Shanghai alone over 10 million square meters. In 2015, the total exhibition area in China reached 108.46 million square meters. There are four cities whose exhibition areas are above 500 million square meters, namely Shanghai, Guangzhou, Beijing, and Chongqing; the total exhibition area in those four cities was 35.96 million square meters, accounting for 33.16% of the total national exhibition area. In addition, there were 25 cities with around 1 to 5 million square meters of exhibition space in 2015, with the total exhibition area of those cities reaching 52.95 million square meters or 48.82% of the nationwide total. Moreover, there were 29 cities with more than 1 million square meters of exhibition area, accounting for 81.97% of the total (see Table 9.2).

9.1.3 AVERAGE EXHIBITION AREA

The average exhibition area refers to the ratio of the total exhibition area and total exhibition numbers. It could reflect the average scale of a city's

TABLE 9.2 Cities with More Than 1 Million Square Meters Exhibition Area in 2015

Ranking	City	Total Exhibition Area (unit=10,000 sq m)	Ranking	City	Total Exhibition Area (unit=10,000 sq m)
1	Shanghai	1,512	16	Ningbo	152
2	Guangzhou	862	17	Suzhou	110
3	Beijing	520	18	Hefei	186
4	Chongqing	702	19	Zhengzhou	230
5	Shenzhen	278	20	Nanchang	115
6	Chengdu	310	21	Xiamen	191
7	Shenyang	310	22	Qingdao	295
8	Changchun	171	23	Changsha	125
9	Jinan	179	24	Tianjin	346
10	Hangzhou	265	25	Harbin	197
11	Nanjing	225	26	Dalian	118
12	Dongguan	340	27	Zibo	217
13	Weifang	138	28	Guiyang	128
14	Xian	260	29	Wuhan	307
15	Fuzhou	102			

Source: 2015 China Exhibition Statistical Reports; 2016 China Exhibition Economic Committee.

exhibition industry in a more scientific way. Comparatively speaking, the large-scale exhibition is capable of attracting more exhibitors and buyers globally and exerts a greater influence worldwide. In 2015, there were 16 cities whose average exhibition areas were above 10,000 square meters (see Table 9.3). Therefore, small and medium exhibitions play a main role in the event industry in China; however, holding a certain amount of large-scale exhibitions could achieve a higher and broader industrial influence.

9.1.4 RANKINGS IN SCALE OF EXHIBITIONS

The scale of an exhibition is a vital indicator to evaluate its significance and influence. In 2015, the number of exhibitions whose exhibit space was around 100,000 square meters to 500,000 square meters ranked in the first place in overall scale rankings, while those with an exhibition area below 100,000 square meters ranked second. The scale distribution of exhibitions in China is shown in Figure 9.1. The number of exhibitions with a scale of 100,000 to 500,000 square meters takes the leading role, followed by those with a scale below 100,000 square meters in the second place; together, those with a scale below 500 thousand square meters occupy 75% of the total market. In addition, large-scale exhibitions whose exhibition area is

TABLE 9.3 Average Exhibition Area in 2015

Ranking	City	Average Exhibition Area (unit=10,000 sq m)	Ranking	City	Average Exhibition Area (unit=10,000 sq m)
1	Harbin	8.2	12	Beijing	1.25
2	Zibo	6.03	13	Jinan	1.21
3	Dongguan	5.67	14	Ningbo	1.12
4	Shenzhen	3.12	15	Hefei	1.02
5	Shanghai	2.02	16	Nanjing	1
6	Guangzhou	1.79	17	Xiamen	0.99
7	Chengdu	1.59	18	Chongqing	0.94
8	Qingdao	1.47	19	Wuhan	0.91
9	Xian	1.44	20	Zhengzhou	0.9
10	Changchun	1.39	21	Shenyang	0.89
11	Tianjin	1.33	22	Hangzhou	0.89

Source: 2015 China Exhibition Statistical Reports; 2016 China Exhibition Economic Committee.

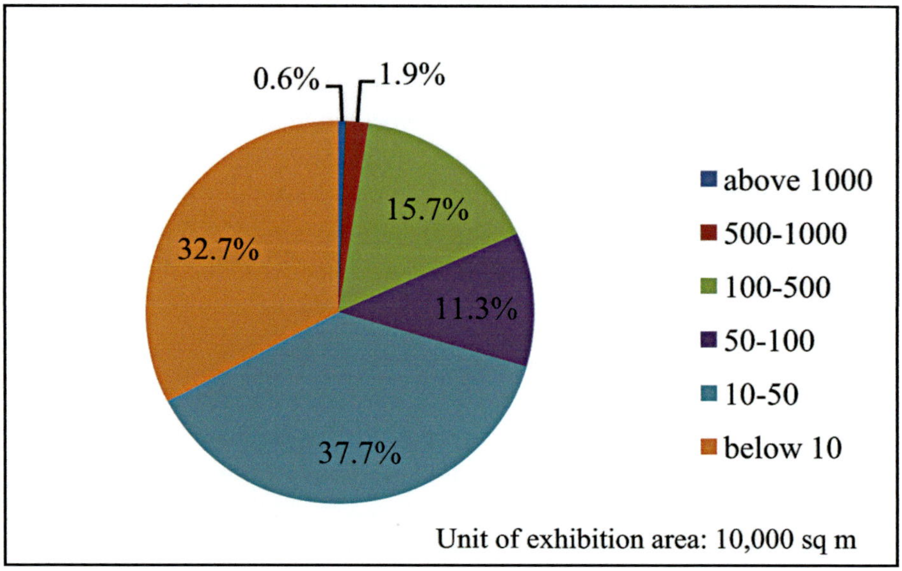

FIGURE 9.1 Distribution of scale differences in exhibitions in 2015 (categorized by the total exhibition area). Source: 2015 China Exhibition Statistical Reports; 2016 China Exhibition Economic Committee.

over 100,000 square meters, play a major role, with mega exhibitions of more than 500,000 square meters occupying 28.9% of the total.

The total exhibition areas of large-scale exhibitions – that is, exhibition areas over 100,000 square meters – in different cities are shown in Table 9.4 and 9.5. The numbers and exhibition areas of large-scale exhibitions in Shanghai, Guangzhou, Shenzhen, and Beijing have the absolute advantage domestically. In Guangzhou, the exhibition area of the Canton Fair, which is held biannually, was 2.32 million square meters in 2015. Excluding the influence of the Canton Fair, the total exhibition area in Guangzhou was 3.39 million square meters in 2015, around 2.54 million square meters less than that of Shanghai. At the same time, the number of large-scale exhibitions in Shenzhen ranks in the third place nationwide.

9.1.5 NUMBER AND AREA OF EXHIBITION VENUES

Exhibition venues are important infrastructure in the development of the exhibition industry, the number and area of which can certainly decide the development level of a city's exhibition industry. China has a large number

TABLE 9.4 Distribution of Exhibitions with an Exhibition Area over 100,000 Square Meters

Provence/ City	Number of Exhibitions	Exhibition Area (unit= sq m)	Province/ City	Number of Exhibitions	Exhibition Area (unit= sq m)
Guangdong	45	7822900	Henan	3	200000
Shanghai	37	5926818	Jiangsu	3	340000
Beijing	10	1404700	Zhejiang	3	360000
Hubei	6	795000	Anhui	2	210000
Liaoning	6	705600	Heilongjiang	2	232000
Shandong	6	1060000	Jilin	2	300000
Tianjin	6	746000	Chongqing	2	260000
Fujian	5	794000	Guizhou	1	120000
Sichuan	5	655000	Shanxi	1	100000

Source: 2015 China Exhibition Statistical Reports; 2016 China Exhibition Economic Committee.

TABLE 9.5 Major Cities with an Exhibition Area Over 100,000 Square Meters

City	Number of Exhibitions	Exhibition Area (unit = sq. m.)
Shanghai	37	5926815
Guangzhou	25	5712900
Shenzhen	13	1420000
Beijing	10	1404700
Tianjin	6	746000
Dongguan	7	690000
Xiamen	2	274000

Source: 2015 China Exhibition Statistical Reports; 2016 China Exhibition Economic Committee.

of exhibition venues of a large scale, with relatively sufficient exhibition area provision. The total exhibition areas in cities with more than 100,000 square meters of indoor exhibition area in 2015 are shown in Table 9.6.

Currently, Shanghai is the city with largest indoor exhibition area in China, with a total exhibition area of 862,100 square meters, followed by Guangzhou with sufficient exhibition equipment, laying a good foundation for large-scale exhibitions; Beijing has many exhibition venues, the largest being the New China International Exhibition Center, with an indoor exhibition area of 106,800 square meters; Shenzhen is going to build the Shenzhen International Convention and Exhibition Center with an area of 500,000

TABLE 9.6 Total Exhibition Areas in Cities with More Than 100,000 square meters of Indoor Exhibition Area in 2015

City	Indoor Exhibition Area (unit=10,000 sq m)	Number of Exhibitions	City	Indoor Exhibition Area (unit=10,000 sq m)	Number of Exhibitions
Shanghai	86.21	12	Harbin	13.6	3
Guangzhou	52.24	6	Dongguan	13.4	3
Beijing	44.79	9	Hefei	13.15	3
Chongqing	32.5	4	Kunshan	13	4
Hangzhou	21.92	6	Tianjin	12.9	3
Qingdao	21.7	3	Wuxi	12.85	5
Wuhan	21.4	4	Shijiazhuang	12.76	5
Jinan	20.99	4	Shenyang	12.76	3
Nanchang	20.05	3	Shantou	12.53	6
Xi'an	17	4	Dongying	12.1	4
Nanjing	16.72	4	Foshan	12	6
Changchun	16.59	4	Shenzhen	11.8	2
Weifang	15.71	6	Guiyang	10.35	2
Chengdu	15.7	4	Xiamen	10	1

Source: 2015 China Exhibition Statistical Reports; 2016 China Exhibition Economic Committee.

square meters, which will be put into use in 2018. Large-scale exhibition venues are mainly in developed MICE (meetings, incentives, conferences, and exhibitions) cities like Beijing, Shanghai, Guangzhou, and Shenzhen, which have an absolute advantage in exhibition venues resources. Additionally, there are also large-scale exhibition venues with an area of more than 100,000 square meters in Wuhan, Qingdao, Nanjing, Chengdu, etc., and the provision of the exhibition area is relatively sufficient.

9.1.6 NUMBER OF MEMBERS APPROVED BY UFI

UFI is so far the most important international organization in the world's exhibition industry, and to become a member of UFI is a symbol of a level of importance in the exhibition industry for companies or organizations. As of June 2016, there were a total of 124 UFI members in China, mainly distributed in Beijing, Shanghai, Shenzhen, and Guangzhou. Among them, there

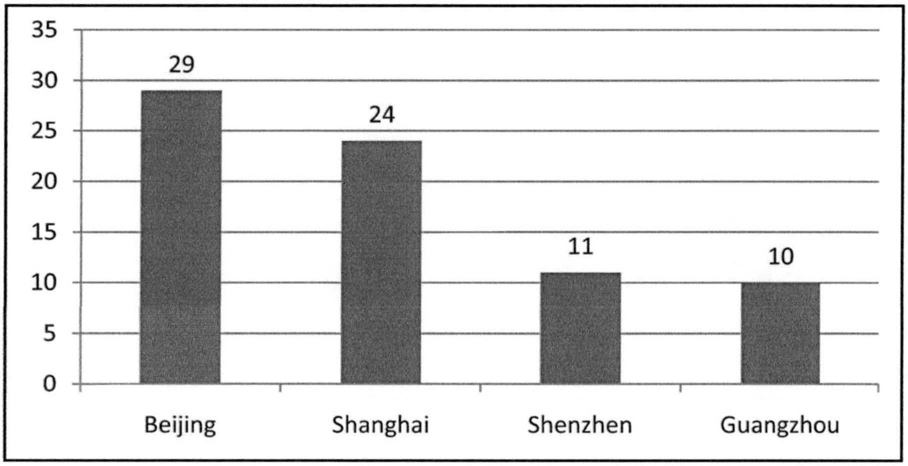

FIGURE 9.2 Number of UFI-approved exhibition organizations in main cities as of June 2016. Source: UFI official website,http://www.ufi.org/

are 29 in Beijing, 24 in Shanghai, 11 in Shenzhen, and 10 in Guangzhou; the number of members in those four cities accounts for 59.7% of the total number of members, forming an obvious differentiated pattern (see Figure 9.2). The developed cities like Beijing, Shanghai, Shenzhen, and Guangzhou are the main bases of the UFI-approved organizations, and Beijing ranks first with 29 members, followed by Shanghai with 24; both these cities enjoy significant advantage.

9.1.7 NUMBER OF EXHIBITIONS APPROVED BY UFI

The "UFI Approved" logo designates a high-quality exhibition trade fair. If an exhibition wants to get UFI approval, its service, quality, and visibility needs to meet certain standards. UFI has very strict requirements on applicant exhibitions' scale, history, proportion of foreign exhibitors, proportion of foreign visitors etc.[1] At present, there are a total of 108 exhibitions with UFI approval in China, which are mainly distributed in Shanghai, Beijing, Shenzhen, and Guangzhou. Among them, there are 30 in Shanghai, 18 in Beijing, 11 in Shenzhen, and 7 in Guangzhou. The distribution of

[1] The application standard by UFI: An international exhibition to be held continuously more than three times;an exhibition area of at least 20,000 m^2;and at least 20% foreign exhibitors and 4% overseas visitors.

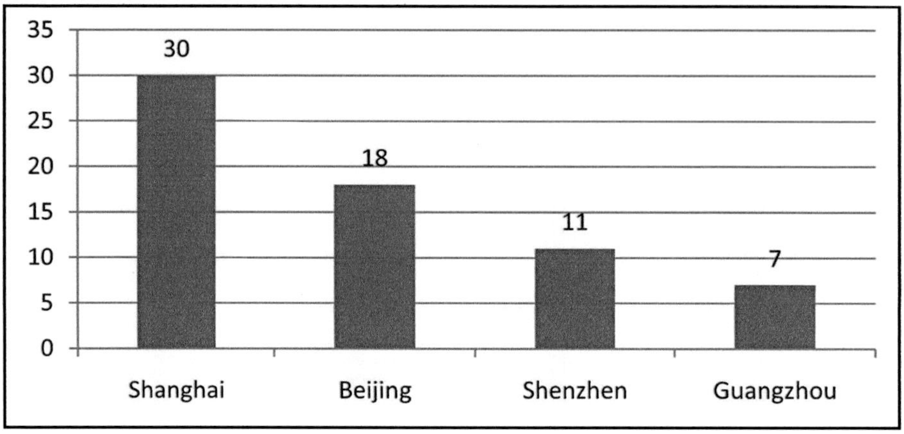

FIGURE 9.3 Numbers of UFI-approved exhibitions in main cities as of June 2016. Source: UFI official website,http://www.ufi.org/

exhibitions with UFI approval in China forms an obvious differentiated pattern, with separation into two groups. The group formed by Shanghai, Beijing, Shenzhen, and Guangzhou has an absolute advantage. Meanwhile, the exhibition distribution within the group is also not in balance, as Shanghai has 23 more than Guangzhou and the gap is obvious (see Figure 9.3).

According to the number of exhibitions and UFI approvals, the exhibition brand development pattern in China is differentiated mainly as follows: The first echelon, including Shanghai, Beijing, Guangzhou, and Shenzhen, has a high level of brand exhibitions and plays an important part in both large-scale exhibitions and UFI-approved ones; the group formed by other cities in China is at a disadvantage, with quite a low level of brand exhibitions and trailing in an obvious gap behind the first echelon.

9.1.8 DOMESTIC EXHIBITION INDUSTRY DEVELOPMENT PATTERN AND TRENDS

Competition in the exhibition industry in China forms three echelons, resulting in a pyramid structure pattern (see Figure 9.4). The first echelon consists of Shanghai, Guangzhou, and Beijing; the second echelon is led by Shenzhen; and the third echelon is led by Tianjin.

The first echelon: Shanghai, Guangzhou, and Beijing as the tip of the pyramid**.** The number of exhibitions is high, the available exhibition area is

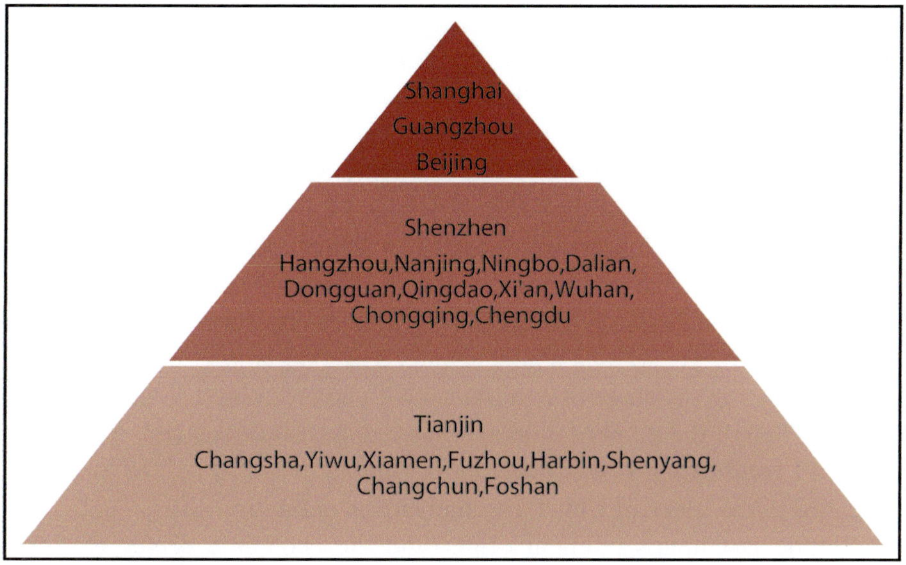

FIGURE 9.4 Domestic competition pattern of the exhibition industry.

large, the degree of internationalization of exhibition projects show that the organizational institutions are of a high level, the infrastructure of venues is first-rate, and the available exhibition area is large.

The second echelon: Shenzhen, Hangzhou, Nanjing, Ningbo, Dalian, Dongguan, Qingdao, Xi'an, Wuhan, Chongqing, and Chengdu as the main body. The number of exhibitions is relatively high, the available exhibition area is large, but the total available exhibition area is insufficient or the degree of internationalization is lower.

The third echelon: Tianjin, Yiwu, Changsha, Xiamen, Fuzhou, Harbin, Shenyang, Changchun, and Foshan as the domestic base. The number and area of exhibitions held is less than those of the first two echelons, but it occupies a certain position in the domestic exhibition competition market for holding some brand exhibitions or cities' own competitiveness and position.

9.1.8.1 The first echelon: Shanghai, Guangzhou, and Beijing

Shanghai is the international financial center and leading city in the Yangtze River Delta and its economic strength in conventions and exhibitions ranks first in the country. It has the absolute advantage in numbers and area of exhibitions held, as well as the number of exhibitions above a designated size, the largest available exhibition area of 490,000 square meters of total indoor venue space, the most exhibitions and show organizer enterprises with UFI certification, high marketization and high degree of internationalization;therefore, Shanghai is undoubtedly the leading city of the first echelon in the competition pattern.

Guangzhou is the largest city and economic center of South China. China's first exhibition, led by the China Import and Export Fair, and China's first largest venue, China Import and Export Fair Venue, played a driving role in the development of the exhibition industry in China, laying a solid foundation for the exhibition industry. The exhibition area of Guangzhou exceeded that of Beijing's in 2012 to rank as the country's second largest, and it occupies the advantage in the share of exhibitions with an area above 100,000 square meters. Though the number of show-organizing institutions and exhibitions with UFI certification is less than that of Beijing, it is still judged as having ascended to the status of China's second largest exhibition city.

Beijing is China's political center and the economic center of North China, with high international popularity. Its number of exhibition-organizing institutions and exhibitions with UFI certification ranks second, following Shanghai. However, the area of exhibitions held in Beijing in 2015 and the number of exhibitions above a designated size was less than those of Guangzhou. The transfer of exhibitions in Beijing to other places is due to frequent political events, traffic jams, and other adverse environmental issues. Beijing, as the capital city in China, has too many city functions nationwide, which leads to adverse impact on the continued development of Beijing's exhibition industry, which is shrinking currently. Based on 2015 data, Beijing is now China's third largest exhibition city.

Shanghai, of the first echelon, is the leading city of the domestic exhibition industry, with Guangzhou and Beijing second and third, respectively; together, they lead in the rapid development in the economics of conventions and exhibitions, and present the development pattern of "one superpower and two poles."

9.1.8.2 The Second Echelon: Shenzhen, Chengdu, Chongqing, and Hangzhou have Differentiation Advantage

The number and area of exhibitions in Shenzhen takes a national leading position, with its average exhibition area ranking first in the country and occupying a certain share among the largest exhibitions in the area above

50,000 square meters. Though the total venue area for Shenzhen is only 139,800 square meters, the 105,000 square meters of its single exhibition space at the Shenzhen Convention and Exhibition Center ranks it at the top. In addition, the degree of internationalization for Shenzhen's exhibition industry is high, and the number of show organizer institutions and exhibitions with UFI certifications ranks as the country's third highest level, second only to Shanghai and Beijing. It has cultivated and introduced a group of brand exhibitions producing important influence at home and abroad. Shenzhen ranks fourth in the domestic exhibition industry and is the leader of the second echelon.

Chengdu and Chongqing occupy decisive positions in the economic belt of western conventions and exhibitions. Both rank at the top in the number and area of exhibitions held, but have the defect of lacking in the degree of internationalization. Under the lead of Shanghai as the foremost city of this industry, the exhibition industry of nearby Hangzhou, Nanjing, and Ningbo have received rapid development, and these three cities rank at the top in the number and area of the type of exhibition held. Though the three cities occupy the advantage in the total available exhibition area, the number and degree of internationalization for exhibitions above the designated scale held are required to be enhanced. Dalian is located in the economic belt surrounding the Bohai Sea of China, with a pleasant climate and developed economy. It can rely on the costal advantages of focusing on carrying out foreign economic and trade fairs. Dongguan is located in the Pearl River Delta Economic Development Zone, with a developed manufacturing industry. Relying on the local industrial system, it is vigorously developing the exhibition industry, and has cultivated many brand exhibitions such as for furniture exhibitions, and occupies a certain market share in the exhibition market. Xi'an and Wuhan are located in Central China and are the core convention and exhibition cities in this region as provincial capitals.

To sum up, the second echelon represents the trend led by Shenzhen and other cities to maintain rapid development based upon various advantages.

9.1.8.3 The Third Echelon: Led by Tianjin, Its Development Level and That of Other Cities to be Enhanced

Tianjin's exhibition industry is located in the economic belt of the Circum-Bohai Sea Region, amid a solid industrial foundation of heavy industry, large port freight volume, and a developed logistics industry, forming a half-hour-urban-economy-circle with Beijing. Its number and scale of exhibitions ranks top among the third echelon, and it occupies the advantage among the share of medium-sized exhibitions with the area of 30,000 square meters to 50,000 square meters. The total area of the Tianjin venue is higher, but due to the restriction of only 54,000 square meters at the Meijiang Convention Center, Tianjin's largest single venue, the number of large-scale exhibitions is less, and the internationalization degree is not high.

Other cities occupy the top position in their convention and exhibition economic belts, but due to a restriction of total available exhibition area or great influence effect of MICE city within the economic belt, they are not in the leading position for conventions and exhibitions, and the development level requires to be improved.

To sum up, the third echelon represents the trend led by Tianjin wherein the development levels need to be improved.

9.2 QUALITATIVE ANALYSIS OF EXHIBITION INDUSTRY COMPETITIVENESS OF MAJOR CITIES IN CHINA

Qualitative judgments on the competitiveness and trends of convention and exhibition cities are important in order to unscramble the situation regarding the exhibition industry in China. This section will qualitatively analyze the opportunities and challenges of five exhibition cities – Beijing, Shanghai, Guangzhou, Shenzhen, and Tianjin – and predict the future competitive landscape.

9.2.1 SHANGHAI

9.2.1.1 Shanghai Market Saturation Analysis

With the best and largest number of exhibition venues nationwide, Shanghai's exhibition industry has strong demand. Both the exhibition number and area rank first in the whole country, showing an increasing trend in the last 5 years. It is predicted that the market of the exhibition industry in Shanghai is nearly saturated, with exhibitions developing in large scale.

In 2015, there were in total 12 professional exhibition venues in Shanghai, with 862,100 square meters of indoor exhibition area in total and an average of 71,800 square meters per exhibition venue, ranking first nationwide. Among these venues, the National Exhibition and Convention Center (Shanghai) is so far the largest indoor exhibition area nationwide, with an indoor exhibition area of 400,000 square meters. In addition, the Shanghai New International Expo Center is the fourth-largest professional exhibition venue, with an indoor exhibition area of 200,000 square meters.

In 2015, there were 749 exhibitions hosted in Shanghai, with a total exhibition area of 15.1155 million square meters, accounting for 8.1% and 13.06% of China's total number of exhibitions and exhibition area, respectively, to rank first in China. The average exhibition area was 20,200 square meters per exhibition. According to statistics, from 2011 to 2015, the average annual growth rate of the number of exhibitions hosted in Shanghai increased slightly, up by 2.23%, and the exhibition area in Shanghai annually increased 11.72% on average.[2]

9.2.1.2 Shanghai Internationalization Pattern Analysis

The exhibition industry is highly international. With Shanghai having the largest number of organizations and exhibitions holding UFI certification, most overseas exhibition companies prefer to host their exhibitions there.

By June 2016, UFI members in China totaled 124, of which the number in Shanghai was 24, accounting for 19.35%, to rank second in China only after Beijing.

(1) **The highest proportion of international exhibitions.** By June 2016, there were a total of 108 UFI-certified exhibitions in China, among which Shanghai had the largest number, 30, accounting for 27.78%.
(2) **The largest number of overseas exhibition companies' subsidiaries.** Among the top 10 exhibition companies with turnover of more than 100 million euros announced by AUMA, the Association of the German Trade Fair Industry,a total of seven companies had set up subsidiary companies or joint ventures in Shanghai.
(3) **The largest number of exhibitions hosted by overseas exhibition companies.** Currently, there are 115 exhibition projects in Shanghai invested in by overseas exhibition companies ranked in the top 10 with turnover of more than 100 million euros as announced by AUMA; the number of projects is the largest in China.

[2] Source: *China Exhibition Economic Development Report 2015.*

9.2.1.3 Shanghai Exhibition Industry Structure Analysis

The Shanghai exhibition industry structure mainly has the following two characteristics:

(1) **A high level of internationalization, with active investment by overseas exhibition companies.** The expanding and opening up of service trade in Shanghai will greatly promote the Shanghai exhibition industry. There are a total of 115 exhibition projects in Shanghai invested in by overseas exhibition companies who rank in the top 10 of turnover of more than 100 million euros according to AUMA, and that number of projects is the largest in China. The advantage is obvious when compared to the 12 projects in Beijing. In addition, the Shanghai New International Expo Center (SNIEC) is jointly invested and built by the Shanghai Lujiazui Exhibition Development Co., Ltd. and the German International Exhibition Group (whose members include Hannover Messe, Messe Düsseldorf, and Messe München). As the first Sino-foreign joint venture and co-operation exhibition center, the Shanghai New International Expo Center has become one of China›s most successful exhibition centers.

(2) **The Shanghai exhibition industry has a mature market-oriented operation standard.** Currently, Shanghai exhibition companies hosting various exhibitions projects are now largely getting rid of relying on government and subsidies, realizing the implementation mechanism of the independent market-oriented operation. According to statistics, among more than 800 exhibition projects in Shanghai, more than 90% are run independently by companies in a market-oriented operation of strong vitality.

9.2.1.4 Shanghai Exhibition Environment Analysis

Gu Jun, deputy director of Shanghai Municipal Commission of Commerce, said in April 2016 that currently the Shanghai exhibition industry is maintaining a rapid development trend, and the 2015 exhibition area of Shanghai ranks first in China; Shanghai has set a clear goal to build an "International Exhibition City" of great influence in the global market in 2020.[3]

[3] Date source: http://finance.sina.com.cn/roll/2016-04-12/doc-ifxrcizs7353402.shtml

According to the *Shanghai Exhibition Industry Development Report*, by the end of 2014, the total exhibition area provided and exhibition capacity of large venues in Shanghai ranked first worldwide, and the number of exhibitions and exhibition area ranked first in China. In 2014, Shanghai held 755 exhibitions of all kinds, accounting for nearly 10% of the total number of exhibitions in China: its 12.4 million square meters exhibition area, accounting for one-eighth of the total national exhibition area and 1.45 times larger than that of second-ranked Guangzhou, saw both the number of exhibitions and exhibition area increased by 17.6% and 54.23%, respectively, compared to the "Eleventh-Five-Year Plan" period.

According to the report, by 2020, the expected indicators of the Shanghai exhibition industry will include 200 professional exhibition companies in Shanghai, more than 30 of the world's leading exhibition companies investing in Shanghai, and more than 35 organizations being admitted to the International Exhibition Management Association. By then, the total exhibition area of Shanghai will reach 20,000,000 square meters, the number of exhibitions with more than 100,000 square meters will reach 50, and the international exhibition will account for more than 80% of total exhibitions. The report also cites the standard of an international exhibition city by UFI, including that the urban income per capita will reach the average level of developed countries, that the city's position will be as a business center, and that the city's service industry will account for more than 50% in GDP.

Thus, Shanghai plans to actively develop as an "International Exhibition City" and to strengthen the international influence and visibility of the Shanghai exhibition industry in a favorable environment.

9.2.2 GUANGZHOU

9.2.2.1 Guangzhou Market Saturation Analysis

Based on the overall use of the venue, the Guangzhou exhibition industry market still has room for further development and large-scale space.

(1) **The total exhibition area supply exceeds 450,000 thousand square meters in Guangzhou**, of which the indoor exhibition area of the Canton Fair venue is 338,000 square meters, and the indoor area of the Poly venue is 67,800 square meters.

(2) **According to an equilibrium analysis of the venue use and exhibition room, the Guangzhou venue has a partial vacancy phenomenon, and numerous exhibition areas have not been fully utilized.** The Canton Fair venue used less than 10 exhibition rooms on the same day at the same time; that is, the time of the venue utilization rate of less than 30% and the vacancy rate of more than 60% was 116 days in total, accounting for 37% of the whole year, so that nearly 50% of the time the venue utilization rate was less than 50%.[4]

(3) **There is a structural shortage in the use of the venue.** In the peak season, especially in March each year, there is a shortage involving the Canton Fair venue, and the exhibition is difficult to fit within the exhibition schedule. However, in terms of the overall situation of the whole year, the supply of the Guangzhou venue is adequate; the structural venue vacancy situation is greater than the lack of venue supply. Therefore, the Guangzhou exhibition industry market reaches close to saturation in March, the market saturation situation of the peak season spike.

9.2.2.2 Guangzhou Internationalization Pattern Analysis

(1) **As the host city of Canton Fair, Guangzhou has a long history and a high degree of internationalization, which is an important factor in promoting the further development of exhibition industry in Guangzhou.**

Guangzhou also has a long history of international trade exhibition. In 1957, under the planned economy system in China, the Canton Fair was China's only foreign trading window. A total of 1,223 foreign merchants from 19 countries and regions participated in the fair at the outset of its holding. Although it has experienced the ups and downs of a long history, the Canton Fair has continued to be held over the past 56 years. It experienced a steady growth period in the 1970s and 1980s, brought about by the "enterprise reform of decentralization" in 1978 and the reform of the foreign trade system around 1982, and a rapid development period from the 1990s. The Canton Fair is a comprehensive international trade event with the longest history, the largest scale, the most variety of goods, the most buyers distributed

[4] Source: Interviews with key figures in Guangzhou exhibition industry.

most widely for the region, with the best deal and credibility in China at present. Further, it has been developed into an import and export trade fair with an exhibition area of 1.16 million square meters and visitors totaling nearly 177,500 including overseas merchants from 213 countries and regions. At the end of 2015, Canton Fair attracted oversea buyers from 193 countries, which are the United Nations members, and it enjoys high degree of internationalization.

(2) **Excluding the Canton Fair, however, the degree of internationalization for other exhibitions in Guangzhou is still low, showing the characteristic of an uneven distribution of the degree of internationalization.** It is mainly reflected in the following three aspects:

(i) The proportion of international exhibitions is low. Exhibitions in Guangzhou are mainly about domestic trade, including the China (Guangzhou) International Building Decoration Fair, ranked as the largest fair of its kind in Asia. The proportion of international exhibitions in Guangzhou was only 17.3% in 2011, much lower than that of the same period in Shanghai where 674 exhibitions were held, including 227 international exhibitions, accounting for 33.7%.[5,6]

According to the interview: Hong Kong's influence range is too small. Our main focus is on the domestic market. And now the domestic market is relatively sluggish. We have to stabilize the domestic market first and go solidly step-by-step. Exhibition scale in Guangzhou is the largest in China. It is very professional and gets good results.

The biggest problem of the Guangzhou exhibition industry is the low degree of internationalization. Foreign exhibitors and buyers are not many and 90% of exhibitors are from the domestic side. In essence, the purpose is to sell Chinese goods to the whole world. But Germany sells the world's goods to the world.

The low degree of internationalization in the Guangzhou exhibition industry is one of the bottleneck. This is related to a lot of factors, including the low city popularity and the lack of historical

[5] *Convention and Exhibition Economic Development Situation in Pazhou Area (2014)* is still being compiled in 2016. So, the related data of 2013 will temporarily be used to reflect the proportion of International Exhibition in Guangzhou.

[6] Source: *Convention and Exhibition Economic Development Situation in Pazhou Area (January 2013).*

participation, the lack of confidence for foreign investment because of poor market environment, and so on.

(ii) The number of overseas exhibition companies and regional headquarters stationed in Guangzhou is higher. Among the top 10 exhibition companies with a global turnover of more than 10 million euros announced by AUMA, six have set up subsidiaries in Hong Kong and five have set up subsidiaries or joint ventures in Guangzhou.

(iii) The number of exhibitions held by overseas companies is high. At present, the number of projects invested in Guangzhou by the top 10 transnational exhibition companies with an annual income of more than 10 million euros is 15, a total which is slightly less than that in Hong Kong. The high entry rate of overseas companies further accelerates the internationalization process of the exhibition industry in Guangzhou.

9.2.2.3 Guangzhou Exhibition Industry Structure Analysis

The structure of Guangzhou exhibition industry has the following two characteristics:

(1) **From the perspective of the absolute quantity of convention and exhibition enterprises, marketization forces represented by private enterprises and foreign-funded enterprises are the main constituents of Guangzhou's convention and exhibition market.** Guangzhou had 201 exhibition enterprises (units) and 5,474 employees in 2012.[7,8] Of those units, 180 were private enterprises and foreign-funded enterprises, accounting for 90% of the total number of enterprises.[9] This proportion will increase with time and rapid development of marketization operations.

(2) **From the perspective of the strength structure of the structure of the convention and exhibition market, though marketization**

[7]The statistics on Guangzhou exhibition industry employees in 2012 are relatively detailed. The statistical data from the most recent two years are not complete. Thus, the employment data of 2012 can be used to explain the phenomenon from the side.

[8]*[NPC and CPPCC Proposal] To Build a World-Class Convention and Exhibition Center To Boost the Development of the New Urbanization*, Guangzhou Municipal Committee of the China Democratic National Construction Association http://nandu.oeeee.com/html/201301/17/17058.html.

[9]*Report on the Work of Promoting the Scientific Development of the Exhibition Industry To Create a New Global Convention and Exhibition Center*, Guangzhou Municipal Economic and Trade Commission.

organization of Guangzhou accounts for 90%, it lacks competitiveness in the convention and exhibition market, and its market share is low. The exhibition scale of state-owned enterprises is relatively large, and its strength is strong. Conversely, though foreign-funded enterprises and Hong Kong-funded enterprises have organized many exhibitions, their scale is relatively small and market competitiveness is relatively low on average. It can be seen from the above comparison analysis that the Guangzhou exhibition industry market is led by the government and national power – characteristic of strong government and national power – and that a minority of high-quality exhibitions account for 70% of the market, with the remaining 30% of the market shared by private enterprises, Hong Kong-funded enterprises, and foreign-funded enterprises. It is a typical oligopoly market.

According to interview:

The commercial atmosphere of the Guangzhou exhibitions is not strong. Governmental exhibition accounts for a relatively large proportion. The commercial atmosphere of Shanghai is great, but most exhibitions in Guangzhou and Dongguan are organized by the government. If the government is involved in exhibitions, the rule has been changed. For example, the government has corresponding subsidy and privilege. In addition, if the exhibition is evaluated via scale rather than quality, exhibitors will be affected by the government and will select the exhibitions organized by the government; thus, selection of these exhibitors is not a commercial choice at all. Private enterprises and foreign-funded enterprises are helpless.

9.2.2.4 Guangzhou Exhibition Environment Analysis

(1) **Guangzhou's hardware facilities for conventions and exhibitions are advantageous in China. This provides a broad space for the increase in scale of exhibitions.** The total exhibition area supply exceeds 450,000 square meters in Guangzhou, and the exhibition area available is relatively abundant.

(2) **Overall, the soft environment of exhibition industry remains to be further improved, although Guangzhou was the first in China to cancel exhibition examination and approval** (see Figure 9.5).

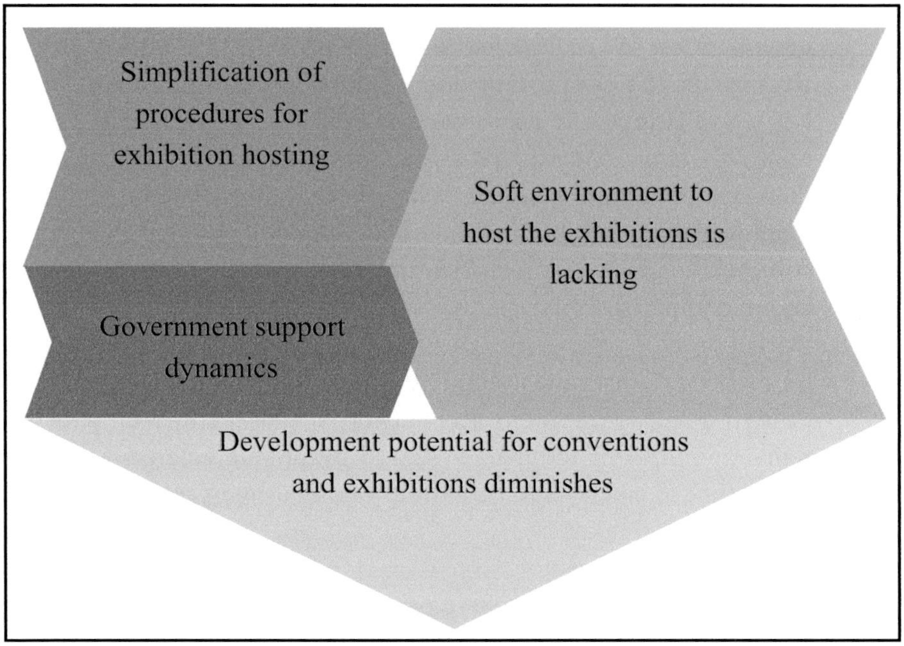

FIGURE 9.5 Guangzhou exhibition-hosting environment.

Guangzhou was the first city to cancel exhibition examination and approval requirements. The procedures for hosting an exhibition have been gradually simplified, and currently, most administrative examination and approval procedures have been cancelled. From July 1, 2010, Guangzhou cancelled the industrial and commercial examination and approval system that had earlier been needed prior to hosting an exhibition. So far, examination and approval for foreign economic and technological exhibitions with an exhibition area of over 1,000 square meters, which had necessitated examination and approval directly by the Guangdong department on foreign economy and trade as entrusted by the original State Council, have had such examination requirements cancelled. A classified examination and approval system was used for foreign economic and technological exhibition with an area of over 1,000 square meters and graded as "national" and "China" in the name of exhibitions. At the start of February 2013, the recorded matter which was cancelled in *The List of Administrative Examination and Approval and Recorded Matter Cancelled, Transferred, and Decentralized in the Fifth Administrative Examination and Approval System Reform* shows that recording for foreign economic and technological exhibitions with an area smaller than 1,000 square meters had been cancelled by the Guangzhou Foreign Economy and Trade Bureau. The cancellation of examination and approval is a signal of the government's deregulation of the exhibition industry in market access. Guangzhou's inadequate conditions for hosting exhibitions are at the forefront of the whole nation and are gradually in line with Hong Kong and Macao.

The simplification for hosting exhibitions is a signal the government is loosening market access to the exhibition industry. However, industry laws and regulations, as well as the industry's own internal standards, have not kept pace with the changes in the deregulation of the centralized distribution of Guangzhou's venues and, as a result, there has been a rapid deterioration of order within the ranks of exhibition hosting, such as the frequent occurrence of overlapping hosting periods or the repetitious hosting of exhibitions. These become important hindrances to the development of Guangzhou's exhibition industry. To a large extent, they squeeze the growing space for new theme exhibition and newly transplanted brands, leading to the weakening of enterprises' market confidence. Intermediary agents such as exhibition industry associations lack function and appeal, and have failed to develop industry norms and standards. The lack of specialized laws and regulations in the exhibition industry has meant the industry and government have failed to form effective management measures. The Guangzhou government's support dynamics for the exhibition industry, then, are insufficient.

Thus, the national aim of broadening exhibition industry market access and competition is an important draw in the development of the exhibition industry, one with a ground-breaking effect on the market-oriented competition of the exhibition industry and new exhibition introduction. Deficiencies in the soft environment for Guangzhou's exhibition hosting, however, form a counter force. Under the push-and-pull of both forces, the attractiveness of Guangzhou's exhibition industry significantly diminishes. Its incremental potential is far lower than the level its industry standing and regional condition should reach.

9.2.3 BEIJING

9.2.3.1 Beijing Market Saturation Analysis

Beijing has a large number of venues but not a large exhibition area for a single venue. It has had negative growth in the both the number and area of exhibitions in the past 5 years, indicating that the demand for the exhibition industry is declining and that the market is reaching saturation levels. The exhibition industry in Beijing is becoming more international and more branded, resulting in greater global influence.

There were nine venues with a total indoor exhibition area of 447,900 square meters in Beijing as of 2015, ranking it third in the country. On average, the exhibition area of a unit venue is 49,800 square meters. Among the venues in Beijing, the New China International Exhibition Center is the largest, with an indoor exhibition area of 110,000 square meters and a rank of tenth in the country.

In 2015, Beijing held 415 exhibitions with an exhibition area total of 5,201,000 square meters, which accounted for 4.47% and 4.48%, respectively, of the country's totals, to rank fourth nationwide. The average exhibition area was 12,500 square meters per exhibition. According to statistics, there has been a negative growth trend in the number and the area of exhibitions in Beijing from 2011 to 2015. The number of exhibitions has decreased by 2.92% and the area of exhibitions has decreased by 7.57%.

9.2.3.2 Beijing Internationalization Pattern Analysis

The exhibition industry of Beijing has a high level of internationalization. It has the most UFI-certified members of exhibition organizers and the proportion of international exhibitions is high. It has a large number of branches and exhibitions established and hosted by well-known overseas exhibition companies.

By June 2016, the number of UFI-certified members in Beijing reached 29, accounting for 23.39% of the total in the country and ranking first among all cities nationwide.

(1) **It has a high proportion of international exhibitions.** Beijing had the second largest number of UFI-certified exhibitions, after Shanghai, with 18 exhibitions that accounted for 16.67% of the total.
(2) **It has a large number of branches or subsidiaries of well-known overseas exhibition companies.** Among the top 10 global exhibition companies identified by AUMA, a total of six have set up subsidiaries or joint ventures in Beijing.
(3) **It has a large number of exhibitions hosted by overseas exhibition companies.** At present, the top 10 global exhibition companies identified by AUMA have invested in a total of 12 projects in Beijing.

In 2013, there were more than 7,000 international conferences in Beijing, which received about 683,000 visitors. Revenue was 1.087 billion RMB, accounting for 9.1% of the country's total conference revenue, an increase of 467.7% compared to that of 2004. The annual growth rate of Beijing was 18.7%. There were 283 international exhibitions in 2013, including 157 medium-sized international exhibitions with an exhibition area of 10,000 to 50,000 square meters and 25 large-scale exhibitions with an exhibition area over 50,000 square meters. The revenue of international exhibitions reached 4.84 billion RMB and increased by 728.6% over 2004, accounting for 49.8% of the total revenue of exhibitions. The international revenues of the event industry accounted for 47.8% or nearly half. In other words, the international level of Beijing's event industry has been increasing.

9.2.3.3 Beijing Exhibition Industry Structure Analysis

Beijing's event industry structure mainly has two characteristics as follows:

(1) **The structure of the conference market has changed: the proportion of government meetings has decreased, and the quality and benefits of conferences has gradually increased.** According to the 2014–2015 Beijing Hotels Conferences Market Report, corporate meetings accounted for about 60% of hotel conferences hosted in Beijing, association meetings accounted for 25%, while government meetings decreased to 15%. With the conference market bubble gradually being corrected, the quality and benefits of meetings will also increase gradually. Data from the 2015 Beijing Statistic Yearbook show that the average number of participants in Beijing conferences was 70.8 persons, an increase of 16% compared with the 2009 level, indicating increased conference space occupancy. A total of 38.4% of the conference space in Beijing exceeded 50% at its occupancy in 2014. Overall occupancy is 42.9% on average, an increase of 4.4% compared with that of 2013.

(2) **The structure of the exhibition market has changed: associations have become the main organizers of exhibitions rather than chambers of commerce.** According to statistics for categories of exhibition organizers in 2016 (see Table 9.7, Figure 9.6), exhibitions in Beijing are mainly organized by associations. Beijing was once the leader of the exhibition industry nationwide, with its wealthy resources of

administration power and headquarters of associations and chambers of commerce. But with weakening administrative power over exhibition resources configuration capabilities and the limitation of venue scale, the traffic factor, and so on, the advantages and development power of the Beijing event industry declined. Currently, Shanghai firmly occupies the leading position. Guangzhou has exceeded Beijing and occupies second place, while Beijing has fallen to third.

9.2.3.4 Beijing Exhibition Environment Analysis

Exhibition industry is seen as a platform to encourage Beijing's world-class urban development and construction and to achieve industrial transformation in the country. The industry policy will continue to be good in the future.

The Beijing Overall Urban Planning 2004–2020 report proposed that the event industry is a key support in the development of the service sector, with the goal of developing Beijing into Asia's most influential international exhibition city. Beijing's Twelfth-Five-Year Plan of Developing the Exhibition Industry proposed to make Beijing into the Asian Exposition City, one of the top five international conference destinations and Asia's leading incentive destination: the leader of China's event industry that would strive to achieve faster growth in the sector than Beijing's overall GDP growth. During the Thirteenth-Five-Year period, Beijing will further consolidate the status of the development of the exhibition industry, adhere to high-end, professional, and international development, and breakthrough to make it an international exhibition city of significant influence.

Overall, the Beijing government has given high priority to the development of the event industry and is helping to expand the international influence of Beijing's exhibition industry through a series of planning and policy exercises.

TABLE 9.7 Categories of Beijing Exhibition Organizers in 2016

Category of organizer	Government	Association	State-owned enterprise	Private enterprise	Foreign-funded enterprise	Sino-foreign-joint venture	Public institution	Total
Quantity	24	162	19	35	14	7	18	279
Percentage	8.60%	58.06%	6.81%	12.54%	5.02%	2.51%	6.45%	100%

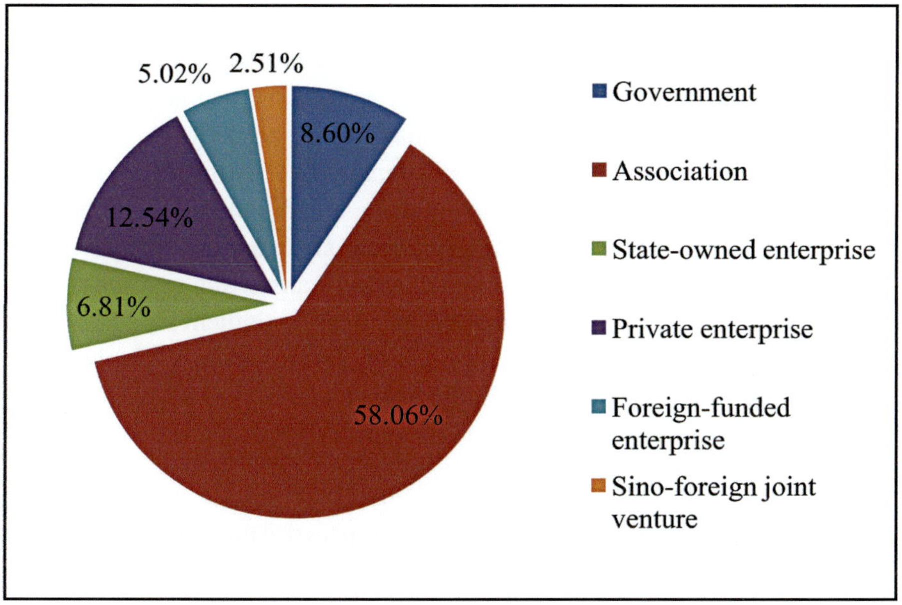

FIGURE 9.6 Categories of Beijing exhibition organizers in 2016.

9.2.4 SHENZHEN

9.2.4.1 Shenzhen Market Saturation Analysis

Shenzhen exhibition industry market demand is strong, but the supply is insufficient; convention and exhibition industry development is severely restricted by the venue size, and the market is close to saturation.

(1) **The utilization rate of the Shenzhen Convention & Exhibition Center in 2015 was 52.71%, ranking fourth nationwide,** with a total exhibition area of 2,730,000 square meters.
(2) **In 2015, due to lack of availability in the venue schedule, 150 exhibitions were rejected;**[10] the high utilization rate of the venue reflects the lack of a large venue in Shenzhen, which greatly limits the rapid development of the exhibition industry.
(3) **The insufficiency of the available exhibition area limits the scale development of the brand exhibition and even leads to an outflow of brand exhibitions.** Take the 71st China International Medical

[10] Source: Interviews with key figures in the Shenzhen convention and exhibition industry.

Equipment Fair in 2015 as an example: there were a total 3,896 medical equipment manufacturing enterprises from 28 countries, and government institutions, hospital buyers, and distributors of more than 150 countries and regions attended; the conference and convention and exhibition center were inundated with participants. According to the organizers, there were still hundreds of domestic and foreign enterprises hoping to participate in the exhibition that could not due to the Shenzhen Convention & Exhibition Center venue – the venue was too limited, and they had to consider transferring to other cities.[11] Similarly, the China International Medical Equipment Fair, Shenzhen International Furniture Expo, China International Optoelectronic Expo, China International Public Security Expo, and other large exhibitions have all been subject to the constraints of the venue area.

9.2.4.2 Shenzhen Internationalization Pattern Analysis

The exhibition industry in Shenzhen started from the late 1980s and has been in the market exploration stage. Since the first China International Hi-Tech Fair (High-Tech Fair for short) was held in 1999, the convention and exhibition economy in Shenzhen has been developing rapidly. The venue area had increased by 20 times by 2006. Annual turnover, the number of exhibitions, and other indicators continue to grow rapidly. The economic effect is remarkable. In 2015, with a total exhibition area of 2.78 million square meters, Shenzhen ranked fourth in China, and the average exhibition area was 37,000 square meters. The number of large-scale exhibitions reached 13. Although there is a higher degree of internationalization for some of the exhibitions, on the whole, exhibitions characteristically show an uneven distribution in the degree of internationalization. The degree of internationalization needs to be further enhanced. It is mainly reflected in the following three aspects:

(1) **Exhibitions in Shenzhen are mainly about domestic trade and the proportion of international exhibitions is low, but partial exhibitions show a higher degree of internationalization.** In 2015, the China International Hi-Tech Fair attracted 128 delegations from 28 countries and international organizations, among which, 21 national delegations along the "One Belt and One Road" participated in

[11] Source: Interviews with key figures in the Shenzhen convention and exhibition industry.

special galleries of the same name. The China International Optoelectronic Exposition, which at present represents the world's largest and most complete industrial chain of optoelectronics professionals, has become the exchange platform for technology and products between optoelectronics industry enterprises at home and abroad, research institutions, investment institutions, and other multilevel parties. In 2015, a total of over 150 social public security enterprises from nearly 40 countries and regions participated in the China International Social Public Security Expo, which received 130,000 buyers and visitors from over 150 countries and regions. The exhibition's scale ranks first in the world for similar professional exhibitions.

(2) **The number of overseas exhibition companies or regional headquarters stationed there has increased.** Among the top 10 exhibition companies with a global turnover of more than 100 million euros identified by AUMA, five have set up subsidiaries or joint ventures in Shenzhen.

(3) **The exhibitions host by overseas companies are of a small quantity.** At present, the number of projects invested in Shenzhen by the top 10 transnational exhibition companies with annual income

TABLE 9.8 Transnational Enterprises Investors in Exhibition in Four Cities (the Top 10 with Annual Income of More Than Euro 10 Million)

Name of Company	Shenzhen	Guangzhou	Hong Kong	Macao
Reed Exhibitions	2	1	1	0
GL Events	-	-	-	-
United Business Media	3	2	13	0
Messe Frankfurt	0	7	0	0
MCH Group	0	0	1	0
Messe München	0	1	0	0
Messe Düsseldorf	1	4	0	-
Deutsche Messe	2	1	0	-
VIPARIS	1	2	0	0
Koelnmesse	0	1	0	0
Total	9	19	15	0

Source: Collected according to the official data of the company websites[1]

[1]Among the top ten companies ranked by business revenue, only Reed Expo and UBM Asia had a complete event list; other companies were only able to provide exhibitions held from Jul. 2015 to Jul. 2016. Thus, the statistical time is limited to Jul. 2015 to Jul. 2016.

of more than 10 million euros is nine (see Table 9.8), which is slightly less than the number of projects in Hong Kong and Guangzhou. The high entry rate of overseas companies further accelerates the internationalization process of the exhibition industry in Shenzhen.

To sum up, the Hi-Tech Fair has accelerated the process of the exhibition industry in Shenzhen. At present, although exhibitions in Shenzhen are mainly about domestic trade and the proportion of international exhibitions is low, partial exhibitions show a higher degree of internationalization and have started the internationalized exhibition effect.

9.2.4.3 Shenzhen exhibition industry structure analysis

The structure of the Shenzhen exhibition industry has the following three characteristics:

(1) **From the perspective of the structure of convention and exhibition organizations, the degree of marketization of Shenzhen's exhibition industry is relatively high; professional convention and exhibition companies and industry associations have become significant entities for organizing exhibitions.** According to the 2015 Convention and Exhibition Development Report of Shenzhen issued by the Shenzhen Exhibition Industry Association (see Figure 9.7), Shenzhen has about 63 organizers at present. They can be divided into state-owned exhibition companies, private exhibition companies, joint venture (foreign-funded) companies, and community organizations according to organization property. There are nine organizers that have joined UFI (also known as the Union of International Fairs). Based on exhibition statistics of the Shenzhen Convention & Exhibition Center in 2015, a distribution diagram of exhibition quantity is shown in Figure 9.7, by exhibition organizer type. Exhibitions organized by nonstate-owned organizations accounted for 71% of the total. Exhibitions organized by joint ventures (foreign-funded) accounted for 16%. Further, except for shopping festivals and trade fairs, exhibitions organized by joint ventures (foreign-funded) account for over 20%. Compared with the previous

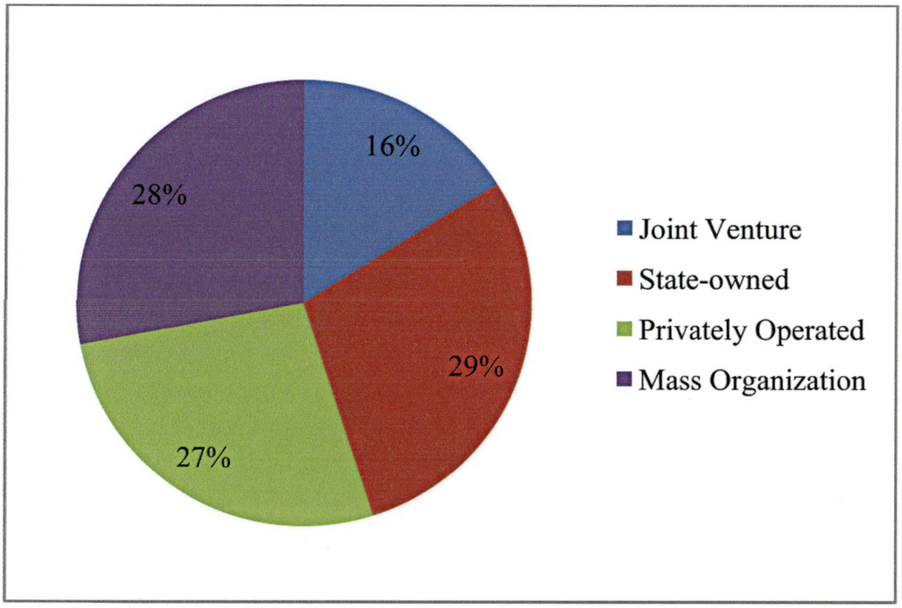

FIGURE 9.7 Proportion of exhibitions in Shenzhenby different organizers, 2015.

year, the exhibition proportion by nonstate-owned organizations increased.

(2) **Marketization degree of exhibitions organized by the government has been constantly enhanced.** The government has not directly participated in trade statistics, exhibition certificate, and catering service work of exhibition since 2005. Meanwhile, it established a relatively solid exhibition industry market operation and policy support system. Abiding by the principle of "marketization-oriented, governmental support," the government invests to construct large convention and exhibition venue facilities but supports the corporatization of convention and exhibition venues and the commercialization of convention and exhibition projects; it provides a certain level of support for important conventions and exhibitions, while common commercial conventions and exhibitions are operated according to market principles.

(3) **The operational strength of Shenzhen convention and exhibition enterprises has been constantly improved to promote the internationalization progress of the Shenzhen exhibition industry.**

However, as a whole, international competitiveness needs to be enhanced. According to the *2015 Convention and Exhibition Development Report of Shenzhen* issued by the Shenzhen Exhibition Industry Association, there are more than 900 organizations engaged in exhibition, exhibition design, and exhibition engineering in Shenzhen at present. These organizations provide professional exhibition and display services for exhibitions around the nation. The output value is nearly RMB 7.8 billion. There are around 55,000 employees in the exhibition and display industry, and 80% of exhibition and display designers have a college degree or above. However, according to AUMA statistics for 2014, the annual business volume of local convention and exhibition enterprises in China was not more than Euro 100 million. The sector lacks convention and exhibition companies at a high level and with strong competitiveness. Even though the total quantity of exhibitions organized in Shenzhen ranks second place in China's exhibition industry, Shenzhen lacks transnational exhibition groups that can occupy overseas markets on a global scale.

9.2.4.4 Shenzhen Exhibition Environment Analysis

(1) **Shenzhen's exhibition industry development is taken seriously by the government. In order to aid the rapid development of the convention and exhibition economy, the government has continually released a series of policy bonuses.** In 2004, the Shenzhen Municipal Government introduced the first *Opinions on Developing Shenzhen's Exhibition Industry* in the nation, in which it proposed guidelines for the internationalization, marketization, and specialization of the exhibition industry's development, with the goal of creating a "well-known MICE city." The exhibition industry has been formally classified into the industrial development planning of Shenzhen as an emerging industry, providing policy guarantees for the rapid development of Shenzhen's exhibition industry. In 2006, the government set up a 20 million RMB special convention and exhibition fund to support the sector's development. *Shenzhen's Financial Contribution Special Fund for Exhibition Industry Management Methods,* printed and issued by the Shenzhen's People's Government General Office, sets up specific provisions for the funding objects, funding methods,

and funding conditions and standards of Shenzhen's financial contribution to the special fund for the exhibition industry. The awards shall be transparent and publicized, and a Shenzhen exhibition industry management group is set up to take the lead in managing and optimizing relevant policies and regulations each year.

Moreover, the Shenzhen Municipal Government values the long-term development of the city's exhibition industry. Besides creating the exhibition industry policy bonus release for the first time, the Shenzhen Municipal Government is also positively exploring a sustainable development path for the exhibition industry. In 2015, it formally established a friendly communication city relationship with Hannover Messe, the famous industrial fair in Hanover, Germany, to promote Shenzhen as a partner in mutually beneficial cooperation in economic and trading investment, cultural creativity, education in science and technology, medicine and hygiene, and conventions and exhibitions, as well as tourism. In addition, the "Pearl River Delta City Exhibition Industry Cooperation and Development Base—Shenzhen DCC Exhibition and Show Cultural Creativity Industry Park" was formally built in Shenzhen, which was helpful in speeding up the integration of resources, the promotion of cross-industry and cross-domain communication and cooperation, and the building of a one-stop high-end service platform for the city exhibition industry of the Pearl River Delta, combining smart show technology, R&D design, creative experience and cultural leisure, and greatly enhancing communication and cooperation in the exhibition industry of the Pearl River Delta and the nation as a whole.

(2) **In terms of hard conditions for hosting exhibitions, Shenzhen is equipped with first-class international communications and logistics, and airport, port, and transportation facilities as well as other infrastructure.** In addition, Shenzhen plans to integrate Bigger Airport Zone development, build a new convention and exhibition center, and correspondingly perfect surrounding service support facilities.

In conclusion, the Shenzhen Municipal Government highly values the convention and exhibition economy, and has taken a series of measures to promote MICE city construction. With the start of construction of the Shenzhen International Convention & Exhibition

Center (SZICEC), the future soft and hard environment for hosting exhibitions will be further optimized.

9.2.5 *TIANJIN*

9.2.5.1 Tianjin Market Saturation Analysis

The number and area of exhibition venues are at a relatively low level; however, there has been a relatively high increase in those figures in the last 5 years. Exhibition industry demand is quite high, but may be restricted by the exhibition venue scale in future development.

In 2015, there were a total of three professional exhibition venues in Tianjin, with 129,000 square meters of indoor exhibition area in total and an average of 43,000 square meters per exhibition venue, to rank 19th among cities in China. The Meijiang Convention and Exhibition Center is the largest professional exhibition venue in Tianjin, with an indoor exhibition area of only 54,000 square meters.

In 2015, 260 exhibitions were held in Tianjin, with a total exhibition area of 3.46 million square meters and an average exhibition area of 13,300 square meters, to rank fifth in China. The number of exhibitions accounted for 2.8% nationally, with the exhibition area accounting for 2.99%. According to statistics, from 2011 to 2015, the number of exhibitions held in Tianjin increased by 11.52% annually on average, and the exhibition area increased by 11.45% annually on average.

9.2.5.2 Tianjin Internationalization Pattern Analysis

The internationalization level is quite low in Tianjin. At the end of 2015, there were no exhibition organizations with UFI certification and the proportion of international exhibitions was quite low, with no overseas exhibition companies in Tianjin or hosting exhibitions there.

The proportion of international exhibitions is quite low. In 2015, there were only three UFI-certified exhibitions, accounting for only 3.9% of the total number of certified exhibitions in China.

No overseas exhibition company has moved into Tianjin's market. Currently, no well-known overseas exhibition companies identified by AUMA have set up a subsidiary company or joint venture in Tianjin.

No overseas exhibition company hosts exhibitions in Tianjin. According to AUMA, of the top 10 exhibition companies with turnover of more than 100 million euros, none have investment projects in Tianjin yet.

9.2.5.3 Tianjin Exhibition Industry Structure Analysis

Exhibition industry development in Tianjin is led by the government, the main development path for the Tianjin exhibition industry in recent years. As a developing trend, the market-oriented operation mode will eventually replace the government's leading exhibitions; however, based on the current situation of Tianjin, government leading will still continue to play a main role in the future development of Tianjin's exhibition industry. At present, the exhibition industry has been developed to the stage of oligopolistic competition; under this circumstance, it will take a quite long time for Tianjin to cultivate a large-scale exhibition brand, which will require the government's coordination and a combination of all kinds of resources to achieve the goal.

9.2.5.4 Tianjin Exhibition Environment Analysis

Tianjin's exhibition industry developed late in the 1990s; the number of exhibitions has increased dramatically, together with an increase in standards, but the exhibition brand is still quite low level. From 2011 to 2015, the number of exhibitions increased by 11.52% annually on average and the exhibition area increased by 11.45% annually on average. Currently, there are only three exhibitions certified by UFI. UFI is the authority of the international exhibition industry, and only the approval of UFI can make an exhibition become a brand.

With regard to the hardware of facilities construction, there are only three professional exhibition venues. In 2003, the Tianjin International Exhibition Center undertook expansion construction, with the exhibition area increasing to 35,000 square meters. Further, in 2003, the Binhai International Convention and Exhibition Center was put into use, with a total area of 98,000 square meters. In 2010, the Meijiang Convention and Exhibition Center was built for the "Summer Davos," with a total area of 98,000 square meters.

Government leading is the main method of Tianjin's exhibition industry development. Among current exhibition organizations, the government still plays the main role, with few professional exhibition companies. The circumstances of having only a few famous exhibitions, more horizontal exhibitions, and severe exhibition theme competition has resulted in a low willingness by domestic and overseas exhibition organizers to hold exhibitions in Tianjin. However, the development of the exhibition industry in Tianjin has been greatly supported by the government, especially with the publication of *Tianjin Exhibition Industry Promotion and Development Methods*, aimed at promoting the development of the exhibition industry in Tianjin by improving and standardizing the exhibition industry development environment, and establishing special exhibition industry development funds mainly to support key exhibition projects and encourage famous exhibition brands at home and abroad to hold exhibitions in Tianjin, which will further benefit the development of the exhibition industry in Tianjin.

To sum up, currently the development of the exhibition industry in Tianjin is mainly government led, which, on the one hand, is lend great support by the government and policy, but, on the other hand, may negatively influence sustainable development in the future for lack of market base. Because of the late development of the exhibition industry in Tianjin, even though it developed quickly in recent years, it severely lacks international exhibition brands and standardization. With government support and strong demand, both the hardware and software environment of the exhibition industry in Tianjin will gradually be developed and promoted.

9.2.6 FUTURE COMPETITION BETWEEN KEY MICE CITIES IN CHINA

Based on a qualitative analysis of five key MICE cities – Beijing, Shanghai, Guangzhou, Shenzhen, and Tianjin – change trends in the competition pattern of these five cities can be identified, as shown in the figure below. The blue box represents the current scale of the exhibition industry, and the red box represents the forecast of the future exhibition industry scale (see Figure 9.8).

(1) **Shanghai – continues to lead:** The gap with other cities is enlarged.
(2) **Guangzhou – limited development:** Facing the pressure of competition from the venue construction in various cities to break through the development limitation and facing the great potential of convention and exhibition development in cities, Guangzhou's exhibition

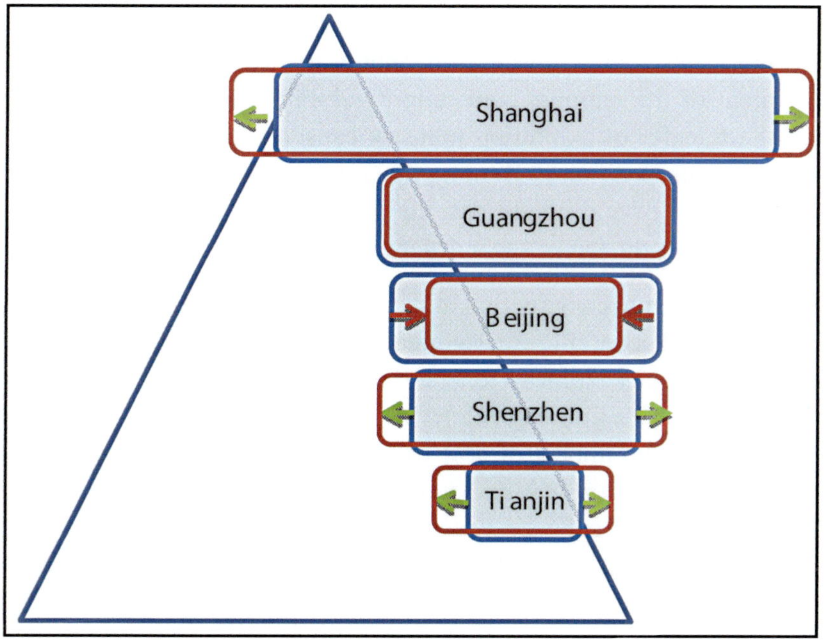

FIGURE 9.8 Future competition between key domestic MICE cities.

industry expansion is affected, and even the phenomenon of exhibition projects diversion occurs.

(3) **Beijing – gradual transfer:** Affected by its unique position of being in the political center, the Beijing exhibition industry faces a series of factors that are adverse to its development. Due to the construction of the Tianjin National Convention and Exhibition Center project, the industry is confronted with a trend toward transfer.

(4) **Shenzhen – potential to ascend to the first echelon:** The exhibition industry is in a rapid development stage. With the construction of an international convention and exhibition center and the breakthrough of the bottleneck of total available exhibition area, the competitiveness of the Shenzhen exhibition industry is being greatly enhanced. Shenzhen has the potential to become a first-tier MICE city. Therefore, the research prejudgment is that the Shenzhen International Convention and Exhibition Center is expected to help Shenzhen ascend to the status of a first-tier MICE city, together with Shanghai, Guangzhou, and Beijing, reorganizing the development pattern of the domestic exhibition industry.

(5) **Tianjin – potential to enter the second echelon:** The Tianjin exhibition industry is still at the primary stage. With Tianjin's powerful industrial foundation and advantage in heavy industry, the settlement of the national convention and exhibition center project, and the transfer of exhibition industry caused by too much urban function superposition in Beijing, the Tianjin exhibition industry has the opportunity and conditions for great promotion in the future, and may enter the list of second-tier MICE cities.

In general, venue construction in various places, changes in the domestic and international economic environment, as well as the comprehensive competitiveness of a city will lead to a new round of reshuffling in the domestic exhibition industry's future development pattern.

Determining the impact of new exhibition halls on the development of the domestic exhibition industry and the venue supply structure as well as how operators might enhance strengths and seize strategic leading position will become key priorities in the future development of exhibition halls.

9.3 QUALITATIVE ANALYSIS OF THE EXHIBITION INDUSTRY COMPETITIVENESS OF HONG KONG AND MACAO IN CHINA

9.3.1 HONG KONG

9.3.1.1 Hong Kong Market Saturation Analysis

The structural shortage in Hong Kong's professional conference, convention, and exhibition venues, led by insufficient professional exhibition area, locational conditions, and uneven support service between the venues, has restricted the incremental development of the Hong Kong exhibition industry; the Hong Kong exhibition market has reached its saturation state.

(1) **There exist two professional venues in Hong Kong:** the Hong Kong Convention and Exhibition Center and the Asia World-Expo. Together, the area available for indoor exhibition is 152,000 square meters.
(2) **Hong Kong venue utilization is close to limitation; however, it is still the main venue of the Hong Kong professional exhibition at this stage:** The conference and exhibition center has strong location

advantages, located in the Wan Chai District of downtown Hong Kong facing the world-famous Victoria Harbor, with shopping, dining, business, leisure, and other supporting services readily available. The Hong Kong Convention and Exhibition Center, with an indoor exhibition area of 66,000 square meters, held a total of 1,113 events from July 2014 to June 2015, of which there were 104 regular exhibitions, 38 large conferences, 66 recreational events, 409 banquets, and 489 other events.[12] In peak Hong Kong exhibition periods (from mid-March to mid-May, and October to mid-November), exhibition rental rates are high and the venue is unable to accommodate new exhibitions.

(3) **AsiaWorld-Expo has supporter status as a Hong Kong convention and exhibition venue, and its utilization by professional trade exhibitions is relatively low**: AsiaWorld-Expo is located near the Hong Kong airport, and is more than half an hour's drive from the Hong Kong Convention and Exhibition Center. In 2015, total leased area was 2,833,000 square meters and more than 300 large-scale exhibition events were held, of which only 33 were professional exhibitions, with the rest being conferences, concerts, sporting events, all kinds of cultural and recreational events, and other convention and exhibition events.

9.3.1.2 Hong Kong Internationalization Pattern Analysis

Based mainly on industrial import and export demand in Asia, the exhibition industry in Hong Kong has a high degree of internationalization. The driving force of the internationalization of the exhibition industry in Hong Kong is not in brand transplantation by transnational exhibition groups or exhibitions, but in Hong Kong's export-oriented economic and trade system, buttressed by its long history of a free port policy, overseas market expansion needs, sound legal systems in Europe and America, and other conditions. This is also the core competitiveness of the development of the exhibition industry in Hong Kong.

[12] Source: *Hong Kong Convention and Exhibition Center data flash*; the official statistics for the Hong Kong Convention and Exhibition Center cover the period from July 1, 2014 to June 30, 2015.

TABLE 9.9 Types of Hong Kong Exhibitions

Category		Characteristic	Example
Local consumer show		An exhibition for the local public consumer market	Book exhibition, delicacy exhibition, wedding banquet / wedding exhibition, video games / cartoon exhibition, pet exhibition
International trade exhibition	Import type	By taking advantage of the geographical position of Hong Kong, international exhibitors account for a certain proportion to attract buyers of local and neighboring regions	HOFEX food and beverage exhibition, electronic exhibition, textile exhibition, building materials exhibition, beauty exhibition, environmental protection exhibition
	Export type	Most exhibitors are Asian light industrial consumer goods manufacturers. Mainly aimed at overseas markets.	Clock and watch exhibition, electronic exhibition, gift exhibition, jewelry exhibition, toy exhibition, fashion exhibition, household goods exhibition

Source: Hong Kong Exhibition Industry Association, 2015.

(1) **As Asia's city of conventions and exhibitions, Hong Kong has a high degree of internationalization and is far ahead of the other five cities.** The Hong Kong exhibition scene is composed of two parts: local consumer shows and international trade exhibitions (see Table 9.9). The international trade exhibition divides into import and export. The Hong Kong exhibition industry is not limited to local trade in Hong Kong for domestic exhibition; it also provides a trade service platform for international exhibition merchants. With the shift of global manufacturing to Asia, and by virtue of its regional advantages, Hong Kong developed an international trade exhibition system constructed on import exhibitions of industrial materials and technologies required locally and in Asia, and export exhibitions of light industrial consumer goods to meet procurement demands of international buyers outside of Asia.

(2) **Exhibitors and merchants in the Hong Kong exhibition structure are characterized by a high degree of internationalization.** According to statistics of the Hong Kong Tourism Board for

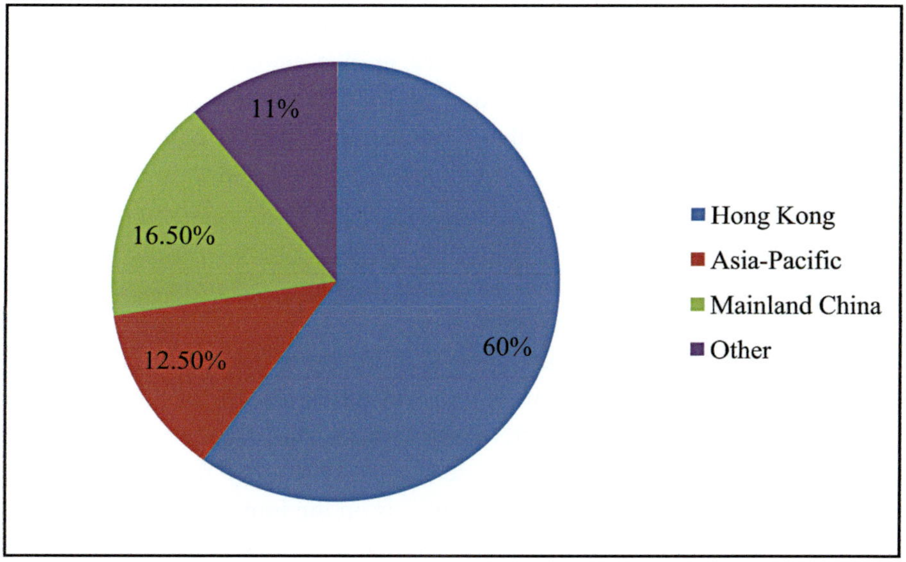

FIGURE 9.9 Hong Kong trade exhibition buyers by regional composition.

exhibitions and conferences, in 2015, 12.5% of buyers came from Asia-Pacific and 11% came from other countries (see Figure 9.9). *According to the interview:* "So we are based on consumer goods for procurement, such as gifts, toys, clothing, consumer electronics, jewelry; origin place is mainly from Greater China, and exhibitors are from Greater China. Their factories are in the mainland, ownership is likely to belong to various countries and its origin place is in mainland."

(3) **There are 19 projects in Hong Kong invested in by overseas transnational exhibition groups, which is slightly more than that in Guangzhou. Among these, UBM Asia has the largest number, at 13.** Thus, the trend of internationalization in the exhibition industry in Hong Kong is not driven by the presence of foreign investment brands. Although the Hong Kong exhibition industry is mainly focus on local brands, the exhibition industry is still highly internationalized. Overseas market development needs, free trade port policy, and a light industry history are the important elements of formation. Hong Kong covers an area of 1,070 square kilometers, equivalent to only 14.4% of Guangzhou's area (7,434 square kilometers), and

has a population of 7 million. As an independent economic system, the local demand from Hong Kong is not large. Coupled with the transfer of manufacturing industry, market demand is limited. Under this geographical and historical environment, Hong Kong's overseas market demand continued to expand and shape the highly export-oriented economy back to the Chinese mainland and the Asian region. Adapting to the needs of Hong Kong's expansion of the international market, the Hong Kong exhibition industry has become an important platform for international trade in Hong Kong. Exhibitors and buyers are mainly international customers.

(4) **Hong Kong's free trade system is an important driving force for the internationalization of conventions and exhibitions. It is also one of the core competitiveness factors that other regions cannot copy.** Hong Kong's free trade system is mainly reflected in three aspects: a) It does not set the controls on the import and export trade. Except for the control of arms, drugs, and international agreements and other relevant provisions of international obligations fulfillment, as well as food hygiene and rice trade controls to maintain the security of Hong Kong, all other import and export goods are not interfered with. b) No tariff barriers. c) The procedures of import and export are simple, with only the need to submit the declaration form for memorandum to the Hong Kong customs. The free trade system is a great convenience for organizers, exhibitors, and customers. This helps to form the strong attraction to international exhibitions.

<u>According to the interview:</u>

Hong Kong is a free port and all exhibits are exempt from customs duties. All exhibits can cross the border except for contraband, which is a great convenience to enrich the exhibits category greatly. Macao is also one of the free ports.

Hong Kong was once a city with developed manufacturing in its history, which it began to transfer to the Pearl River Delta in the 1980s. Under the export-oriented economy and free trade system, coupled with its status as an international financial center, a sound legal system in Europe and the United States, and other soft power, Hong Kong became the most suitable trading center for the circulation of capital in the Asian region. The outstanding trading image and the image of a traditional manufacturing industry base further strengthened the international competitiveness of the Hong Kong exhibition industry by centering it on international consumable procurement, so that the degree of internationalization in the Hong Kong exhibition industry took the lead.

9.3.1.3 Hong Kong Exhibition Industry Structure Analysis

Hong Kong has more than 100 exhibition service suppliers based on its excellent convention and exhibition foundation and resources. Many branches or subsidiaries of transnational exhibition companies or groups have been set up in Hong Kong, and an international exhibition industry chain has been formed.[13] The exhibition industry format of Hong Kong has the following characteristics:

(1) **Marketization competition environment.** The development of the Hong Kong exhibition industry is completely driven by marketization forces. The government does not attend to exhibitions. The Hong Kong exhibition industry is composed almost entirely of local enterprises, foreign-funded enterprises, and the Hong Kong Trade Development Council, at proportions of 50%, 20%, and 26%, respectively. These three represent a triopoly.

(2) **Oligopolistic economy of the small number of convention and exhibition enterprises (see Figure 9.10).** Some 68% of conventions and exhibitions in Hong Kong are organized by eight convention and exhibition enterprises or organizations. Of the 46 convention and exhibition organizations that held exhibitions in 2013, 38 organizations just held one or two exhibitions, accounting for 82%.[14] Among the eight organizations that have held more than two exhibitions, five are local enterprises, two are foreign-funded enterprises, and one is the Hong Kong Trade Development Council. Competitiveness among local enterprises is strong. The Hong Kong Trade Development Council, Global Sources, and UBM Asia are the organizations of Hong Kong that have held the most exhibitions.

(3) **The market advantage of the Hong Kong Trade Development Council is large, and the development space for private enterprise is small.** The predecessor of the Hong Kong Trade Development

---

[13]General Situation of Development of the Hong Kong Exhibition Industry, Hong Kong Exhibition Industry Association.

[14]At present, the Hong Kong Trade Development Council has not updated the latest data for 2014 and 2015; relevant data in 2013 can be used for making the situational judgment.

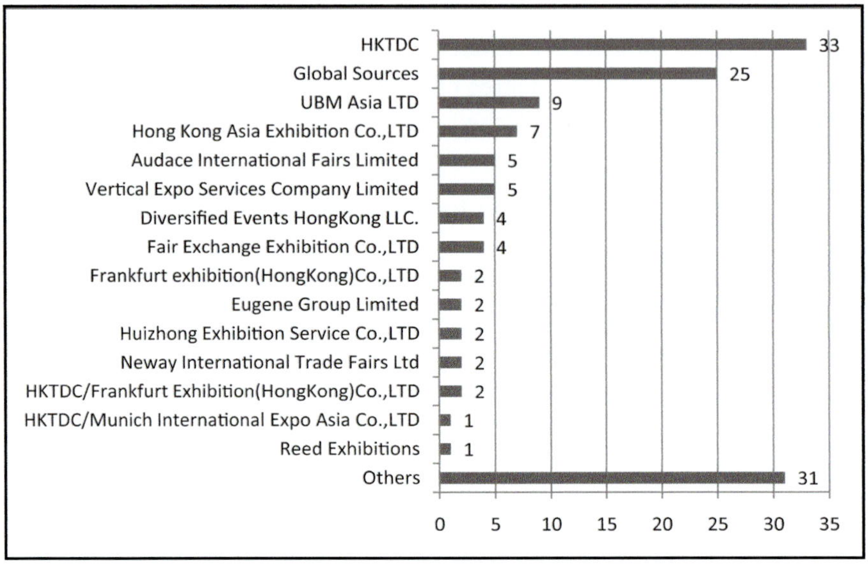

FIGURE 9.10 Distribution diagram of exhibitions organized by all convention and exhibition enterprises of Exhibition scheduling of the Hong Kong Convention and Exhibition Center and exhibition scheduling of Asia World-Expo, 2013.

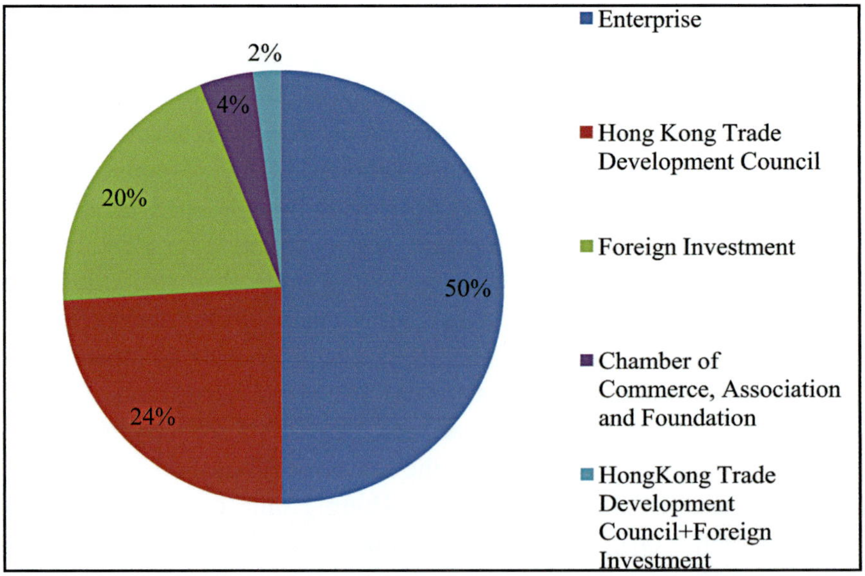

FIGURE 9.11 Market shares of various convention and exhibition enterprises of Hong Kong, calculated as per convention and exhibition projects. Source: Exhibition scheduling of the Hong Kong Convention and Exhibition Center, and exhibition scheduling of Asia World-Expo, 2013.

Council (HKTDC) is the subordinate department of the Industrial and Commercial Administration, the statutory organization authorized by the Hong Kong government at present to conduct trade promotion globally and implement enterprise management (see Figure 9.11). A total of 85% of expenditure of the HKTDC is from its own operation; 15% is from governmental subsidy. It is a nonprofit organization. Integrating the international network resources promoted in its many years aimed at advancing the development of mid- and small-sized enterprises of Hong Kong, the HKTDC has become the one organization that has held the most exhibitions in Hong Kong. International networking and nonprofitability are core competitive aspects of exhibition development by the HKTDC. Other convention and exhibition enterprises cannot be compared. It has set up over 40 offices worldwide. With the accumulation of many years of commercial resources, it is difficult for other local convention and exhibition organizations to surpass. By operating as a non-profit and promoting mid- and small-sized enterprise, the HKTDC has overcome the defects of general market operation. It is difficult to affect the lead status of the HKTDC in the global exhibition industry due to those two factors, which has reduced the market confidence of local convention and exhibition enterprises in Hong Kong to a certain extent. In addition, market direction is adjusted to overseas markets such as the Chinese mainland.

(4) **Internationalization of the exhibition industry.** Several famous organizers set up headquarters in Hong Kong in 2015 for organizing events in Hong Kong and the Chinese mainland. Six companies among the top 10 exhibition companies identified by AUMA with a global business volume of more than Euro 100 million have set up subsidiaries in Hong Kong. The HKTDC is a unique organizer whose global business volume is higher than Euro 100 million in Hong Kong. Business volume in 2014 was Euro 2.225 billion. At the same time, it is also one of two companies identified by AUMA in Asian-Pacific regions.

9.3.1.4 Hong Kong Exhibition Environment Analysis

(1) **With its free port history, advanced infrastructure, and sound European and American legal systems and arbitration center, Hong Kong has become one of the cities with a superior environment for hosting exhibitions in Asia.** In recent years, the Hong Kong government's support for the exhibition industry has further enhanced the situation. The government's support has focused on the creation of a hosting exhibition environment. In recent years, it began to enhance capital support, but that did not attract convention and exhibition projects in the manner of direct financial contribution. Hong Kong's exhibition industry mainly operates through private convention and exhibition enterprises, and the government does not get involved in exhibition hosting. In 2008, the Hong Kong government allotted 0.15 billion HKD for the development of the exhibition industry over a 5-year period. The fund is specially planned by the "MEHK Hong Kong Meeting and Exhibition Extending Department" as a whole and is dedicated to Hong Kong's convention and exhibition promotion, one-stop service provision, and the enhancement of exhibition merchants' travel experience.

(2) **In terms of hard conditions for hosting exhibitions, Hong Kong is a transportation hub of Asia and equipped with first-class international communications, logistics, airport, port, and transportation facilities, and other infrastructure.** Hong Kong is one of the important ports around the world. In 2012, the port throughput was 23.126 million containers. At the same time, it is also an aviation hub, with 180 airlines and waypoints, of which, 136 are international waypoints. Half of the world's population can arrive in Hong Kong within 5 hours. Hong Kong has also built two specialized convention and exhibition venues, whose service quality is universally praised. The surrounding service support facilities of the Hong Kong Convention and Exhibition Center are complete. The high level of support and the convenience of transportation and logistics make Hong Kong well-endowed to overcome the basic hard conditions to host exhibitions.

(3) **In terms of the soft environment for hosting exhibitions, important components for Hong Kong are its free port policy, its "one**

nation, two systems" principle, a complete European and American legal system, an arbitration system, and convention and exhibition theme protection. These are the core elements of competitiveness to attract international investment.

The free port policy, which has lasted for 200 years, is an important basis for the free economy and trade in Hong Kong. Today, Hong Kong is the freest economic system in the world, continuing to hold first place in the ranks of global economic freedom jointly published by the Heritage Foundation and the Wall Street Journal for 19 years. In 2013, Hong Kong scored 89.3 among 177 economies, and though it fell by 0.6 points in the last year, it was still the highest around the globe.

Under the "one nation, two systems" policy, the political system and style are quite connected with foreign countries. Foreign investment does not need to adapt to a new system, thus reducing the possibility of non-acclimatization. Hong Kong inherited Libreville economy during the UK's colonization, with the dynamic commercial and trading environment of the market. A sound commercial and trading system was established. The open and free market environment greatly enhanced the industry atmosphere for the exhibition industry.

The connectivity and guarantee of a sound European and American legal system provide a systematic environment for the development of the exhibition industry. On the one hand, it significantly reduced legal systematic barriers between Hong Kong and foreign countries, creating a strong adaptability to international investment and being very attractive to international capital. On the other hand, due to the trading history established in the UK and US over years, the legal system thereof provided a sound guarantee to trading industry.

The Hong Kong International Arbitration Center has been established for over 25 years, based on an international vision and a highly-developed legal and commercial structure. Since then, it has become a leading dispute settlement service institution in Asia. In 2011, the Hong Kong International Arbitration Center handled 502 private cases, of which 275 were arbitration cases, 127 were disputes of domain name, and 100 were mediated cases. The total amount involved came to 3.8 billion dollars. The advancement of arbitration services has provided a more ordered and normative market environment for the development of the exhibition industry.

The theme protection of Hong Kong's exhibition industry is guarded by venue, which provides a strict three-month theme protection to professional exhibitions. Although there is no specific communication and coordination between the venues, due to the risks brought about by the special distance between the two major exhibition venues (one located near Wanchai, and the other, at the airport; a distance of a 30-minutes car drive) and the influence of the differentiation of the venue positioning, cut-throat competition such as hosting rival exhibitions at the same time is rare and industry self-discipline prevails to a certain extent.

With plans to protect the value of intellectual property rights by making relevant laws and establishing a "fast action group" targeted at the exhibition industry, both customs and organizers will provide relevant intellectual property rights protective measures.

In conclusion, the environment for hosting exhibitions in Hong Kong has obvious international appeal, which is also the core driving force behind the continuous development of the exhibition industry there.

9.3.2 MACAO

9.3.2.1 Macao Market Saturation Analysis

At present, the development of the Macao venue is ahead of the convention and exhibition market and is not saturated; there is a very large space to introduce increments.

(1) **The Macao exhibition industry started late, and the current gross of the exhibition industry is low.** Macao as a venue had a total area of 74,700 square meters in 2015; although the overall number of annual conferences and exhibitions held was 831, only 61 exhibitions were held in the whole year, accounting for 7.3% of the convention and exhibition events.[15]

(2) **At present, the Macao venues are mainly hotels and government public facilities, without professional convention and exhibition venues and dominated by multifunctional halls and conference halls;** these include Macau's grand hotels, a tourism event center, the Macao Cultural Center, Macao Science Center, and Macau Tower, etc. Among them, the Venetian Macau exhibition center is the main professional convention and exhibition venue in Macao, with 75,000

[15]Source: Macao Convention & Exhibition Industry Association

square meters of exhibition space. Thus, there is still a lot of room for development.

9.3.2.2 Macao Internationalization Pattern Analysis

The Macao exhibition industry mainly includes consumer shows, comprehensive exhibitions, and entertainment exhibitions. The sector entertained 5,607 exhibitors and 144,866 professional visitors in 2015. Only 19.6% of exhibitors and 10.5% of professional visitors are from regions other than Macao, the Chinese mainland, and Hong Kong. Top 10 exhibition groups whose annual income is more than 10 million euros as summarized by AUMA in 2015 are not located in Macao. It can be seen that the influence area of the Macao exhibition industry market is still limited to the local region, the Chinese mainland, and the Hong Kong market, and that internationalization has a large enhancement space.

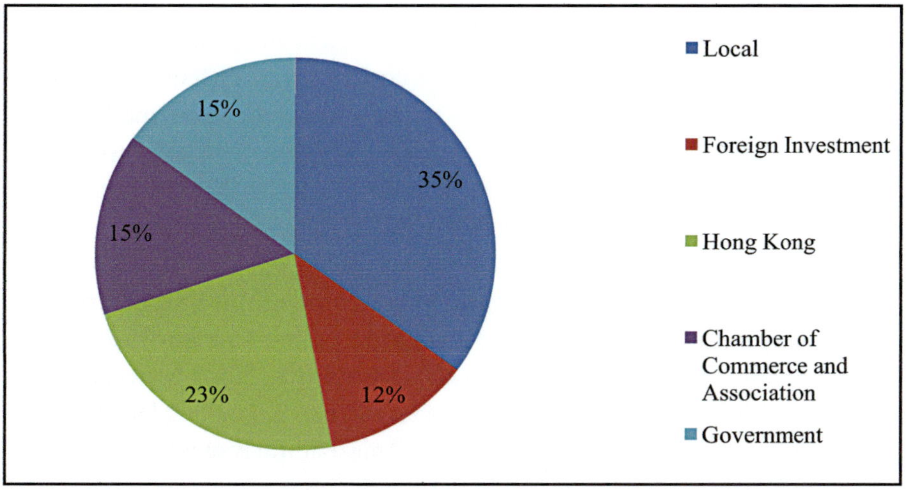

FIGURE 9.12 Diagram of market shares of various convention and exhibition enterprises of Macao, calculated according to convention and exhibition projects. Source: Macao convention and exhibition website.

9.3.2.3 Macao Exhibition Industry Structure Analysis

Macao is in the initial stage of its exhibition industry, and the degree of specialization for the exhibition industry is not high. Still being in the initial stage, the structure of the exhibition industry is diversified only by non-consumable exhibitions, according to the statistics of Macao. The sector is composed of government, local Macao enterprises, Hong Kong enterprises, and foreign-funded enterprises (see Figure 9.12). Few Guangzhou enterprises will organize exhibitions in Macao. Market forces of several parties are relatively even, with no leading force yet. However, the exhibition industry of Macao is still at its preliminary development stage: some organizers are not professional exhibition organizers; they are mainly large groups, hotels, and cultural transmission companies.

9.3.2.4 Macao Exhibition Environment Analysis

Macao's exhibition industry started just recently in the Pearl River Delta, and both the soft and hard conditions of the convention and exhibition sector need to be developed.

(1) **In terms of hard conditions, transportation and logistics industries are the weaknesses of Macao.** Macao airports lack direct airlines, as most flights must be changed in Hong Kong; it is also inferior in port freight volume and bearing capacity to surrounding cities' ports such as Suigong dock. Macao differs greatly from Hong Kong and Guangzhou in terms of transportation and logistics. In terms of hardware facilities for conventions and exhibitions, the Venetian Convention and Exhibition Center in Macao is the only professional exhibition facility, with an available exhibition area of 77,000 square meters.

(2) **In terms of the soft environment for conventions and exhibitions, Macao has also inherited a free port policy and has the characteristics of high economic freedom similar to Hong Kong.** In 2011, in a global economy freedom index, Macao ranked No. 19 of the 179 global economies, and No. 5 in the Asia-Pacific region. However, the industries in Macao are not diversified, and it is not as outstanding as Hong Kong in terms of its commercial and trading environment. Benefiting from the rapid development of tourism, Macao has positioned

the city as a world tourism and leisure center, and its industry greatly depends on the gaming industry and tourism. Because of this, the city's environment emphasizing leisure and ignoring commerce and trading makes Macao more suitable for holding conventions, impeding the development of exhibition events. As the leisure nature of the gaming industry and tourism is in conflict with the atmosphere of commercial and trading conventions and exhibitions, the trade side is negatively affected. Thus, being a world tourism and leisure center actually becomes a negative element in the development of Macao's exhibition industry. Under this environment for hosting exhibitions, the exhibition industry plays a supporting role in Macao's economic development; Macao's exhibition industry is mainly characterized by conference industry development, which is in sharp contrast with Guangzhou and Hong Kong.

However, Macao's exhibition industry is important to the government. It has given powerful policy support, which mainly includes the establishment of professional institutions, project cooperation, and funding support. In 2010, Macao established the Exhibition Industry Development Committee to specifically be in charge of the development of Macao's exhibition industry, including formulating measures, convention and exhibition services, and outward promotion. In 2011, the Macao Economic Services Bureau (known by its Portuguese initials of DSE) established a convention and exhibition comprehensive service department, a convention and exhibition policy development group, and a foreign cooperation work group. Thus, we can see the degree of emphasis laid on Macao's convention and exhibition sector by the government. In terms of cooperation projects, the central government encourages Macao to cooperate with other cities in the Pearl River Delta region under a *Closer Economic Partnership Arrangement (CEPA)* cooperation frame. In September 2012, the national Commerce Department and Macao Economy and Finance Department signed the *Agreement on Improving Cooperation in the Exhibition Industry* to encourage both parties to provide policy support for exhibition industry cooperation in funding, customs, tax, etc. The two parties jointly developed several brand convention and exhibition events in Macao, promoting the growth of Macao's exhibition industry and its surrounding industries. In terms of funding support, on Jan. 1, 2013, Macao's *Convention and Exhibition Event Incentive Plan* was formally introduced, providing a series of funding support for convention and exhibition events reaching its standards, composed of basic assistance and financial support. The basic assistance includes assisting in publicity, coordinating government department connections, and assisting in competitive bidding. The financial support includes accommodation subsidies, food and beverage and accommodation subsidies, hosting honorable guests' subsidies, publicity and promotion subsidies, and simultaneous interpreting subsidies. The support of exhibitions includes subsidies for location rental, accommodation, hardware, opening and closing ceremonies, qualified buyers, logistics, promotion and publicity, etc. Macao's convention and exhibition incentive plan is the most powerful fund support of the three cities of Guangdong, Hong Kong, and Macao, and it is an important advantage in the development of Macao's exhibition industry. Additionally, Macao is one of the cities, that is, most closely related to Portuguese-speaking countries. This also provides an advantageous international stage for its publicity and marketing in convention and exhibition.

To sum up, Macao's exhibition industry environment is more suitable for the development of the conference industry, but the great fund support from the nation and the Macao government has a stimulating effect on Macao's exhibition industry that cannot be ignored.

9.4 DEVELOPMENTS AND TRENDS OF EXHIBITION AND VENUE

Currently, the exhibition industry is transforming from the sales exhibition to one of industrial creation. The communication and exchange between enterprises and the spread of new knowledge have become two characteristics of convention and exhibition events. **Venue, as the carrier of convention and exhibition events, is going through an upgrade from 4.0 Era to 5.0 Era.** Looking back on the development history of the global exhibition industry in the last 200 years and on the development and changes of venue in China, 5.0 Era has the following features:

Diversified carrying capacity, such as exhibitions, conventions, and large-scale events, etc., and the capacity for allowing many kinds of events to be held simultaneously.

Communication and interaction for industrial creation are taken as functional orientation, and more space is required for social communication, interaction, and exchange.

Further, more emphasis is placed on the experience and benefits of venue users such as organizers, exhibitors, and professional visitors. Customer

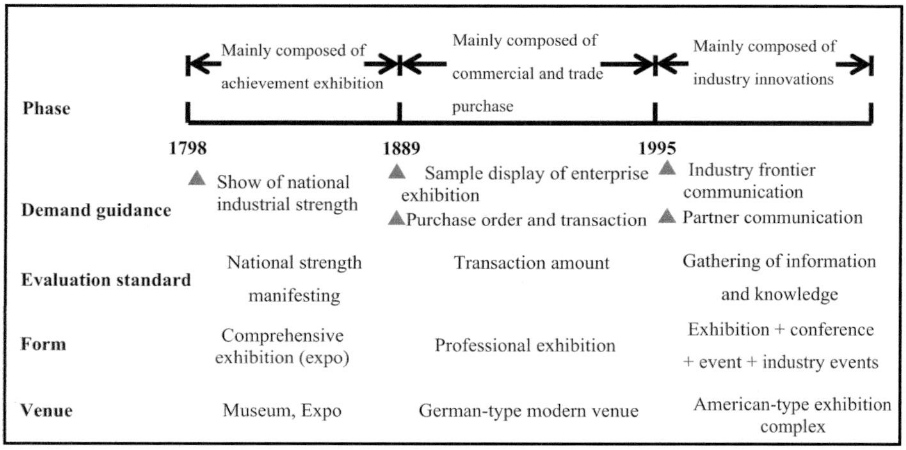

FIGURE 9.13 Development and evolution process figure of the global exhibition industry.

performance evaluation and management is a new development trend (see Figure 9.13).

9.4.1 FUNCTIONAL EVOLUTION OF EXHIBITIONS: FROM TRADING TO INDUSTRIAL INNOVATION

9.4.1.1 Fairs period focusing on achievement exhibition (1798–1889)

In the 18th and 19th centuries, the purely demonstrative art exhibition as an achievement exhibition and the pure publicity national industry exhibition appeared. Exhibitions at that time focused on the exhibition of national achievements.

The industrial fairs of modern times derived from the French Public Fair for Industrial Products in 1798, which was the first national industrial fair organized by the government in the world. In the years following, industrial fairs featured a strong sense of demonstration and publicity; a rigorous organization system appeared, driven by the industrial revolution. Many countries imitated France's lead to hold industrial exhibitions. However, the exhibitions at that time were only domestically oriented and there were almost no foreign exhibitors due to the popularity of protectionism.

The Great Exhibition of Industry of All Nations, held in 1851,was an important milestone in the history of the global exhibition industry and the

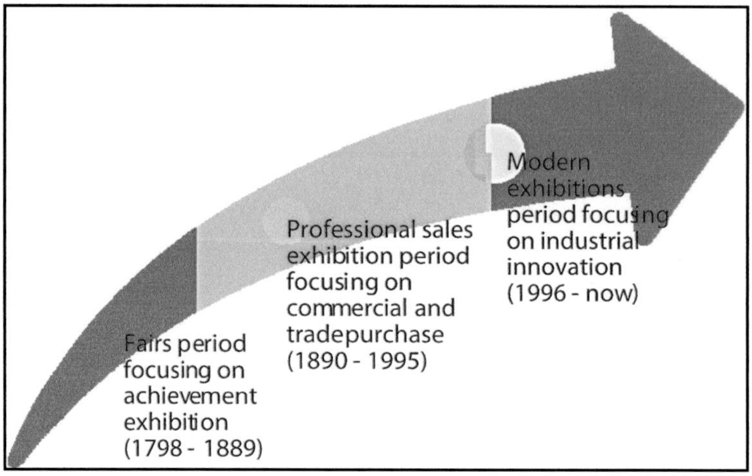

FIGURE 9.14 Functional evolution of exhibitions.

first international exhibition in the world. This exhibition intended to facilitate trading and cooperation among countries and share global resources and markets through the exhibition events – the initial purpose of modern exhibitions. It was the precursor of the current World Exposition.

In general, exhibitions at this stage were used to demonstrate the industrial power of a country. They were led by national governments and broke boundaries between countries for international communication, but lacked the commercial and trading market function.

9.4.1.2 Professional Sales Exhibition Period Focusing on Commercial and Trade Purchase (1890–1995)

After the industrial revolution, the commodity economy was promoted to an important position in country development. The commercial and trade function of exhibitions was highlighted, and the exhibitions transformed from comprehensive ones to professional ones.

The beginning of the modern exhibition industry is represented by the first sample exhibition held in Leipzig, Germany. The sample fair featured both the marketability of bazaars and the demonstrative function of industrial exhibitions. Adopting the method of demonstration and with the purpose of transactions, it was the earliest form of modern commercial and trade exhibitions.

After World War II, professional exhibitions appeared and developed. World War I had a great impact on the economies of many countries and had damaged the international free trade environment. The countries looked for a new approach to facilitate the development of their economies. The comprehensive trading exhibition and fair emerged at the right moment. During 1916–1919, many countries held exhibition events. Among these exhibitions, the international fair of French was the most successful. After World War II, economic reconstruction and educational advancements in science and technology became the critical work of countries. Comprehensive exhibitions were difficult to adapt to the demands of local markets as industry upgraded more rapidly and the division of labor was refined. Thus, the professional exhibition became the leading form of the exhibition industry in 1960s. The professional exhibition organizes the exhibitors and visitors and limits the accessibility to the public by focusing on a certain industry. It can reflect a certain industry and the overall development conditions of related industries, and has a strong market function.

People at this stage deemed the exhibition as a place to sell a product or service and sign a contract. The purpose of participating in the exhibition was oriented to a successful deal, and the return on investment (e.g., orders submitted) was the main criterion to evaluate an exhibition (see Table 9.10). Exhibitions at this time focused on the key administration of customers (KAM), which can be divided into the recognition of key potential users, customer penetration and negotiation, cooperation and communication, establishment of cooperative relations, seeking for new cooperative opportunities, etc. The exhibitions at this time can be classified as having three functional levels, taking the exhibitors as the core, namely a sales function, a marketing function, and a network function.[16] The exhibitors sell the products not only to the customers, but also target industry analysts, purchasing influencers, and suppliers. In addition, the exhibitors engage in creating diversified relations with competitors, government officers, partners, exhibition organizers, and the industry association.

In brief, "professional" and "commerce and trade" are the significant characteristics of this stage, and the two characteristics are maintained until recently. Since then, the success of an exhibition has relied on the professional

---

[16] Rosson, P., & Seringhaus, F. H. (1995). Visitor and Exhibitor Interaction at Industrial Trade Fairs [J]. Journal of Business Research, 32, 81–90.

TABLE 9.10 Reasons for Participating in an Exhibition of Exhibitors and Model for Development Stages of Customer Relations

Development stage	Reasons for visiting an exhibition (%)	Reasons for participating in an exhibition (ranked by degree of importance)
Pre-KAM: Identify key potential customers	Find new companies (12%), carry out commercial contact (6%), compare products and services (7%)	Meet new customers, release new products, meet new distributors, promote old products
Early KAM: Customer penetration, detect where the supplier is popular	Get technology or product information (21%)	Contact old customers and distributors, strengthen company image, get orders
Mid KAM: Realize cooperation, strengthen the position of a popular supplier	Discuss specific questions/ communicate with experts (10%)	Contact old customers and distributors
Cooperation establishment: Build the cooperative consciousness, create a common culture, target customers	Discuss specific questions/ communicate with experts (10%)	Contact old customers and distributors
Interactive: Continue to improve, share the benefits, semi-fusion status	Without real function. At this stage, the enterprises are close to each other. They even share marketing actions, including the display on the exhibition	Without real function
Dissolution: Separation	Seek new customers, new products, new development, and new companies	Meet new customers and distributors, get orders

Source: Blythe, 2002[17].

visitor to a larger extent. Learning about the demands of visitors, budgets, and the evaluation of exhibition benefits is quite important to exhibitors and the organizers of exhibitions. Such concepts transform traditional neighborhood exhibitions to production-based and visitor-oriented exhibitions.

9.4.1.3 Modern Exhibitions Period Focusing on Industrial Innovation (1996–Now)

Following traditional resources such as capital and land, knowledge becomes the critical resource of enterprises in obtaining competitiveness.

[17]Blythe, J. Using Trade Fairs in Key Account Management[J]. Industrial Marketing Management, 2002, 31: 627–635.

The knowledge-based economy is the hot subject of the world's current economy. Meanwhile, the function of exhibitions has transformed from commercial and trade purchase to one of industrial innovation.

First, under the backdrop of the knowledge economy, international professional exhibitions have become hotspot carriers for the global spread of industry knowledge. The large-scale international exhibition is becoming the gathering hall and arena of suppliers and buyers for whole industries and even the site of the generation of industry standards. The flagship exhibition is often the annual event of an industry. It can attract global attention and even lead the development direction of the industry in the future. The functions of an exhibition have gone far beyond the meaning of marketing channels. The exhibition shows the cutting-edge findings and products of an industry. Nonselling events such as comparing products, learning about competitors, testing the market response, and collecting industry information are carried out in the exhibition. It is also an important driving force for the continuous innovation and improvement of enterprises, which will bring a deep influence on the sales plan and strategic decision and policy making of the enterprise in the future. The intangible benefits generated deserve more attention. At the same time, to meet the demands of industrial communication between exhibitors and professional visitors and the demands of obtaining cutting-edge information, the exhibition has begun to transform from the pure exhibition to a form of "exhibition + convention." The exhibition becomes a collecting and distributing center of industry information. It transforms the model of purchasing meeting and trading fair to the modern exhibition. The marketing function is weakened gradually. In a manner of speaking, the exhibition becomes an irreplaceable platform for industrial communication and information spread.

Second, the information obtained through exhibition participation will react on the industry through production decisions of the enterprises and the subsequent research and development generated. In the meantime, the holding of the flagship exhibition also becomes a sign that a country or a region takes a lead in the industry, which is greatly beneficial to the establishment of national and regional industry image and the industrial position. Exhibitions play a significant role in facilitating industrial innovation regardless of whether it is on the industrial level or on the regional and national level. Multifunctional features combining exhibition, convention, and events of the large-scale exhibition become more significant. The international large exhibition is becoming the gathering hall and arena of the suppliers and buyers of the whole industry and even the site generator of industry standards.

Third, with the changes in the functions of exhibitions, the forms of exhibitions become more diversified as well. The convention and exhibition events do not take a single form anymore as majority, but provide a number of conventions, forums, and awarding events according to communications between the exhibitors and the professional visitors and the latest trend of an industry. The Frankfurt Book Fair is called the "Mecca of the World Publishing Industry." While the Frankfurt Book Fair was held in 2012, all kinds of events, including a high-end convention for the book industry, demonstration events of "future classroom," cosplay cartoon performances, fairs and sales of bookshelf and bookcase, etc., were held at the same time. It fully reflected the concept of the organizers to "show the forming process of a book" for the book fair. **Within the few days of the exhibition, the global or regional outstanding enterprises in the book industry gathered together to discuss the latest trends of industrial development and learn about the latest industry concepts under the leadership of industrial leaders. The forms of facilitating convention with exhibition and of contributing exhibition with convention have become increasingly popular. The convention and exhibition center has higher requirements for the carrying capacity of multiple business formats and the ability of comprehensive service.**

To sum up, the functions of an exhibition have been transformed from commercial and trade purchase to industrial innovation. The exhibition creates an increasingly close relationship with the local industry and generates a relationship of bilateral interaction. As a result, the productive service feature of exhibitions has gained global attraction. The position of exhibitions in the economic development of a country is manifest. The single form of the exhibition has been gradually broken, and the model of "facilitating convention with exhibition and contributing exhibition with convention"has become mainstream to drive industry communication and industrial innovation.

Case 1: America Game Show E3

The game show E3, as the abbreviation of Electronic Entertainment Exhibition, is the largest commercial exhibition of computer games in the world and the largest game convention "Electronic Entertainment Expo/Exposition".

The most attractive point of the E3 game show is the press conferences of large-scale game manufacturers. In the short three days, Sony, Microsoft, and other game manufacturers would launch more than 10 press conferences to show the new games and game hosts. At the press conference, the game designers would demonstrate how to play the game and show its largest selling point. Finally, they would invite the visitors to try the game. Sometimes, you have to line up for several hours for trying to play popular games. For the game host, the demonstration tends to be description and interpretation of the hardware parameters and design optimization.

Besides the press conference, the other important content of E3 is the conferences of insiders. Although the processes of these conferences would not be open to the outsiders, they are more important for the insiders who attend these conferences. These conferences have different functions. Some are held for sharing industry experience, some for business negotiation, and some for study and discussion. That is to say, media reporters, game commentators, game exhibitors, and visitors have different conferences to attend. With press conferences and other conferences, E3 game shows met the demands of the participants for market expansion and experience share.

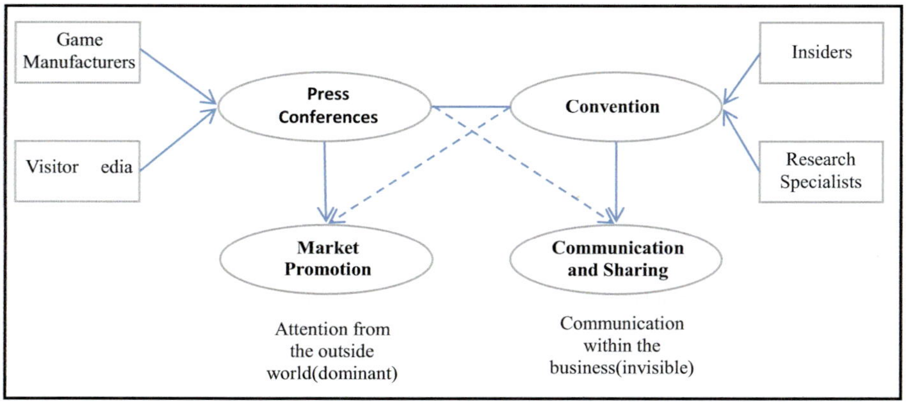

FIGURE 9.15 Operating mechanism of E3 game show.

The following figure shows the main operating method of the E3 game show (see Figure 9.15). It can be seen that the press conferences and the conferences are the two main composition pieces. The main participants of press conferences are game manufacturers and media visitors. The purpose and function of the press conference is warming up for the upcoming games or game hosts. Thus, the various game manufacturers strive to shock their press conferences and impress the visitors to attract extensive attention from the outside world. On the contrary, the main purpose of the conferences is to discuss the development trend of games, share the latest and coolest design concept, and facilitate the development of the whole game industry, because the participants are insiders of the game industry or some researchers. Thus, such conferences do not pay attention to the reaction of outsiders, but the influence on the game industry. The annual advertising video of E3 can certify this opinion, because there are only hot gameplay demos and some COSPLAY scenes, but nothing to do with the conferences. The advertising video is made for the visitors and the common players who cannot access the exhibition, i.e. the “dominant” section. On the other hand, the “hidden” section – conferences – will not appear. Additionally, what is worth mentioning is that the conferences and the press conferences are independent from each other to a large extent, because they are totally coincident in time, and the sections are separated.

Case 2: Germany's Hanover Industrial Exhibition (HANNOVER MESSE)

The German Hanover Industrial Exhibition (HANNOVER MESSE) is a typical representative which is honored as the barometer of the industrial development of the world. Its exhibition theme in 2016 was “industrial integration—find the solutions!”. Around 190,000 visitors from more than 100 countries or regions all over the world were attracted to this exhibition.[17] The new concepts “industry 4.0” and “intelligent plant” in the exhibition generated a focus on the industrial integration.[18] The industry deems that it plays an important role in driving the “fourth industrial revolution.”[19]

[17]Source: Report of German Hanover Industrial Exhibition after exhibition in 2016, official website of Hanover Industrial Expo, website: http://www.hannovermesse.com.cn/Pa/?CID=87

[18]Source: Official website of Hanover Industrial Expo, website: http://www.hannovermesse.de/en/news-trends/integrated-industry-next-steps/

[19]Source: Sohu Securities, Hanover Industrial Expo pushes forward the fourth industrial reform, website: http://stock.sohu.com/20140409/n397921294.shtml

Scenes where various intelligent technologies are applied in the manufacturing industry were shown at the exhibition, which gave a practical experience to the people about industry 4.0. The solutions demonstrated at the exhibition covered from mechanical modification to the integration of complete production lines, while the collection and analysis of big data injected fresh impetus for industrial development. The professional visitors took this opportunity to master and invest in the latest technology to respond to the future challenge.

In the meantime, 101 conferences and special events were held in the exhibition period. In addition, sharing and discussion about cutting-edge topics such as industrial automation, intelligent plant, energy, industrial parts and components, and contracting technology etc. were carried out. Among them, the forum "Industry 4.0 Encounters Industry Internet" is an extremely excellent example. The forum attracted more than 8,000 participants who were urged to learn about the latest technology, standards, and business model of the industrial integration field.

As referred by the committee member Oettinger, "German Hanover Industrial Exhibition is not only the global leading industrial trade fair, but a leader in industrial digitizing. For the European Commission, Hanover Industrial Exhibition has become an important platform for sharing information and ideas and communicating the future development of Europe."

9.4.1.4 SUMMARY OF CHANGES IN EXHIBITION FUNCTIONS

To sum up, the functions of exhibitions have evolved from fairs focusing on achievement exhibition, to professional sales exhibitions focusing on commercial purchase, to modern exhibitions focusing on industrial innovation. With economic development, the revolution of industry demand,and the continuous iterative update, the demands on the functional positioning of the venue change as well. Venue positioning needs to consider the following three factors:

- First, the single development model of venues does not conform to the development trend anymore, and communication-integrating exhibitions, conferences, and events have become the standard configurations for the development of the convention and exhibition center.
- Second, positioned from the integrated development of the economy and the industry, the exhibition industry becomes the mainstream, and the convention and exhibition are not deemed as the industrial island anymore.

- Third, media and intelligent method should be fully utilized to improve the benefits of organizers, exhibitors, and professional visitors.

9.4.2 FUNCTIONAL EVOLUTION OF EXHIBITION VENUE: FROM SINGLE DEMONSTRATION TO COMPREHENSIVE FUNCTIONS

The exhibition venue is the platform and carrier for the development of the exhibition industry. Its functional construction changes with the evolution of the functions and forms of the exhibitions. The development of global exhibitions experienced four stages.[20] Due to the different beginnings and progress of the global exhibition industry, it is difficult to summarize its development from the global level, and this section divides the development history of exhibition halls in China by era.

9.4.2.1 1.0 Era: Oriented by the Demonstration of National Achievements (Before 1959)

In the development stage focusing on the demonstration of national achievements, the exhibition venue mainly acted as a place where the development of national and local industry was demonstrated. It served for the construction and image demonstration of the administrative region. The exhibits were mainly the achievements in various fields covering international economy, trade, science and technology, culture and politics, military, etc. The construction of exhibition venues lacked electrical equipment and did not consider the demand of intense demonstration of industrial trades. Take Beijing Exhibition Center as the representative.

9.4.2.2 2.0 Era: Oriented by the Demonstration of Local Industry and Agriculture (1960–1979)

From the 1960s to the 1970s, to solve the problem of feeding and clothing the whole nation, the country vigorously developed agriculture and industry. At that time, the local agriculture and industry had a strong demand for

[20]Contents of the chapter is based on material arrangement provided by the Zhuhai International Convention and Exhibition Center.

demonstration. Therefore, the venue focused on the construction and operation of the achievements in the agriculture and industry of new China. The venues in the 2.0 era have the following features:

- Chinese style.
- Landscape-style construction and layout, large area occupied, relatively small available exhibition area.
- No specialized and electrified structure and layout.
- Typical examples of venues in the 2.0 era were the National Agricultural Exhibition Center and the Guangdong Agricultural Exhibition Center.

9.4.2.3 3.0 Era: Oriented by Commercial Function Development (1980–2000)

A batch of modern exhibition venues appeared with the occurrence of professional trade shows to meet the functions of product display and purchasing for the trade show. The venues in the 3.0 era have the following features:

- The planning and design and the electrical layout of the modern exhibition venues are relatively complete, which ensure their capacity for undertaking the show of heavy industry products such as machinery.
- Single function and do not have conference and recreational facilities.
- Small available exhibition area and intensive development.
- Most venues located in the central city with convenient transportation.
- Typical examples for 3.0 era venues are SNIEC Shanghai and CIEC (old venue). The occurrence of 4.0 era venues brought down the number of shows for 3.0 era venues and made them transform into consumer shows.

9.4.2.4 4.0 Era: Oriented by Scale Development of Exhibition Area (2000–Now)

With the development of the professional trade show and the increasing emphasis of governments and industries, the trade show is appealing to more professional visitors, which evolves into a trend of scale development. After stepping into the 21st century, regardless of the exhibition area or the capacity for bearing people flow and material flow of 3.0 era, the venue cannot meet the demand of industry development. Therefore, new venues are constructed everywhere, and 4.0 venues emerge at the right moment. 4.0 era venues have the following characteristics:

- Scale-oriented development and exhibition area leads the demand.
- Improved hardware facilities and electrical layout, but intelligent construction and sustainable development are applied less.
- Take the exhibition as the main function, and insufficient auxiliary facilities for conference, food, and beverage.
- Most are far away from the central city at the beginning; thus, they have a high requirement for passenger transport.
- Typical examples at this stage are the China Import & Export Fair Complex Guangzhou Venue (338,000 square meters) and SNIEC Shanghai (200,000 square meters).

9.4.2.5 5.0 Era: Oriented by Diversified Matching Development

Following the tendency of diversified development, the concept of "convention and exhibition center" is stressed continuously. Diversified development is an important characteristic for 5.0 era venues. The diversified development is driven by two forces.

- First, after entering the development period that is oriented by industrial innovation, the communication demand between exhibitors and visitors increases, and the large-scale exhibitions in the form of "exhibition + conference + event" increase as well. Therefore, the diversified facilities have become an important standard for the practicability of venues.
- Second, most venues with a scale development are located in a suburb, far away from the central city. Exhibitors and visitors stay in the venue most of the time. It is especially necessary for the auxiliary facilities of diversified businesses such as food and beverage, office, and recreation to meet the basic demand of exhibitors and professional visitors and to improve the word of mouth. In the 5.0 era, a batch of venues under the concept of a large-scale exhibition complex combining "exhibition, conference, food and beverage, accommodation, and recreation" appears with the following features:
  - Balanced multiformat development of exhibition, conference, food and beverage, accommodation, and recreation.

- Perfect electrical layout, excellent expansion capacity.
- Considers the demand of sustainable development, focus on green and environmental protection, and intelligence.
- Convenient transportation.
- The development of 5.0 era venues in foreign countries takes a lead, especially in Suntec of Singapore and Las Vegas in America.

Case: Suntec Singapore Convention and Exhibition Center

Located in the comprehensive development zone of Marina Center in Singapore, Suntec is one of the largest business development zones. This city center covers 650,000 square meters, including the world's top-level Singapore International Convention and Exhibition Center, four 45-floors and one 18-floors office building, one 4-floors shopping center, and the Fountain of Wealth. The underground parking lot can park 3,200 vehicles. The convention and exhibition building has 6 floors, covering 20,000 square meters. The exhibition hall is on the 4th floor, and the non-column convention center is on the 6th floor, which can accommodate 12,000 representatives.

In particular, the Suntec Convention and Exhibition Center has 42,000 square meters of free-available venue and 26,830 square meters of exhibition area. It is divided into several small exhibition halls, which are equipped with embedded ditches to install data communication equipment. Furthermore, the non-column convention hall in the international convention and exhibition center covers 12,000 square meters, which can accommodate 12,000 participants. It is also equipped with an innovative folding seat system, advanced audio-visual devices, lighting equipment with theatrical effects, and a simultaneous interpretation system with 12 languages.

As the largest shopping center of Singapore, the Suntec Shopping Center covers 840,000 square meters and is composed of four theme areas, namely corridor (upscale souvenir boutiques), tropical (living and home products and services), recreational center (Carrefour), and fountain platform (restaurants, bars, and gourmet shops). The Suntec Shopping Center was granted Tourism Award by the Singapore Tourism Board in 1998 and obtained the General Best of Show and the Best of Show in Commerce/Retail in the global excellent construction awards in 1999.

Moreover, Suntec has a Kinderworld Entertainment Complex, five theaters, and a virtual reality theme park.

Suntec faces the Central Business District across a river. More than 700 companies will settle in Suntec after it is completed. The number of tourists in each month will reach 2 million. About 15,000 persons work there every day, more than 50,000 vehicles access it, and more than 10,000 vehicles can park there without the problem of traffic jams.

9.4.2.6 Summary of Changes in Exhibition Venue Functions

The domestic exhibition venues have experienced 1.0–4.0 eras, and the venue 5.0 is leading the mainstream now. The development tendency of venues can be reflected in three aspects:

(1) Increasingly significant demand in business show and business communication; venues develop from the single space to the diversified spaces;
(2) The convention and exhibition center and the concept of complex gain more attention and develop from single function to multifunction;
(3) The demand in multifunction and intelligence on the venues has been improved gradually, and the experience and benefits of organizers, exhibitors, and professional visitors receive more attention.

KEYWORDS

- **competitiveness**
- **exhibition industry**
- **UFI**

REFERENCES

Blythe, J., (2002). Using trade fairs in key account management [J]. *Industrial Marketing Management*, *31*, 627–635.

Rosson, P., & Seringhaus, F. H., (1995). Visitor and exhibitor interaction at industrial trade fairs [J]. *Journal of Business Research, 32*, 81–90.

CHAPTER 10

TOURISM HIGHER EDUCATION IN CHINA: PROFILE AND ISSUES

ZHANGXIN YIN[1] and FANG MENG[2]

[1]*Tourism Department, College of Business, Hunan First Normal University, Yuelu Qu, Changsha, Hunan, China*

[2]*School of Hotel, Restaurant and Tourism Management, University of South Carolina, South Carolina, United States*

CONTENTS

ABSTRACT

This chapter provides an overview of tourism higher education in China. It reviews the history, development, current status, and challenges of China's tourism higher education. Multiple issues are discussed, including program administration, curriculum design, faculty qualifications, degree program setup, and student career perception/expectation. Future development of tourism higher education in China is also discussed with recommendations from tourism scholars and government administration.

10.1 INTRODUCTION

Higher education in tourism studies has a history of less than 40 years in China. With China's reform and opening-up policy, and to meet the increasing personnel demand due to rapid development of the tourism industry in China, an education department was founded by the China National Tourism Administration (CNTA) in 1978. The aim was to establish a tourism education system and provide academic and professional programs at the national level in China (Zhang, Chong, and Ap, 1999),which marked the beginning of China's tourism education (Xu and Zhang, 2004). Nanjing Tourism School was the first to be established in 1978, followed by Shanghai Institute of Tourism the year after, which offers associate programs[1] (Tao, 1997).

Sponsored by CNTA in 1980, the first 4-year undergraduate program with bachelor's degree[2] was launched with the setup of the Department of Tourism and Hotel Management in Zhejiang University. In addition, CNTA provided funds for other universities to offer undergraduate tourism programs to meet urgent needs of tourism higher education in China. By late 1980s, China's tourism higher education was initially structured, with CNTA as the steering body and several other universities such as Nankai University, Hangzhou University, Northwest University, Beijing International Studies University, and Sun Yat-Sen University playing the key roles (Du, 2003). Meanwhile, a growing number of universities and institutes established tourism departments based on their existing programs (Du, 2003) with annual recruits of 1,300 students nationwide (Bao and Zhu, 2008).

Regarding graduate programs in tourism higher education, Zhejiang University was also the pioneer university to provide the first postgraduate program with a master's degree in tourism economics, accredited by Academic Degree Commission of the State Council in 1990 (Tian, 2014). It has also offered a doctoral program since 2003 and accepted post-doctoral scholars since 2005[3].

10.2 CURRENT STATUS OF TOURISM EDUCATION IN CHINA

10.2.1 TOURISM EDUCATION SYSTEM

China's tourism education has formed a complete system with hierarchies. It consists of two categories:

[1]Students in associate program will be granted a graduation certificate without academic degree.

[2]Students in undergraduate program and above will be granted a graduation certificate and an academic degree. Undergraduate program in this article refers to a 4-year study.

[3]www.som.zju.edu.cn. School of Management, Zhejiang University.

1) secondary vocational schools with vocational programs; and
2) institutes of higher education with four levels, namely, associate programs, undergraduate programs (bachelor's degree), postgraduate program (master's degree), and doctoral program (PhD degree) (Zhang and Fan, 2005) (Figure 10.1).

Students in associate programs usually spend 2–3 years in college to obtain a college diploma at the end of study. The hierarchical link between undergraduate program and associate program has been established. Those who would like to pursue an advanced degree are given the chance to take an exam in the last year to enter a higher education level. If students pass the exam, they will have 2 more years in a college or university to earn a bachelor's degree.

10.2.2 SCALE OF DEVELOPMENT

During the last 20 years, China's tourism education expanded rapidly. Statistics demonstrate that there were only 622 colleges and schools providing tourism programs with 139,200 students in 1995, and the numbers rose to 1,136 with 566,500 students in 2005. The numbers continued to increase and reached 2,307 tourism colleges and schools with 797,000 students in 2015 (Figures 10.2 and 10.3).

The number of secondary vocational schools experienced a slight fluctuation in the past 20 years, whereas the number of institutes of higher

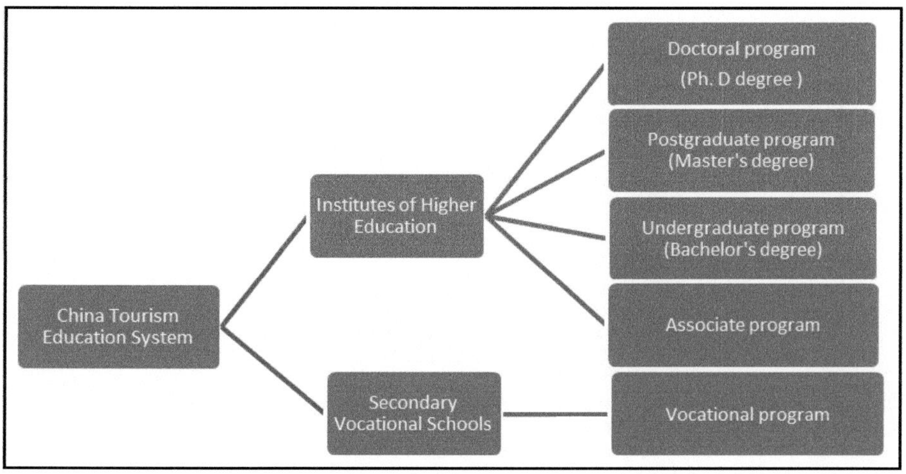

FIGURE 10.1 China tourism education system.

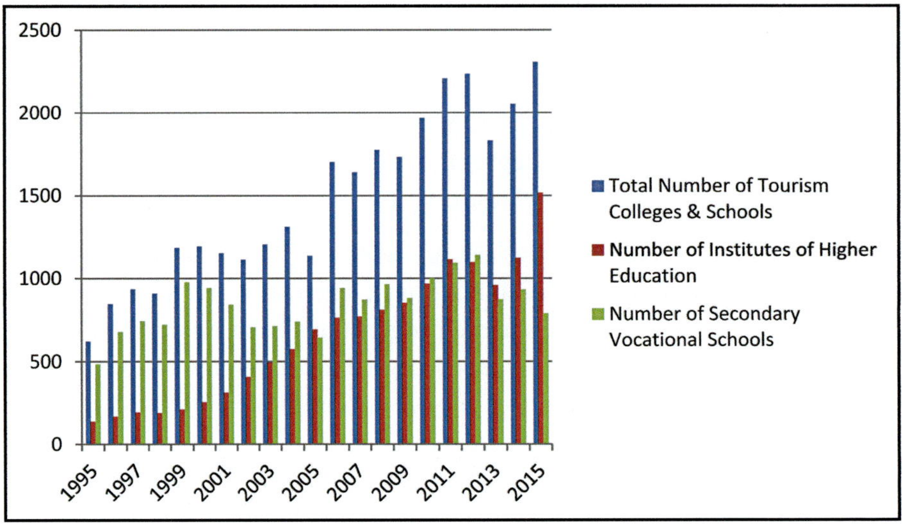

FIGURE 10.2 Number of tourism colleges & schools (1995–2015). Source: CNTA, Yearbooks of China Tourism Statistics, 1995–2015.

education had a steady increase and exceeded the former in 2013, which made higher education the main body of tourism education in China.

The number of tourism students at institutes of higher education has a higher growth rate than the number of secondary vocational schools, as

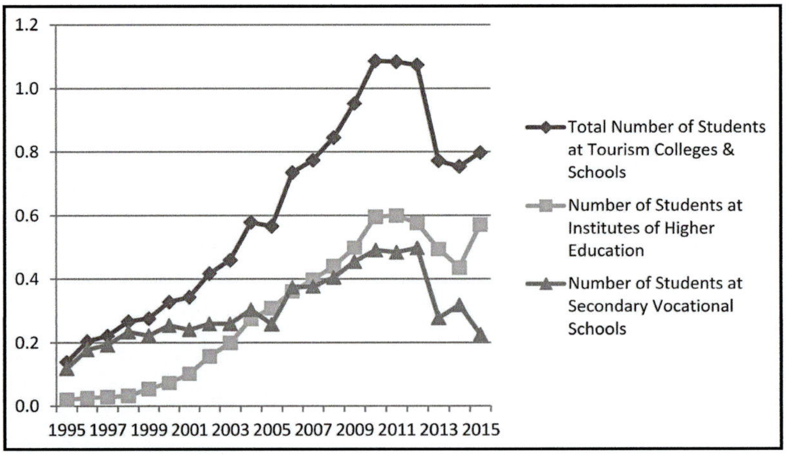

FIGURE 10.3 Number of students at tourism colleges & schools (1995–2015) (million) Source: CNTA, Yearbooks of China Tourism Statistics, 1995–2015.

more students tend to pursue higher education instead of attending vocational programs. Enrollment at higher education institutes has grown significantly over the past two decades, while the number of students at secondary vocational schools has been continuously shrinking.

According to Du (2003), the development of China tourism education can be divided into three stages:

1) Initial Stage from 1978 to 1990. A tourism education system was formed gradually with the hierarchical tourism programs under the direct guidance and financial support from CNTA.
2) Fast Development Stage from 1990 to 2012. The scale of China's tourism education experienced a rapid increase, and the overall quality of teaching improved. Since 1997, China's tourism higher education has been experiencing the educational reform and internationalization of tourism programs, which are associated with the increase in the scale of development, hierarchy of programs, diversification of tourism programs, and quality of tourism education. An example of internationalization is as follows: approved by Ministry of Education, Tianjin University of Commerce and Florida International University (FIU) established a cooperative hospitality management program. Since 2004, the program has graduated more than 2,000 students with a Bachelor of Science Degree from FIU.
3) Adjustment Stage from 2012 to now. The Ministry of Education of China adjusted the structural contexts of *the Catalog of Disciplines and Majors for Undergraduate Programs at General Higher Institutions* in 2012. Tourism Management, formerly listed under Business Administration in 1998, was upgraded to be an equal category of major in 2012 (Table 10.1). Some colleges with 2- or 3-years associate programs were upgraded to universities and started to provide undergraduate programs (bachelor's degree) for students. Some secondary vocational schools were upgraded to colleges and began to offer associate programs. All the adjustment brought the changes that were reflected on the numbers after 2012. With this adjustment, the number of institutes offering tourism higher education began to rise, while the number of secondary vocational schools continued to decrease.

TABLE 10.1 Adjustment of Tourism Management on the Catalog of Disciplines and Majors for Undergraduate Programs (Bachelor's degree)

Degree Programs	Categories of Discipline	Categories of Major	Major
Undergraduate Program (1998)	Management	Business Administration	Tourism Management
Undergraduate Program (2012)	Management	Tourism Management	Tourism Management
			Hospitality Management
			Exhibition Economics and Management
			Tourism Service Management & Education

Source: China Ministry of Education, the Catalog of Disciplines and Majors for Undergraduate Program, 1998 & 2012.

10.2.3 STUDENT ENROLLMENT IN TOURISM EDUCATION HIERARCHY

According to the statistics from CNTA, there were 2,307 tourism colleges and schools in 2015, of which 1,518 were institutes of higher education, accounting for 65.80% of tourism education in China. Among the 571,000 tourism students in the institutes of higher education, 37.65% enrolled in bachelor's, master's, and doctoral degree programs, and 62.35% in the 2–3 years' associate programs. On the other hand, there were 789 secondary vocational schools with 226,000 students study in 2 or 3-years vocational programs (Table 10.2).

- Doctoral Program: In 2015, among all the 1,518 institutes of tourism higher education, 50 offered doctoral programs in tourism-related disciplines. With 257 new entrants and 201 graduates, there were 947 doctoral students at the doctor's level.
- Postgraduate Program: Students on postgraduate program are awarded Master of Science or Master of Tourism Administration degrees (MTA). A total of 156 institutes recruited students for Master of Science and 72 institutes for MTA in 2015. Altogether 1,619 students (for both degree programs) were recruited by institutes in tourism-related disciplines, along with 1,298 graduates and 4,029 registered students.
- Undergraduate Program: Students enrolled in tourism undergraduate programs study for 4 years in universities for Bachelor of Manage-

TABLE 10.2 Students Enrollment in Tourism Education Hierarchy (2015)

	Institutes of Tourism Higher Education (Total Number of Institutes) 15,187, Total Number of Students (571,000)				Secondary Vocational Schools	Total
	Doctoral Program (PhD degree)	Postgraduate Program (Master's degree)	Undergraduate Program (Bachelor's degree)	Associate Program	Vocational Program	
Number of Tourism Institutes, Colleges & Schools	50	156 (Master of Science), and 72 (Master of Tourism Administration)	583	1,075	789	2,307
Number of Enrollment	257	1,619	55,611	110,935	93,000	261,422
Number of Graduates	201	1,298	46,888	——	88,000	——
Number of Registered Students	947	4,029	209,986	—— (356,0388)	226,000	797,000
Proportion of Registered Students	0.12%	0.51%	26.35%	44.67%	28.36%	100%

Source: CNTA, Statistics of China Tourism Education and Training, 2015.

ment. The total number of institutes of higher education offering tourism undergraduate program had reached 583 by the end of 2015, with a student body of 209,986, which accounted for 26.35% of total students in China's tourism education.

- Associate Program: As of 2015, there were 1,075 colleges offering associate programs,with an enrollment of 110,935 students in total. With regard to the number of registered students, the associate program has the biggest student body, which accounts for 44.67% of the total tourism students in China.
- Vocational Program: In 2015, secondary vocational schools recruited 93,000, along with 88,000 graduates and 226,000 registered students.

10.2.4 PROGRAM SETUP AND MISSION/OBJECTIVES IN TOURISM EDUCATION HIERARCHY

In 2011, the Office of the State Council Academic Degrees Committee and the Ministry of Education in China launched the updated *Catalog of Disciplines and Majors for Degree Programs and Personnel Development (2011 Version)*, which aimed to regulate and promote the development of postgraduate and doctoral education in terms of program and degree setup. In 2012, the Ministry of Education modified and launched the *Catalog of Disciplines and Majors for Undergraduate Programs at General Higher Institutions (2012 Version)*, serving as the guideline for undergraduate recruitment and major setup. However, the program setup of tourism higher education in practice is very complicated, and there are more than 30 tourism-related program titles in universities, colleges, and schools at different levels of education, encompassing almost all aspects of tourism industry and activities (Zhang & Fan, 2005).

10.2.4.1 Doctoral Program

The education objective for the tourism doctoral program is to foster researchers with creative academic ideas, theory foundation, and rigorous research methods in tourism-related disciplines. Tourism doctoral candidates are fostered in a broad discipline context. According to the *Catalog of*

Disciplines and Majors for Degrees Programs and Personnel Development (2011 Version), Tourism Management, Tourism Enterprise Management, and Agriculture & Forest Management are classified into the Discipline of Management. A total of 27 institutes offering these tourism-related majors confer Doctor of Management (among them, 24 institutes offer Tourism Management program). Another 14 institutes offering Geography and Ecology program (under Discipline of Science) confer Doctor of Science (Tian, 2014). Other tourism-related majors classified into Disciplines of Economics, Engineering, Agriculture, and History confer doctor's degree of their specific disciplines (Yu and Zeng, 2016).

10.2.4.2 Postgraduate Program

There are two types of postgraduate program: 1) Master of Science, which is granted to full-time postgraduates studying for 2–3 years and focusing on academic research; 2) MTA, mainly awarded to part-time postgraduates(Cai and Zhang, 2015) with flexible study plans ranging from 2 to 5 years. The mission/objective of postgraduate programs with a Master of Science is to foster tourism talents with a scientific attitude and ability to do research, such as literature review, basic research methods, and data collection (Zhang and Fan, 2005). Programs for MTA aims to produce leaders in tourism industry, who are expected to acquire applied knowledge from cases with tourism economic and managerial theories.

Compared to doctoral programs, there are similar tourism-related disciplines for Master of Science but have more majors due to more flexibility entitled by Ministry of Education. Program for MTA started student recruitment in 2010. It recruits only students majoring in Tourism Management under the Discipline of Management. MTA enrolls students with industry experience and allows students to work full time and study part-time to earn their degree. Each student in the MTA program usually works with two mentors, one from the academic institute and the other from the industry. Hands-on case study is a popular and highly promoted teaching method. Students do practical research projects in the industry, and their papers can be investigative reports or case study reports with particular focus.[4]

[4] MTA instructive training program (Trial).

10.2.4.3 Undergraduate Program

The mission and objective of tourism undergraduate program is to foster composite talents in students who have a broad knowledge background with the capability of working in tourism administrative departments, the tourism industry, or tourism schools (Zhang and Fan, 2005). They should be acquainted with the development trends of the tourism industry, master the knowledge of operation and management of tourism enterprises, and be able to analyze and solve problems (Zhang and Fan, 2005).

To meet the diversified personnel needs of the tourism industry, undergraduates are recruited in multiple majors such as Tourism Management, Hospitality Management, Exhibition Economics & Management, and Tourism Service Management & Education, which are all classified into the Discipline of Management in accordance with the *Catalog of Disciplines and Majors for Undergraduate Programs at General Higher Institutions (2012 Version)* (Table 10.1).

Statistics of China Tourism Education and Training (2015) showed that the number of students in different majors were imbalanced. For example, there were 151,995 students majoring in Tourism Management, which accounted for 72.38% of the entire student body in tourism education, while 35,089 students registered in Hospitality Management and accounted for 16.71%, followed by students in the Exhibition Economics & Management (15,620 students, 7.44% of total tourism students). Students in Tourism Service Management & Education are represented in the remainder (Figure 10.4).

10.2.4.4 Associate Program

The associate program is designed to meet educational objectives for training tour guides, junior managers, and professionals for travel agencies, hotels, parks, or related businesses. Students are required to acquire basic knowledge of economic and managerial theories (Zhang and Fan, 2005).

There are 13 tourism-related majors that aim to meet the personnel demand in the tourism industry. One college usually has several majors at the same time. Numbers of students in different majors are uneven. In 2015, a total of 799 colleges recruited 48,043 students majoring in Tourism Management, followed by 644 colleges with 43,306 new entrants in

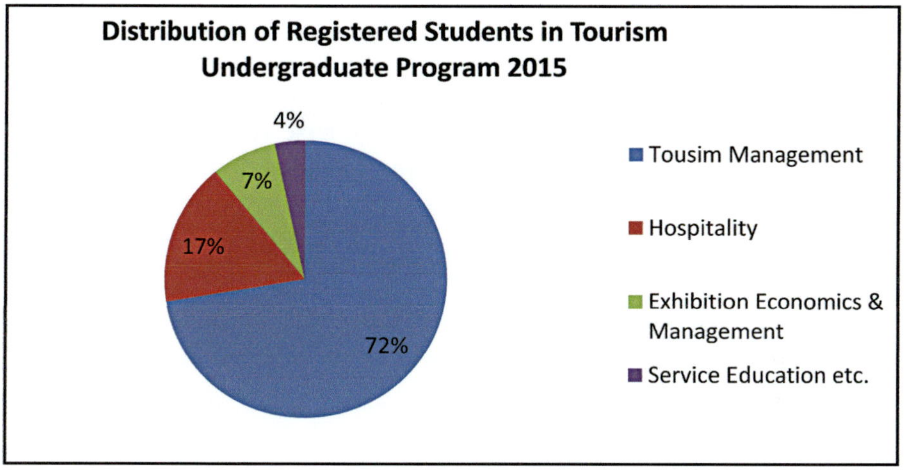

FIGURE 10.4 Distribution of registered students in tourism undergraduate program 2015 Source: CNTA, Statistics of China Tourism Education and Training, 2015.

Hospitality Management. These two majors have dominant priority in students' major choice and accounted for 82% at the level of associate program. Representing 7%, Exhibition Planning & Management with 8,090 freshmen in 177 colleges, took the third place in this level. Other majors such as Tour Guide, Foreign Affairs Tourism, and Leisure Service & Management recruited smaller number of students and account for the remaining 11% (Figure 10.5).

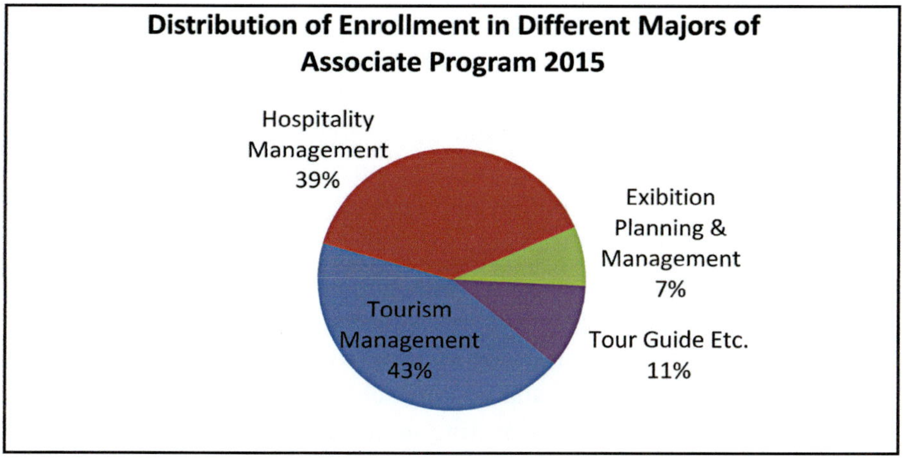

FIGURE 10.5 Distribution of enrollment in different majors of tourism associate program 2015 Source: CNTA, Statistics of China Tourism Education and Training, 2015.

10.2.4.5 Secondary Vocational Schools

Secondary vocational schools are the training bases for front line service staff and supervisors in the tourism industry. Professional programs focus on practical skills instead of a broad theory base (Shen, 1997). Majors in secondary vocational schools are more diverse and random. The top 3 majors are tourism management and service, luxury hotel operation and management, and tour guide service, with registered students of 97,000, 56,000, and 14,000, respectively. The total number of students in these three majors accounted for 73.89% of the entire secondary vocational student population(Statistics of China Tourism Education and Training, 2015).

10.2.5 PROGRAM-RUNNING MECHANISM

Currently, state-owned institutes and schools are still the main stream of tourism education in China. Zhang and Fan (2005) reported three types of tourism program setup in China's higher education system, namely, independent institutes (e.g., Guilin Tourism University), tourism schools (e.g., School of Tourism Management in Beijing International Studies University), and tourism departments/programs (e.g., Tourism Department of Business School of East China Normal University).

Various explorations in administrative mechanisms have been actively undertaken especially in tourism institutions of higher education. Private invested schools and programs have developed rapidly in recent years (Du, 2003; Zhang and Fan, 2005). Joint programs with partners such as government departments and enterprises have been set up (Du, 2003). Zhang, Lu, Hu, and Adler (2010) investigated the internationalization of tourism higher education in China and found great attention and efforts made by universities and colleges. Cooperation and exchange programs with overseas hospitality and tourism management program (HTM) are found popular in many tourism institutes. Renowned educators and professors abroad have been invited to teach or give lectures, while Chinese students and faculties are supported by such programs to visit overseas HTM departments or schools as exchange students and visiting scholars. Some institutes of tourism higher education started recruiting international students mainly from Asia and Africa.

10.2.6 CURRICULUM DESIGN

Curriculum design is closely associated with program setup (Wu, Hu, and Zhang, 1998). Tourism programs in different universities and institutes are based on diverse disciplines such as economics, management, geography, and history, which makes a great difference in curricula, especially for doctoral and postgraduate programs.

Curriculum design is also constrained by education regulations (Lam and Xiao, 2000). For undergraduate programs, the curriculum consists of three parts:

1) Foundational Courses. As students at this education level are granted Bachelor of Management, foundational courses in the Discipline of Management can be found in this part, such as Management, Economics, Statistics, Marketing, Economic Law, etc. (Zhang and Fan, 2005).
2) Tourism and Hospitality Major Courses. For this part, specific major courses are offered, such as Tourism Psychology and Introduction to Tourism.
3) Overall Skill Development Subjects. English, service attitude, and communication are the most valuable ones (Lu and Adler, 2009).

For associate and vocational programs, more hands-on, skill-oriented courses are provided in accordance with the educational objectives and industry demands.

Student internships in the tourism industry as well as social practice are required in undergraduate, associate, and vocational programs (Zhang and Fan, 2005). To ensure students have hands-on skills and a realistic evaluation of working experience, they are required to undergo a certain period of practical training (internship) in hotels, travel agencies, and enterprises in tourism attraction sites (Lam and Xiao, 2000).

10.2.7 TOURISM FACULTY

Faculty in tourism programs in China have various education backgrounds. In the early stage of China's higher tourism education, many faculty members used to be transferred from other related disciplines such as geography, business administration, and foreign languages (Lam & Xiao, 2000; Du, 2003).

With a 38-year history, China's tourism education has cultivated a new generation who major in tourism, receive systematic professional education, and now teach or conduct research in tourism in institutes of higher education. With the support of cooperative programs, the former have upgraded their knowledge structure by leading students' internship and interacting with tourism enterprises, while the latter put emphasis on enriching their teaching practice and research. There is increasing number of faculty members with overseas education background who know international HTM program mechanism and research publication very well (Zhang, Lu, Hu, and Adler, 2010).

Requirements for tourism faculties vary in different educational hierarchy. In tourism institutes of higher education, according to the *Annual Report of China Tourism Education* issued by China Tourism Education Association, faculty with doctoral degree accounted for 23.87% of the total, while 57.08% had a master's degree, and 19.05% of the teachers still have not received postgraduate education (Yu and Zeng, 2016). Institutions with doctoral and postgraduate programs, as well as research universities with undergraduate programs have put remarkable emphasis on faculty members' educational background and the academic degrees they obtain, and value faculty's research achievement to a great extent. With regard to the application-oriented universities, colleges and vocational schools, faculties are required to be familiar with practical aspects of the tourism industry in addition to their fundamental teaching qualifications. Faculty who obtain both teaching/research and professional industry capabilities are called *Double Type Teachers* or *Dual-qualification Teachers*, indicating evaluation of faculty by institutes of higher education and vocational colleges and schools at different levels.

10.3 CURRENT ISSUES IN CHINA'S HOSPITALITY AND TOURISM EDUCATION

10.3.1 INCONSISTENT TOURISM DEGREE PROGRAM SETUP

The Ministry of Education in China launched the *Catalog of Disciplines and Majors for Degree Programs and Personnel Development* in 2011 as a guideline for postgraduate and doctoral programs, and the *Catalog of Disciplines and Majors for Undergraduate Programs at General Higher*

Institutions in 2012 for undergraduate programs setup. Both published catalogs separated all the academic disciplines into three different levels, the top being "academic degree-conferring categories of disciplines," followed by "first-order disciplines (categories of major)" and "second-order disciplines (major)." However, Tourism Management degree programs were assigned to different categories of majors in these two government documents (Table 10.3).

In the bachelor's degree programs, "Tourism Management," as a first-order discipline (category of major), is categorized under the "Management" category of discipline. However, the master's and doctoral programs are categorized under "Business Administration", a first-order discipline (category of major) under "Management"; therefore, the master's and doctoral programs of Tourism Management are in the second-order discipline (Major). Consequently, bachelor's degree programs are first-order disciplines, but master's and doctoral degree programs are second-order disciplines, which represent inconsistency and confusing academic program setup.

In China's higher education system, disciplinary construction refers to a discipline's degree of maturity. Colleges within a university are usually structured based on first-order disciplines. Therefore, there are only very few colleges of tourism in China (such as Sun Yat-Sen University and Beijing Union University), and most tourism doctoral degree programs are set up under other departments or schools such as geography, business administration, social sciences, and other humanities disciplines (Bao and Lai, 2016).

TABLE 10.3 Tourism Degree Programs in Different Disciplines and Majors

Degree Programs	Categories of Discipline	First-order Disciplines (Categories of Major)	Second-order Disciplines (Major)
Doctor/Master (2011)	Management	Business Administration	Tourism Management
Bachelor (2012)	Management	Tourism Management	Tourism Management
			Hospitality Management
			Exhibition Economics & Management
			Tourism Service Management & Education

Source: China Ministry of Education, 2011 and 2012.

10.3.2 INEFFECTIVE CURRICULUM DESIGN

China's higher tourism education has been established on well-structured hierarchies, aiming to develop specialized personnel of different types, including operational, managerial, mid- and high-level or executive administrative, and academic fields. Consequently, various degree programs have been set up to meet the diversity of personnel needs. However, curriculum design still overlaps among the degree programs at different levels and ignores actual market demand (Wu, Hu, and Zhang, 1998; Lu, 2008), which represents that the strategic goals and positioning of personnel development are largely ambiguous among the degree programs at different levels in China's higher tourism education.

- Curriculum overlaps in degree programs at different levels. There is no clear strategic distinction among degree programs at different levels in China's tourism education. For example, the curriculum of associate programs is a mini or core version of the undergraduate programs; the postgraduate education usually simply repeats some core courses of undergraduate programs, and the curriculum design of vocational and associate programs do not show any essential distinction.
- Curriculum overlaps in different majors in the same-level degree programs. For example, the curriculum design and course outlines of different majors such as Tourism Management and Hospitality Management are almost identical in the undergraduate programs in some higher education institutions.
- Lack of tourism-specific curriculum design. In China's tourism higher education, tourism majors or programs have generally originated from other disciplines or departments such as geography, economics, management, and history. Therefore, many tourism courses have been closely associated with the "parent" discipline by simply adding the term "tourism" in front of the pre-established courses – for example, tourism geography, tourism economics, tourism marketing, and tourism psychology, etc.
- Inconsistency in tourism curriculum design. There is a great difference in the curriculum design in China's universities and colleges due to the various "parent" disciplines that originate the tourism program. The program setup, educational objectives, and student recruitment of each school have a close connection to tourism curriculum development.

Although a student internship in the tourism and hospitality industry is required by the Ministry of Education, the length of internships varied from one year to a few weeks for associate programs, and half a year to a few weeks for undergraduate programs among different universities and colleges (Zhang and Fan, 2005).

With regard to the teaching materials in China's higher tourism education, Du (2003) reported three stages in the development of teaching materials in tourism: the stage of void, featuring the development of teaching manuals by faculties transferred from other disciplines to tourism education); the stage of import, by introducing other disciplines' theories and knowledge as well as translating foreign tourism publications; and the stage of self-development, featuring faculty members' developing and publishing their own textbooks. However, duplication and plagiarism are serious issues in many textbooks, and there has been a lack of textbooks and reference materials in postgraduate and doctoral education, along with outdated contents and systems of teaching in many universities and colleges (Du, 2003). On the other hand, in terms of research, some popular web search engines such as Google Scholar are still unavailable in China, which to some extent limits the tourism faculty's access to scholarly literature.

10.3.3 MISMATCH OF STUDENT CAREER PERCEPTION/ EXPECTATION AND INDUSTRY DEMAND

A large percentage of graduates from tourism programs, especially from undergraduate programs and beyond, are not employed in the tourism industry. A study reported that junior and senior undergraduate students commonly perceived that the tourism major covered a broad range of subjects but lacked focus and practical or hands-on aspects (Xu and Zhang, 2004). In addition, half of the undergraduate students who had the internship experience reported that they would change their major or career if they have chance in the future.

The reasons are multifaceted and originated from the employment mechanism of tourism enterprises, undergraduate tourism education, and students' expectation of tourism jobs. On the one hand, many hospitality and tourism enterprises tend to ignore new employees' educational background; so, everyone has to work up from the lowest level. There is no efficient mechanism to screen promotion opportunities for new employees with higher academic degrees and capabilities. On the other hand, undergraduate tourism programs in China emphasize theoretical aspects of management without paying much attention to actual skill development, which is an essential focus of tourism profession. Therefore, tourism students in China commonly lack practical training and real-world experience in tourism enterprises, and thus have unrealistic expectations of their career in the tourism field. They are likely to encounter reality shock when they start their internship or first job after graduation. For example, many undergraduate students do not expect themselves to work from entry level position and are mentally unprepared for the hard work in the tourism field. They are demotivated as they do not have a management position or their work has very limited management component; thus, they cannot achieve their self-value perception or self-actualization. In addition, undergraduate students are not satisfied with the salary paid at entry level jobs in the tourism field, and some choose to pursue a higher level degree to avoid this situation. Therefore, the majority of tourism program graduates who started their first job in the tourism industry are employed outside the industry (Xu & Zhang, 2004; Zhang and Fan, 2005). Last but not the least, in Chinese traditional values, tourism is a service industry, which indicate inferior, servile jobs only for inexperienced youth in hotels, restaurants, and attraction sites. People commonly perceive that there is no need to take higher education for this hands-on, technical job. Tourism programs do not have as high a profile as many other disciplines and majors.

10.4 FUTURE DEVELOPMENT

10.4.1 PROMOTE AND UPGRADE TOURISM MANAGEMENT TO BE A FIRST-ORDER DISCIPLINE

In China's higher education system, disciplinary construction is crucial as it reflects disciplinary status, research, curriculum design and training schemes, the impact on society, and the growth of bachelor's, master's, and doctoral programs. In 2012, the government upgraded the undergraduate program of tourism management from a second-order discipline (major) to be a first-order discipline (category of major), which indicates the important progress of tourism as an academic discipline (Ma, 2016). However, postgraduate and doctoral students in tourism majors still have to be in the "parent" school or department of business administration, geography, economics, etc. due to its second-order disciplinary status. Tourism and hospitality faculty have been restricted to follow the hiring and promotion criteria of business administration. Along with the rapid growth of the tourism industry in China, more efforts and investment are needed to improve existing tourism education institutions in terms of the upgrading of master's and doctoral degree programs to obtain consistent disciplinary status and seamless connection from the undergraduate education to postgraduate and doctoral education.

10.4.2 IMPROVE TOURISM CURRICULUM DESIGN

Existing tourism education curriculum design in China overemphasizes the tourism management and service function, which has led to course overlap and restricted perspectives of students. Based on the multidisciplinary and interdisciplinary nature of tourism, tourism education institutions should broaden the curriculum design to focus more on the political, social, and cultural aspects of tourism, and facilitate students' understanding on the strategic role of tourism on industrial integration in China. The tourism industry has significant impact on host residents' quality of life and well-being, public resources protection and utilization, local culture and heritage recognition, ethnical understanding, and even international affairs. It is essential to broaden the perspectives of tourism education and improve the quality of tourism personnel as well as change the bias of the general public toward the tourism profession in particular (Yu and Zeng, 2016).

10.4.3 DEVELOP PERSONNEL HIERARCHY IN TOURISM

It is important to establish the hierarchy of tourism education based on market need and set national standard guidelines for tourism education practices (Lam and Xiao, 2000). To meet the market's diverse need of tourism personnel, tourism education institutions need to closely interact and cooperate with tourism enterprises to understand the actual and changing demand, and adjust the educational objectives, program setup, and curriculum design accordingly. Tourism education institutions should broaden their perspectives and provide tailor-made education programs based on market demand, not regulations and existing faculty of categories of major (such as the strict and trivial regulations/guidelines of the business administration discipline) (Du, 2003). In addition, to have a better linkage between the education/

training path and career path based on market demand, tourism education institutions in China should further distinguish the objectives and practices of curriculum design at different levels so as to accommodate the hierarchical career path of diverse tourism personnel needed.

10.4.4 CONCLUDING REMARK

China's tourism higher education has a short history but has grown fast in the past 40 years in terms of program setup at different levels, curriculum design, student enrollment, and internationalization. There are still issues and problems in tourism higher education in many aspects. However, with the significance of the tourism industry in China's economy and on-going tourism education reform, tourism programs at different levels will gradually develop graduates with broader disciplinary perspective and skills to meet the diverse needs of today's tourism industry.

KEYWORDS

- **challenges**
- **curriculum**
- **faculty**
- **higher education**
- **programs**

REFERENCES

Bao, J. G., & Zhu, F., (2008). On the shrinking of China's tourism undergraduate education and way out—Thoughts about thirty years for development of tourism higher education. *Tourism Tribune*, *23*(5), 13–17.

Bao, J. G., & Lai, K., (2016). Connotation and necessity of upgrade for tourism management discipline. *Tourism Tribune*, *31*(10), 14–16.

Cai, J., & Zhang, Y., (2015). Thinking on education of master of tourism administration in China. *Forestry Education in China*, *33*(3), 36–39.

CNTA, Personnel, Labor & Educational Department (1998). A report on China's tourism education.

Du, J., (2003). Reforms and development of higher tourism education in China. *Journal of Teaching in Travel & Tourism*, *3*(1), 103–113.

Lam, T., & Xiao, H., (2000). Challenges and constraints of hospitality and tourism education in China. *International Journal of Contemporary Hospitality Management*, *21*(5), 291–295.

Li, Y. Q., (2013). The evaluation system and index connotation of "Double Type" teachers in tourism vocational college. *Tourism Forum*, *6*(5),105–110.

Lu, S., (2008). Study on Education of Tourism of Henan Province. *Master Thesis*.

Lu, T., & Adler, H., (2009). Career goals and expectations of hospitality and tourism students in China. *Journal of Teaching in Travel & Tourism*, *9*, 63–80.

Ma, B., (2016). Investigation on logic and thought of upgrading tourism discipline. *Tourism Tribune*, *31*(10), 25–32.

Shen, B. J., (1997). Thought on establishment of tourism discipline and tourism higher education. *Tourism Tribune*, Supplementary Issue of Tourism Education, 21–24.

Tao, H. J., (1997). My understanding of the development stages of China's tourism education. *Tourism Triune*, Supplementary Issue of Tourism Education, 6–9.

Tian, L., (2014). Annual China tourism education report on postgraduate and doctoral program. China Tourism Publication House, Beijing.

Wu, B., Hu, X., & Zhang, L., (1998). A research on the structure of China's tourism education system. *Journal of Guilin Tourism Institute*, *9*(3), 65–71.

Xu, H. G., & Zhang, C. Z., (2004). A comparative analysis of overseas and Chinese tourism education and its enlightenment. *Tourism Tribune*, (S1), 26–30.

Yu, C. G. & Zeng, G. J. (2016). Personnel training and industry demand on tourism management Discipline. *Tourism Tribune*, *31*(10), 18–19.

Zhang, H. Q., Chong, K., & Ap, J., (1999). An analysis of tourism policy development in modern China. *Tourism Management*, *20*, 471–485.

Zhang, L., Lu, T., Hu, H., & Adler, H., (2010). An exploratory study of the internationalization of tourism higher education in China. *Journal of Human Resources in Hospitality & Tourism*, *9*, 33–46.

Zhang, W., & Fan, X., (2005). Tourism higher education in China: past and present, opportunities and challenges. *Journal of Teaching in Travel & Tourism*, *5*(1–2), 117–135.

CHAPTER 11

LEISURE AGRICULTURE AND RURAL TOURISM DEVELOPMENT IN CHINA (2006–2016)

HONG XU, CONGLIN ZHAO, and XINYING MA

Nankai University, Nankai Qu, 300071, China

CONTENTS

11.1 RURAL TOURISM DEVELOPMENT IN CHINA

The development of rural tourism in China has developed in a fast pace in last 20 years. At present, rural tourism has become a major component of China's tourism, welcomed by the majority of tourists. According to the rural tourism statistics released by the China Tourism Academy, during 2016 October holiday, the number of rural tourism was 129 million person-time, accounting for 69% of the same period of tourism trips. The country has become one of the main destinations for tourists to choose their holiday.

11.1.1 STATISTICAL ANALYSIS OF THE OVERALL DEVELOPMENT OF RURAL TOURISM IN CHINA

Domestic rural tourism began rapid development around 2008, which is closely related to China's national tourism policy. Looking at the tourist number of rural tourism, in 2008, the numbers of rural tourists in China is only 300 million people, followed by the annual rural tourism trips increasing year by year. In 2013, the number reached 1 billion people for the first time. This number is more than three times in 2008, 2.5 times of that in 2010. From Table 11.1, we can see that the number of rural tourists increased from 400 million in 2010 to 800 million in 2012, and the tourist trips are doubled in three years. From this, we can see that the domestic rural tourism maintains a relatively rapid growth in 2008 to 2013, and this steady growth has continued since 2014. In 2015, the number of tourists arriving in the countryside shows a burst of growth, reaching a historical high of 2.2 billion, an increase of 83.33%. Comparing the figures from 2008 to 2015, the number of rural tourism trips ranged from 300 million to 2.2 billion, taking into account only 7 years, with an average growth rate of 34.66%. Specific statistics are given in Table 11.1.

During the same period, domestic tourists also increased steadily. In 2008, the number of domestic tourists in China was 1 billion 710 million, reaching the highest level of 4 billion in 2015. Although it reached the highest level in history, in 2015, the number of people is only 2 times more than in 2008. This is due to the large amount of the domestic tourism base. At the same time, it also reflects another phenomenon, that is, compared to rural tourism, the number of domestic tourism growth is relatively stable, with the average growth rate of 12.18%, far below the 34.66% growth rate of rural tourism, not showing an explosive growth. Especially in the last 3 years, the annual growth rate is about 10%, which fully shows that China's tourism market is in a healthy state of operation.

With regard the proportion of the amount of rural tourism accounting for the domestic tourism, from Table 11.1, it is evident that the proportion of the number of rural tourism increased yearly. In 2008, the proportion is 17.54%; and then the number is 22.73% in 2011, the first time when the number is more than 20%. In 2013, the proportion of rural tourism reached 33.23%, about one-third of the total number of domestic tourism, until 2015, when the number of rural tourism accounted for 55%; for the first

TABLE 11.1 Comparative Analysis of Rural Tourism Statistics and Domestic Tourism Statistics

Year	Number of village tourists			Number of domestic tourists			The percentage of rural tourism (%)
	Number of people (100 million)	Annual growth rate (%)	Average growth rate (%)	Number of people (100 million)	Year-on-year growth (%)	Average growth rate (%)	
2008	3	---	34.66%	17.1	6.30%	12.18%	17.54%
2009	3.4	13.33%		19	11.10%		17.89%
2010	4	17.65%		21	10.53%		19.05%
2011	6	50%		26.4	25.71%		22.73%
2012	8	33.33%		29.57	12%		27.05%
2013	10	25%		32.62	10.30%		30.66%
2014	12	20%		36.11	10.70%		33.23%
2015	22	83.33%		40	10.77%		55%

Source: The Yearbook of China Tourism from 2008 to 2015, relevant news reports from China National Tourism Administration, National tourism working conference materials.

time, this number was more than half, reaching the highest level in history. In other words, in the whole year of 2015, more than half of the tourists choose to travel to the country. This not only fully illustrates the rapid development of rural tourism, but also shows that China's domestic tourism preferences of residents have gradually changed from urban tourism and coastal tourism in the past to rural tourism.

In contrast, the changes in the number of rural tourism and domestic tourism tourists show that the rapid development of rural tourism is due to the good momentum of economic development of the country as a whole and the key role of the national policies and measures. There was an explosive growth of rural tourism from 2014 to 2015, and in this period, the national policy of 2014 and 2015 mentioned the need to vigorously develop rural tourism and leisure agriculture. It is the introduction of these policies that stimulate the rapid development of the rural tourism market. Secondly, the development of rural tourism in China is closely related to the implementation of the paid leave system. Since 2007, the state canceled the May first Golden Week holiday; increased three traditional festivals, namely Ching Ming Festival, Dragon Boat Festival, and Chung Yeung Festival; and began to implement paid leave system. These changes in the system not only alleviated the congestion caused by holiday travel, but most importantly changed people's travel habits. People's travel habits gradually change from long-term travel to short tours, and for tourists, the rural areas around the city are undoubtedly their best choice.

11.1.2 STATISTICAL ANALYSIS OF THE RURAL TOURISM RECEPTION

With the development of rural tourism, not only the number of tourists is increasing yearly in terms of supply, the number of tourism attraction villages and towns to carry out rural tourism in China is also increasing. According to the statistics of the relevant departments, from 2008 to 2010, the number of tourism villages and towns in the country is about 50,000. In 2011, the number exceeded the five million mark, reaching 53,000, and by 2014, the number of villages and towns have doubled to 10.6 million. Many villages and towns gradually complete the construction of tourism urbanization through the development of rural tourism, and many farmers' lives have also improved. Many of the farmers are no longer engaged in the simple agricultural life as in the past and gradually carry out tourism-related work. Relevant departments predict that by 2020 China will have more than 150,000 villages and towns that carry out rural tourism activities.

In some villages and towns, agritainment (farm house), a unique business model is rapidly promoted and developed. In 2008, there were 1.28 million farmhouse operators nationwide and 1.5 million in 2010. While the development of the farmhouse reached a stagnant period in the next three years, with a slow development and the farmhouse operators remained at a level of slightly more than 1.5 million. In 2013 to 2015, the number of emerging farmhouses saw a rapid growth and increased to 300,000 in just 3 years (Table 11.2).

Because of rural tourism and farmhouse management, many farmers have been benefited directly or indirectly from employment and income generation. In 2009, due to the development of rural tourism, there were more than one million 590 thousand farmers with new jobs. The income of farmers increased to 25.7 billion, driving agricultural sales revenue to 35.2 billion. In 2013 and 2014, the number of farmers who benefited greatly increased, and more than 30 million of farmers have benefited from the development of rural tourism. In 2015, the farms engaged in rural tourism operation was approximately 20 million people countrywide, and the number of farmers benefited indirectly reached 70 million. By 2020, it is expected that there will be more than 80 million farmers who will benefit from the development of rural tourism.

11.1.3 STATISTICAL ANALYSIS OF RURAL TOURISM REVENUE

The development of rural tourism in China has not only brought about rapid growth of rural tourists, but also considerable tourism revenue. In 2008, in the initial stage of domestic rural tourism, income was at a low level of only 56 billion. With the continuous development of rural tourism, tourism

TABLE 11.2 2008–2015 the Change of Leisure Agriculture and Rural Tourism in the Number of Farmhouse (10,000)

Year	2008	2009	2010	2011	2012	2013	2014	2015
Number of farmhouse	128	135	150	>150	>150	170	200	220

Source: China leisure agriculture and rural tourism in-depth research and investment strategic planning analysis report.

revenue also showed a strong momentum of growth. Revenue in 2010 was 120 billion, twice of 2008. Revenue growth in 2011 nearly doubled that of 2010, with an increase of 80%. The annual income growth showed an increasing trend in the next few years, up to 2015, when a record high of 440 billion was reached. In Figure 11.1, you can see three prominent peaks of income growth in 2010, 2011, and 2014. Comparing these three peaks, we find that the peak year is the year when the country's rural tourism policy was promulgated. For example, in 2009, the National Tourism Administration promulgated the "Rural Tourism Development Program," and the role of this policy was soon reflected in the tourism revenue for 2010. In the year of 2014, the central government proposed that the development of rural tourism could be an important form of rural industrial structure adjustment to improve the attractiveness of rural tourism and increase the investment in rural tourism, thereby greatly stimulating development and increasing rural tourism revenue. Rural tourism revenue showed a substantial increase in 2014 and 2015.

11.1.4 RURAL TOURISM ENTREPRENEURSHIP

In recent years, the country has vigorously promoted widespread entrepreneurship and innovation, and it can be said that in all walks of life, a national entrepreneurship boom has been launched; the field of rural tourism is no exception to this phenomenon. Rural tourism entrepreneurship also shows

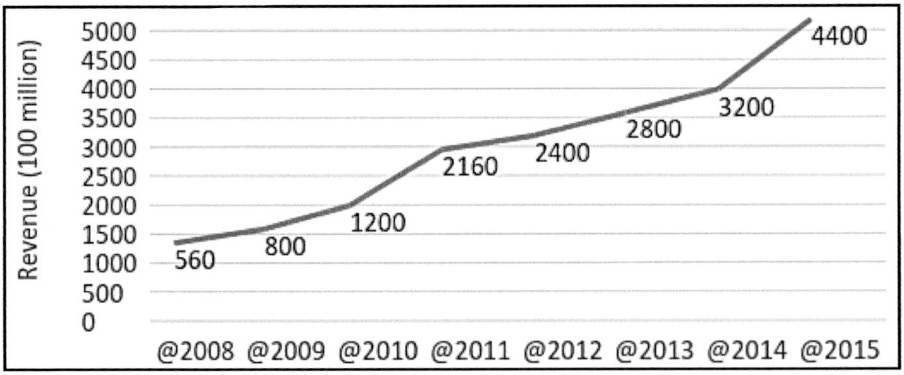

FIGURE 11.1 Rural tourism revenue from 2008–2015 (Source: The Yearbook of China Tourism from 2008 to 2015, relevant news reports from China National Tourism Administration, and National tourism working conference materials).

a good trend; the state not only created 100 rural tourism business bases in the country but also organized more students, peasants, and people with special talent to join the rural tourism creative industry. Guided by policy measures, this aims to further promote the development of rural areas and add more jobs for the rural areas through this method. At the same time, this model is predicted to play a positive role in promoting the construction of urbanization. Through the farmers in situ urbanization, farmers and college student groups can acquire more benefits. Relevant state departments have been identified that will organize and guide 10,000 college students, returning home migrant workers, people with professional artistic talents, and youth entrepreneurship groups to join the rural tourism development from 2015 to 2017. Simultaneously, while carrying out rural tourism and "tens of thousands of" brand creation activities, the 1000 "China Rural Tourism Model Village," 1000 "China Rural Tourism Model Households," 10000 "China Rural Tourism Rich Leaders," and 10000 "Gold farmhouse" will be launched. By 2020, the country will have over 3 million rural tourism operators, and the number of rural tourists will reach 4 billion. China's rural tourism will step into a new level, and the market and the scale will be further expanded, which will attract financial investment into rural tourism.

11.1.5 THE DEVELOPMENT OF LOCAL RURAL TOURISM IN CHINA

The policy of rural tourism provided a powerful guarantee for its development in 2009, when the State Council issued "*The Views on Accelerating the Development of Tourism*," pointing out the use of ethnic villages and ancient towns to construct characteristics of a rural tourism town. Under the support of the policy, many local governments have increased the investment in rural tourism and gave preferential treatments and subsidies in land, taxes, and other aspects. Some local governments directly issued rural tourism consumption coupons to local residents in order to stimulate the development of local rural tourism. At all levels, government efforts have aided local rural tourism in achieving a good development trend. Taking Beijing as an example, the development of rural tourism has shown good momentum in recent years, not only in the number of tourist trips, but the tourism income has also shown an upward trend, despite a small decline in rural tourism revenue in 2014. In terms of employment, the development of rural tourism provides jobs for more farmers. Specific as shown in Table 11.3:

TABLE 11.3 Statistical Analysis of Rural Tourism Data in Beijing (2010–2015)

Year	Rural tourism reception households (ten thousand households)	Rural tourism practitioners (ten thousand people)	Rural tourism person-time		Rural tourism income	
			Number of people (ten thousand person-times)	Year-on-year growth (%)	Tourism revenue (100 million yuan)	Year-on-year growth (%)
2010	1.4	6	3328.5	11.30%	25.1	17.90%
2011	1.5	6.4	3511.8	5.50%	30.4	20.9
2012	1.6	6.8	3635.7	3.50%	35.9	18.20%
2013	1.6	7	3750.9	3.20%	37.6	4.50%
2014	1.7	6.9	3825.4	2%	36.2	-3.70%
2015	1.6	--	4043	5.70%	39.2	8.30%

Source: Compiled according to the Beijing Bureau of Statistics rural tourism related statistical data over the years.

The development of rural tourism is now in the transformation and upgrading period. The rural development model, business model, and marketing model are changing. The future development in practice will need to focus on solving the problems such as integration of new technology into rural tourism, improvement of economic quality of rural tourism, and enhancement of the rural tourism added value. Although the proportion of rural tourism has now accounted for more than half of domestic tourism, the future development of rural tourism should also continue to expand the market size and further improve the rural tourism in the tourism market share, increase the frequency of revisiting tourists, and integrate the rural tourism resources. This will not only help the development of the economy but also play a positive role in the environment and so on.

11.2 LEISURE AGRICULTURE AND RURAL TOURISM LITERATURE OVERALL REVIEW

The fast growth of rural and leisure agriculture tourism stimulates academic research in this area. In order to better statistically analyze rural tourism and leisure agriculture research topics, and understand excitable issues of China over the past decades, this chapter especially selects 10 domestic mainstream research journals. Rural tourism and leisure agriculture industries involve rural agriculture, ecology, and tourism. Therefore, this chapter chooses the core journals in the two fields; the chosen journals should have a strong correlation with rural tourism and leisure agriculture studies to ensure accurate and scientific research. Specific selection criteria involve three core tourism journals, including the Tourism Tribune, Tourism Science, and Tourism Forum; three core journals for agriculture and rural areas, including World Agriculture, Rural Economy, and Agricultural Economy; two core periodicals for geography, including Human Geography and Economic Geography; and two journals mainly publishing tourism, namely Journal of Beijing International Studies University, and Ecological Economy. By using the CNKI advanced retrieval function, the theme is set for "rural tourism" or "leisure agriculture," and literature sources are reviewed from the selected 10 core journals for the time period from January 1, 2005 to December 31, 2015. Following this, each document searched is reviewed to ensure that the research direction focuses on rural tourism and leisure agriculture. A total of 523 documents were collected.

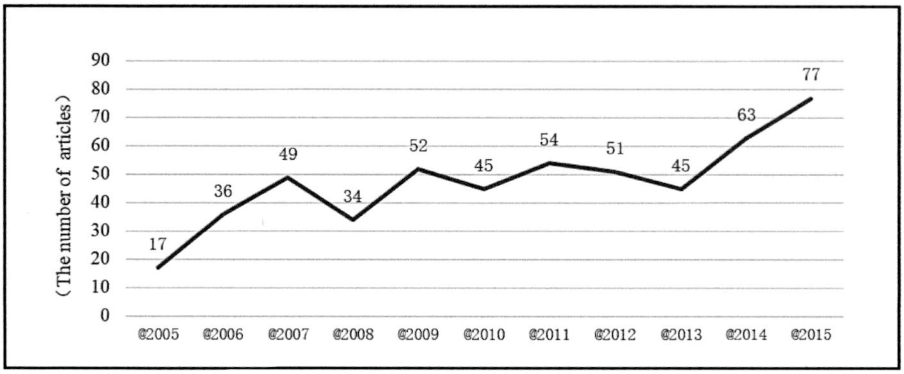

FIGURE 11.2 Literature quality trend from 2005-2015. Source: Based on CNKI search.

11.2.1 THE QUANTITY TREND OF DOCUMENTS

The 523 articles were classified according to the published year, and the quantity of articles devoted to the topic of focus was noted.

As the line graph shows below, the first peak about rural tourism and leisure agriculture research appeared in 2007. The number of articles surged nearly three times from 17 to 49 since 2005, which is directly linked with the national tourism theme "China rural tourism 2006" and "Chinese Urban and Rural Harmony Tour 2007." The information put forward by the government is pushing more scholars' concern for this field. From 2008 to 2011, the amount of relevant literature, despite an occasional drop, has shown a steady upward trend, and the growth rate is relatively stable. From 2011 to 2013, there is a slight decline in the articles devoted to the topics. From 2013 to 2015, tourism research ushered in an explosive growth, reaching the highest value of 77, which exactly coincides with the government's proposals researching a number of rural tourism and leisure agriculture policies at this stage. The trend also shows that rural tourism and leisure agriculture are more significantly practice-oriented. Related studies are often based on the needs of national industrial development, and research results often become the basis for rural tourism industry development.

11.2.2 ANALYSIS OF PAPERS PUBLISHED IN JOURNALS

In the selected journals, Agricultural Economy, accounting for 32.12% of published articles, ranked first and Tourism Tribune contains 84 publications, accounting for 16.06%, ranking second. This fully demonstrates the agriculture and tourism attribute of rural tourism and leisure agriculture. Other journals contain relatively the same amount of papers (Table 11.4).

Three categories of tourism journal literature are basically related to rural tourism compared to leisure agriculture and prefer academic topics; agricultural economic journals contain more leisure agriculture literature than rural tourism literature, which shows that the leisure agriculture industry's own property, is more biased toward the agricultural industry. In addition to magazine preferences, there is a lack of leisure agriculture research at present.

11.2.3 RESEARCH CONTENT AND PERSPECTIVES

11.2.3.1 The Main Contents of Rural Tourism

11.2.3.1.1 Concept

In the study of the concept of rural tourism, most scholars are concerned with the research of He (2002) and Liu (2006). These two papers are pioneer research for a large number of references for the later studies, and many of the concepts are defined on this basis. He (2002) points out that rural tourism is defined as activities in rural areas, with rural, natural, and humanistic subjects for tourist attractions. Liu (2006) defines rural tourism as "rural tourism means tourism activities, with a combination of rural areas and farming related custom, countryside scenery for attractions, attracting tourists to have a rest, sightseeing, experience and learning." With the development of rural tourism, there was a gradual shift from sightseeing to holiday,

TABLE 11.4 Paper Volume

Journal	Articles	Proportion	Journal	Articles	Proportion
Tourism Tribune	84	16.06%	World Agriculture	31	5.93%
Tourism Science	13	2.49%	Rural Economy	38	7.27%
Tourism Forum	36	6.88%	Agricultural Economy	168	32.12%
Human Geography	11	2.10%	Journal of BISU	39	7.46%
Economic Geography	37	7.07%	Ecological Economy	66	12.62%
			In total	523	100%

Source: Based on CNKI search.

vacations became one of the main purposes of visitors for rural tourism, and changes in the industry attracted the attention of scholars. Guo (2010) pointed out that rural tourism is a kind of new tourism operating activities based in rural areas, involving utilization of rural unique natural environment, idyllic landscape, production management form, folk culture and customs, farming culture, and farm village resources, to offer sightseeing, leisure, experience, entertainment, shopping, and holiday activities for the city tourists. The following researchers made a number of definitions about rural tourism, which are basically similar to the aforementioned definitions.

11.2.3.1.2 Development Model

Rural tourism pattern is receiving more and more attention from scholars, and the research gradually matures after 2006. Scholars have different views and perspectives on the development model. Summarized together, there are two main perspectives, namely community participation and resource characteristics.

1) **Community Participation:** Development of rural tourism requires not only government and corporate support, but the participation of local rural residents also plays a vital role. Participation of local residents allows them to reap their own benefits from the development of rural tourism, which is also conducive to improve the social status of the residents. Yang and Wang (2006) in accordance with democratic and social development conditions proposed four community participation models, respectively. They are as follows: traditional, administration-led, residents and government joint participation, and residents' full participation. Zou and Wang (2007) used Beijing DaYing Village as an example to discuss the community-led development model. Wang (2009) for Guangxi Ping An Zhaicun research shows that in terms of tourism development and cultural heritage protection, the "Elite Model Management" can play a better role. Zhou and Jiang (2009) proposed three kinds of endogenous community-led development patterns, namely the basic-level organization leading mode, the share-holding operating mode, and the professional cooperatives mode. According to Guo (2010) based on the research of the Shangri-la YuBeng community, which uses the "rotating" model,

the participation of community can solve the phenomenon such as disorderly competition and conflicts of interest. Guo (2011) analyzed the operation mechanism and framework of "rural communities and tourist attractions symbiosis mode." It is noteworthy that Cai et al. (2013) conducted field research on three villages in Zhejiang and pointed out that the effectiveness, fairness of community participation, and tourisms stage of development are very important to the development of the community participation pattern. Methods such as comparative analysis, field investigation, and document analysis were utilized. Li (2013) discussed the community-led model of rural tourism with tourism poverty alleviation and pointed out the important role and problem of community-led mode in poverty alleviation. Additionally, Wang and Zhang (2014) summarized the previous community models and summed up the "Farmers + Farmers," "Enterprise + Farmers," "Enterprise + Community + Farmers," "Government + Enterprises + Tourist Association + Travel Agency," "Joint Stock Cooperative System," and "Government + Travel Agency + Enterprise + Community residents" as six modes, with the advantages and disadvantages of each model.

2) **Resource Characteristics:** Rural tourism development is inseparable from its' rural resources, and different resources tend to have their special characteristics. Therefore, deciding how to select the appropriate development mode according to different resources drew many scholars' attention. Ma (2007) based the research on rural tourism development in Sichuan and summarized the proposed village-style rural tourism cluster development mode, garden-style special industries rely mode, courtyard leisure resort mode, and the ancient street style folk tourism small town mode. Xu (2009) examined the axis system theory study and presented rural tourism space structure pattern of Ningbo. Liu (2011) focused on the characteristics of the city–rural farmhouse tourism spatial structure function and discussed six kinds of farmhouse form modes, namely, the folk experience pattern, business entertainment street pattern, natural ecological pattern, motels pattern, and modern ecological agriculture pattern. According to the special geographic conditions and geographical features in Sichuan ethnic areas, Chen (2011) proposed wilderness and suburban rural tourism. Gao (2015) summed up the "Luodai mode" and

"agricultural mode," according to the unique cultural resources and management in the process of Chengdu rural tourism development. Yu Daisong (2015) argued that the past simple farmhouse mode is difficult to adapt to the existing needs of tourists, and tourist reception facilities should be upgraded. According to the concept of the urban complex, Daisong proposed the development model of rural tourism complex, namely haplotype rural tourism complex, regional rural tourism complex, and remote platforms rural tourism complex.

11.2.3.1.3 Planning and Development

Tourism planning and development has always been a stimulating issue. Fan (2009) draws on landscape ecology theory and pointed out the rural tourism spatial elements areas – gallery – group – edge planning ideas. Zhang and Bao (2009) discussed the reasons for selecting tourism as the leading industry in countryside and proposed a "starting point-power" hypothesis. Luo Chang (2006) studied the mechanism to protect the interests of Ethnic Village Community Participation in Tourism Development. Guo (2009) explored how to choose the rural tourism development model in economically developed areas and analyzed the role of government. Luo and Huang (2009) applied the concept of circular economy to rural tourism and explored the rural tourism development of cycle economy. Wang (2011) explored the rural tourism development of the western ethnic minority villages; Wu and Zhu (2012) proposed the "five win model" based on six stakeholders (the government, enterprises, residents, tourists, resources, and environment) and conducted empirical research on Hainan Maogan scenic area planning as a case study. Han and Wang (2009), in accordance with the interaction between "urban" and "rural" and the movement law of tourism flow, proposed the "city-village" extremely variable model and pointed out that the three northeastern provinces are able to carry out related tourism product developments on this basis. Zhang and Zhang (2009) analyzed rural tourism development decision paths by the analytic hierarchy process (AHP). Liao (2014) used Taiwan rural landscape as an example and presented three approaches to develop rural tourism based on the "Satoyama Initiative."

11.2.3.1.4 *Effect*

Effects of rural tourism are an important part of the rural tourism study and are also one of the topics scholars are willing to research. Topics of interest include the impact of rural tourism on the economy, culture, and ecology.

1) **Effects on Economy:** Rural tourism has an important influence on economic development, generally acting on the income of local farmers, the adjustment of industrial structure, employment of farmers, and the resulting income inequality. Influence in these areas has aroused great attention of scholars; thus, the economic role of rural tourism has become a rousing issue. Zhang et al. (2006) investigated the contribution and impact of rural tourism development on rural economics. Zou (2008) analyzed some problems in tourist towns such as economic decline and how rural tourism interests monopolized by a few as tourism promotes rural construction. Feng (2009) studied the effects of rural tourism on the Beijing-Tianjin corridor local residents and on economic and social elements by using a questionnaire survey. Wang (2010), from both quantitative and qualitative points of view, explored the impact of rural tourism on the rural employment structure, quality, and farmers' income interest through field research. Huang (2011) discussed the income gap between rich and poor farmers in Southern Anhui rural areas due to the development of rural tourism. He (2014) compared six different types of peasant household family characteristics, livelihood strategies, and livelihood capital under the influence of rural tourism by designing a farmers' livelihood capital evaluation index system.
2) **Effects on Culture:** The culture here mainly refers to the rural culture, including farming culture, folk culture, etc. Scholars have different research perspectives, mainly in the rural culture feature analysis (Sun et al., 2010); rural folk cultural heritage (Liao, 2014), protection and mining (Zhang, 2008; Hu, 2009; Zhang, 2015); and rural tourism with rural folk culture development (Zhang and Zhang, 2007; Cao, 2012; Ning, 2015). Li (2011) analyzed the dual attributes of rural culture, "rustic and heritage," and proposed three rural culture protection mode: "eco-museum, rural big stage, and landscape carnival." Xie Yanjun (2015) constructed the path of protecting rural heritage by establishing a model for the protection and utilization of

rural heritage, the cultivation of rural sense of place, the carrier of rural cultural memory and the "show-gaze" model of heritage.

3) **Effects on Ecology:** The effects of rural tourism on the ecology concern scholars most. Rural tourism and rural ecological environment are interdependent and mutually restrained. Rural tourism development will promote the local government and relevant organizations to protect the local environment and enhance environmental awareness. However, with the increase in tourists, the garbage brought by visitors causes some pollution and destruction of the environment. Therefore, how to promote the harmonious development of rural tourism while preserving the ecological environment has become enthusing research. Huang (2007) analyzed the necessity of environmental protection in the process of rural tourism development. Cao and Chen (2008) examined the rural tourism and environmental issues in western ethnic areas and proposed measures to develop eco-tourism communities and establish government-led environmental protection mechanisms. Li (2014) found that a variety of ecological services of natural ecosystems can be used to develop rural tourism, which can also effectively reduce the harmful ecological footprint. Li and Wang (2015) discussed ecological transformation of rural tourism.

11.2.3.1.5 Problems and Strategies

Problems and countermeasures for rural tourism research have been a focus from the early stages of rural tourism development. Many scholars have done such research to provide support for the reality. For instance, Po (2010) through the Chengdu case study pointed out that a single product type, no outstanding features, low management level, and poor marketing and brand awareness are the major issues for domestic rural tourism at this stage. Liu and Li's (2013) study showed that there are large-scale problems such as inadequate infrastructure and poor environmental awareness of staff regarding rural tourism, and introduced the sustainable development model to solve the problems. Addressing environmental issues, Zheng and Zhou (2007) and Mo (2011) studied sustainable development and low-carbon development of rural tourism separately. Rural tourism under the urban and rural overall development has become an important topic. Li (2015) discussed the rural tourism development strategy under urban and rural balancing. Luo (2015) analyzed the basic situation and formation mechanism of rural tourism value system and then analyzed the way to construct rural tourism in the context of urban and rural overall planning.

11.2.3.1.6 Other Related Topics

The research on rural tourism in the present stage still includes tourists' and residents' perception, such as the demand mechanism in rural tourism (Tao, 2015); tourist behavior and satisfaction (Wang and Luo, 2006; Tang and Zhai, 2008); local residents' attitudes toward rural tourism and their sense of belonging (Du, et al., 2013; Jia and Wang, 2015); upgrading of rural tourism industry (Yang, 2011); and rural tourism destination image cognition (Guo and Wang, 2015).

In general, the research scope of domestic rural tourism is extensive, research topics are diversified, and research methods are mainly qualitative empirical research. This also shows that the study of rural tourism has a strong practical value, providing guidance to the development of the industry.

11.2.3.2 The Main Contents of Leisure Agriculture

11.2.3.2.1 Concept

The definition of leisure agriculture is mainly focused on industrial function, industry convergence, leisure, and sightseeing. Zhang (2006) believes that leisure agriculture is to increase the function of leisure-based agricultural production, which will not only eliminate the single production function of agriculture, but also increase the cultural attributes of agriculture. Guo (2007) proposed leisure agriculture as a new industry based on agriculture for the purpose of leisure by means of service. This new industry is aimed at urban tourists, coupling agriculture and tourism, the first and tertiary industries. Mao (2008) argued that leisure agriculture is a series of leisure activities full of agricultural characteristics provided to visitors, taking advantage of rural natural ecology and cultural environment, through design and planning management. Zhang (2012) argued that leisure agriculture industrialization is essentially a kind of emerging industry form with a set of entertainment, tourist resort, scientific research and education, demonstration, taking into consideration agricultural production, farmers' lifestyle, and rural amorous feelings for enterprise operation and scale development.

11.2.3.2.2 Development Model

The study of the leisure agriculture development model can not only enrich the relevant theories but also provide guidance for the practice. For example, Guo et al. (2007) summarized the previous models and puts forward the model of facility agriculture, a science and technology park. Guo et al. (2008) summed up pastoral agricultural tourism, folklore tourism, farmhouse tourism, village township tourism, leisure tourism, science education tourism, and return to nature tourism as seven leisure agricultural modes, and their segmentation was discussed in each of the mode segmentation. Hu (2011) discussed the development model of leisure agriculture in Hangzhou with the theory of tourism spatial structure. Feng and Dai (2012) put forward the systematic protection, emphasizing overall and resource sustainable development, regional differences and coordination principles, and agricultural landscape treatments based on the agricultural landscape characteristics of "Production and Ecology and Life" function. Niu (2014) summarized six modes pertaining to the development of domestic leisure agriculture, exploring the agricultural exhibition, farming participation, ecological tourism, folk culture, peasant life experience, and rural holiday entertainment. Hong et al. (2014) researched on leisure agriculture in Guangdong Province and examined three modes, namely farm participation, folk experience, and science education.

11.2.3.2.3 Present Situation Analysis

For the study of the present situation of leisure agriculture, domestic scholars generally adopt the way of empirical studies through field investigations and analyze the destination's development status. For example, Zhang et al. (2013) researched and analyzed the overall spatial layout of Hunan leisure agriculture and some key parks, and put forward specific strategies on how to promote the development of leisure agriculture in Hunan. Miao et al. (2014) use the content analysis method to analyze the types, spatial distribution, and tourist satisfaction of Guangxi leisure agriculture scenic spots. Some other scholars studied this field through the model and quantitative analysis methods, such as Liu (2015) who focused on Beijing residents' leisure agriculture demand behavior characteristics and influencing factors through the use of the Heckman model and pointed out that poor reception facilities and service environment are the key limiting factors. Xu et al. (2015) used the quantitative analysis method to study 483 nationwide leisure agriculture and rural tourism demonstrations focusing on the spatial distribution characteristics and influencing factors. Xiantang conveyed that resources, transportation, and tourism market have a greater impact on the development of domestic leisure agriculture. Some other literature focused on discussions regarding leisure agriculture promotion strategy qualitatively (Li, 2015; Wang and Ge, 2015).

11.2.3.2.4 New Rural Construction

The research on the relationship between new rural and leisure agriculture has always been an important topic, and leisure agriculture has a huge role in promoting the construction of new rural areas (Wang, 2007; Zhou and Huang, 2012). Zeng, Li, and Zeng (2011) and Xu and Lv (2012) respectively probed the leisure agriculture development in the southeast area of Chongqing and the northern Jiangsu area with regard to the new rural construction and put forward specific strategies.

11.2.3.2.5 Discussion

Compared with rural tourism, the research on leisure agriculture is obviously insufficient. On the one hand, the research depth is not enough; on the other hand, the research methods are mostly qualitative analysis and there is little quantitative analysis. Cross-disciplinary research on leisure agriculture is relatively inadequate, and most of the literature is still concentrated on the agriculture field. In the future, it should cover the research and development of leisure agricultural products, consumer behavior, and marketing strategy to promote the popularization of leisure agriculture and industrial upgrading.

11.2.4 Review and Prospect

11.2.4.1 Review

At present, the research on rural tourism and leisure agriculture in China has achieved some results, but the results are mainly focused on the development and planning of rural tourism, ecological environment protection, rural development strategy, development model, and so on. The basic theoretical research is not enough. It explains the dependence of rural tourism on resources, simultaneously showing that the research of rural tourism and leisure agriculture at the present stage is still at the macro level, with a lack of in-depth discussion of the relevant issues. The research topic also lacks innovation, as the repetition of the research problem is prominent. These problems are more obvious in the area of leisure agriculture.

In the research method, the qualitative research trend of rural tourism and leisure agriculture is obvious. Although there are some studies using quantitative research methods, the number is relatively small. Meanwhile, rural tourism is less geared toward interdisciplinary research. There are few studies on rural tourism from the perspective of sociology, management, or economics. The research method system of rural tourism in China is not yet mature.

11.2.4.2 Prospect

There are quite rich results from the research on rural tourism; so, the study on basic theory and basic concepts should be strengthened. In terms of research topics, how to promote rural tourism experience in the era of mass tourism; how to construct rural marketing channels through the internet environment, the interactive mechanism between the development of urbanization and rural tourism and leisure agriculture; and how to guide the innovation of rural tourism through the policy will be some important research directions. How to carry out interdisciplinary research on rural tourism and leisure agriculture is also a subject that deserves attention.

Rural tourism and leisure agriculture not only have an important impact on the tourism industry itself, but they also have a far-reaching impact on the country's economic, social, cultural, and other aspects. Going forward, more attention must be paid to this field in hopes of attracting more scholars to study rural tourism and leisure agriculture.

KEYWORDS

- **leisure agriculture**
- **literature review**
- **rural tourism**

REFERENCES

Cai, B., Tao, Z., & Lang, F., (2013). A Comparative study on Rural Tourism Community Participation Mode: Taking three villages in Zhejiang Province as Examples. *Commercial Research, 10*, 191–196.

Cao, D., & Chen, G., (2008). Environmental problems and sustainable development of rural tourism in the western ethnic areas. *Ecological Economy, 10*, 109–112.

Cao, X., (2012). Cultural mapping: A new method of community involvement and the practice in cultural rural tourism. *Tourism Tribune, 12*, 67–73.

Chen, X., (2011). Upgrading the rural tourism in Sichuan nationality region on the basis of location analysis. *Journal of Southern Agriculture, 42*(9), 1168–1171.

Du, Z., Su, Q., & Jiang, L., (2013). A structural mode of residents' sense of community in rural tourism destinations and its application: a case study of Anji county in Zhejiang province. *Tourism Tribune, 28*(6), 65–74.

Fan, C., & Li, B., (2009). Spatial pattern of countryside tourism based on the theory of landscape ecology. *Economic Geography, 29*(4), 683–687+697.

Fan, Y., & Xie, Y., (2015). Memory, display and gaze: a research on the synergy of protection and utilization about rural cultural heritages. *Tourism Science, 1, 11*–24+87.

Feng, H., & Zhao, J., (2009). Study on residents' perception to tourism influence and exploring countermeasures in "Beijing Tianjin passageway"—A case study of Yang Jiaying village, Yongqing county, Hebei province. *Journal of Anhui Agricultural Sciences, 37*(14), 6674–6677.

Feng, X., & Dai, G., (2012). The Protection of agricultural landscape characteristics in rural tourism development. *Tourism Tribune, 8*, 104–111.

Gao, N., (2015). Research on rural tourism development model – A case study of Chengdu area. *Modern Business, 24*, 44–45.

Ge, Z., & Zhang, S., (2015). Research on leisure agriculture at western ethnic region: A case study of Ningxia. *Ecological Economy, 31*(9), 132–136+155.

Guo, C., & Liang, M., (2009). Study on the developing model of rural tourism in the developed areas. *Guangdong Agricultural Sciences, 3*, 215–218.

Guo, F., Wang, K., Zhang, J., & Li, R., (2015). Rural tourism destination image of the case in "five golden flowers" Chengdu: Based on the text mining of blogs. *Tourism Tribune, 30*(4), 84–94.

Guo, H., (2010). The Significance, situation and prospects of the development of leisure agriculture in China. *Chinese Journal of Agricultural Resources and Regional Planning, 31*(1), 39–42.

Guo, H., & Lv, M., (2008). The present situation and countermeasures of leisure agriculture in China. *Economic Geography, 4*, 640–645.

Guo, H., & Ren, G., (2007). Study on the Present situation and countermeasures of our country's leisure agriculture development. *Journal of Beijing International Studies University, 1*, 66–71.

Guo, W., (2010). Study on the "alternate system mode" regarding rural residents' participation in tourism development and community empowerment effectiveness—A case study of Shangri La Yubeng community, Yunnan Province. *Tourism Tribune, 1*, 76–83.

Guo, Y., (2011). A study on community-scenic symbiosis model on rural tourism. *Resource Development and Market, 27*(2), 187–189.

Guo, Y., Wu, H., Ma, L., Zhang, J., & Wu, W., (2007). Study on the Urban agriculture development model. *Ecological Economy, 11*, 131–135.

Han, B., & Wang, J., (2009). On the rural tourism development model of the three northeastern provinces—based on "city-village" growth poles model. *Journal of Beijing International Studies University, 3*, 50–55.
He, A., Yang, X., Chen, J., & Wang, Z., (2014). Rural tourism development on farmer households' livelihood impact - A case study of Qinling Mountain. *Economic Geography, 12*, 174–181.
He, J., & Li, L. (2002).A study on the conceptions of rural tourism. *Journal of Southwest China Normal University (Philosophy & Social Sciences Edition), 28*(5), 125–128.
Hong, J., Wan, Z., Xiao, G., & Cong, R., (2014). Development situation, main mode and countermeasure of Guangdong leisure agriculture. *Guangdong Agricultural Sciences, 41*(16), 198–201+205.
Hu, A., (2011). Structural layout and development of leisure agriculture mode: As an example of Hangzhou . *Ecological Economy, 1*, 104–107+112.
Hu, Y., (2009). The development and protection of rural tourism and rural culture. *Journal of Anhui Agricultural Sciences, 37*(21), 10303–10304.
Huang, D., (2007). Analysis on the environmental problems and countermeasures in the development of rural tourism. *Ecological Economy,* 10, 118–121.
Huang, W., Ding, Y., & Shen, F., (2011). A Study on the negative influence of south Anhui rural tourism on the environment—A case study of Xidi and Hongcun. *Journal of Anhui Agricultural University (Social Sciences Edition), 20*(2), 24–26+101.
Jia, Y., & Wang, D., (2015). Changes in residents' perception of impact and attitudes towards tourism development over time. *Tourism Tribune, 5*, 65–73.
Li, F., (2011). Study on protection models based on the binary attributes of rural cultural landscape. *Area Research and Development, 30*(04), 85–88+102.
Li, W., (2015). Some considerations about the development of leisure agriculture in Liaoning. *Agricultural Economy, 7*, 74–75.
Li, X., (2013). A study on pro-poor rural tourism mode subject to community based development. *Ecological Economy (Academic Edition), 2*, 349–351.
Li, X., (2015). Overall Ideas and countermeasures of rural tourism in the perspective of urban and rural areas. *Agricultural Economy, 5*, 61–62.
Li, Y., & Jin, L., (2014). Study on the Ecological footprint structure and characteristics of rural tourism—A case study of Liu Gou village, Yanqing County, Beijing. *Resource Development and Market. 30*(09), 1147–1149+1152.
Li, Y., & Wang, C., (2015). Study on the ecological transformation of rural tourism under the new urbanization in China. *Agricultural Economic Problems, 6*, 29–34+110.
Liao, G., (2014). A brief discussion on the agricultural culture in the development of rural tourism. *Agricultural Economy, 8*, 41–42.
Liao, H., (2014). Pathways to sustainable rural tourism: Satoyama approaches for developing rural tourism in Taoyuan, Taiwan, China. *Tourism Tribune, 29*(6), 76–86.
Lin, Z., Lv, W., Wu, R., & Mo, X., (2013). Gender differences in entrepreneurial motivations for agri-tourism operators: The case of Taiwan. *Tourism Tribune, 28*(5), 89–98.
Liu, D., (2006). Several discriminations in rural tourism, agricultural tourism and folklore tourism. *Tourism Tribune, 21*(3), 12–19.
Liu, H, & Li, S., (2013). Ecological civilization perspective of rural tourism intensive sustainable development roadpath. *Ecological Economy, 4*, 138–141.
Liu, H., & Huo, S., (2015). An analysis of the demand behavior of urban residents' leisure agriculture - Based on the micro survey data of Beijing. *Journal of Agro technical Economics, 4*, 90–97.

Liu, X., Wang, X., Zhai, Z., & Chang, F., (2011). An analysis of the spatial structure of rural tourism and the promotion of its from based on the theory of urban daily system—A case study of Lantian county. *Human Geography, 5*, 138–142.

Lu, Z., Zhang, W., & Tang, J., (2009). An Empirical study on brand image of rural festival tourist activities—A case of Luoping rape bloom festival. *Tourism Tribune, 24*(5), 61–66.

Luo, S., Huang, Y., & Wang, L., (2009). Study on circular economy development model of rural Tourism —A case of Hongyan village tourist spots, Gongcheng, Guilin. *Tourism Forum, 2*(6), 886–889.

Luo, Y., (2006). A study on the assuring mechanism of the interest of community participation in tourism development of ethnic village. *Tourism Tribune, 21*(10), 45–48.

Luo, Y., (2015). Study on the Value system of rural tourism in the context of urban and rural development. *Agricultural Economy, 09*, 67–68.

Ma, Y., Zhao, L., Song, H., Guo, Q., & Liu, M., (2007). Study on the Chinese rural tourism development pattern—A case of Chengdu. *Economic Geography, 2*, 336–339.

Mao, S., (2008). The distinction between recreational agriculture, touristy agriculture and urban agriculture. *Special Zone Economy, 10*, 133–135.

Miao, H., Ma, J., & Zhang, H., (2014). Research on leisure agriculture development and demand characteristics in Ningxia -Based on the content analysis of network text. *Research on Development, 02*, 104–108.

Mo, Y., (2011). Study on rural tourism development in view of low carbon ecology—A case study of Lishui. *Ecological Economy, 4*, 102–104+111.

Ning, L., (2015). Guizhou traditional rural tourism and folk sports and culture interactive development—A case study of Miao village in Xijiang Southwestern Guizhou. *Guizhou Ethnic Studies, 36*(08), 193–196.

Niu, J., (2014). Urban leisure agriculture mode and countermeasures. *Ecological Economy, 1*, 124–127+143.

Pu, S., (2010). Study on the present situation and countermeasures of rural tourism —Taking rural tourism of chengdu as an example. *Ecological economy, 5*, 119–123.

Sun, Y., Cheng, S., Zhong, L., & Min, Q., (2010). Assessment on Tourism resources potential for agricultural heritage sites: A case study on Qingtian county in Zhejiang province. *Resources Science, 32*(6), 1026–1034.

Tang, D., & Zhai, Y., (2008). A study on rural tourists' selective behaviors among different age groups. *Tourism Tribune, 23*(10), 68–71.

Tao, Y., (2015). An empirical study of the demand mechanism and appeals-alienation of rural tourism. *Journal of tourism, 30*(7), 37–48.

Wang, B., & Luo, Z., (2006). Survey on visitor satisfaction with services of rural tourism in Beijing. *Journal of Beijing Union University (Humanities and Social Sciences), 4*(4), 38–43.

Wang, J., (2010). Rural tourism development on local farmers' employment effects - A case study of Jiangxin island, Nanjing. *Guangdong Agricultural Sciences, 37*(12), 166–169.

Wang, J., (2011). Rural tourism development of western minority village based on the construction of new countryside. *Tourism Forum, 4*(1), 36–39.

Wang, L., (2009). On the elite governance of cultural heritage in rural tourism communities—discussion about the election in Pingan stockaded village, Guangxi province. *Tourism Tribune, 24*(5), 67–71.

Wang, S., & Zhang, Y., (2007). Leisure agriculture and the construction of new socialist countryside. *Rural Economy, 2*, 74–77.

Wang, S., & Zhao, Y., (2015). The countermeasures and suggestions for the development of modern leisure agriculture in Liaoning. *Agricultural Economy, 4*, 50–52.

Wang, T., & Xian, Y., (2009). Study on development decision-making path of recreational belt around metropolis (ReBAM) rural tourism based on probability model. *Tourism Tribune, 24*(11), 30–35.

Wang, X., & Zhang, L., (2014). A Study on community participation mode and mechanism in rural tourism. *Tourism Overview (second half). 7*, 111–112.

Wu, D., Zhu, T., Wang, Y., Zhang, Y., & Wang, X., (2012). The five-win model of rural tourism development—An example of the planning in the Maogan scenic spot. *Journal of Beijing International Studies University, 5*, 1–8.

Xu, J., & Lv, H., (2012). Research on sightseeing and recreational agriculture development based on new countryside construction. *Anhui agricultural science, 40*(8), 4741–4743.

Xu, Q., (2013). Study on the spatial agglomeration of rural tourism based on the theory of "pole-axis system"—A case study of Jiangshan, in Zhejiang. *Economic Geography, 4*, 174–178.

Xu, X., Liu, D., Hu, J., & Hou, J., (2015). Spatial distribution characteristics and influencing factors of rural tourism destination – the case study of national level leisure agriculture and rural tourism demonstration sites. *Economic Geography, 9*, 182–188+207.

Yang, A., (2011). Understanding rural tourism upgrading from the industrial fusion optimization perspective. *Tourism Tribune, 26*(4), 9–11.

Yang, X., & Wang, Q., (2006). A study on resident participation in tourism planning and development at urban and rural destinations. *Tourism Tribune, 21*(4), 32–37.

Yu, D., & Wei, Q., (2015). Building rural tourism complex to promote sichuan rural tourism upgrading. *West Forum on Economy and Management, 03*, 40–43.

Zeng, J., & Zeng, W., (2011). Discussion on development strategies of recreational agriculture in the view of new rural construction. *Journal of Anhui Agricultural Sciences, 39*(32), 19913–19914.

Zhang, G., & Ulan Montoya, (2012). Study on Our country's leisure agriculture industrialization and its model. *Inquiry into Economic Issues, 10*, 30–37.

Zhang, J., (2015). Study on the Ancient villages folk culture change under the influence of rural tourism in central Zhejiang province. *Economic Forum, 9*, 105–107.

Zhang, W., & Yan, L., (2006). The Social and economic benefits, problems and countermeasures of rural tourism development in China. *Journal of Beijing International Studies University, 3*, 17–24.

Zhang, X., & Bao, J., (2009). Tourism Development and rural vicissitudes: the hypothesis of "origin-dynamics". *Tourism Tribune, 6*, 19–24.

Zhang, Y., & Wang, L., (2008). Digging the Rural culture to promote the sustainable development of rural tourism. *Agricultural Economy, 12*, 70–71.

Zhang, Y., & Zhang, Y., (2007). Rural culture and development of rural tourism. *Economic Geography, 27*(3), 509–512.

Zhang, Z., (2006). The object, essence and characteristics of leisure agriculture. *Chinese Rural Economy, 3*, 73–76.

Zheng, W., & Z, Z., (2007). On the basic features and realization approaches of sustainable rural tourism. *Ecological Economy, 9*, 127–130.

Zhou, B., & Huang, W., (2012). On the interaction of leisure agriculture development and constructing of new socialist countryside. *Ecological Economy, 2*, 97–100.

Zhou, Y., Jiang, J., & Wang, X., (2009). A study of community-driven endogenous rural tourism development model. *Tourism Science, 23*(4), 36–41.

Zhu, H., Zhang, H., Fu, Z., Yuan, Z., Zhang, J., Chen, M., & Huang, H., (2013). Development strategies and spatial layout of leisure agriculture in Hunan province. *Economic Geography, 33*(4), 132–134+154.

Zou, T., (2008). Mode and policy for rural tourism accelerating building a new socialist countryside. *Journal of Fujian Agriculture and Forestry University (Philosophy and Social Sciences), 11*(3), 31–34.

Zou, T., Wang, Y., & Cong, R., (2007). On the community-based model of rural tourism—A case study of Da Ying village. Tong Zhou District, Beijing. *Journal of Beijing International Studies University, 1*, 53–59.

CHAPTER 12

A REVIEW OF STUDIES ON CHINA TOURISM DESTINATION COMPETITIVENESS DURING THE PAST DECADE

JINGNA WANG

College of Tourism and Service Management, Nankai University, China

CONTENTS

ABSTRACT

This chapter aims to review the literature of tourism destination competitiveness (TDC) and examine the primary TDC research achievements in the recent 20 years. First, this chapter reviews the important theoretical basis and mainstream ideas of TDC, expounds the concept of TDC in detail and introduces a few tourism destination competitiveness models (TDCM) that are widely used today. Second, it combs development of the influencing factors and evaluation index of TDC. Third, the chapter will give a brief introduction of the latest Chinese empirical research achievements and evaluation methods of TDC. Fourth, from TDC definition, supply and demand perspectives and indicator selection, it will discuss the problems and challenges of the TDC research is facing, provides an outlook of the future directions and new path in TDC research. Fifth, this chapter will explore the strategies of enhancing TDC based on the perspective of a city in three aspects in the Chinese context. Finally, the chapter use Shenzhen as an example of destination city to explore how the destination develops, maintains, and enhances its competitiveness in a contemporary China context.

12.1 INTRODUCTION

Downturns in the global economy have created more market opportunities for tourism in recent years. Tourism has become the mainstay of many countries' or cities' economy. At the same time, consumers have become more experienced and more demanding with the wide use of network and information technology that leads to greater levels of competition among tourism destinations (TDs). Under these circumstances, many researchers have highlighted the importance of destination competitiveness (DC) in the field of tourism research and launched many additional studies (e.g., Pearce, 1997; Crouch and Ritchie, 1999; Faulkner, Oppermann, and Fredline, 1999; d'Hauteserre, 2000; Dwyer and Kim, 2003; Wang, Hsu, and Swanson, 2012). The Travel and Tourism Research Association (TTRA) recently claimed that destination performance and competitiveness are one of the top two management research priorities that are critical to decision makers over the next decade (Williams, Stewart, and Larsen, 2012). This also confirmed that how to develop, maintain, protect TDs, and strengthen their own competitiveness is a big challenge of tourism.

Many scholars have conducted research on the two major themes in tourism destination competitiveness (TDC) and obtained a wealth of research results in the recent two decades: (a) Developing a conceptual model or modifying existing models. (b) Exploring the influencing factors and determinants of TDC to evaluate DC empirically. The former attempts to provide a comprehensive conceptual framework that identifies key success factors in determining DC. These studies provide systematic guidelines and models to explain the comprehensive tourism value chain of DC (Ritchie and

Crouch, 1999, 2003; Buhalis, 2000; Hassan, 2000; Dwyer and Kim, 2003; Mazanec, Wöber, and Zins, 2007; Kunst, 2009). Based on previous studies, the latter group develops operational measures for each component of the DC model in order to provide indices of DC (Mihalic, 2000; Kozak, 2001; Melian-Gonzalez and Garcia-Falcon, 2003; Hudson, Ritchie, and Timur 2004; Enright and Newton, 2005; Botti, Peypoch, Robinotc, and Solonadrasana, 2009; Cracolici and Nijkamp, 2009; Kayar and Kozak, 2010; Zhang, Gu, and Zhang, 2011).

This chapter aims to review the essential discussion of TDC and examine the primary TDC research achievements in the recent 20 years. First, this paper reviews the important theoretical basis and mainstream ideas of TDC, expounds the concept of TDC in detail, and introduces a few TDC models (TDCM) that are widely used today. The influencing factors and evaluation index of TDC will be also examined. The chapter will give a brief introduction of the latest Chinese empirical research achievements of the TDC evaluation methods. Then, it will discuss the problems and challenges the TDC research is facing and provide an outlook of the future of new directions and new paths in TDC research. Finally, this chapter will explore the strategies of enhancing TDC based on the perspective of a city from three aspects in the Chinese context.

12.1.1 THE CONCEPT AND STRUCTURE OF TOURISM DESTINATION COMPETITIVENESS (TDC)

TDs are places where tourist activities mainly happen. From the perspective of demand, tourists are faced with the increasingly diverse destination choices. From the perspective of supply, destination management organizations are in a highly competitive era. When it became obvious that the tourism industry had grown steadily to a prosperous level in the global economy (Kayar & Kozak, 2010), understanding the factors that drive DC is of particular interest to both researchers and policymakers (Tsai, Song, and Wong, 2009).

12.1.1.1 The Origin of TDC

Early researches focused on the source, forms, and features of TDC, which included studies of traditional destination image, destination attraction, lifecycle of the destination, decision-making of tourists, and stakeholders related to tourism in the tourism area. In the 1990s, international competitiveness was introduced to tourism research. These views of competitiveness are associated with three major groups of thought. They are: (1) comparative advantage and/or price competitiveness perspective; (2) strategy and management perspective; and (3) historical and socio-cultural perspective (Dwyer and Kim, 2003). These views are related to the country-specific economic characteristics of competitiveness, firm-specific characteristics, and social, political, and cultural characteristics of competitiveness.

The theory of comparative advantage and the theory of competitive advantage are more suitable than many other mature theories to be the theoretical basis of TDC research. The theory of comparative advantage is one of the classical theories of international trade. It states that the comparative advantage of primary production factors such as land, labor, and natural resources is the key to determine the success of competition. Extended to DC, comparative advantage refers to advantages of resources endowment of a destination, including natural resources, human resources, knowledge resources, and capital resources. The differences in resource endowment of a destination determine the direction of development and the strategic plan of a TD, so that the TD can investigate and develop comparative advantages to form competitive industries and improve competitiveness in the marketplace.

Michael Porter's theory of competitive advantage (Diamond model) states that the international competitive advantage of a country depends on the integration of four basic elements: the factors of production, demand conditions, related industries, corporate strategy organizations, and two auxiliary elements (acts of government and opportunities). Many scholars took the diamond model as the most basic element on which to build TDCM. Though Porter's Diamond model refers to a nation's competitive advantages, it can be applied to a region or destination (Vanhove, 2005). If a region or destination can make effective use of its resources, it still can obtain competitiveness (Crouch and Ritchie, 1999).

Ritchie and Crouch explain that the success of destinations comes from the integration between resources and management by using the concepts of comparative and competitive advantages. The Crouch-Ritchie (C-R) model established by them is also based on the theory of competitive advantage, and other scholars conducted additional research to improve and perfect it, thus forming influential models such as the Dwyer and Kim model.

In recent years, the resource-based perspective played a very important role in the analysis of competitive advantage (Grant, 1991; Day, 1994). Fewer studies in DC briefly introduced the resource-based perspective into TDC, but they failed to integrate that perspective into TDC research (Dwyer and Kim, 2003; Melian-Gonzalez and Garcia-Falcon, 2003; Lee and King, 2006, 2008; Cracolici and Nijkamp, 2008). The author suggests that only when there are detailed and in-depth analyses of the state of resources and sharing a consistent understanding of destination development strategy for all relevant actors, can a TD achieve use of resources sufficiently and effectively. Therefore, further studies on the resource-based view (RBV) theory will help action bodies of TDs to build a careful framework for the study of TDC and reach agreement on competitive strategies.

12.1.2 ANALYSIS ON THE CONNOTATION OF TDC

Definitions of TDC are mostly based on a competitive strategy theory perspective, focusing on destination resources and abilities in the use of resources. Such views indicate that DC is an organic combination of all relevant capabilities and emphasizes on the comprehensive ability of the destination. For example, after many years of TDC research, Crouch and Ritchie (2000a) pointed out that a destination's competitiveness is the ability to expand travel income and attract more tourists by providing a satisfactory and memorable experience for tourists, at the same time improving the local people's quality of life through tourism and protecting preservation for future generations. Hassan (2000) indicated that TDC should be "the ability of a destination to create and integrate added value products that sustain its resources while maintaining market position relative to other competing destinations." Buhalis (2000) also explained that TDC could be the ability to make a long-term success of a destination and ensure the sustainability of local resources so that it can satisfy all stakeholders. These definitions stated that TDC depends on the ability of all relevant action bodies to add value to existing resources and stressed that the sustainability of the effective use of resources will generate strategic assets that meet the interests and demands of stakeholders.

Meanwhile, some scholars highlighted the role of TDC in the market from the theory paradigm of location advantage-company performance and explained that the performance of a TD should manifest as a destination market position or market share; they used economic indicators (e.g., market share and tourism revenues) to reflect the competitiveness of a destination. D'Hauteserre's (2000) considered that TDC is the ability of a TD to maintain and enhance its market position and share over time. Yoon (2002) argued that TDC is the ability of a TD to create and integrate value-added products so as to maintain its market position. Buhalis (2000) put forward that TDC is the ability to occupy a position of initiative in the competitive market.

With the traditional view that TDs are regarded as well-defined geographical areas, such as a country, an island or a town, being replaced by a new concept of the modern TD, it is increasingly recognized that a destination can also be a perceptual concept. This can be interpreted subjectively by consumers, depending on their travel itinerary, cultural background, purpose of visit, educational level, and past experience (Vlahović, 2010). Some studies focused on customer experience value, re-examined the theory of competitive strategy, and explored the definition and framework of TDC. Dwyer and Kim (2003) argued that the manifestation of competitiveness is a destination's ability to provide better products and services than another destination for visitors in their important experience. Lee and King (2009) believed that TDC is the ability to obtain a sustained competitive advantage and convey a better travel experience than other similar destinations. Kunst (2009) pointed out the sustainable competitiveness of any TD is basically determined by its ability to effectively distinguish itself from competing destinations by means of a particular set of emotion-driven tourist experiences that are hard to imitate. Wang and Pizam (2011) pointed out that the resources of a TD create a lasting and memorable link for tourists between the physical environment and an interpersonal relationship. If the destination is able to realize the potential of these resources and conduct independent marketing, it is possible to embark on a competitive road of sustainable development.

Chinese scholar Long (2010) explained that comparative advantages changed tourism competitiveness from the perspective of supply and demand to one of competitiveness based on the tourist experience. Pi (2015) proposed that customer experience value is the essence of competition in TDs. To defeat competitors is only a by-product of a superior experience and not the goal of TD competition.

It is important to note here is that TDC is a relative concept. A TD is a geographical space where tourism resources cluster, but is not an administrative boundary (Pike, 2008). It can be a theme park, an island, a town, or a state/province, and it can also be a country or an international zone. Development scale, space scale, destination organization, demographics, geography, climate and weather, culture, infrastructure, attractions, politics, management, and other aspects are variables in different TDs. Therefore, there are common inherent characteristics among destinations which are directly competing (Assaker, Hallak, Vinzi, and O'Connor, 2014). The competitiveness of the TD is evaluated in order to determine the status of a destination with respect to other similar destinations (Haahti, 1986; Henderson, 2000). Kozak and Rimmington (1999) suggest that we first need to determine what destinations are direct competitors to compare different TDCs. Competitiveness is determined by results compared with direct competitors. Enright and Newton (2004) emphasized the importance of considering competitiveness in specific environments and pointed out that the strength of competitiveness in a certain destination is represented by the results of comparing it to different competitors. Therefore, the competitiveness of a TD is similar to the competitiveness of enterprises. Without competition, competitiveness is not meaningful. Competitiveness can be explained by being compared with competitors. If competitiveness is measured without competitors, it can only reflect the current situation and attributes of a TD. Only by comparing all aspects with its competitors, can it reflect the relative competitiveness of a destination and that will be a future reference to clearly guide destination development.

It is not hard to see that there is a certain difference in "TDC" that the above research maintained. The multidimensional characteristic of TDC and the multifaceted results of competition performance lead to the failure of TDC studies to agree on a widely acceptable concept of DC. Although, with the development of TDC research, scraping these diverse and scattered fragmented theories together, we can outline the logical thread of the definition of the TDC concept—"resource advantages-unique ability-position advantage-destination competitiveness." But the additional clarification of a definition of the connotation of TDC is still an urgent problem to be solved in this research field. The problem of defining the competitiveness of a TD and clarifying the manifestation and performance of TDC should be solved. The answers will surely become a guide and standard for the development of TDC research.

12.1.3 MODELS OF TDC

A TD is not directly equal to ordinary goods. The essential difference between them lies in that the tourists' experience of the tourism product is co-created by a number of participants (Wang and Pizam, 2011). The formation of TDC should not only be based on the comparative advantage and competitive advantage theory, but it also needs analysis from the perspective of the system theory in order to better understand the relationship of all kinds of factors on competitiveness in TDs and their influences on each other.

Based on Potter's Diamond model, Ritchie and Crouch (2000, 2003) proposed a complex model of TDC and took into account competitive advantages and the comparative advantages as well as the micro and macro environment. The core of the model has five dimensions: (1) supporting factors and resources, including infrastructure, accessibility, facilitating resources, hospitality, enterprises, etc., which are the basis for a successful TD; (2) core resources and attractors, which encompass the constructs physiography and climate, culture and history, mix of activities, special events, entertainment, superstructure, and market ties, describe the main attraction of the TD; (3) destination management, which can improve the core resources' attraction and strengthen the quality and efficiency of supporting factors and resources, adapt to a potential barrier (such as seasonal activity) (Wang, Hsu, and Swanson, 2012), and is composed of organization, marketing, quality of service/ experience, information /research, human resource management, finance and venture capital, visitor management, resource stewardship, and crisis management; (4) destination policy, planning and development, including philosophy/ value, vision, positioning/branding, development, competitive/ collaborative analysis, monitoring and evaluation, and audit; (5) and finally, qualifying and amplifying determinants consisting of location, safety/security, cost/value, interdependencies, awareness/image, and carrying capacity (Crouch, 2011).

The C-R model of TDC made a detailed description and analysis of the complex relationship of influencing factors, which had a wide influence on understanding and evaluating TDC. Their research provided guidance and encouragement for further studies. Based on this model, other research tried to improve the traditional C-R model from different aspects (e.g., Mihalic, 2000; Dwyer and Kim, 2003; Enright and Newton, 2004, 2005; Kim, Borges, and Chon, 2006; Cracolici and Nijkamp, 2009). However, the C-R model makes it difficult to measure the whole set of various tourism competitiveness determinants, which reduces the applicability of this model (Kunst, 2009). Alternatively, tourists' experiences are not dependent on the magnitude of each element but on the tourism market which is structured by competitive factors (Long, 2010). Thus, the C-R model has some drawbacks.

Dwyer and Kim (2003) found that the C-R model only pay attention to the perspective of supply and ignore the perspective of demand. They developed the integrated model of TDC, made with a combination of the main elements of national and firm competitiveness and the main elements of DC. The model is similar to Crouch and Ritchie's framework, but adds some different aspects to explain the determinants of DC.

The model is made up of resources (including endowed resources, created resources, and supporting resources), destination management, situational conditions, demand conditions, destination competitiveness indicators, and quality of life indicators. With reference to the destination's resources/attractions base, Dwyer and Kim not only distinguish between inherited and created resources but also stress the importance of supporting factors (Kunst, 2009). Inherited resources contain both natural and cultural resources; created resources consist of tourism infrastructure and superstructure, special events, variety of available activities, entertainment and shopping; and supporting resources comprise capital infrastructure, service quality, accessibility, hospitability, and market linkages. In contrast to the C-R model, Dwyer and Kim's model explicitly acknowledges demand as an important factor, such as the demand's perception of the destination, the demand's preferences, and the potential demand's awareness of the tourist destination, and adds socio-economic prosperity as the required outcome. Although this model is also mostly of conceptual significance, its practical application would require a huge effort to determine the competitive capacity of a TD (Kunst, 2009).

Heath (2003) determined that existing models do not deal adequately and integratively with certain issues. For example, existing studies do not adequately emphasize the importance of human capital as a key determinant of TDC and do not attach enough attention to the essential linkages between communication and information management. Therefore, Heath (2003) proposed a new model that contains the following key factors: the foundation, an essential base for competitiveness; the cement, which binds and links respective facets; the building blocks, which are essential to make tourism "happen" in a destination; and the roof (the key success drivers). This model contains four levels that include the customer experience, balance between stakeholder engagement and acquired benefits, and a holistic approach to destination marketing and strategy (e.g., destination image and branding, competitive positioning, target markets, innovative promotional strategies, visitor satisfaction management) and other factors. Thus, Heath's model should be considered mostly for the merit of its conceptual-cognitive contribution (Kunst, 2009). However, whether the elements in his model can be used to apply for empirical purposes and compare the key determinants among destinations needs to be examined further.

Chinese scholars Guo and Cao (2004) indicated that the existing competitive model is too general to be used as guidance on specific TDC. Through a survey questionnaire of 64 related professional doctoral students, they received six key questions on which to focus; then, they constructed the 6 factor linkage model, which describes the relationship between them. The model is shown in Figure 12.1. They put the visitor experience and the quality of residents' life as two key dimensions into the model. At the same time, circulation and interaction of the left and right sides of the model explain the key factors of TDC and the relationship among those factors. But this model only used qualitative analysis and had not yet carried out empirical testing.

In addition, Yi (2006) made a reconstruction based on elements lacking in the D-K model and established five factors of TDC from the questionnaire and path analysis. The model factors were divided into three categories. The first category included tourism resources and support factors. They were the antecedents of other elements. Elements of the second category were

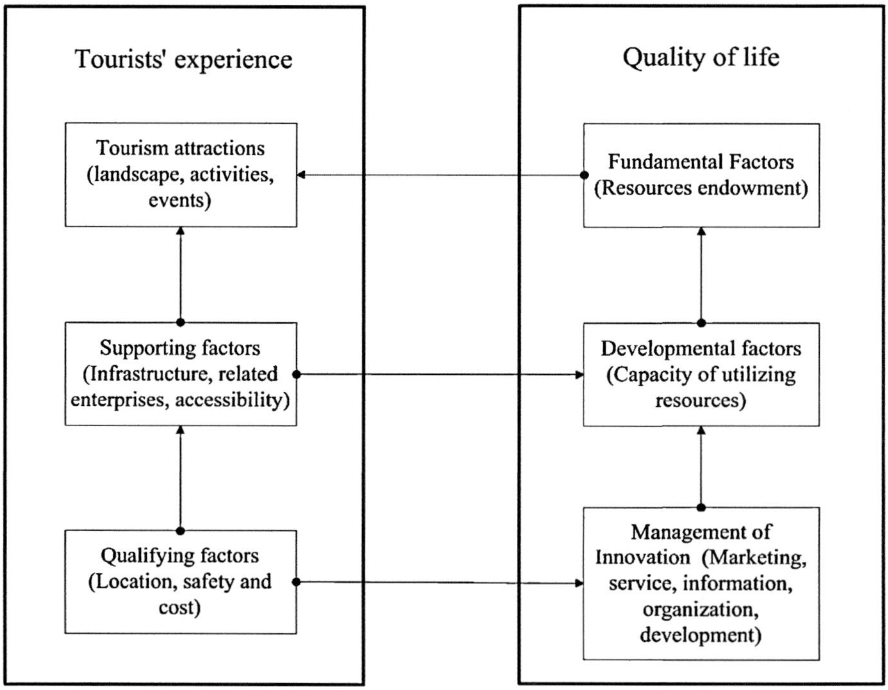

FIGURE 12.1 The 6-factor linkage model. (Source: Guo, and Cao, 2004).

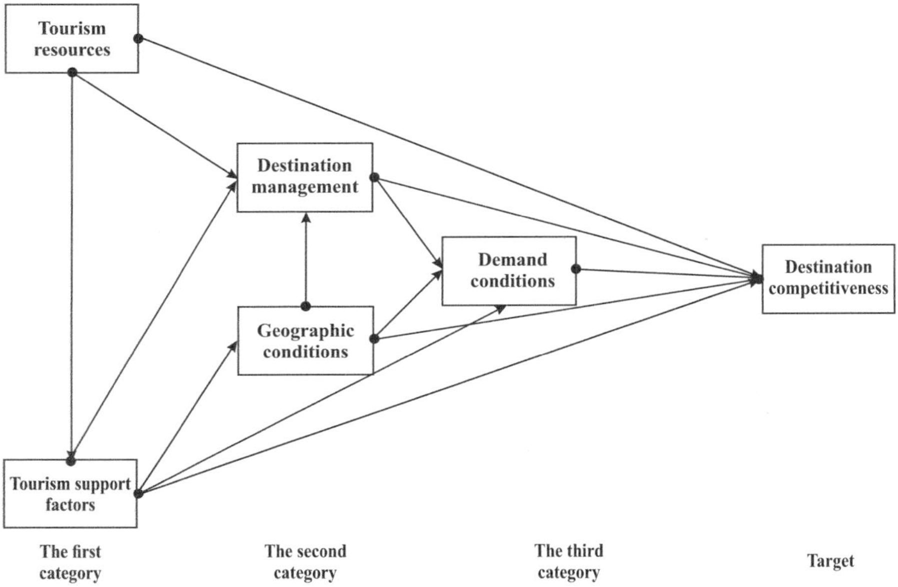

FIGURE 12.2 Five-factor model (Source: Yi, 2006).

destination management and geographic conditions. Elements of first and second categories influenced elements of the third category, demand conditions, which ultimately affected TDC (shown in Figure 12.2).

12.2 THE INFLUENCING FACTORS AND EVALUATION RESEARCH ON TDC

12.2.1 EMPIRICAL STUDIES ON THE INFLUENCING FACTORS AND EVALUATION INDEX SYSTEM OF TDC IN CHINA AND FOREIGN COUNTRIES

12.2.1.1 Influencing Factors of TDC

The C-R model based on Potter's competitive advantages and comparative advantages includes five main influencing factors of TDC: core resources and attractions, supporting factors and resources, destination management, amplifying and qualifying determinants, and destination policy, planning, and development. This research provides guidance and inspiration to further studies.

12.2.1.1.1 Core Resources and Attractions

Core resources and attractions are the main factors that constitute the destination attraction and also are the primary cause and the core incentive factors of choosing a tourism destination.

Core resources can be divided into physiography and climate, culture and history, mix of activities, special events, entertainment, and superstructure. Crouch (2011) used the analytic hierarchy process (AHP) to rank each component and attribute. The result was that core resources and attractions are the most important and determinant factors for TDC. Among them, physiology and climate are the most important determinant components. Having a rich cultural and historical heritage was ranked as the second most important determinant factor.

12.2.1.1.2 Supporting Factors and Resources

Although it was found that the destination-supporting factor had a relatively smaller impact on a destination's competitiveness, this factor is an essential prerequisite for the success of tourism destinations (Wang, Hsu, and Swanson, 2012). Supporting factors and resources generally include general infrastructure, quality of service, and accessibility of destination, hospitality, and enterprise/market ties. In his empirical study, Crouch (2011) also found tourism infrastructure as a third important determinant component in DC. Assaker, Vinzi, and O'Connor (2011) found that the infrastructure and environment had a direct positive impact on generating tourism activities and revenue. As such, destination management organizations must be concerned with infrastructure and tourism superstructure. For example, improving reception facilities might include tailoring the space, layout, quality, and type to the flow rate, composition, and consumption level of the targeted tourism market (Wang et al., 2012). Enright and Newton (2004) indicated that TDC includes not only the specific factors of tourism attraction but also the enterprises or organizations involved in tourism products and tourism services.

In the early studies of TDC, "core resources and attractions" and "supporting factors and resources" were the main influencing factors of measurement, because they can explain the comparative advantages and competitive advantages to a large extent. With the further development of TDC research, studies have found the importance of destination management.

12.2.1.1.3 Destination Management

The component destination management refers to activities (e.g., marketing, resource stewardship) that can enhance the appeal of core resources and attractors, strengthen the quality and effectiveness of the supporting factors and resources, and best adapt to the underlying constraints (e.g., seasonality) (Wang et al., 2012). It mainly includes destination marketing management, service experience management, information management, human resource development, environmental management, and crisis management. Destination management places more emphasis on the "service experience" based on the concept that the tourism destination is actually the combination of a variety of different elements forming a comprehensive customer experience (Bejou and Palmer, 1995). This requires all stakeholders to coordinate and cooperate with each other, focusing on tourist demand, and creating greater customer experience value in order to withstand the competition. That tourism firms should ensure that their products are continually updated is consistent with respondents' agreement that destination managers and tourism firms should continue to create experiences in their destinations that differentiate themselves from other destinations and that operators should become "experience providers" developing personal encounters and authentic experiences (Dwyer et al., 2016).

As information technology changes the way visitors receive and use information, technological innovation will promote further understanding and experiences of the cultural and natural landscape of travelers (Molz, 2013). The success of tourism enterprises will continue to depend on their efforts to add value to products and services through the use of technology producing competitive advantage (Buhalis, 2000). The greater the environmental complexity that can be handled by a firm, the higher is the level of its adaptability and the better are the chances of its long-term survival (Tuominen, Rajala, and Moller, 2004). Environmental management of TDC impact was mainly reflected in two aspects. On the one hand, it can increase tourism enterprises operating costs. On the other hand, environmental management improves demand for the TD, while environmental management bringing new tourism demand can compensate for the costs. Environmental quality and the perception of the product that tourists purchase have a close relationship. Environment management can bring economic benefits for the tourism sector (Dwyer & Kim, 2003). In addition, having a crisis management plan in place is an important issue for populated tourist destinations (Wang et al., 2012). Moreover, based on the destination's market positioning research, TDs should reinforce promotional activities to improve competitiveness.

12.2.1.1.4 Qualifying Determinants

The qualifying determinants moderate, modify, or mitigate destination competitiveness by filtering the influence of the other components (Gomezelj and Mihalĭc, 2008; Wang et al., 2012). These factors can also be referred to as situational conditions that determine the potential upper limit of destination demand beyond the scope of the destination management organization's control or influence. Qualifying determinants mainly include destination location, safety, cost (i.e., transportation costs, the effect of exchange rates, and the cost of living in a tourism destination) and dependencies between destinations of a competitive or complementary nature. Gomezelj and Mihalĭc (2008) state that micro level situational conditions include company competition: value for money in destination tourism experiences, value for money in accommodations, the use of information technology by firms, and value for money in shopping items. But they were less competitive in the areas of co-operation between the public and private sectors, access to venture capital, the investment environment, the use of e-commerce, and manager capabilities. Assaf and Josiassen (2011) identified 30 determinants, which they grouped into eight drivers of tourism performance, including five qualifying determinant sub-dimensions: security, safety, health; economic conditions; and tourism price levels.

12.2.1.1.5 Demand Factors

With the deepening of TDC research, scholars recognized the comprehensive measurement of TDC cannot be confined to the supply perspective and should give more opportunity to consider the demand side, that is, to meet visitors' preferences and needs is the direct result of the DC. Dwyer and Kim (2003) first took into account demand conditions and determined that demand factors play an important role in determining TDC. Whether the destination has competitiveness depends on the tourists' motivation. Different motivations cause different tourists' purchase patterns. If demand is effective, the experience of tourism products and the expectation of tourists are matched (Dwyer et al., 2016). Therefore, the specific indicators of demand factors include destination awareness, destination perception, and destination preference. In further empirical studies, Dwyer et al. (2016) indicate that refreshing tourism products is important because of changing consumer values and competition. This should be based on customer orientation and also requires competitor analysis and acknowledgment of customer needs and global trends.

12.2.1.2 Empirical Studies on the Evaluation Index System of TDC

DC is a relative concept and also has multidimensional features, involving many different factors; so, it is always difficult and controversial to measure TDC. As the premise of TDC studies is a selection index and validation of the mutual relationship among indices, we must understand the impact of every index on competitiveness and their interaction with systematic perspective before confirming indicators. Therefore, the current TDC evaluation index system is mostly derived from the main factors in the existing mature destination competitiveness model.

Many research studies put forward influencing/decision factors of TDC and made empirical measurements on relevant evaluation indicators. For example, Dwyer and Kim (2003) conducted a survey on the stakeholders of the tourism industry in South Korea and Australia, and proposed the decision factors and evaluation indicators of TDC. The evaluation index system is subdivided into successive and creative resources, support factors, destination management, industry environment, demand factors, and market performance indicators. They also classified the TDC indicators as "rigid indicators" and "soft indicators." "Rigid indicators" refers to the objective and quantitative evaluation index, also known as economic performance indicators such as tourism numbers, travel expenses, economic contribution of tourism, economic prosperity index, tourism investment, price competitiveness index, and government support. "Soft indicators" refers to the perception of tourists and subjective or qualitative indicators.

It should be noted that different countries have different tourism resources, which may result in the difference of tourism product type and consumption structure. At the same time, the factors that determine DC may vary in products and target market in different locations (Enright and Newton, 2005).

Because of the different analysis units or different analysis perspectives, the quantitative evaluation of TDC must have different research models. Therefore, many analyses still need more detailed work. For example, Enright and Newton (2004) combined with the features of Hong Kong to refine the indicators so that they can get the TDC of Hong Kong with the aid of the C-R model. This chapter compiled evaluation methods and indicators of the empirical studies on TDC over the past 20 years, as shown in (Table 12.1).

From the above table, the evaluation indicators of TDC can be divided into two categories: the obvious indicators (rigid indicators) and the recessive indicators (soft indicators). The obvious indicators reflect the final result of TDC, which mainly includes practical ability and potential ability. The practical ability can be reflected by tourism income, prices, person-time, and tourist per capita cost, and the potential ability can be measured by the tourism complaint ratio, the employment of tourism, tourism investment, etc. The recessive indicators reflect the status competition of similar tourism destinations sometime in the future, mainly from market surveys. It includes quality of life of destination residents, tourism resources level and destination image, government management, environment, the local economic support, and so on. TDC studies on "soft indicators" are quite controversial. "Rigid indicators" have fewer differences, but "rigid indicators" lack dynamic comparison and prediction (Wang, 2009); therefore, a TDC evaluation index system should be constructed by both "soft indicators" and "rigid indicators" and needs to be evaluated completely.

12.2.2 EVALUATION METHODS OF TDC

The present research has shown some methods for evaluating the competitiveness of TDs and its determinants. Before Crouch & Ritchie's research, studies on the TDC mainly used qualitative evaluation, but today, studies of various countries is no longer confined in qualitative research (such as the Delphi method) and focus more on the quantitative research, quantifying all kinds of indicators and then conducting extensive, meaningful analysis. Common methods are the AHP, factor analysis, principal component analysis (PCA), structural equation modeling (SEM), partial least squares path model (PLSPM), panel data model, and cluster analysis. In particular, the use of the panel data model makes it possible to measure potential competitiveness.

TABLE 12.1 Evaluation Methods and Main Evaluation Indicators of TDC

Author	Destination	Methodology	Data Sources	Main Evaluation Indicators
Kozak, Rimmington (1999)	Turkey and the other competitive destinations	Variance analysis	Questionnaire	Tourists' motivation, tourists' satisfaction or dissatisfaction with destination attributes, and seasonal competition, etc.
Uysal, Chen, Williams (2000)	Virginia and other 10 states in the U.S. Mid-Atlantic region	Descriptive statistical analysis Important performance analysis	Questionnaire	The characteristics of travel (travel distance, the scale of tourism, destination, season, destination type); the importance of factors: 48 attributes
Wang, Wu (2000)	Taiwan, Hongkong and the Association of Southeast Asian Nations (ASEAN)	Three stages least squares regression analysis, Optimal scale regression analysis	WTO Tourism statistics yearbook	Dependent variable: person-time; independent variables: price, exchange rate, time, special events
Dwyer, Forsyth, Rao (2002)	Australia and other 18 destinations	Variance analysis	The World Bank, International visitors survey	Price competitiveness index
Huybers, Bennett (2002)	Queensland	Multiple logistic regression analysis	Questionnaire	The degree of environmental damage, tourists demand
Sahli, Hazari,Sgro (2003)	19 OECD countries	Linear regression	Public data	Market share, price competitiveness, per capita income, real exchange rate, national passenger transport comparative advantage, hotel operation rate, relative density of tourists
Toh, Khan, Lafling (2004)	Singapore, Thailand, Malaysia, Hong Kong	Shift-Share analysis, SSA	The World Bank	Number of visitors

TABLE 12.1 (Continued)

Author	Destination	Methodology	Data Sources	Main Evaluation Indicators
Enright, Newton (2004)	Hong Kkong	Important performance analysis (IPA)	Questionnaire	15 attractions attributes, such as safety, navigation, nightlife, special events, etc., 37 enterprises related indicators, such as political stability, high international accessibility, convenient transportation, etc.
Mangion, Durbarry, Sinclai (2005)	3 tourism destinations in the Mediterranean (Malta, Cyprus, Spain)	Seemingly unrelated regressions, Wald Test, Multiple linear regression	The World Bank, Public data	Destination relative price (accommodation and transportation), price elasticity, expenditure elasticity
Enright, Newton (2005)	Hong Kong, Singapore, Bangkok	T-test, Variance analysis, F-test	Questionnaire	15 attractions attributes, such as safety, navigation, nightlife, special events, etc., 37 enterprises related indicators, such as political stability, high international accessibility, convenient transportation, etc.
Kim, Guo, Agrusa (2005)	Mainland outbound tourism destinations	Multi-dimension analysis, Interactive least squares analysis	Questionnaire	Destination attributes, preference of tourists
Gooroochurn, Sugiyarto(2005)	200 countries	Confirmatory factor analysis	Public data	Price, openness, communication facilities, infrastructure, culture, history, social development, environment and human resources
Yi Lirong(2006)	Seven regions of China	SEM	Questionnaire	Tourism resources, support factors, location conditions, regional tourism management, demand conditions

Author	Destination	Methodology	Data Sources	Main Evaluation Indicators
Mazanec, Wöber, Zins (2007)	197 countries around the world	Structural equation model, Least square method	WTTC data	8 potential variables such as openness, heritage and culture, infrastructure, communication facilities, social competitiveness, education, tourism price competitiveness and environmental protection, and 25 evaluation indicators
Gomezelj, Mihalic (2008)	Slovenia	Descriptive statistical analysis T- test	Questionnaire	6 evaluation indicators, such as endowment resources, creative resources, support factors, environment, destination management, demand, and 85 sub indexes.
Cracolici, Nijkamp (2009)	6 areas in the south of Italy	Factor analysis	the 2001 ACNielsen SITA survey on Italian tourist habits and behaviors	Regional Tourist Attractiveness(RTA) Destination Competitiveness Indicator(DCI)
Zang Dexia (2009)	Qingdao, Dalian	Factor analysis	Questionnaire	Tourism competitive performance, tourists' satisfaction and residents' happiness index
Hong Zhang, Chaolin Gu, Luwen Gu, et al(2011)	16 cities in Yangtze River Delta of China	TOPSIS & Information entropy	China statistical yearbook 2006	Tourism resources endowment, capacity, tourism employment ability, sustaining power
Zhang Yi, Zhang Ning, Fang Xu-Hong, Huang Zhong-Hao (2011)	China	IPA	Expert Scoring	Potential competitiveness, environmental competitiveness, realistic competitiveness
Wang Chunyang, Huang Fucai (2011)	Zhangjiajie, China	EFA & CFA	Questionnaire	Tourism resources, tourism facilities, infrastructure, support elements, destination management, quality of service

TABLE 12.1 (Continued)

Author	Destination	Methodology	Data Sources	Main Evaluation Indicators
Chunyang Wang, Maxwell K. Hsu, Scott R. Swanson (2012)	China	EFA	Questionnaire (snowballing type, the first batch of tourism practitioners)	Tourism resources, infrastructure, destination support factors, destination management, tourism superstructure
Ivo Mulec , Nicholas-Wise (2013)	Serbia's Vojvodina Region	Mean and standard deviations (SD)	Online survey: www.esurveyspro.com	Heritage, artificial resources, support factors, destination management , scenario, demand factors
Guy Assaker, Rob Hallak, Vincenzo Esposito Vinzi, et al. (2013)	154 countries	PLSPM	Euromonitor International	Total arrivals, tourists' expenses and revenue
Stanislav Ivanov (2013)	140 countries	Regression analysis	WTTC	Destination environment, business environment and infrastructure, cultural resources and natural resources
Jeong-Yeol Park, Soo Cheong (Shawn) Jang (2014)	30 countries	Gravity model	Tourism statistics yearbook	Dependent variable: passenger flow; independent variables: environment, climate, culture, history, infrastructure, accessibility, price, tourism superstructure and other 16 indicators
Dwyer, Dragićević, Armenski , Mihalič, & Knežević Cvelbar. (2014)	Serbia	IPA	Questionnaire (Tourism practitioners)	Sustainable tourism development, marketing, risk management, climate change, innovation and product development, tourism and hospitality education

Author	Destination	Methodology	Data Sources	Main Evaluation Indicators
Yinggao Zhu, Qianjing Zhu, Zhiwei Zhu (2014)	16 cities in Yangtze River Delta of China	Self-organizing map	Yangtze River Delta statistical yearbook 2011, WNCHS, NHCCS, et al.	Revealed competitive advantages (tourism performance, tourism operation ability), potential competitive advantages (tourism professionals, tourism resources), environmental sustaining power (natural support, economic support and social support)
Trinidad Domínguez Vila, Simon Darcy, Elisa Alén González (2015)	Spain and Australia	Factorial analysis, k-means clustering analysis	the secondary data from the web's official sources for all tourist destinations	17 secondary indicators: Core resources and attractions, supporting factors and resources, limitation and amplification factors, destination planning and management
Marco Cucculelli, Gianluca Goffi (2015)	Italian Destinations of Excellence	Principal component analysis	Collected by a web survey	Core resources and key attractions, tourism service, overall infrastructure, conditions and support factors, destination policy and development, destination management, demand factors

1. **Delphi method.** It is based on system procedures and makes use of anonymous comments that experts shall not discuss with each other, does not have horizontal linkages, and only has a relationship with investigators. Through many rounds of investigation of experts on questions of a questionnaire, after repeatedly consulting, classifying, and modifying, the final results are aggregated into an agreement among experts. This method is a widely used and accepted method, collecting experts' views in a particular field such as tourism (e.g. Chang, Hsu, Choi, and Sirakaya, 2006; Lee, Song, and Mjelde, 2008; Spenceley, 2008; Williams and Pan, 2008; Han and Zhang, 2015).
2. **AHP.** It is widely used in the evaluation of TDC. This method explains the system of multiple hierarchies and gives weight of every index. The respondents score each item and draw the final evaluation results of TDC. The method combines qualitative and quantitative analysis, and its logic is very clear. However, the weight of each index will be affected by the subjective decision of the respondents. It has been used to evaluate the quality of service and TDC (e.g., Wan, Li, and Zhang, 2001; Tsaur, Chang, and Yen, 2002; Su, Yang, and Gu, 2003; Huang, 2015).
3. **Factor analysis.** It is based on the correlation between variables, which makes the correlation between the same group of variables much higher and the correlation between different groups of variables relatively lower. Factor analysis can achieve the purpose of reducing dimensions and classify the variables, therefore, this analysis has been widely used in the assessment of validity of TDC (e.g., Yi and Fu, 2006; Zang and Huang, 2007; Cracolici and Nijkamp, 2009; Zang, 2009; Vila, Darcy, and González, 2015)
4. **PCA.** This does not take into account any random factors, and subjective decisions can reduce the correlation between the original indicators, and after the reduction of indicators, it can accurately draw and sort results (Zhang et al., 2011). The PCA method is generally used in TDC research (e.g., Zhang and Zhou, 2005; Huang, Li, Zheng, and Li, 2006; Cracolici and Nijkamp, 2009; Wang, Hsu, and Swanson, 2012; Cucculelli and Goffi, 2015). It is important to note PCA is only effective in large data with complex evaluation.
5. **Importance performance analysis (IPA).** It identifies the relative importance of service or product attributes and shows the

performance of these indicators. These two perspective become the vertical axis and the horizontal axis, and all attributes are displayed in the coordinate. This method is helpful to demonstrate the importance and performance of the TDC in the four charts and to put forward improvement methods. Some studies on TDC used IPA (e.g., Uysal, Chen, and Williams, 2000; Enright and Newton, 2004; Zhang et. al., 2011; Dwyer et al., 2016).

6. **Clustering analysis.** This analysis has been used extensively in TDC evaluation and research (e.g., Enright and Newton, 2004; Gooroochurn and Sugiyarto, 2005; Huang et al., 2006; Spencer & Holecek, 2007; Vila et al., 2015). This method of group research divides a group into relatively homogeneous groups (clusters). Its principle is that individuals in the same cluster have significant similarities, while individuals in different clusters have obvious differences. It is mainly used in exploratory research, where the results of the analysis can provide a number of possible solutions. Scholars choose the final solution to meet the needs of their subjective judgment and further analysis. It can effectively distinguish options according to similarities, but cannot effectively express the details of the difference between them.
7. **SEM.** It is a method of establishing, estimating, and testing a causality model. The multivariable analysis is used to explain the relationships between multiple variables and multiple concepts. Statistically, by looking for some observable variables as latent variables (indicators), SEM can analyze relationship between the latent variables and not only can make a clear analysis on the overall value of every single indicator but also to analyze the relationship between the single indicator. Some scholars use this method to test a comprehensive causality model to understand tourism competitiveness (e.g., Yi, 2006; Mazanec et al., 2007; Wang and Huang, 2011; Assaker et al., 2011).
8. **Panel regression analysis.** It uses the characteristics of cross-section data from horizontal analysis and the characteristics of time series data from vertical analysis. Thus, it is the special combination of cross-section data and time series data. In the panel data model, the interpretation of the regression coefficient can not only explain the variation in different time periods but also explain the difference in the different research monomer (cross-section). Based on characteristics of the dual feature of the panel data model, the model used in

competitiveness analysis can solve the measurement of sustainable competitiveness (e.g., Mangion, Durbarry, and Sinclai, 2005; Croes, 2011; Park and Jang, 2014).

In addition to above evaluation methods, many scholars tried to use other methods to explore determinant factors and the relationship between those factors of TDC. Examples include the following: Zhang, Gu, and Gu (2011) combined technique for order preference by similarity to an ideal solution (TOPSIS) and information entropy and conducted an empirical evaluation of TDC in the 16 cities in the Yangtze River Delta. Zhu, Zhu, and Zhu (2014) used the information entropy-based weighting method for the determination of the weights of all the evaluation aspects. The self-organized mapping neural network is proposed to give a more comprehensive classification of tourism developments. Assaker et al. (2014) used PLSPM to test network relationship between destination and its determinant factors.

12.2.3 CHALLENGES OF THE EXISTING RESEARCH ON TDC

Along with the development of TDC research in recent 20 years, new research is emerging. TDC has been greatly expanded in the content and method, and has formed a more mature research field. However, there are still some problems and challenges in the current research.

12.2.3.1 The Definition of Dc is not Unified, Which Limits the Applicability of the TDC Model

Destination can be a country, a city, or a scenic spot. However, in order to evaluate DC more accurately, the research object should be limited to a certain range. The existing research is launched from the three layers of the TDC.

12.2.3.1.1 Research on the National Level

Previous studies in DC are mainly focused on the national level of DC. (Faulkner, Oppermann, and Fredline, 1999; Kozak and Rimmington, 1999;

Dwyer, Mistilis, Forsyth, and Rao, 2001; Heath, 2003; Kayar and Kozak, 2010; Kunst, 2009; Mazanec, 2011).

Competitiveness on the national level is the result of interacting factors that influence: a) economic performance of the corporate sector; b) the efficiency of the public sector; c) the predominant business climate; and d) the availability of suitable infrastructure and superstructure (Garelli, 2006, cited by Kunst, 2009). On the national level, a set of objectives that the destination is expected to achieve through building and enhancing its competitiveness includes attracting more visitors and satisfying their needs better than their competitors can; providing a high standard of living and a real income for the destination's citizens, and contributing to the prosperity and the well-being of the country (Crouch and Ritchie, 1999; Dwyer and Kim, 2003; Dwyer et al., 2004; WEF, 2008, 2011). A few authors argued that these indicators are not sufficient in determining the future direction of competitiveness and are of no great practical relevance (Hassan, 2000; Dwyer & Kim, 2003; Kunst, 2009). The main reason for this phenomenon lies in an essential difference between indicators of DC and the factors enhancing the competitive capability of a destination. Indicators of DC are static and indicate only the past or current performance, which is a comprehensive strength of tourism, rather than a relative competitiveness of a TD. Because they cannot predict future development, one can think of them as reflective factors. The influencing factors are composed of formative factors and determinants, which increase or decrease competitive capacity of a tourist destination. Further, because they are dynamic and changing over time, one can use them to predict the future.

With regard to China, the geographical distribution and seasonal distribution of tourism resources are not uniform, and the simple weighted average cannot express capabilities of a TD accurately. At the same time, the administrative policies, management capacity, and tourism resources of various tourism cities are different; moreover, international visitors only tour a few cities that cannot represent the whole country, so that it is difficult to generally measure the tourism competitiveness of a country. In addition, the index that failed to exhibit tourism performance criteria is inappropriate as a TDC evaluation indicator. Park (2014) also pointed out that when selecting a country as the research object, it needs more detailed and comprehensive data to identify the role of variables. It is also an objective existence of challenges.

12.2.3.1.2 Research on the City/Region Level

In the past decade, a few scholars have put forward views opposing national level research. Hassan used a destination as a strategic business unit for analysis (Hassan, 2000). Another pioneer was Bordas, who maintained that competitiveness should not be established between countries but between clusters and tourist business. He believed that competitiveness of certain tourist products is more important than competitiveness of a country or destination in a tourist sense (Bordas, 2003). Kunst (2009) also pointed out the competitiveness of a destination's integral experiential mix mainly corresponds to the specific perception by the visitors and is less associated with the level of its socio-economic, political, and regulatory development. From the above discussion, it is questionable to use a country as a unit for DC analysis. Focusing on competitiveness of a specific tourism destination makes more sense.

It is worth noting that more and more empirical studies of DC based on city or region found different conclusions and brought some new thoughts to guide the practice of DC (Enright and Newton, 2004, 2005; Cracolici and Nijkamp, 2008; Botti et al., 2009). Botti et al. (2009) found that tourist arrivals at a destination depend on attracting the tourists' perception.

Zang and Huang (2007) explored TDC and the influencing factors of Chinese seaside cities through the questionnaire in Dalian, Beijing, Nanjing, Guangzhou and Kunming; especially in Tianjin and Jinan, they found that the influence of natural attractions, resources and environment maintenance, social disaster, the destination accessibility and popularity, and destination management are different for TDC of Chinese seaside cities.

Zhang et al. (2011) tested tourism reception capacity, economic development factors, eco-environmental quality, and resources endowment of the Yangtze river area and found that resources endowment was less important than other factors. Ivo Mulec (2013) evaluated the potential and general competitiveness of Vojvodina, Serbia, based on the D-K model. Zainuddin, Radzi, and Zahari (2013) from the tourists' perspective searched for perception of TDC while taking tourist involvement as a moderator variable. Wang and Huang (2011) took Zhangjiajie, China, as an example to determine the relative importance of each influencing factor of TDC using SEM and drew the conclusion that the most important influencing factors are tourism resources, destination management, tourism facilities, destination support factors, infrastructure, and service quality; among them, destination management is the most important.

12.2.2.1.3 Research on the Tourism Company Level

Some research has narrowed the focus on representative local enterprises and resorts that play an important role of attracting and serving tourists. For example, d'Hauteserre (2000) made an analysis of the US Foxwoods Resort Casino to figure out how this casino can attain high competitiveness. Hudson, Ritchie, and Timur (2004) tested competitiveness of Canadian Ski Resorts on the basis of the C-R model. Currie, Wesley, and Sheehan (2012) compared service quality and capabilities of 5 yacht harbors in Canada to study whether different enterprises can result in different competitiveness levels. Hallmann, Muller, and Feiler (2014) introduced related factors of the C-R model into winter sports tourism, then explored the adaptability of a destination competitiveness model to the demand-side, and then analyzed the impact of different factors of TDC on tourists' perceived satisfaction.

As a matter of fact, research focused on a scenic spot or a tourism enterprise cannot reflect the strength of a local tourism destination's competitiveness because that TD is a complex of different resources, any part of which cannot determine the destination's competitiveness. This kind of evaluation on competitiveness is only suitable for large, vertically integrated companies. Nevertheless, small business on their own cannot play a decisive role in changing TDC and cannot eliminate the impact of policymakers and other relevant departments on destination management and the construction of competitiveness. With regard to China, the role of market forces on tourism has kept a low profile; the power of destination management is concentrated in the government administrative department. Enterprises are small in scale, and their capabilities are limited. For these reasons, whether it is reasonable for research to focus on enterprises to test TDC should be further explored.

From the discussion above, if we want to compare destination competitiveness among different destinations, we first need to determine which destinations are direct competitors. Assaker et al. (2013) indicated that only those destinations in direct competition have common internal features. In other words, it is meaningful to make a comparison of TDC among those destinations providing homogeneous tourism products, then it can show the comparative advantages and competitive advantages intuitively. The purpose of evaluating TDC is not only to understand the strength of TDC, but more importantly to determine differences between competitors so as to do better than your competitors' to gain market share. In other words, one of the important questions in current DC research is to look for the suitable analysis unit of DC. It may be a good way to narrow DC research to the city level rather than the more complicated and confusing national level.

12.2.3.2 Taking a Second Look at Supply and Demand Perspectives, Expanding The Scope of TDC Theory

12.2.3.2.1 From the Tourist Perspective

A TD is a collection of different products and experiences and provides an overall experience to tourists. Tourism experiences related to sightseeing, activities, entertainment, hotel stays, food consumption, and interaction with staff and local people generate the combined tourist perception of the destination and the impact of destination competitiveness (Ballantyne, Packer, and Falk, 2011). A destination's competitiveness lies in providing better products to meet the needs of tourists (Dwyer and Kim, 2003). Tourist demand determines destination positioning, marketing, and purposes of the trip (shopping/sightseeing/experience), and then, the tourists determine how they perceive the destination. Tourists' satisfaction determines the destination's reputation and the possibility if tourists will return to visit the destination again, which may impact on potential tourists.

The existing research on evaluating of TDC only evaluates tourism demand. Dwyer and Kim (2003) first took demand into account and considered specific indicators: destination consciousness, destination perception and destination preference. However, those indicators cannot be used directly as a quantifiable evaluation criterion. Afterward, further studies took demand into consideration as an important factor of the TDC model, but only in the Dwyer & Kim's model. Until recently, researchers began to introduce other tourist factors into destination studies. Pansiri (2014) combined tourists motivation and destination competitiveness, while using gap analysis in their research on perception of tourists' needs and supplier perception of tourist demand. They expected to help managers to determine why people travel, and the experience they have at a destination. Zainuddin et al. (2013) suggest that the tourism experience and tourist participation are the causes of the perception of TDC; moreover, these factors can impact on the decisions of tourists, the construction of destination image and future behavioral intentions. Thus, the relationship between customer value experience and TDC will arouse more and more researchers' concern to systematically analyze the internal connection of the relationship which will be a hot issue and cause difficulty in future research.

Furthermore, the relative position of the TDC not only depends on the changes of each index but also depends on the changes in tourism demand structure. Even if every index of destinations remain the same, but the demand structure of tourists have changed, then the orientation of tourism demand and the direction of tourist flows will certainly change (Long, 2010). Future research needs to have a clear grasp of the essence of the customer experience and take the impact of the tourism experience on the TDC index structure into studies on the competitiveness evaluation paradigm.

12.2.3.2.2 From the Destination Perspective

There are two different answers in strategic management to the question of how a superior competitive position is achieved. One is Porter's framework and the other is the RBV approach. The RBV is a return to an analysis of internal aspects with the aim of achieving a firm's superior performance. To a certain extent, the RBV carries competitive advantage a step forward in the strategic management field. Grant (1991) made progress on resource-based theory by identifying "capacities" from the concept of "resources" and placed them side-by-side in strategic management, so as to form a two-dimensional view of RBV. Capability is defined as the capacity for a team of resources to perform some task or activity (Grant, 1991). Therefore, resources are the source of a firm's capabilities, but capabilities are the main source of its competitive advantage (Grant, 1991).

It is very interesting that some current DC literature has involved the content of capabilities, but failed to apply the approach of RBV to analyze destination competitiveness (Bordas, 1994; Crouch and Ritchie, 1999; Buhalis, 2000; Ritchie and Crouch, 2000b; Cracolici and Nijkamp, 2008; Kayar and Kozak, 2010;). For example, although Ritchie and Crouch made no mention of capabilities, they defined DC as the factors that can utilize resources effectively; they claim that it is important for a destination to utilize its resources effectively (Crouch and Ritchie, 1999; Ritchie and Crouch, 2000b).

Further studies on TDC based on a supply perspective should explore the sources of competitiveness integrating RBV into DC. Additional studies on the influencing factors of TDC divide those factors into formative factors, determinants, and indictors to explore the essential difference of various competition factors to impact on competitiveness. Formative factors refer to resources that form the essential base for competitiveness, including endowed resources, created resources, and supporting factors; determinants of DC refer to capabilities, which under DMOs, is the capacity for team building by all individual players to integrate and utilize resources to achieve value-added activities. Indicators of DC are a reflection of competitiveness and an index of the strength of DC. They are explicit factors.

12.2.3.3 Reflection on the Paradigm of Competitiveness Evaluation, Having a Deep Exploration of Indicator Choice

12.2.3.3.1 Reflection on the Competitiveness Model

The existing TDC models mostly are based on Potter's Diamond model (such as the C-R model and the D-K model). These models expand the TDC theory but still have two issues.

First, the essence of tourism is an incredible experience. Only when tourists have a good perception of and experience in a destination, can a tourism destination become a popular stop for tourists.

Therefore, in tourism experience, interaction should be the main source and representative characteristic of the experience value. Interaction is one of the important determinants forming the TDC and also has an impact on the destination experience and evaluation of tourists. As Gentile, Spiller, and Noci (2007) suggested, the value generated due to interactions between customers and enterprises can have a potential influence on the measurement of traditional performance (market share, sales, and profitability) and intangible assets (brand equity and customer equity). In the interaction between tourists and destination tourism enterprises, tourists and destination service people, tourists and the destination environment, tourists to tourists, TDs should grasp environmental changes sensitively when developing marketing plans and marketing activities.

We need to consider experience-driven innovation constantly, consider the functions and characteristics of tourism products, and determine elements of the customer experience, in order to control changes of tourists' demand structure and increase tourist consumption.

Because the tourism experience is not determined by the size of each TDC factor, the tourism circumstance is structured by competitive factors. Existing competitiveness evaluation models are based more on the perspective of supply and have not focused on the tourist interaction of the tourism experience and value co-creation. Therefore, the construction of a destination model still needs to increase additional factors from the demand side in the future.

Secondly, implicit in the actual operation process of the evaluation paradigm of TDC, which is built on Potter's model, is an assumption: there is a linear correlation or positive correlation between various competitive factors and tourism competitiveness (Long, 2010). In fact, many factors may not be directly related to TDC; however, there are some nonlinear relations with a turning point. Long (2010) considered traffic accessibility as the focus and found that improvement of traffic conditions make small/medium-sized tourism cities marginalized. The time distance between small/medium-sized cities and regional central cities is shortened due to the improvement of traffic conditions. Some overnight visitors will, therefore, transform into day-trippers, such as Suzhou, Kaifeng, Luoyang, and Jiaozuo in China. When traffic conditions have been greatly improved, the average residence time in these cities may be shortened dramatically. Therefore, for some noncentral cities, the improvement of traffic conditions may not enhance tourism competitiveness, but may weaken their competitiveness.

There are a number of factors, such as safety factors, fog and haze, which are threshold of TDC. Below the threshold, when factors have a decisive effect on TDC, the impact of any other indicators on TDC will be ignored (Long, 2010). For example, the China Tourism Research Institute in Beijing prepared the *Chinese Inbound Tourism Development Annual Report 2014,* which pointed out that since January 2013, Beijing and cities in east-central China with serious haze was one of the main factors affecting the decline of tourist arrivals and tourist satisfaction in China in the past two years.

A point worth noting is that internal factors and their relationship can form an organic combination. These factors constitute a stage or scene, whether they can "perform(ance)" wonderfully or not only depends on the number of various factors but also depends on the mutual cooperation of various factors. Therefore, these factors and the effect of TDC are closely related, or we can say that there is a structure effect.

12.2.3.3.2 The dilemma of Indicators Selection

TDC is the result of long-term development, and it is also facing changes in the environment and the challenge of competitors; thus, TDC is dynamic. The life cycle of many destinations, after a burst of growth, then stops or faces recession, such as Hamm, Germany, Lo Tova Lou, and New Zealand. (Pike and Page, 2014). At present, the evaluation indicators of TDC are mostly a reactive index, which cannot reveal the development potential of a destination. The evaluation of TDC should add some factors which can reflect trends of future development, such as non-repeatability, scarcity, development and damage degree of a destination resource, investment in new tourism products, product innovation, and tourism education.

The relationship between the factors and TDC is not a linear relationship. There are more complex non-linear functions. But the relationships of a traditional competitiveness evaluation model between aspects, indicators, and secondary indicators are parallel by default and cannot completely reflect the real competitiveness of a tourism destination.

In addition, an evaluation model often involves dozens of or even hundreds of indices. In this case, it is difficult to evaluate TDC for respondents and it is hard to ensure the authenticity of replies to questionnaires, which could also increase the cost of data collection. The while indices are not completely independent; they have a certain relevance. For example, if a destination has strong economic capability, its infrastructure construction will be more superior, and development of the industry driven by the economy will affect the quality of the environment. The internal relationship between the indices also influences the accuracy of the evaluation on TDC to a certain extent.

Therefore, future studies of TDC evaluation, on the one hand, should pay more attention to comparative research of the destination. The relative value will be used instead of the absolute value to evaluate TDC. On the other hand, they can classify indices according to the actual situation, evaluating and comparing indicators of different levels, making TDC evaluation be more practical. Moreover, the predictive indices are needed to add to the competitiveness evaluation model of a tourism destination.

12.3 STUDY ON THE IMPROVEMENT OF TDC FROM THE PERSPECTIVE OF A SINGLE TOURIST CITY

The 2016 Report on China's Tourism Development pointed out that since 2000, the number of domestic tourists has sustained continuous growth, which promotes China stepping into the era of mass tourism. China is becoming the country with the largest number of domestic tourists. China's total tourism revenue is more than 4 trillion yuan in 2015, of which domestic tourism revenue accounted for 85.8% of total national tourism revenue %, becoming China's most important tourist market. Further, from the inbound tourism market, China has become the world's fourth largest tourist reception country. In 2015, the number of inbound tourists reached 133 million and tourism foreign exchange earnings reached $1136.5 million. Currently, the development of China's tourism industry is not confined to Beijing, Shanghai, Guangzhou, and the southeast coastal cities and famous tourist areas, but almost all the provinces and cities include tourism as a strategic pillar industry. Therefore, this China-based paper analyzes the findings and deficiencies of existing studies from the following three aspects: the current situation of TDC and its effect on the economy from the input-output perspectives; the relationship between the government and the tourism market; and the development of tourism destination marketing strategy in this social media era, hoping to present for readers a more comprehensive theory and practice of TDC development in China.

12.3.1 ANALYSIS ON THE INPUT-OUTPUT EFFICIENCY OF TDC

12.3.1.1 Current Situation of Input/Output Efficiency of Chinese Provinces and Cities

Economy of scale of the development of urban tourism, to a certain extent, reflects the strength of TDC, that is to say:

The input size of urban tourism materials and tourism total output, and the relationship between them, is one of the significant factors that impact the TDC. Many researchers have adopted the input-output analysis method to evaluate tourism on the impact of the economy (Lee and Taylor, 2005).

Li (2001) first introduced the output model to tourism research by using Guangdong Provincial input-output data. The quantitative analysis of related and ripple effect shows that the tourism industry has a strong industrial association, complementary consumption, and a strong influence on the industry. He pointed out that the Chinese tourism industry plays an important role in the national economy; not only does it have the opportunity and conditions to become a new economic growth point, but it has a strong radiation and spreading effect on the national economy and can promote the development of related industries. Zhang and Kan (2003) using input-output analysis found that the Shanghai tourism industry has the features that a high investment and high output, and the high return to society. At the same time, two scholars found that the Shanghai tourism industry is mainly based on the outbound market and international markets. Fixed asset investment produced a "controlling" rather than an "inducing" effect for the production capacity of the Shanghai tourism industry. Zuo (2007) introduced the structure of income distribution as an important supplementary indicator to evaluate the role of social and economic development in a destination. They found a serious imbalance in the first distribution structure of national income in the Hunan Province. The main benefit belongs to owners of capital not tourism practitioners in the development of tourism. It will not help to stimulate tourism development and may lead to a widening income gap. Wang and Shi (2007) on the basis of a Gansu Province input-output table found that the stimulating effect on social and economic development of tourism in Gansu Province is strong. It has helped to increase the total output of various departments of the national economy, but gives little push to other industry demands. Feng (2009) indicated that the TDC evaluation model is similar to the input-output model of companies. Destination resource endowments and various support facilities are components of destination investment; passenger flow, income, and local residents' welfare are the performance results of destination output. The operation process of destination management is the same as the production process. The input-output efficiency of a destination is the intuitive performance of competitiveness. This study taking 31 provinces, cities, and autonomous regions in China as the objects of the study, based on input-output efficiencies, obtained a comprehensive comparison of TDC. The results showed there is a "weakened from east to west" structure of input-output efficiency in China tourism destinations. Moreover, the utilization efficiency of tourism resources is low. Among them,

Shanghai is the most efficient tourist destination in China. On the contrary, some destinations that have weak competitiveness are lacking resources and effective planning and development, and they are also weak in investment in labor, capital, and other soft elements.

Zhang and Shi (2015), by using panel data of 31 provinces (cities, districts), in China, from 2003–2012 and variation coefficient methodology, tested the tourism economic contribution to the provinces (city, district) TDC; they found that some destinations in remote areas have poor accessibility and are away from the tourist market economy, which is mostly located in the northeast, northwest, and southwest of China. Although these destinations have a low TDC, the tourism resources with distinct regional characteristics, high quality, and strong attraction, coupled with the local governments has great attention paid to the development of the tourism industry. Further, the economic contribution of tourism to the local economy also showed a rising trend. Tianjin, Hainan, Chongqing, and Guizhou provinces (autonomous regions) have abundant tourism resources and an excellent reputation, making tourism a pillar industry in regional economic development. Their tourism economic contribution to the local economy is very significant. Unexpectedly, tourism advantages and resource advantages of Beijing, Guangdong, Jiangsu, Zhejiang, Shandong provinces (cities) are obvious. There is high traffic accessibility, a high level of per capita income, and a strong DC, but tourism's economic contribution to TDC is weak. Zhang and Zhang (2014) took empirical research on the tourism competitiveness of 16 cities in Anhui Province, based on an input-output perspective, and found that urban competitiveness depends not only on the production investment amount of a city, but more on the rational allocation of various tourism elements. Further, what leads to the big difference of urban TDC is not only the business tourism difference caused by differences of urban tourism sources and economic scale, but also the tourism destination's own characteristics (traditional tourism destination or emerging tourist destination).

12.3.1.2 Suggestions on Improving Input-Output Efficiency

Tourism destinations with high competitiveness have a high level of economic advantages and location advantages, and have a high input-output efficiency in China. However, from the input-output index, their strong competitiveness mainly comes from high investment, especially high investment of capital resources. This mode of economic growth fueled by investment is not conducive to the development of urban destination competitiveness. To enhance the competitiveness of a tourism destination, we need to change the path from high input and high output into low input and high output (Feng, 2009). On the one hand, destinations based on consolidated resource advantage and capital advantage, need to establish their tourism professional service system, improve tourism service, and urban tourism resources that play a coordinating role in integration, enforcing sites' cooperation to develop together and expand the attraction of the destination's tourism resources. On the other hand, destinations need to implement diversified industrial development, break the boundaries of the industry, and gradually integrate with relevant industries to improve the TD's product system, thereby enhancing the industrial level.

For destinations that have ordinary competitiveness, the reason tourism development is slow is the unbalanced growth of the regional internal tourism elements, which brings the bottleneck effect to the TDC. These cities are lacking high-quality tourism professionals or are lacking high-quality tourism resources, or its tourism investment scale is small. This leads to tourism resources with low quality, lack of attraction, tourism products that are too simple, low scale of tourism investment, and tourism destinations with low attraction so that they cannot meet the needs of tourists. Therefore, we should balance the input of each factor's resources and avoid excessive investment into a single resource. At the same time, the destination government needs innovation of the tourism industry, which should also build a flexible investment and financing mechanism, stimulate enthusiasm of market economic participants in the area of tourism development and management, and increase the tourism enterprises' capital operation ability. In addition, a development strategy of human resources is needed to make the TD change to a knowledge-intensive destination. Cities with weak TDC lack sufficient attention investment in tourism elements for local government. There is a certain gap between them and other destinations in some aspects such as input elements, output performance, or resource utilization and efficiency. Therefore, when enhancing the competitiveness of these destinations, they need to look to government as the leader and focus on spatial layout, market situations, product creation, and other important factors of the tourism industry, systematically developing regional tourism planning. They should also focus on establishing a tourism safety plan and market environment, guiding social capital to the tourism industry, introducing and cultivating tourism professionals, building a soft index of destination competitiveness, and realizing rapid development.

12.3.2 THE RELATIONSHIP BETWEEN A DESTINATION GOVERNMENT AND A TOURISM MARKET

Since the 1980s, the impact of the government on tourism development has gradually become an important topic in China's tourism industry. What attitude the government should adopt? What role to play have become a hot and interesting topic in the field of tourism research. Taking "government" and "tourism" as key words to search, during the period from 1989 to 2000, the literature on the influence of government on tourism development revealed only 5 articles; for the 10-year period from 2001 to 2010, literature on government and the development of tourism increased significantly to 167 units (Kuang, 2011); from 2010 to 2016, the research related to the government showed rapid growth, with an increase to more than 300 units. This research theme focused on the following topics: the relationship between government and the market in the development of the tourism industry; government behavior and function in tourism marketing; and competition-cooperation relationships between local governments. The relationship between government and the market is a major theoretical issue and also becomes an urgent question that needs to be seriously reflected on and solved. Therefore, this section discusses the relationship between the government and the tourism market.

12.3.2.1 Re-examination of a Government-Led Tourism Development Strategy

The government-led tourism development strategy that the National Tourism Administration officially put forward in China has been implemented for nearly 20 years since 1997. Development based on practical experience has led to a significant related research on the development of government-led tourism strategy. But why did the Chinese tourism industry implement the government-led development model? The studies can be roughly divided into two categories (Xu, 2013). One category took the perspective of research based on the characteristics of the tourism industry and applied concepts such as public good, externality, information asymmetry, market failures, and other theories to test the necessity of government intervention or government-led models (for example, Liang, 2005; Wang, 2005). Another category from a historical perspective considered international comparisons and environmental characteristics to investigate the necessity of the government-led model. Xu (2013) reviewed relevant literature and found that the "root cause" of the government-led tourism industry model in China derived from funding requirements of building infrastructure, the needs of policy support, and other special conditions in the initial stage of the tourism industry. In the meantime, the tourism market faced economic systems reform and environmental pressures. Government intervention can improve the factor conditions, demand conditions, supporting industries, governance structure, and market competition environment of China's tourism industry, and can further enhance the international competitiveness of the tourism industry (Zhang, 2006).

However, Chinese researcher Shangzheng (2005) pointed out that implementation of a Chinese government-led tourism development strategy has taken more than 20 years to enhance the social, economic, and cultural status of the tourism industry, rapidly improving international market visibility and competitiveness of the tourism industry in China. However, there are also five major negative effects: it depressed the development of the tourism market in favor of government achievements to a certain degree; resources allocation by government made tourism officials complacent, leading to inaction and neglecting to capture market opportunities; government was directly involved in micro production and business activities, so that part of tourism business operations have a strong administrative character, resulting in non-separation, property rights between government and enterprises, and low economic benefit. Zhang argued that the government should give way to a market orientation, and the market should play a basic role in allocation of resources, and at the same time, play its role creating a good environment promoting the tourism industry.

Today, domestic and international economic situations and environment are changing. In 2012, the 18th National Congress of the Communist Party of China proposed that the "market should play a fundamental role in resource allocation to a greater and broader extent," "promoting the functions of the government to create a good development environment, providing high-quality public services, maintaining social fairness and justice". The development and summary in practice causes us to examine and reflect on the role of the Chinese government in economic development. Future research is needed to clearly define "government intervention" and "government-based" boundaries, and to seriously explore the government-led boundary, establish the role of operational definition and evaluation standards of the government's role, and achieve a reasonable balance between the government-led tourism strategy and the market.

12.3.2.2 The Relationship Between the Government and Other Stakeholders in the Tourism Market

Establishing a social-economic relationship must embody a certain relationship of benefits, and the benefits dominate the social and historical activities of people. In the process of tourism economic development in China, for different players, such as local governments, tourism developers, nonprofit organizations, tourists, community residents and competitors, the balance of interests among them, achieving the maximization and optimization of benefits distribution, is the key to urban tourism development. It can enhance the overall tourism destination's sustainable competitiveness. Some scholars of game theory analyzed multiple game relationships of tourism destination stakeholders, trying to determine an effective guarantee to improve a destination's competitiveness.

Li and Yang (2012) believed that the government, as tourism resource ownership and public affairs manager, holds a unique and important position in the development of a tourism economy and occupies the dominant strategic position in local tourism development. The development of nonprofit organizations is not perfect, and its role in tourism economic development is weak. Therefore, the core scenic spots of a destination have become a tool for some local governments to realize their own interests, and the government is concerned about the economic benefits and political benefits resulting from focusing on these core scenic spots. Liu and Chen (2012) pointed out that in Shanghai and Shenzhen, from 2003 to 2010, the number of tourism public companies directly or indirectly controlled by the government was as high as 85%. They used unbalanced panel data analysis and compared nongovernment companies and the tourism public companies controlled by the central government; they demonstrated that public companies controlled by local government showed better operating performance. What should be noted is that there is a phenomenon that rent-seeking behaviors in government purchase caused a waste of public resources and government control caused unfair competition of small- and medium-sized tourism enterprises. Lv and Zheng (2014) using Yangzhou Caiyi Street as the object of their study pointed out that government guidance, resident's participation, and businesses cooperation improve the tourism environment, community development, and urban public interests, thus achieving sustainable development of urban tourism. Among them, government plays a very important role in form of public service agencies. Xu (2015) using evolutionary game theory studied how government and enterprises could achieve a win-win result in the development of low carbon tourism. They pointed out that in the early stage of development of China's low carbon tourism investment, the government can improve the investment environment for investors and give special funds to support such preferential policies in order to achieve optimal results between government and enterprises. As a result of the travel agency credit crisis in China's tourism market, through game model analysis, Lu (2016) found that consumers' distrust of travel agencies, travel agency dishonesty business practices, and related government systems have a close relationship; therefore, the government should strengthen supervision, punish bad faith business practices strictly, while at the same time, reward companies operating in good faith.

Local government plays two roles in China's development of tourism destinations: as a regulator which is representative of the public interest, seeking social and environmental benefits; and as a stakeholder pursuing their own interests, such as political achievements, reputation and performance, bonus and promotion. As for the other role, government-owned tourism enterprises have resources and information advantages which non-state-owned enterprises are unable to obtain, which might be unfair competition for nonstate owned companies. In order to achieve its political objectives, local government will enhance performance in the short term, possibly causing waste or destruction of public resources and the negative effects to sustainable development is obvious. From the perspective of the greater society, it is not conducive to the comprehensive benefits of society and culture. Therefore, while China's economy has entered a new development stage, local government should think about how to guide the development of the tourism industry. Further, when the market plays a fundamental role in resource allocation, it needs to think carefully how to achieve the government-led, enterprise-based, market-oriented operation.

In conclusion, the development of China's tourism industry has made remarkable achievements in 20 years, but in the process, the phenomenon of government "absence" and "offside" has always existed. At present, the development of China's tourism industry has entered a new stage to accelerate the transformation and industrial upgrading of the industry, changing from a government-oriented to market-oriented approach, from an extensive model to an intensive model, from quantity growth to quality and efficient development, from a single function to comprehensive functions, which are the basic targets and development directions of tourism development in the future. How a destination government takes a scientific approach to planning tourism industry development, how to guide tourism investment and financing, how to supervise and standardize the tourism market environment, and how to cooperate with relevant industrial departments are interesting questions that need to be further discussed.

12.3.3 DESTINATION'S MARKETING STRATEGY IN THE ERA OF NEW MEDIA

With the rapid development of information technology, the popularity of smart phones and more mature and rational consumers, destinations are facing one of the most important topics: how to find more effective marketing tactics and strategies to improve TDC. Paying attention to marketing innovation, and enhancing the scientific and professional marketing levels can cause government to solve, control, implement and reply to many practical problems of tourism marketing, which can then strengthen tourism destination marketing performance and achieve superior destination competitiveness.

The marketing approach of destination governments in China is mostly based on traditional marketing channels such as travel transactions, special presentations, massive propaganda material, and advertisements on television and in newspapers, magazines, and other traditional media. With the development of network media in recent years, the Internet created many convenient ways for public communication, with many social networks (WBL, microblogging, photo sites), public and official websites, OTA and travel UGC, video websites, web celebrities, live modes and so on. These new sources of communication are more active than traditional media. Because the access to information for visitors has changed dramatically, destination government, as having the leading role in building and spreading the destination image needs to think and adjust how to promote the tourism destination according to the destination market and look to marketing improvement opportunities, so as to enhance destination competitiveness. With practical experience, research on this topic is becoming abundant.

Some researchers believe that the Internet is the most important media for Chinese tourists collecting tourism information. The TD's government developed and operated the official tourism website. Because of the authority and objectivity of its information, the government plays an important role in TD marketing communication. How to comprehensively evaluate the overall marketing functions of the official website and how to achieve the overall marketing goal of the tourism destination are the top priorities of official tourism websites. In 2008, Zhang and Hu pointed out that there are repetitive constructions, less effective propaganda, and a convergence image of Chinese tourism websites. Most official websites have simple content, a single image, incomplete information, and slow update speed, so that they lack attractiveness for consumers to return. Those websites cannot meet the consumers personalized travel demand. Based on five aspects, namely information function, interactive function, function of trade, relationship management, and technical function, Zhang, Li and Ma (2011) constructed an evaluation index system of Chinese tourism websites, and by means of coupling model validation confirmed that the interactive function of the official websites is the weakest, and that the level of network marketing in China's economically developed eastern provinces is higher than the less developed western provinces. Wu and Han (2012) conducted an empirical evaluation of the official tourism websites of 33 provinces, cities, and districts in China and found the destination official website trapped in spontaneous construction, lacking reasonable cognition about the importance of integrated marketing and brand image-building, and understanding the tourists' psychology of need inadequately; showing local characteristics deficiently, and needing more room for website construction. Wang (2014) using evaluation analysis of website influence and the investigation of website structure and content indicated that the Provincial Tourism Bureau attaches great importance to the network of related tourism information. The websites provide more comprehensive tourism information, station search and interactive features, friendly links, or related website links; it has a certain influence and radiation force, and its recognition and awareness are high. But there are still some issues neglected in the sites, such as the inclusion of the site map, website promotion, slow access speed, a certain chaos to content arrangement, single expression form of information released, and slow update information.

Yang, Wu, Zhang, Jiang, and Li (2014) using ROST Content Mining based on text analysis to test the projected image of Zhangjiajie and found that the network marketing of the destination website failed to build a clear, expected image. There are other scholars from the official WeChat and micro-blog exploring effective marketing and promotion of tourism products. Yi (2015) considered Guizhou Province as an example and found that the Tourism Bureau in undeveloped areas established WeChat platforms to adapt to the trend that tourists like to use mobile terminal equipment to obtain information and communication, but the reality is that WeChat cannot provide image promotion and product marketing without professional management, lacks original content, and interacts with users infrequently.

Some scholars found that both the Internet and traditional word-of-mouth had an important and broad impact on consumers. The Internet word-of-mouth is formed by a variety of different sources of information and positive or negative comments on a product or company from potential or real consumers through the network. Xu (2015) found consumers who initially have a positive perception, attitude, or travel intention of a destination, when they see a detailed, negative word-of-mouth comment on the destination, would change their first impression and positive attitude, and decline the general evaluation of the destination's brand, generating a brand equity dilution effect. Lai, Tang and Zhu (2011) pointed out that a number of negative Internet comments, number of blogs, a negative word-of-mouth ratio, and the number of pictures in a blog showed a significant correlation with the customer perception of a scenic region. The Internet word-of-mouth has an impact on tourists' decision.

Therefore, under the environment of network media, when depending only on a single destination official tourism website, building the destination brand image is not enough. We must use effective cooperation among different medias and promote the establishment of a unified tourism destination image in order to enhance regional tourism industry competitiveness.

Liu, Song, and Chang (2014) considering Beijing as the research sample, looking at the Chinese-English version of the Beijing Tourism Website, Ctrip, Mafengwo, Baidu Tourism, and TripAdvisor, five tourism websites, through the analysis of network content, found the difference between constructing and displaying the destination character symbols of the official website and nonofficial website. The official website introduced Beijing in detail, trying to build comprehensive tourism destination symbols, especially highlighting Beijing's status as an international metropolis and China's political center, economic center, and cultural center. In the nonofficial websites, publishers who attained much attention in posts and have a lot comments and praise play the role of "opinion leader." Their comments tend to focus on spreading the characteristics of a tourism destination as recreation. This conclusion confirmed the conclusion proposed by Mei and Yang (2010): the image construction of a tourism destination should be completed by all sources of a destination to build a joint marketing network, including enterprises which have tourism resources, local governments, industry associations, promotion and communication agencies, tourism service sellers, and leading complementary enterprises (Mei and Yang, 2010). Currently, it is much more theoretical and of practical significance to analyze how to carry out joint marketing activities to improve TDC.

In conclusion, in the new media age tourism destination, governments should effectively use their own resources and improve the performance of their own tourism marketing; make an alliance of tourism organizations, tourism enterprises and network communication/media to innovatively allocate resource distribution; turn various market demands into new opportunities for destination development over time; develop a corresponding marketing strategy; form a comprehensive marketing effort and establish a good reputation through social evaluation of tourism consumer behavior, which encourages and enhances positive tourists' decision-making, developing a larger scope of the market. Future research on these issues will make a useful supplement to the theory of TDC.

12.4 DISCUSSION AND CONCLUSION

In the past 20 years, research on TDC has developed dynamically. Academia kept up with the times, which resulted in significant research findings that have far-reaching influence on social science, etc. However, existing research focus, theories, and the evaluation dimensions still have room to consider and explore.

Based on the general consensus that TDC is comparative competitiveness, researchers need to compare their research objects with real competitors when making an accurate evaluation and measurement of TDC. Evaluating competitiveness on a narrow or specific level, such as the city, resort, or local level, is most meaningful. The result of the evaluation may effectively guide destination policy makers and all the providers to enhance the competitiveness of a destination rather than just evaluate the existing general strength of s destination.

Because DC is always associated with a tourism product, the analysis of consumer perceptions of competitiveness is better than that just considering destination managers as interviewees to evaluate TDC. In the future, it is necessary to incorporate the relevant factors of tourists' perception and experience into the evaluation of TDC, so that in the measurement of TDC, the research from the destination managers can accurately grasp the characteristics of the destination resource advantages, explain policy and plan and develop information. At the same time, the researchers need to include tourists' experiences and perception from a demand perspective to make an effective evaluation of TDC. These can better determine the gap between supply and demand during the construction of TDC, discern the disadvantages and advantages of the destination, adjust the strategic development direction, develop a clear market position, and realize an effective construction scheme of TDC.

Despite the number of similarities between a firm and a destination, existing studies have paid little attention to what RBV researchers have learned by assessing the competitiveness of firms. It is suggested that integrating the current theory of RBV into destination competitiveness research can push the DC theory development further. Blending current DC theories with RBV may help to analyze systematically the cause/effect relationship of DC. Therefore, future research should blend RBV into the DC field in order to better understand and analyze the mechanism of the competitive advantage of a destination, and hence find suitable theoretical support for indicators of DC.

In reality, at present, most indicators belong to a reactivity index, can only measure and evaluate the past and present state of a destination and lack predictive evaluation on influencing indicators of destination competitiveness (or instance, "increasing numbers of passenger makes the destination resource continually disrupted, for a long time, competitive advantages will be reduced"), and leading to reference value is low for strategic planning of a destination in the future. Therefore, adding the predictive index is an improvement for a future TDC evaluation model.

China's tourism industry is expected to become a new economic growth point, promoting the development of related industries. However, there are still some problems which hinder the rapid development of tourism and the establishment of the TDC. The following questions whether the government-led strategy need converting; how to develop the new urban development strategy; how to deal with the government and the tourism market, especially the relationship with stakeholders; and how to use the new medium of the Internet to conduct joint marketing to establish a good brand image need more research in theory and practice.

12.5 THE VITALITY OF SHENZHEN'S TOURISM INDUSTRY—FROM THE PERSPECTIVE OF DC

When researching a destination example of the improvement of China's tourist competitiveness, we choose Shenzhen as our target city to explore how the destination develops, maintains, and enhances its competitiveness.

Shenzhen is a major city in the south of Southern China's Guangdong Province. It is located on the east coast of the Pearl River Estuary, bordering Hong Kong international metropolis to the south. The municipality covers an area of 1,991.64 square kilometers with a total population of 14.6 million at the 2016 census. Shenzhen has a tropical zone maritime climate with a humid clime and plenty of sunshine year round, which contributes to the abundant yield of fruits. It is also known as "the Capital of Design," "the City of Innovation," and "the Traffic Leader City."

Shenzhen is the only harbor city in China that owns ports, skyline, highways, and railways with multiple means of transportation and is the intersection of mainland China and overseas destinations. The volume of inbound tourists from Shenzhen contributes to 50% of the national total every year (Chi, 1999). Shenzhen international airport has established almost 100 airlines in total; sea transportation from Shekou Port, Chiwan Port, and Yantian Port serve businesses worldwide; GuangJiu railway, JingJiu railway, and the Guangshen highway facilitate the inland traffic surge. The traffic network in the Pearl River Delta region has been greatly enhanced.

Under the leadership of Mr. Deng Xiaoping, Shenzhen was singled out to be the first of the five special economic zones (SEZs) in 1980. Since then, Shenzhen has played an important role in leading and practicing the Reform and Opening Policy and Modernization Strategy for these 30 years. After 2007, the tourism impact in Shenzhen ranked the area fourth of the main cities in China for many years. In 2013 and 2014, Shenzhen was ranked first in the number of inbound tourists to China.

Within 36 years, Shenzhen has developed into a modern city that has thousands of people, a powerful economy, harmonious society, well developed infrastructure, and beautiful atmosphere from a less developed county that had only little more than 30,000 people and very limited traffic. It has achieved a miracle in the history of world industrialization, urbanization, and modernization[1].

With the rapid change of time and preference of tourists during the past 30 years, some tourist cities including Dalian, Zhuhai, and Zhang Jiagang have experienced a rapid rise and decline. Other cities like Kunming, Jinan, and Qin Huangdao have turned from important traditional tourist destinations into tourism interchange stations gradually. However, during the past 30 years, Shenzhen has increased resources in the process of tourism development, due to its efforts in concept innovation, mechanism innovation, and product innovation and has achieved consistent improvement in tourism competitiveness. Therefore, this article reviews Shenzhen for its advantages and the cause of the competitiveness as a tourist destination.

12.5.1 EARLY 1980s–90s: THE FIRST PEAK WAVE OF THE TOURISM DRIVEN BY SPECIAL ECONOMIC ZONE POLICY AND THE ECONOMY

Before Shenzhen was singled out as a SEZ, Luohu, where Shenzhen is located, was the port for in and out of Hong Kong, with a limited capacity for transit travel (Chen, Yu, and Mou, 1992). With additional changes, the economy in Shenzhen has developed rapidly, which largely enhanced tourist competitiveness. Tourism in Shenzhen has achieved its first peak wave.

During the years 1980 to 1988, tourism in Shenzhen focused on business and business-oriented service resorts and SEZ shopping. To further attract tourists from Hong Kong and Macao and to solve accommodation problems

[1] Highlight of Shenzhen. (2012, November 06). SZNews.com. Retrieved from http://www.sznews.com/zhuanti/content/2012-11/06/content_7365464.htm.

of the business traveler, Shenzhen established Xili Lake, Xiangmi Lake, Shiyan Lake, Silver Lake, East Lake and Dameisha Beach, Xiaomeisha Beach, Shekou Sea World, Shenzhen Bay Hotel, Tourist Center, and Xiyong Resort and is China's first city of domestic resort tourism (Chen, Yu, and Mou, 1992). With the antique buildings, western style buildings, ancient temples, and quiet gardens, the environment in the resorts and attractions is elegant, attracting a lot of business travelers. With the development of the tomb of Song Dijing, Left Fort established by Lin Zexu, Dongshan Pearl Farms and Sha Tau Kok Street duty-free area, Shenzhen has developed a tourist destination advantage with unique sightseeing and shopping districts.

After the 1989, with the development of the urban construction, a lot of "star" hotels have been established and tourist accommodations have moved into the center of the urban area. Tourism in periphery urban area have not achieved further development. Shenzhen, as a border Special Economic Zone (SEZ), has seen the developing of business travel with a decline of sightseeing travel. Meanwhile, with the opening of Splendid China in Oversea Chinese Town, Shenzhen entered the antique-cultural tourism stage.

From 1989 to 1992, Shenzhen, with traditional cultural resources, cozy modern accommodations and contemporary culture sightseeing and entertainment tourism, has attracted overseas tourists who are willing to exploring the charm of 5,000 years of Chinese civilization. With the influence of Deng Xiaoping's southern tour and the strong power of China's Tourism Year marketing campaign, Splendid China and China Folk Culture Valley improved the taste and power of the tourist product, causing tourism in Shenzhen to enter a new era.

Zhuhai, also one of the Special Economic Zones (SEZ), has been through rapid improvement in the early 80s and then declined and reached a plateau. There was barely any increase in inbound tourists during the years 1987-1995 (Long, 2010). It is not because of the decrease of the absolute score of Zhuhai's tourist Competitiveness Index, but the relative score. On one hand, there is a lack of cultural resources in Zhuhai. On the other hand, the developing speed of culture attraction products is relatively lower than that of its competitors. For instance, the construction speed of Zhuhai's Theme Park was slower than that of Shenzhen's. After completion of the Pearl Land and new Yuan Ming Palace, a lack of creativeness in the concept and the similarity to the "Window of the World" resulted in a decline of tourists' curiosity, generating a disappointing result. By 1992, Zhuhai Pearl Land had a cumulative loss of 26 million yuan. Additionally, the primary and secondary tourist markets underperformed those of Shenzhen. All the factors mentioned above led to the stagnation of tourism in the past 10 years.

12.5.2 MID AND LATE 1990s TO EARLY 2000: THE ECONOMY DRIVEN SECONDARY RAPID GROWTH FEATURED WITH THEME PARK

With the additional development of China's economy, the advantages of SEZ was not effective anymore, and the attraction of tourism was largely decreased by the early 90s (Long, 2010). After 1993, with decreased interest of Hong Kong and Macao tourists in Splendid China and Folk Culture Valley, the tourist numbers dropped 12% and 32%, respectively, compared with 1992. Moreover, the haphazard tourism facilities and operation, for example, the lack of baggage transfer service and a tourist group parking lot in the railway station, together with an increase of the departure ports and the speed up of processing passengers, resulted in another decline of Shenzhen's tourism.

Shenzhen's tourism department prepared and restructured the tourist concept, tourist resources, tourist plan, tourist culture and tourist product. The theme park was regarded as the primary attraction supporting the further development of Shenzhen's tourism industry. Besides, new attractions will be established every 2–3 years to maintain demand and facilitate further development. This strategy successfully realized the transformation of Shenzhen's tourism driven mechanism and helped Shenzhen achieve a second rapid increase in the number of inbound tourists in the mid and late 90s. Meanwhile, the volume of business travelers increased substantially. For example, Splendid China has attracted 8,000 tourists per day for 3 years (Li and Wang, 1995). The opening of China Folk Culture Valley contributed to the third peak year (Li and Wang, 1995). Though tourist volume of the two attractions decreased to 3,000 and 4,000 per day, respectively, the opening of the "Window of the World" theme park in 1994 largely improved the volume of visitors to Splendid China and China Folk Culture Valley, thus generating a positive impact. The Happy Valley theme park, opened in 1998, providing a more effective form of entertainment for teenagers. Less than a decade, Overseas Chinese Town has launched four large-scale tourist attractions with different cultural themes (Table 12.2).

TABLE 12.2 The Theme Park of Shen Zhen Overseas Chinese Town

Theme Park	**Splendid China**	**China Fork Culture Valley**	**Window of the world**	**Happy Valley**		
Theme	Famous sights in China	Chinese folk customs	World attractions	Amusement park		
				Phase I	Phase II	Phase III
Opening date	Sept. 1989	Oct. 1991	Jun. 1994	Oct. 1988	May, 2002	May, 2005
Feature	Static display	Performance entertainment		Interactive experience		

At the same time, with the opening and refining of the wild zoo, botanical gardens, Dapeng Bay Resort, and other scenic spots, Shenzhen formed a pattern of a modern city with two large tourist attractions located on the east and west side respectively. The Western area has the concept of "Splendid China, Window of the World, China Folk Cultural Valley, Happy Valley," showing the interaction between Chinese and western culture in a joyful and peaceful atmosphere. The Eastern area focuses on the concept of "sunshine, beach, sea, nature", highlighting pleasure and relaxing leisure time. Shenzhen, with the theme park feature, is heaven for a vacation.

In conclusion, during this period of time, the success of Shenzhen's tourism development comes from creative concepts and the nurturing of a significant share of the tourist theme park consumption market. It has achieved the "artificial imitation landscape -- artificial real landscape -- the combination of real landscape and landscape" and "static landscape exhibition-- dynamic performance entertainment -- project actively participation" theme park product development model and became the typical representative of China's theme park tourism. All these efforts have motivated the rapid development of Shenzhen, making it a unique city and a leader in China's tourism industry.

In comparison, tourism in Dalian has declined since 2000. The reason for the decrease in tourist competitiveness is quite straightforward. In the 1990s, most cities in China had poor environmental conditions, while Dalian developed an environmental advantage and made it one of its tourist resource attractions. With the development of China's urbanization, more and more cities have achieved improvement of their environment. Therefore, environment is no longer the main reason for making travel decisions. Besides, the tourism spatial layout in Dalian is not balanced. Dalian only focused on the development and construction of several coastal scenic spots, lacking a comprehensive tourist resort plan. In addition, the city's recreational business district was mainly for commercial use. The recreational function was not obvious and the time period tourists stayed was too short; sightseeing tourism accounted for a large part but did not form a complete tourist route; the coastal tourism products of Dalian were aging, single, lacking in features, interest and participation. The change in tourist demand preference has weakened the relative advantage of the tourist competitiveness in Dalian, a while new competitive advantage has not been developed yet, hindering further development of Dalian's tourism.

12.5.3 EARLY 21ST CENTURY: THE THIRD PEAK WAVE MOTIVATED BY MARKET DRIVEN CITY SEASHORE TOURISM

Shenzhen is a coastal city with a long coastline. During the 20 years' urbanization and the industry-first development pattern, Shenzhen was more like an inland city rather than a coastal city, with no trace of seashore. Faced with the strong momentum of theme park development, the Shenzhen municipal government and the tourism department have been considering how to get rid of the theme-park based, artificial landscape and achieve a breakthrough in the business tourism-oriented single tourism structure situation. With economic growth and the expansion of the city, leisure tourism is the trend of future development. Seashore tourism has features that are valued by tourists. It is also the kind of tourism that has achieved rapid development worldwide. Taking advantage of the abundant coastal tourism resources in Shenzhen and developing the vacation tourism, marine tourism, adventure tourism and some other coastal tourism products featured with interactive participation and entertainment, could to a large extent balance the tourism products in Shenzhen. Therefore, when the tourism industry in Shenzhen entered a more mature development stage by the end of the 1990s, the development of coastal characteristics and diversified tourism has become the new direction of the development of Shenzhen's tourism industry[2].

After the year 2002, based on a "retreat two into three" city development strategy, seashore tourism was developed with the support of the government. Dameisha Coastal Resort Area, Xiaomeisha Coastal Resort Area, Sea World, Minsk World, Mangrove Seashore Park, and Dapeng Peninsula have been established gradually and provide a beautiful landscape by the waterfront boardwalk. On March 26, 2006, the Shenzhen 4th Municipal People's Congress approved the "Shenzhen National Economic and Social Development eleventh five-year-plan" (2006–2011). In accordance with the plan, Shenzhen will take various measures to build the city into an influential international tourist city and a beautiful seashore tourist city.

Shenzhen also achieved a rapid development of tourism diversification during this period. In 2003, the "Culture Supporting Strategy" was established. The government continued to increase investment in creative industries by integrating cultural tourism resources and establishing OCT-LOFT creative group, Shenzhen F518 Creative Fashion Park, Shenzhen Museum, Dafen Oil Painting Village, Guanlan Print, Wen Bo Palace, Bantian handmade street, GuanShanYue Art Museum, and other cultural facilities and cultural industry clusters, improving Shenzhen's tourism product structure and forming a series of new landscapes that show the cultural charm of Shenzhen.

The Shenzhen Tourism Cultural Festival has various forms of activities (more than 170 recorded). The larger ones including the Shenzhen International Tourism and Culture Festival, Shenzhen Gold Coast Tourism Festival, Shenzhen Shajing Golden Oyster Festival, Window of the World International Beer Festival, etc. The International Magic Festival held by Happy Valley is one of the world's largest magic festivals, attracting the world's top masters to attend every year[3].

The development goal of tourism in 2004 was one of the core components of urban development in Shenzhen. The development pattern of

[2] A brief history of the development of the tourism industry in Shenzhen. (October 25, 2006). SZNews.com. Retrieved from http://www.sznews.com/zhuanti/content/2012-11/06/content_7365464.htm.

[3] Tourism and leisure in Shenzhen. (2010, January, 18).SZnews.com. Retrieved from http://news.qq.com/a/20100804/001579.htm.

"Big Tourism" was primarily established with more extensive development space[4]. In the year 2005, Shenzhen had a record of 57.82 million visitors, achieving tourism revenue up to 42.1 billion yuan, exceeding 40 billion yuan for the first time. On November 19, 2008, Shenzhen was officially approved by the United Nations Educational, Scientific and Cultural Organization (UNESCO) to join the global creative city network and was awarded the "Design Capital" designation. Shenzhen, the sixth "Design Capital" of the world, became the first city in China to be listed in the network[5].

Tourism in Jinan, the spring city, started in 1986. In 1990, Jinan was assigned to one of the coastal economic zones, improving the tourism environment of the city. In the summer of the same year, the four famous spring groups resumed recreating marvelous sights and driving tourism development in Jinan. Jinan became the first group of "China's excellent tourism city" in the year 1998, ranking 16 among 54 cities in China. It achieved an extraordinary growth of tourism in the 1990s. However, after 2000, more scenic spots with lower quality tourism products were developed through extensive investment, making Jinan less competitive than its competitors, whose tourism projects were well developed and tourism products outstanding. Lacking enough competitiveness, tourism in the spring city suffered. The market shuffled and Jinan's tourism status fell rapidly. It turned into a "transfer station of tourism" gradually. Visitors would not see Jinan as a travel destination, but a stopover for half a day then hurrying on to Taishan, Qufu or other coastal cities. "Keeping the visitors" in the city has been the crux of tourism in Jinan. For the primary reason, we found that Jinan has very abundant natural resources, but does not have tourism products with unique features and high quality. The various forms of tourism demand could not be satisfied naturally. At the same time, Jinan municipal government did not take action to innovate the tourism product and motivate various economic principals in the market to participate in tourism development and management. Significantly, the tourism industry was not incorporated or included in the economic development plan of the whole city.

[4] A brief history of the development of the tourism industry in Shenzhen. (October 25, 2006). SZNews.com. Retrieved from http://www.sznews.com/zhuanti/content/2012-11/06/content_7365464.htm.

[5] The current economic and social development of Shenzhen in 2012. (April 28, 2012). Baidu's Wenku database. Retrieved from http://wenku.baidu.com/view/cc964cd784254b35eefd349b.

So far, Shenzhen has established a tourism resources system that includes land, water, biological, cultural relics, artificial landscape and dozens of other types of landscape, becoming a famous international emerging tourist city that brings together shopping, tourism, exhibition, and vacation options. Here, we quote the words of Chi Xiongbiao, the deputy director of the Shenzhen Municipal Tourism Administration, "It's important to own more tourism resources, but it's definitely not the only factor. The key and unique tourist advantage is the innovation and creation, and the perfect combination of the modern city culture and the tourism of Shenzhen." It really points out the essence of tourism destination competitiveness.

12.5.4 2011–PRESENT: ESTABLISHING THE INTERNATIONAL TOURISM CITY IMAGE THROUGH INNOVATION AND SELF-DEVELOPMENT

Globally, during the early stages of tourism development, a boomtown will more or less mimic a more developed city. When developing to a certain stage, having accumulated abundant resources and strategic abilities, the boomtown will start innovation and self-development, presenting a clearer tourism position.

The development of Shenzhen's tourism follows this model after the year 2010. With 30 years' tourism development, exploration and accumulation, Shenzhen has achieved astonishing results, representing "the Coast of South China Sea, the Fashion Capital". Shenzhen was listed as one of the top tourist destinations of world in 2010 by The New York Times. In early 2016, Shenzhen ranked seventh among the world's 100 tourist destination cities.

Shenzhen's tourism has been featured in "Theme Park," "Urban Scenes," "Coastal Leisure," and "the Golf Capital,"[6] Shenzhen has successfully operated around 20 various theme parks, with the number of tourists, turnover and profits, and other economic indicators ranking first among the major cities in China. Futian Central Area CBD has become the high-end tourism distribution center, playing an important role in urban scenes tourism. The coastal leisure attraction has been quite influential. Dameisha Beach, Xiaomeisha Beach, Wave Riding Yacht Club, the F1 Motor Yacht Championship, the China Cup, and other coastal tourism projects and marine tourism activities have been most remarkable activities. Moreover, Shenzhen has 15 golf clubs. The Mission Hills Golf Club, with 216 holes, is one of the largest golf clubs in the world.

[6]Cai, H. (2010). The Four characteristics of Shenzhen Tourism. Shenzhen Special Zone Daily, *11*,16.

Based on the information in Table 12.3 and Table 12.4, Shenzhen's tourism is booming. Inbound overnight tourists maintained first place among the large- and medium-sized cities for a long time, and international tourism income has been ranked fourth place in China. Shenzhen's status has been further strengthened as China's important tourist destination and outbound tourism distribution center. Compared with similar cities, Shenzhen has a strong tourism competitiveness.

Shenzhen, supported by mature hospitality products, a large number of leading enterprises with good quality, and perfect industry systems and excellent demonstration effect, has significant advantages among tourist cities in China. Shenzhen has developed a more perfect public service system, with more convenient tourism infrastructure, the implementation of the Shenzhen airport 24-hour clearance policy, the opening of the Xiamen-Shenzhen railway, and the increasingly perfect highway system. Shenzhen's tourism network and Tourism Advisory Service stations are providing 24 hours of Shenzhen tourism information. The internationalization of information symbols of tourism service facilities further improve the language and travel environment for overseas tourists. In addition, Shenzhen has established unique catering, entertainment, shopping, and other ancillary services. The abundant tourism resources and tourism support factors have laid a good foundation for Shenzhen to form a competitive advantage of a tourism destination.

Shenzhen has excellent primary and secondary markets (Bao, 1994). As China's largest SEZ, Shenzhen has large amount of business travelers; the number of foreign tourists has remained stable for many years and that of

TABLE 12.3 Shenzhen 2010–2015 Inbound Tourism

Year	2010	2011	2012	2013	2014	2015
Inbound tourists (million)	102.060	110.455	120.643	121.489	118.218	121.870
Overnight tourists (million)	16.758	17.120	16.910	16.682	16.112	16.465
Tourism Receipt of Foreign Exchange (billion) Yuan	3.180	3.746	4.329	4.531	4.566	4.968

TABLE 12.4 Shenzhen 2010–2015 Tourism Income

Year	2010	2011	2012	2013	2014	2015
Tourism Income (million) Yuan	62.877	73.732	83.976	96.112	109.165	124.480
Year-on-year increase	15.45%	17.26%	13.91%	14.45%	14.19%	14.03%

domestic tourists has slightly increased by a certain proportion, making Shenzhen a unique city that has a broad third market that other cities do not have. Shenzhen Municipal Bureau of Tourism, the Destination Management Department, established five major tourism brands, "Coastal Romance, Theme Park, Cultural Creativity, Sports and Leisure, Urban Style,"[7] centering around the goal of the construction of an international seaside tourism city and focusing on creating a "Creative Shenzhen, Fashion Capital" tourism brand. At the same time, the Shenzhen government has strengthened the market order and tourism quality supervision, actively innovating management tools and constantly optimizing the tourism environment. It focused on the needs of tourists and provided a strong guarantee for forming tourism destination competitiveness. Experience management, information management, safety management, environmental management, and a series of effective destination management activities and strategies, together with superior geographical advantages, have strengthened the competitiveness of Shenzhen's tourism.

In future development, Shenzhen's tourism industry is going to face new challenges. The severely limited carrying capacity of the city; the scarcity of the land used for tourism projects; the aging of the tourism product structure; the lack of convergence between the tourism and the Internet, creativity, culture and sports; and the further requirement of public services development will be the issues Shenzhen has to take into account. Whether Shenzhen, the "World Tourism miracle" evaluated by the International Tourism Organization, will achieve astonishing development in the future remains to be seen.

KEYWORDS

- **destination government**
- **evaluation method**
- **index system**
- **input-output efficiency**
- **marketing**
- **resource-based view model**
- **tourism destination competitiveness**
- **tourism market**

[7]13th Five Year Plan of Shenzhen Tourism Development. (October 24, 2016). Shenzhen Tourism Office. Retrieved from http://www.sz.gov.cn/wtlyjnew/xxgk/ghjh/fzgh/201610/t20161024_5010916.htm.

REFERENCES

Assaf, A. G., & Josiassen, A., (2012). Identifying and ranking the determinants of tourism performance: A global investigation. *Journal of Travel Research*, *51*(4), 388–399.

Assaker, G., Hallak, R., Vinzi, V. E., & O'Connor, P., (2014). An empirical operationalization of countries' destination competitiveness using partial least squares modeling. *Journal of Travel Research*, *53*(1), 26–43.

Assaker, G., Vinzi, V. E., & O'Connor, P., (2011). Examining the effect of novelty seeking, satisfaction, and destination image on tourists' return pattern: A two factor, non-linear latent growth model. *Tourism management*, *32*(4), 890–901.

Ballantyne, R., Packer, J., & Falk, J., (2011). Visitors' learning for environmental sustainability: Testing short-and long-term impacts of wildlife tourism experiences using structural equation modeling. *Tourism Management*, *32*(6), 1243–1252.

Bao, J., (1994). A preliminary study on the theme park layout. *Geographical Research, 13*(3), 83–89.

Botti, L., Peypoch, N., Robinot, E., & Solonadrasana, B., (2009). Tourism destination competitiveness: the French regions case. *European Journal of Tourism Research*, *2*(1), 5.

Buhalis, D., (2000). Marketing the competitive destination of the future. *Tourism management*, *21*(1), 97–116.

Cai, H., (2010). The four characteristics of Shenzhen tourism. *Shenzhen Special Zone Daily, 11*, 16.

Chen, C., Yu, L., & Mou, G., (1992). Research on the development of Shenzhen's Tourism. *Urban problems, 4*, 13–19.

Chi, X., (1999). The construction of the regional tourist center in Shenzhen. *China Opening Journal, 1.*

Cracolici, M. F., & Nijkamp, P., (2009). The attractiveness and competitiveness of tourist destinations: A study of Southern Italian regions. *Tourism management*, *30*(3), 336–344.

Croes, R., & Wang, Y., (2007). A comparison of destination competitiveness mode—taking Orlando and lAs Vegas as An example [J]. *Tourism Tribune*, *7*, 006.

Crouch, G. I., (2011). Destination competitiveness: An analysis of determinant attributes. *Journal of Travel Research*, *50*(1), 27–45.

Crouch, G. I., & Ritchie, J. B., (2000). The competitive destination: A sustainability perspective. *Tourism management*, *21*(1), 1–7.

Currie, R. R., Wesley, F., & Sheehan, L., (2012). Inter-enterprise destination competitiveness. *Tourism Planning & Development*, *9*(2), 165–182.

Daniels, M. J., Norman, W. C., & Henry, M. S., (2004). Estimating income effects of a sport tourism event. *Annals of Tourism Research*, *31*(1), 180–199.

Day, G. S., (1994). The capabilities of market-driven organizations. *Journal of Marketing*, 37–52.

D'Hauteserre, A. M., (2000). Lessons in managed destination competitiveness: the case of Foxwoods Casino Resort. *Tourism Management*, *21*(1), 23–32.

Dwyer, L., & Kim, C., (2003). Destination competitiveness: determinants and indicators. *Current issues in tourism*, *6*(5), 369–414.

Dwyer, L., Dragićević, V., Armenski, T., Mihalič, T., & Knežević Cvelbar, L., (2016). Achieving destination competitiveness: an importance–performance analysis of Serbia. *Current Issues in Tourism*, *19*(13), 1309–1336.

Dwyer, L., Forsyth, P., & Rao, P. (2000). The price competitiveness of travel and tourism: a comparison of 19 destinations. *Tourism management*, *21*(1), 9–22.

Dwyer, L., Mellor, R., Livaic, Z., Edwards, D., & Kim, C., (2004). Attributes of destination competitiveness: A factor analysis. *Tourism Analysis*, *9*(1–1), 91–101.
Enright, M. J., & Newton, J., (2004). Tourism destination competitiveness: a quantitative approach. *Tourism Management*, *25*(6), 777–788.
Enright, M. J., & Newton, J., (2005). Determinants of tourism destination competitiveness in Asia Pacific: Comprehensiveness and universality. *Journal of Travel Research*, *43*(4), 339–350.
Faulkner, B., Oppermann, M., & Fredline, E., (1999). Destination competitiveness: An exploratory examination of South Australia's core attractions. *Journal of Vacation Marketing*, *5*(2), 125–139.
Feng, X., Shen, H., & Hu, X., (2009).Chinese tourism destination competitiveness evaluation and empirical research. *Journal of East China Normal University (Natural Science Edition)*, *41*(5), 101–107.
Gentile, M. S. M., (2013). Perceived destination competitiveness of Langkawi island, Malaysia: A preliminary finding. *Procedia-Social and Behavioral Sciences*, *105*, 801–810.
Gentile, C., Spiller, N., & Noci, G., (2007). How to sustain the customer experience: An overview of experience components that co-create value with the customer. *European Management Journal*, *25*(5), 395–410.
Gomezelj, D. O., & Mihalič, T., (2008). Destination competitiveness—Applying different models, the case of Slovenia. *Tourism Management*, *29*(2), 294–307.
Gooroochurn, N., & Sugiyarto, G., (2005). Competitiveness indicators in the travel and tourism industry. *Tourism Economics*, *11*(1), 25–43.
Grant, R. M., (1991). The resource-based theory of competitive advantage: implications for strategy formulation. *California Management Review*, *33*(3), 114–135.
Guo, S., & Cao, N., (2004). An explanation of tourism destination competitiveness, *Nankai Business Review*, *7*(2), 95–99.
Hallmann, K., Müller, S., & Feiler, S., (2014). Destination competitiveness of winter sport resorts in the Alps: how sport tourists perceive destinations?. *Current Issues in Tourism*, *17*(4), 327–349.
Han, G., & Zhang, S., (2015). The research of influencing factors of skiing tourism destination competitiveness based on Delphi method. *China Winter Sports*, *2*, 71–75.
Hassan, S. S., (2000). Determinants of market competitiveness in an environmentally sustainable tourism industry. *Journal of travel research*, *38*(3), 239–245.
Heath, E., (2003). Towards a model to enhance destination competitiveness: A Southern African perspective. *Journal of Hospitality & Tourism Management*, *10*(2), 124–141.
Highlight of Shenzhen, (2012). *SZNews.com.* Retrieved from http://www.sznews.com/zhuanti/content/2012–11/06/content_7365464.htm.
Huang, L., (2015). Study on the influencing factors of international competitiveness of tourism destination in Chengdu City. *Tourism Overview*. *11*. 164–165.
Hudson, S., Ritchie, B., & Timur, S., (2004). Measuring destination competitiveness: An empirical study of Canadian ski resorts. *Tourism and Hospitality Planning & Development*, *1*(1), 79–94.
Kayar, Ç. H., & Kozak, N., (2010). Measuring destination competitiveness: an application of the travel and tourism competitiveness index (2007)[J]. *Journal of Hospitality Marketing & Management*, *19*(3), 203–216.
Kim, H., Borges, M. C., & Chon, J., (2006). Impacts of environmental values on tourism motivation: The case of FICA, Brazil. *Tourism management*, *27*(5), 957–967.

Kozak, M., & Rimmington, M., (1999). Measuring tourist destination competitiveness: conceptual considerations and empirical findings. *International Journal of Hospitality Management*, *18*(3), 273–283.

Kuang, Y., (2011). Review and enlightenment of the government's influence on tourism development in China in recent years. *Tourism Overview Monthly, 03*.

Kunst, I., (2009). Tourist destination competitiveness assessment-approach and limitations. *Acta Turistica*, *21*(2), 129–159.

Lai, S., Tang, X., & Zhu, M., (2011). A study on the influence of Internet word-of-mouth on the choice of tourism destination. *Management Review, 23*(6), 68–75.

Lee, C. F., & King, B., (2006). Assessing destination competitiveness: An application to the hot springs tourism sector. *Tourism and Hospitality Planning & Development*, *3*(3), 179–197.

Lee, C. F., & King, B., (2009). A determination of destination competitiveness for Taiwan's hot springs tourism sector using the Delphi technique. *Journal of Vacation Marketing*, *15*(3), 243–257.

Lee, C. K., & Taylor, T., (2005). Critical reflections on the economic impact assessment of a mega-event: the case of 2002 FIFA World Cup. *Tourism Management*, *26*(4), 595–603.

Li, H., & Wang, X., (1995). The Secret of the success of three scenic spots in Shenzhe. *Tourism Tribune, 5*, 30–33.

Li, J., Li, G., & Jiang, B., (2001). An analysis of enterprise relationship and enterprise spread in the tourist industry-taking Guangdong as an example. *Tourism Tribune*, *16*(3), 19–25.

Li, Q., & Yang, C., (2012). Local government competition: an important perspective to understand the phenomenon of China's tourism economy. *Journal of Hunan Finance and Economics College, 28*(1), 78–84.

Liang, L., Cao, X., & Xu, Y., (2005).A study of the role of government in the development of modern tourism. *Journal of Northwest A&F University (Social Science Edition), 4*.

Liu, C., Song, B., & Chang, Y., (2014). A study on the cognitive symbol of tourism destination image based on network analysis: a case study of Beijing. *Southeast Communication, 7*, 42–46.

Liu, J., & Chen, G., (2012). A study on the relationship between the government control, the balance of power and the operating performance of Tourism Listed Companies. *Tourism Science, 26*(1), 51–59.

Long, J., (2010). Paradigm of tourism competitiveness: Reflection and inspiration. *Tourism Science, 24*(2), 26–39.

Lu, L., (2016). An analysis of the evolution game behavior of the government, travel agencies and consumers in the tourism market. *Journal of Beijing Polytechnic College, 15*(2). 27–30.

Lv, K., & Zheng, L., (2014). From conflict to cooperation: the relationship between tourism development and local residents integration: government guiding type community participation in the practice and Enlightenment of Yangzhou Caiyi Street project. *Urban Planning, 3*, 78–82.

Mazanec, J. A., & Ring, A., (2011). Tourism destination competitiveness: second thoughts on the world economic forum reports. *Tourism Economics*, *17*(4), 725–751.

Mazanec, J. A., Wöber, K., & Zins, A. H., (2007). Tourism destination competitiveness: from definition to explanation?. *Journal of Travel Research*, *46*(1), 86–95.

Mei, N., & Yang, P., (2010). The Construction of the cooperative marketing network of tourism destinations. *Human Geography*, *4*, 147–151.

Melian-Gonzalez, A., & Garcia-Falcon, J. M., (2003). Competitive potential of tourism in destinations. *Annals of Tourism Research*, *30*(3), 720–740.

Molz, J. G., (2013). Social networking technologies and the moral economy of alternative tourism: The case of couchsurfing.org. *Annals of Tourism Research*, *43*, 210–230.

Mulec, I., & Wise, N., (2013). Indicating the competitiveness of Serbia's Vojvodina Region as an emerging tourism destination. *Tourism Management Perspectives*, *8*, 68–79.

Pansiri, J., (2014). Tourist motives and destination competitiveness: A gap analysis perspective. *International Journal of Hospitality & Tourism Administration*, *15*(3), 217–247.

Park, J. Y., & Jang, S., (2014). An extended gravity model: Applying destination competitiveness. *Journal of Travel & Tourism Marketing*, *31*(7), 799–816.

Pearce, D. G., (1997). Competitive destination analysis in Southeast Asia. *Journal of Travel Research*, *35*(4), 16–24.

Pi, P., (2015). An integrated model of tourism destination competitiveness-based on customer-experience value. *Journal of Bohai University (Philosophy and Social Science), 06*, 55–60.

Pike, S., (2008). *Destination Marketing: An Integrated Marketing Communication Approach.* London, Elsevier.

Pike, S., & Page, S. J., (2014). Destination marketing organizations and destination marketing: A narrative analysis of the literature. *Tourism Management*, *41*, 202–227.

Ritchie, J. R., & Crouch, G. I., (2010). A model of destination competitiveness/sustainability: Brazilian perspectives. Revista de Administracao Publica, *44*(5), 1049–1066.

Ritchie, J. B., & Crouch, G. I., (2003). *The Competitive Destination: A Sustainable Tourism Perspective*. Cabi.

Ritchie, J. R. B., & Crouch, G. I., (2000). Are destination stars born or made: must a competitive destination have star genes. In: *Lights, Camera, Action-31st Annual Conference Proceedings*.

The current economic and social development of Shenzhen, (2012). *Baidu's Wenku Database.* Retrieved from http://wenku.baidu.com/view/cc964cd784254b35eefd349b.

The 13th Five Year Plan of Shenzhen Tourism Development, (2016). *Shenzhen Tourism Office.* Retrieved from http://www.sz.gov.cn/wtlyjnew/xxgk/ghjh/fzgh/201610/t20161024_5010916.htm.

Tourism and leisure in Shenzhen, (2010). *SZnews.com.* Retrieved from http://news.qq.com/a/20100804/001579.htm.

Tsai, H., Song, H., & Wong, K. K., (2009). Tourism and hotel competitiveness research. *Journal of Travel & Tourism Marketing*, *26*(5–6), 522–546.

Tuominen, M., Rajala, A., & Möller, K., (2004). Market-driving versus market-driven: Divergent roles of market orientation in business relationships. *Industrial Marketing Management*, *33*(3), 207–217.

Vila, T. D., Darcy, S., & González, E. A., (2015). Competing for the disability tourism market–a comparative exploration of the factors of accessible tourism competitiveness in Spain and Australia. *Tourism Management*, *47*, 261–272.

Vlahović, S., (2010). Destinations' competitiveness in modern tourism. *Tourism & Hospitality Management*, *Sept.*1332–1348.

Wang, C., & Huang, F., (2011). A study on the influencing factors of tourism destination competitiveness- Based on the case of Zhangjiajie: SEM. *Contemporary Economic Management, 33*(4), 63–71.

Wang, C., (2009). *Tourism Science, 23*(3), 28–34.

Wang, C. Y., Hsu, M. K., & Swanson, S. R., (2012). Determinants of tourism destination competitiveness in China: *Journal of China Tourism Research, 8*(1), 97–116.

Wang, H., (2006). A brief history of the development of the tourism industry in Shenzhen. *SZNews.com*. Retrieved from http://www.sznews.com/zhuanti/content/2012–11/06/content_7365464.htm.

Wang, L., & Shi, P., (2007). Analysis of tourism industry association and industry spreading in gansu province. *Geography and Geo-Information Science, 23*(1), 68–72.

Wang, Q., (2005). Role of the market, government manners and the development of China's tourism industry. *Journal of Beijing Second Foreign Language Institute, 1*, 20–25.

Wang, X., (2014). The current situation of provincial government tourism website construction. *Journal of Modern Information, 34*(12), 90–94.

Williams, P. W., Stewart, K., & Larsen, D., (2012). Toward an agenda of high-priority tourism research. *Journal of Travel Research, 51*(1), 3–11.

World Economic Forum, (2008a). The travel and tourism competitiveness report 2008. Retrieved from https://members.weforum.org/pdf/Global_Competitiveness_Reports/TTReport/TTfullreport.pdf.

World Economic Forum, (2008b).The global competitiveness report 2008–2009. Retrieved from https://members.weforum.org/pdf/GCR08/GCR08.pdf.

World Economic Forum, (2011). The travel and tourism competitiveness report. Retrieved from http://www.weforum.org/reports/travel-tourism-competitiveness-report-2011.

Wu, X., & Han, N., (2012). A study on the evaluation of brand image building based on the local government tourism portal - A case study of the 33 provinces, cities and regions in China. *Tourism Forum, 5*(1), 92–97.

Xu, F., (2015). The evolutionary game between government and enterprises in the development of low carbon Tourism. *Journal of Commercial College of Guizhou, 28*(2), 55–58.

Xu, X., Sun, F., & Wang, L., (2015). Dilution effects of online negative word-of-mouth on brand equity for tourism destination: Moderating effects of familiarity and susceptibility. *Human Geography, 25*(12), 113–120.

Xu, Y., (2013). A re-examination of the government-based tourism development model: Based on the perspective of literature analysis. *China's Administrative Management, 12*, 013.

Yang, X., Wu, J., Zhang, X., Jiang, S., & Li, K., (2014). Analysis of the projection image of tourism destination based on Web Text: the case of Zhangjiajie. *Journal of the Graduates Sun Yat-Sen University (Natural Sciences, Medicine), 1*, 82–97.

Yi, H., (2015). Study on the operation and management of the government-based tourism in Underdeveloped Areas: A case study of Guizhou province. *Journal of Xinyang Normal University: Philosophy and Social Science Edition, 35*(2), 59–63.

Yi, L., (2006). Evaluation of regional tourism competition based on SEM. *Journal of Chongqing University: Natural Science Edition, 29*(10), 154–158.

Yi, L., & Fu, Q., (2006). An empirical study on the influencing factors of tourism destination competitiveness. *Journal of Chongqing University: Natural Science Edition, 29*(8), 154–158.

Yoon, Y., (2002). *Development of a Structural Model for Tourism Destination Competitiveness From Stakeholders' Perspectives*, (Doctoral dissertation, Virginia Polytechnic Institute and State University).

Zang, D., & Hu, X., (2008). A study on actuality and countermeasure of web marketing in Tourism destination. *Science-technology and management, 10*(4), 90–92.

Zang, D., & Huang, J., (2006). An analysis and understanding of the connotation of "tourism destination competitiveness". *Tourism Tribune*, *21*(12), 29–34.

Zang, D., (2009). A study on the evaluation system of tourism destination competitiveness based on factor analysis. *Journal Beijing International Studies University, 31*(9), 20–27.

Zhang, H., & Zhang, J., (2014). Research on tourism destination competitiveness based on the analysis of input output efficiency: A case study of 16 cities in Anhui Province. *Journal of Anhui University, 6*, 150–156.

Zhang, H., & Shi, H., (2015). Research on the tourism destination competitiveness and the contribution degree of tourism economy-A case study of 31 provinces in mainland China. *Journal of Arid Land Resources and Environment, 12*, 216–221.

Zhang, H., Gu, C. L., Gu, L. W., & Zhang, Y., (2011). The evaluation of tourism destination competitiveness by TOPSIS & information entropy–A case in the Yangtze River Delta of China. *Tourism Management*, *32*(2), 443–451.

Zhang, L., Li, J., & Ma, Y., (2011). The coupling analysis of the tourism destination network marketing system and the tourism industry development. *Economic Geography*, *31*(2), 339–345.

Zhang, S., (2005). The inevitable transformation of government-based tourism development strategy. *Tourism Science, 1*, 5–8.

Zhang, W., & Kan, Y., (2003). An analysis of tourism industry association and industry in shanghai city: *Social Sciences, 8*, 21–27.

Zhang, X., (2006). The leading position of the government in the development of the tourism industry at present stage. *Special Economic Zone, 11*, 230–231.

Zhu, Y., Zhu, Q., & Zhu, Z., (2014). Modeling, evaluation and analysis of tourism destination competitiveness: A case study of the Yangtze river delta of China. *Asia Pacific Journal of Tourism Research, 19*(8), 932–949.

Zuo, B., Li, X., & Bao, J., (2007).Tourism national income and its initial distribution pattern-A case study of Hunan province. *Tourism Tribune*, *22*(1), 10–15.

INDEX

A

B